Nᴇᴡ Aᴘᴘʀᴏᴀᴄʜ ᴛᴏ Lᴇɢᴀʟ Tʀᴀɴꜱʟᴀᴛɪᴏɴ

Susan Šarčević

New Approach to Legal Translation

Kluwer Law International

The Hague • London • Boston

Published by Kluwer Law International
P.O. Box 85889
2508 CN The Hague, The Netherlands

Sold and distributed in the USA and Canada by
Kluwer Law International
675 Massachusetts Avenue
Cambridge, MA 02139, USA

Sold and distributed in all other countries by
Kluwer Law International
Distribution Centre
P.O. Box 322
3300 AH Dordrecht, The Netherlands

A C.I.P. Catalogue record for this book is available from the Library of Congress

Printed on acid-free paper

Cover design: Alfred Birnie bNO

ISBN 90 411 0401 1

© 1997 Kluwer Law International

Kluwer Law International incorporates the publishing programmes of Graham & Trotman Ltd, Kluwer Law and Taxation Publishers and Martinus Nijhoff Publishers

Table of Contents

Abbreviations

ABGB	Allgemeines bürgerliches Gesetzbuch = Austrian Civil Code
BGB	Bürgerliches Gesetzbuch = German Civil Code
BGE	Bundesgerichtsentscheidungen = decisions of the Federal Court
CLEF	Common law en français
EEC	European Economic Community
EU	European Union, formerly EC: European Communities
ICNT	Informal composite negotiating text of LOS 1982
ILC	International Law Commission
ISO	International Organization for Standardization
LOS 1982	UN Convention on the Law of the Sea of 1982
LSP	Languages for special purposes
OECD	Organization for Economic Cooperation and Development
RSC	Revised Statutes of Canada / Lois révisées du Canada
SC	Statutes of Canada / Lois du Canada
SL	Source language
TL	Target language
UN	United Nations
UNCLOS III	Third UN Conference on the Law of the Sea
UNCTAD	UN Conference on Trade and Development
UNIDROIT	Institute for Unification of Private Law
ZGB	Zivilgesetzbuch = Swiss Civil Code
ZPO	Zivilprozeßordnung = German Code of Civil Procedure

Language Codes

AR	= Arabic
CH	= Chinese
DA	= Danish
DE	= German
EN	= English
ES	= Spanish
FR	= French
GR	= Greek
IT	= Italian
NL	= Dutch
PT	= Portuguese
RR	= Rhaeto-romanic
RU	= Russian

Table of Figures

Acknowledgment

Figures 10, 11, 12 (partially), 13 and some parts of the text relating thereto are reprinted from the author's article 'Conceptual Dictionaries for Translation in the Field of Law' (*International Journal of Lexicography* Vol.2 No.4, 1989:277–293) by permission of Oxford University Press.

Introduction

Although translations of legal documents are among the oldest and most important in the world, legal translation has long been neglected in both translation and legal studies. Far from being recognized as an independent discipline, legal translation is regarded by translation theorists merely as one of the many subject areas of special-purpose translation, a branch of translation studies often snubbed for its alleged inferiority. Even more surprising is the low profile attributed to legal translation by lawyers. In our era of multilingualism, translation plays a major role as a medium of communication in municipal, supranational,[1] and international law. Translations of legal texts lead to legal effects and may even induce peace or prompt a war. Concerned about the grave consequences occasioned by past translation errors in treaties, Kuner comments: 'The growing trend toward providing authentic texts of treaties in four or more languages poses dangers to the peace and stability of the international order' (1991:953).

As a result of the increasing demand for the free movement of people, goods, and capital, legal translation affects all of us in one way or another. International trade, for example, could not function without legal translation. Similarly, the success of the Single European Market and the European Union is partly dependent on translation. The translation of municipal law has a relatively long tradition in plurilingual countries such as Belgium, Canada, and Switzerland. In response to the increased emphasis on equal language rights, the European Council has recently adopted a special Charter to protect the language rights of ethnic or minority groups in multi-ethnic societies.[2] Among other things, the Charter recognizes the right of minorities to use their own language in judicial affairs, thus increasing the demand for translations of national and regional legislation and regulations.[3]

---

1. The term *supranational* describes the special position of a regional law such as European law which falls between international and municipal law.
2. The draft project of the European Charter of Regional and Minority Languages was formally submitted to the Committee of Ministers of the Council of the European Council by virtue of Resolution 192/1988 (*see* Woehrling 1989:134). The Charter was adopted by the Council of Europe in 1992 (European Treaty Series 148, Strasbourg 5.X.1992). By emphasizing the relevance of the Union to the citizen, the Maastricht Treaty on European Union, which entered into force in 1993, marks a new phase in the development of citizen's rights and language rights in Europe.
3. For example, the region of Trentino/South Tirol had received autonomous status in 1948, which was newly negotiated in 1972. Nonetheless, German was not declared an official language until the Presidential Order of 1988. As a result of the European Charter (*see* note 2 above), implementation finally commenced in January 1992 (*see* Bauer 1994:71).

1

Compared with the immense quantity of legal translations produced daily, the literature on legal translation is meager indeed. As a result of the importance attached to the letter of the law, most studies are devoted to questions of terminology, while textual and pragmatic considerations tend to be ignored. There appears to be no consensus among lawyers and linguists on acceptable translation techniques, let alone on a theoretical approach to legal translation. Some linguists deny that modern linguistics (Mounin 1979:17) and even translation theory (Weston 1991:1) are of much use in the practice of legal translation. In the past, both linguists and lawyers have attempted to apply theories of general translation to legal texts such as Catford's concept of situational equivalence (Kielar 1977:33) and Nida's theory of formal correspondence (Weisflog 1987:187, 191). Although some translators claim that principles of general translation theory may be applied to legal translation (Koutsivitis 1988:37), at the same time it is argued that special methods and techniques are required to guarantee reliability when translating legal texts (Bocquet 1994:i). The latter view is generally confirmed by Canadian jurilinguists[4] who agree that legal texts are subject to special rules (Didier 1990:161), thus implying that they also require special methods of translation. Despite considerable progress made by jurilinguists in Canada, they still rely heavily on contrastive linguistics and the linguistic theory of translation presented by Vinay and Darbelnet in their classic book *Stylistique comparée du français et de l'anglais*, first published in 1958 (e.g., Didier 1990:250, 293). Since then, the theory of translation has come a long way, especially under the influence of German-speaking theorists. Nonetheless, the linguistic approach to translation is still evident in new works by Jean-Claude Gémar (1995, vols. I and II), where he acknowledges the influence of classic linguists such as Fedorov (1953) and Vinay and Darbelnet but disregards recent trends in translation theory introduced primarily by German scholars (*see* Gémar 1995–I:17).

Translation has traditionally been regarded as a process of interlingual transfer. In this sense Catford defined translation as 'an operation performed on languages: a process of substituting a text in one language for a text in another' (1965:1). Despite the importance of language, German translation theorists no longer regard translation as a process of transcoding languages. Liberated from the alienating bonds of traditional translation, the translator is no longer a passive mediator whose main task is to reproduce the source text (Wilss 1988a:3; Hönig and Kussmaul 1982:14). Today the main emphasis in translation theory has shifted from interlingual to cultural transfer (Vermeer 1986:33; *also* 1992a:31), as a result of which translation is widely regarded as a 'cross-cultural event' (Snell-Hornby 1988:46) and the translator as a cultural operator (Hewson and Martin 1991:133). Having assumed the role of an active text producer, the translator consciously selects a translation strategy on the basis of extralinguistic factors (Neubert and Shreve 1992:5), especially the function (purpose) of the target text (Reiß and Vermeer 1984:96) and other conditions of the communicative situation of reception (*see* Nord 1993:9–20); Kussmaul 1995:55–72). Translation is currently regarded as a complex form of action or, as Vermeer puts it, 'eine komplexe Handlung, in der jemand unter neuen funktionalen und kulturellen und sprachlichen Bedingungen in einer neuen Situation über einen Text

---

4.   On the term *jurilinguiste see* Chapter 4, at 4.7.2 and note 18.

(Ausgangssachverhalt) berichtet...' (1986:33). Thus translation theory has become a theory of action (Holz-Mäntärri 1986:354) in which the translator is a responsible decision-maker (Wilss 1992:50–68). By helping translators evaluate the pragmatic aspects of the particular communicative situation, the *theory of action* becomes a *theory in action* (*cf.* Newmark 1988:8) which presupposes intuition and encourages creativity as part of translator competence (Wilss 1988a:108–140, *also* 1992:1–14; *cf.* Kiraly 1995:14–16).

In view of the numerous restrictions in the translation of legal texts, it is legitimate to ask whether legal translation is compatible with the theory of action proposed by theorists of general translation. This and other questions are dealt with in this interdisciplinary study which attempts to correct the fallacies and traditional views on legal translation held by both linguists and lawyers. The present study is not bound to any particular languages, as is Alvarez Calleja's recent work *Traducción Jurídica (Inglés Español)* (1994), nor to the translation situation in a particular country, as is Didier's chapter on legal translation (1990:207–309) and the national reports from the XIIth International Congress of Comparative Law (*Les Cahiers de Droit* 1987, No. 4). While the purpose of this book is not to lay down specific guidelines on 'how to' or 'how not to' translate legal texts, it attempts to cultivate translator competence by making translators aware of the 'dos and don'ts' of legal translation. Above all, it attempts to provide a new approach to legal translation by proposing a theoretical framework in which the translator assumes the role of an active participant in legal communication. Legal translators have traditionally been denied all freedom to make decisions. Now, thanks to dissidents who dared to defy the *status quo* of tradition, they have finally gained new responsibility and decision-making authority. Since linguistic decisions can also have legal consequences, such authority must be exercised with caution. As responsible decision-makers, legal translators must know exactly how far they can stretch their limited freedom and still respect the restraints of their profession.

A theoretical approach to legal translation must also be practice oriented. Thus legal translation is regarded as an act of communication in this study. In an attempt to illustrate how plurilingual legal instruments are interpreted and applied by the courts, case-law is presented whenever possible. The book is divided into two main Parts, one theoretical, the other practical. While Part I (Chapters 1 – 4) attempts to provide a theoretical framework for the translation of legal texts, Part II (Chapters 5 – 8) shows how translators put language into action to achieve the desired legal effects in practice. Examples are presented of plurilingual legislation from Canada, Switzerland, and Belgium, as well as multilingual treaties and conventions of international law and European law. Excerpts from plurilingual judgments of the Belgian Court of Cassation and the European Court of Justice in Luxembourg are also cited.

Setting the tone for the interdisciplinary nature of this study, Chapter 1 provides basic information on legal texts and legal translation, distinguishing legal texts from other texts and showing why legal translation is special. Chapter 2 presents a historical survey of legal translation from Roman law to the present day. Dominated by literal translation for over one thousand years, legal translation did not experience a major 'emancipation' until late in the twentieth century. Chapter 3 contains a comprehensive analysis of legal translation as an act of communication within the mechanism of the law. The main emphasis is on text reception, i.e., the interpretation and application of parallel texts by the courts. Focusing on text production, Chapter 4 analyzes the changing role of the legal translator. Finally incorporated in the drafting process, legal translators are becoming emancipated text producers in their own right. Attempts to coordinate the situational factors of text production have resulted in new bilingual drafting methods which have succeeded in revolutionizing legal translation.

Legal translators can be effective in their new role as text producers only if they are able to produce texts that achieve the intended legal effects. Among other things, this presupposes legal competence and a basic knowledge of the characteristics of legal texts. With this in mind, Chapter 5 introduces translators to the structure of normative legal texts and, in particular, to the basic elements of legal rules. Since most legal texts deal with various forms of legal action, translators must be able to formulate legal speech acts which lead to the desired results. Chapter 6 raises the question of creativity, showing to what extent legal translators can be creative and still respect the restraints of the profession when translating legislation of municipal law. Focusing on plurilingual communication in international and supranational law, Chapter 7 shows that the main emphasis in the translation of multilingual, multilateral instruments is still on achieving interlingual concordance. Subject to additional constraints, translators strive to preserve the unity of the single instrument by producing parallel texts whose terminology, syntax, and style correspond as closely as possible. Devoted to terminological problems, Chapter 8 sheds light on the decision-making process of translators in their search for adequate equivalents. One of the greatest challenges facing legal translators is being able to compensate for terminological incongruency. The concluding remarks in Chapter 9 deal with questions relating to the future of legal translation as a means of communication in the law. When linguistic means fail to ensure the reliability of parallel texts, legal means are the last resort.

1 Translation Theory and Legal Translation

1.1. FILLING A GAP IN TRANSLATION STUDIES

Translation theorists who have attempted to apply theories of general translation to legal texts have frequently made misleading statements and even failed to recognize the proper communicative function of legal texts. On the other hand, lawyers who have written on legal translation tend to disregard the text and deal exclusively with terminology. This is also misleading because legal translation involves much more than terminology. Despite the emphasis on preserving the letter of the law, legal translation is not a process of transcoding, i.e., translating a string of words from one language into another. As in other areas of translation, the basic unit of legal translation is the text, not the word. Attempting to fill a gap in translation studies, this study focuses on the translation of legal texts.

Since legal texts are subject to legal criteria, it follows that a theory for the translation of legal texts must take account of legal considerations. In the same token, it cannot disregard basic issues of translation theory. In an attempt to provide a systematic approach to legal translation, this Chapter deals with fundamental issues of translation theory such as text typologies, the communicative function of legal texts, and the classification of legal texts. Attempting to correct misconceptions about legal texts, it is shown how legal texts differ from other texts and, in particular, how legal translation differs from the translation of other special-purpose texts. As in general translation, pragmatic considerations are important in legal translation and should be taken into account when determining translation strategy.

1.2. TEXT TYPOLOGIES FOR TRANSLATION

For a long time it was believed that a translation had to be either literal or free and that the type of text is decisive in determining how it should be translated. This led to the creation of text typologies, the first of which were based on subject-matter. Although legal texts were historically most closely related to biblical texts (*see* Chapter 2, 2.2), they were totally ignored in early text typologies. On the contrary, biblical texts were recognized as an independent text type at least as far back as 340 A.D. At that time, Hieronymus distinguished between biblical texts which were to be translated literally (*verbum e verbo*) and non-biblical texts which could be translated freely (*sensum de sensu*) (Kloepfer 1967:28).

When attention was later focused on literary translation, theorists spoke of literary as opposed to non-literary texts (*see* Leonardo Bruni's *De interpretatione recta* of

1420). Although Pierre-Daniel Huet dealt primarily with the translation of literary texts in his *De interpretatione* (1680; expanded edition of *De optimo genere interpretandi*, 1661), he was one of the first to touch upon scientific translation as well. Recognizing that scientific texts confront translators with particular demands, Huet viewed scientific translation as one of the 'foremost tasks of civilization' and one which had been 'absurdly neglected' (in Steiner 1977:265).

At the beginning of the nineteenth century, Schleiermacher made a distinction between the translation of works of art (literary and scientific texts) which he referred to as *Übersetzen* and the translation of worldly texts (common matters from 'business and everyday life') which he referred to as *Dolmetschen* (in Störing 1963:39). At that time, the *Dolmetscher* was the 'interpreter' who translated 'commercial documents, the traveller's questions, the exchanges of diplomats and hoteliers' (Steiner 1977:251). Regarding the terminology of worldly texts as practically the same in most languages, Schleiermacher concluded that such matters can be translated by a mechanical process of interlingual substitution (in Störing 1963:42). As a result, *Dolmetschen*[1] was regarded as an inferior type of translation requiring neither hermeneutics nor creativity.

According to Schleiermacher's classification, scientific texts included philosophical texts and texts of the humanities as well as texts of the natural sciences (Kloepfer 1967:10). Later, a clear distinction was made between literary texts, on the one hand, and technical and scientific texts, on the other. While literary texts included philosophical texts and texts of the humanities, technical texts and texts of the natural sciences were classified as technical and scientific texts. Referring to Schleiermacher, literary critics began to use the term *Übersetzen* to denote the translation of literary texts, whereas all other translation was regarded as *Dolmetschen* (Kloepfer 1967:10), thus placing technical and scientific texts on the same level with Schleiermacher's category of worldly texts. These two groups of texts later developed into what is currently known as special-purpose texts or *Fachtexte*, *textes en langue de spécialité* (*cf.* Snell-Hornby 1986:18).

1.2.1. Special-purpose texts

After the Second World War, Andrei Fedorov included commercial texts and official documents as well as technical and scientific texts in the group of special-purpose texts mentioned in his book *Vvednie v teoriju perevoda*. Rejecting the view that the translation of such texts is inferior, Fedorov emphasized that special-purpose texts can be translated correctly only if the translator possesses excellent knowledge of the particular subject-matter (1954:196–320). At about the same time, Casagrande recognized four text types: special-purpose or pragmatic texts (as he referred to

---

1.   Schleiermacher's notion of *Dolmetschen* should not be confused with its current sense of 'oral translation.' Today O. Kade's distinction between *Übersetzen* and *Dolmetschen* (translation and interpretation) as written and oral translation has been accepted in general translation theory (*see* O. Kade 1981:5; *also* Reiß 1995:48). In German the generic term *Translation* encompasses both *Übersetzen* and *Dolmetschen*.

them), aesthetic-poetic texts, religious texts, and ethnographic texts (1954:335). His text typology later served as the basis for Jumpelt's study *Die Übersetzung natur-wissenschaftlicher und technischer Literatur*, one of the first post-war studies devoted to specialized translation. Classifying all special-purpose texts as pragmatic, Jumpelt distinguished between four groups: technical texts, texts of the natural sciences, texts of the social sciences, and other texts.[2] His group of texts of the social sciences included the following fields of specialization: sociology, economics, politics, finance, and law. Although Jumpelt's analysis is restricted to texts of the exact sciences (technology and the natural sciences), he acknowledges that different techniques are used to translate texts of the social sciences. Basing his comment on terminological rather than textual considerations, he simply notes that translation studies had not yet been carried out on texts of the social sciences. Nonetheless, he does not hesitate to conclude that all special-purpose texts have an informative function (1961:26–27).

1.2.2. Function of special-purpose texts

In 1971 Katherina Reiß made a significant contribution to general translation theory by proposing a translation-oriented text typology based not only on subject-matter but first and foremost on the function of particular texts. Basing her text typology on Karl Bühler's tripartite classification of the functions of language (1934), Reiß classified texts as expressive, conative or informative (1971:32). In later studies Reiß provides numerous examples to support her empirical findings. Regarding creative writing as subjective or author-centered, she classifies literary texts as expressive, whereas persuasive or addressee-oriented texts such as editorials, polemics, advertisements, propaganda, and purpose novels are classified as conative. Finally, objective texts in which the main intention of the author is to convey information are classified as informative. Among others, these include notices, reports, philosophical texts, treatises, *laws and contracts* [emphasis added] (1976:9–10). By assuming that the function of all special-purpose texts is informative, Reiß made the same mistake as Jumpelt.

As a result of the new emphasis on function, translation scholars increasingly turned their attention to the pragmatic aspects of texts, analyzing the function of language in various texts and, in turn, the function of such texts in the communication process. Still regarding specialized translation as inferior, some theorists denied that pragmatics are important in the translation of special-purpose texts (Andersen 1974:164, cited in Wilss 1977:129). On the other hand, members of the Leipzig School defended specialized translation, insisting that pragmatic aspects need to be taken into account in such translations as well (Neubert 1973:19). Nonetheless, it was not until the late 1970s that LSP research (languages for special purposes) began to have a markedly pragmatic orientation (Möhn and Pelka 1977:68). Not by chance,

---

2. Jumpelt's group of 'other texts' includes documents, official documents, diplomatic texts, commercial correspondence, advertisements, press reports and commentaries, radio reports, and military texts (1961:25).

the Third European Symposium on LSP held in August 1981 was devoted to 'Pragmatics and LSP.' The results, however, were not entirely encouraging. In particular, Weber took it upon himself to prove that the formal linguistic characteristics of special-purpose texts are determined by the function of the particular text. To this end, Weber proposed creating a typology of special-purpose texts in which texts would be classified in accordance with Halliday's functional categories as 'predominantly instrumental, regulatory, interactional, personal, heuristic, imaginative or representational' (Weber 1982:227). Weber himself was disappointed with the results of his analysis, which convincingly implied that special-purpose texts have a single function, i.e., representational. This apparently confirmed earlier assertions by Jumpelt and Reiß that special-purpose texts are strictly informative. Not to be outdone, Weber analyzed the data on which he had based his analysis. This led him to the conclusion that previous LSP studies had been decidedly one-sided: They had been restricted almost exclusively to texts of the exact sciences (1982:229).

Determined to compile a comprehensive translation-oriented typology of special-purpose texts, LSP scholars gathered in 1987 at a symposium in Hildesheim for the purpose of developing a special-purpose research strategy based on the principles of text linguistics (Arnzt 1988:3). Despite interest in the project, it appears that only limited progress was made. Not discouraged, Hartmut Schröder attempts to promote LSP pragmatics by emphasizing the importance of analyzing extralinguistic factors which affect forms of social action in special-purpose communication (1993:xi; *cf.* Poulsen 1990:33).

By now it should be clear that a typology of LSP texts can be empirically adequate and formally consistent only if it is applicable to all types of special-purpose texts, including texts of the social sciences. Attempting to present a comprehensive model of specialist communication, Sager acknowledges the importance of communicative function in special-purpose texts. While maintaining that the sender's motivation 'is most frequently to inform the recipient in the restricted sense of augmenting, confirming or modifying his current state of knowledge,' Sager also recognizes two secondary communicative functions: interrogative and directive. In his words, the interrogative function 'requires a reversal of roles so that the sender seeks information from, rather than offers information to the recipient,' whereas the directive function is 'an attempt to elicit modification of behaviour via an effect on knowledge' (1990:102). At this point Sager does not cite examples of special-purpose texts with directive and interrogative functions.

1.3. WHY ARE LEGAL TEXTS SPECIAL?

In special-purpose communication the text is formulated in a special language or sublanguage[3] that is subject to special syntactic, semantic and pragmatic rules (*cf.* Lerat 1995:12; *also* Sager, Dungworth and McDonald 1980:2, 6). Legal texts are formulated in a special language generally known as the *language of the law*

---

3. The term *sublanguage* reflects the fact that a special language is part of general or ordinary language (*see* Sager 1993:29; *also* Lerat 1995:18–20).

(Mellinkoff 1963:3), *langage du droit* (Cornu 1990:17), *lenguaje de la ley* (Iturralde Sesara 1989:29). In keeping with Sager's definition of special-purpose languages,[4] the language of the law is used strictly in special-purpose communication between specialists, thus excluding communication between lawyers and non-lawyers. Concerned primarily with language, Gémar identifies six subdivisions of the language of the law: the language of the legislator, judges, the administration, commerce, private law, and scholarly writings (doctrine) (1995–II:116–122). Not only are there subdivisions of the language of the law, but as Gémar points out, each legal system has its own language of the law; hence, it is more precise to speak of *languages* of the law. Bound to a particular legal system, each language of the law is the product of a specific history and culture (Gémar 1995–II:105, note 37). Therefore, it follows that the characteristics of the French *langage du droit* described by Gémar (1995:109–131; 1990:717–738) do not necessarily apply to English and German, nor do those of the English language of the law described by Mellinkoff (1963:11–32) apply to French and Spanish, etc. This study is not concerned with characteristics of languages of the law but rather with language usage in legal texts or, as Cornu puts it, 'le langage du droit en action' (1990:75). Above all, legal translators must be able to use language effectively to express legal actions that achieve the desired legal effects.

1.3.1. Identifying the function of legal texts

Like other texts, a legal text is a 'communicative occurrence' produced at a given time and place and intended to serve a specific function (de Beaugrande and Dressler 1981:3; *cf.* Baden 1977:183; *also* Hegenbarth 1982:54–85). Although it is precisely the function of legal texts that makes them special, translation theorists tend to place them on equal footing with other special-purpose texts, thus failing to recognize their primary function. In this respect, Reiß continued to regard laws and contracts as informative texts:

> Ein Gesetz informiert... über einen Sachverhalt, der vom Textempfänger zur Kenntnis zu nehmen und zu berücksichtigen ist, wenn er sich keinen Sanktionen aussetzen will. Ein Vertrag informiert über einen Sachverhalt und Rechte und Pflichten von Vertragspartnern, die in diesem Text den Inhalt ihres Übereinkommens schriftlich fixieren. *In beiden Texten kann es sich nur um Exemplare des informativen Typs handeln* [emphasis added] (Reiß and Vermeer 1984:208–209).

Although laws and contracts are informative to a certain extent (as all texts are), this is not their primary function. This fact was recognized by Peter Newmark who also proposed a text typology based on Bühler's model of language functions. Unlike Reiß, he cited laws and regulations as examples of conative, i.e., vocative texts,

---

4. In an earlier book Sager defines special languages as 'the means of linguistic communication required for conveying special subject information among specialists in the same subject' (Sager, Dungworth and McDonald 1980:210. On characteristics of special languages *see* Sager at 1990:99 and 1993:40).

9

which he briefly described as 'directive' and 'imperative' (1982:13–15). For some unknown reason, however, Newmark later changed his mind and reclassified statutes and legal documents as expressive texts (1988:39). This is to be regretted because in so doing, he places legal texts in the same category as serious imaginative literature, autobiography, essays, and personal correspondence. While Newmark does not return to this subject in later works (1991 and 1993), Reiß does in her Vienna lectures (1995). Still convinced that laws and contracts can only be informative texts, she repeats the very same passage cited above (1995:85). A different approach is taken by Sager. While he does not mention legal texts in earlier works (1986, 1990), he not only refers to laws and regulations in his 1993 book but suggests that they have different functions for different readers. In his words, laws and regulations have an informative purpose for the general reader and a directive one 'for the specific group of people listed,' i.e., for those affected by the particular text (1993:70). Though coming closer to the truth, Sager's conclusion is still misleading.

But why all the confusion over the function of legal texts? Taking a closer look at Bühler's tripartite classification, we see that the informative function (*Darstellungsfunktion*) dominates texts which focus on objects and/or facts by 'describing' a state of affairs in the 'real' world, whereas the expressive function (*Ausdrucksfunktion*) is characterized by sender-oriented texts intended to 'enrich' the world. Finally, the conative function (*Appelfunktion*) is addressee-oriented and is used in texts aimed at 'changing' the world by provoking the addressee to action (*Provokation zur Tat*) or by imposing a certain behavior on the addressee (*Verhaltenssteuerung*) (Reiß 1976:9). From the latter examples, it follows that conative texts include not only persuasive but also regulatory texts, a fact that Reiß overlooked in her earlier analysis of conative texts (1976:76) and again in her Vienna lectures (1995:83).

Legal instruments such as laws and contracts are primarily regulatory in nature. In this sense, laws are generally defined as rules of conduct or instruments of social regulation, whereas contracts regulate the conduct of the contracting parties. Thus it follows that regulatory instruments are conative texts and as such are characterized by frequent use of the imperative. Without mentioning legal texts, Bühler himself made a point of emphasizing that texts dominated by the imperative are conative. Although Reiß acknowledges Bühler's statement (Reiß and Vermeer 1984:207), she fails to recognize the special function of the imperative in such texts (Reiß 1976:56). Furthermore, she recently goes so far as to suggest that Bühler was mistaken about the use of the imperative in conative texts. From her point of view, the use of the imperative is typical of informative texts. This time, however, she does not mention laws but rather instructions explaining how to use something (*Gebrauchsanweisungen*) (1995:83). A philosopher and sociologist, Jürgen Habermas also commences his *Theorie des kommunikativen Handelns* (1981) by referring to Bühler's classification of language functions; however, there is no doubt in his mind that legal texts such as laws and contracts have a regulatory function and thus fall under Bühler's category of conative texts (1981:376).

1.3.2. Bipartite system of classifying legal texts

In legal theory the tripartite classification of language has generally been replaced by a bipartite system in which language has two primary functions: regulatory and informative, i.e., prescriptive and descriptive, as they are referred to in legal terms (Kelsen 1991:149–155). Accordingly, texts with a primarily expressive function such as pladoyers in criminal proceedings are excluded from the definition of legal texts in the sense used here.[5] Generally speaking, legal texts can be divided into the following three groups according to their function: 1) primarily prescriptive, 2) primarily descriptive but also prescriptive, and 3) purely descriptive (*cf.* Bocquet 1994:2).

Legal texts whose function is primarily prescriptive include laws and regulations, codes, contracts, treaties and conventions. Such texts are regulatory instruments containing rules of conduct or norms. Accordingly, they are normative texts which prescribe a specific course of action that an individual ought to conform to or, as Kelsen puts it, will be subject to sanction (Kelsen 1991:22–23, 133–135). Today it is generally agreed that normative instruments prescribe how the members of a given society shall act (command), refrain from acting (prohibition), may act (permission) or are explicitly authorized to act (authorization) (*see* Weinberger 1988:60–64).

It should be noted that not all normative texts are legal texts. In particular, religious texts such as the Ten Commandments and the Laws of the Firstfruits in *Exodus* are normative texts prescribing standards of behavior in the form of commands and prohibitions. The difference between legal and religious commands and prohibitions, at least in the Christian world, is that the former are vested with the force of law and thus are coercive in the sense that violations are punishable by law. On the other hand, in theocratic societies, divine rules of conduct constitute the law. For example, the two primary sources of Islamic law are the Koran, the sacred book of Islam, and the *Sunna*, the traditional or model behavior of the Prophet, God's Messenger. For this reason, Islamic law often shows little interest in civil sanctions (David and Brierley 1985:457).

The second group of legal texts consists of hybrid texts that are primarily descriptive but also contain prescriptive parts. These include judicial decisions and instruments used to carry on judicial and administrative proceedings such as actions, pleadings, briefs, appeals, requests, petitions, etc. Whereas the first two groups of legal texts contain legal instruments used in the mechanism of the law, the texts in the third group are not legal instruments although they may have an indirect impact on the law. The third group includes purely descriptive texts written by legal scholars such as legal opinions, law textbooks, articles, etc. Such texts constitute what is known as legal scholarship or doctrine, the authority of which varies in different legal systems.

This study deals primarily with legal texts belonging to the first two groups, in particular with normative texts such as constitutions, codes, statutes, treaties, inter-

---

5.   Legal texts may contain some expressive elements; however, even this is rare. Kurzon refers, for example, to the prosadic features of a bank loan form (1986:25).

national conventions, etc. These are documentary sources of law, i.e., the primary origins from which the law of a particular system derives its authority and coercive force. In the common law countries, the judicial decisions of superior courts, i.e., the statements of law made in the *rationes decidendi* of such decisions are also recognized as a source of law. Case law, as it is called, developed as a distinct authoritative source by virtue of the rule of precedent which obliges judges to observe the decisions made by their colleagues of higher courts. This development was much less pronounced in the continental civil law systems derived from Roman law. On the other hand, works of legal scholarship have always been more authoritative in these systems (*see* Vanderlinden 1995:343–351). Customary law, an unwritten source of law, is not dealt with in this book.

1.4. LEGAL TRANSLATION

For the most part, modern translation theorists no longer regard translation as a mechanical process of transcoding one language into another. Nor is a text regarded as 'a string of words and structures to be converted into a string of equivalents' (Snell-Hornby 1988:75). Primarily under the influence of German scholars, the main emphasis in general translation theory has shifted from language to the cultural aspects of translation (Hönig and Kussmaul 1982:50; Vermeer 1986:33). As Wilss warns, however, a concept of translation cannot be based solely on cultural aspects (1992:39; *cf.* Lambert 1994:17–26). Above all, the translator must take account of the communicative function of the target text and the elements constituting the sociocultural situation in which it is produced (Snell-Hornby 1988:44).

The law of a country or region is certainly influenced by its culture. In fact, some legal anthropologists claim that legal studies cannot be separated from culture, i.e., legal culture (Wróblewsky 1987:11). Nonetheless, in regard to translation, trans-lators of legal texts are concerned primarily with legal, not cultural transfer. Back in 1974 L.-J. Constantinesco, a well-known comparative lawyer, defined legal translation as a double operation consisting of both legal and interlingual transfer. As he correctly emphasized, legal transfer constitutes the principal operation:

> Il s'agit, d'aboutir, par une traduction linguistique faite d'une langue à l'autre, à une transposition juridique faite d'un droit à l'autre. Dans ce processus, la traduction linguistique est secondaire; c'est la transposition juridique qui représente l'opération principale (1974:147).

Although Constantinesco used the term *transposition jurdique*, it was clear to him that legal translation is not a mere process of transposing or substituting concepts and institutions of the source legal system by concepts and institutions of the target legal system, in other words, by transcoding legal terminology. Today, when Hadi talks about the limitations of *transposition juridique*, he is clearly referring to the process of transcoding legal terms from one legal language into another (1992:53). Other lawyers, however, use the term *transposition juridique* in a broader sense. In particular, Tallon makes a point of distinguishing *transposition juridique* from 'ordinary translation' or *transposition linguistique* which, in his opinion, is a mechanical process involving language. Emphasizing the diversity of *transposition juridique*, Tallon is one of the few lawyers to acknowledge that the process of legal translation varies depending on the communicative situation (Tallon 1995:342; on *transposition linguistique* in law, *see* Crépeau 1995:51–53). For Didier, the term *transposition juridique* is synonymous with *legal translation* which he regards as a double operation including interlingual transfer. After abandoning the confusing definition of *transposition juridique* in his 1990 book,[6] Didier defines the term as follows: 'La transposition juridique est l'opération de transfert d'un message juridique émis dans une langue et dans un système juridique, vers une autre langue et un autre système juridique' (1991:9). While this process involves the translation of terminology, this is only one aspect of legal translation.

From Didier's definition it follows that, when lawyers talk about translation 'd'un droit à l'autre,' what they mean is translation from one legal system into another – from the source legal system into the target legal system. Unlike medicine, chemistry, computer science, and other disciplines of the exact sciences, law remains first and foremost a national phenomenon. Each national or municipal law, as it is called, constitutes an independent legal system with its own terminological apparatus and underlying conceptual structure, its own rules of classification, sources of law, methodological approaches, and socio-economic principles. As David and Brierley put it:

> [Each legal system] has a vocabulary used to express concepts, its rules are arranged into categories, it has techniques for expressing rules and interpreting them, it is linked to a view of the social order itself which determines the way in which the law is applied and shapes the very function of law in that society (1985:19).

Due to differences in historical and cultural development, the elements of the source legal system cannot be simply transposed into the target legal system. As a result, the main challenge to the legal translator is the incongruency of legal systems. Despite this incongruency, comparative lawyers have succeeded in identifying fundamental similarities in certain legal systems so as to warrant their classification into legal families. Although consensus has not yet been reached, René David proposed the following classification: Romano-Germanic law (continental civil law), common law, socialist law, Hindu law, Islamic law, African law, and Far East law (David and Brierley 1985:20–31). Insisting that considerable differences exist among certain civil law countries, Zweigert and Kötz divide Romano-Germanic law into Romanic law, Germanic law and Scandinavian law (1984: I:80–82). This, however, does not affect translation *per se*. For our purpose, it is more important to note that, despite fundamental similarities among its constituent legal systems, a legal family does not correspond to a biological reality. Moreover, the differences between the various legal families are sometimes enormous, thus complicating the task of comparative lawyers and translators as well. David's following comment on the

---

6. In his 1990 book, Didier defines *transposition juridique* as follows: 'C'est-à-dire la transposition d'un discours juridique propre à un système juridique vers un autre système juridique dans la même langue' (207).

difficulties of comparative legal analysis sheds light on the legal barriers encountered by translators:

> The absence of an exact correspondence between legal concepts and categories in different legal systems is one of the greatest difficulties encountered in comparative legal analysis. It is of course to be expected that one will meet rules with different content; but it may be disconcerting to discover that in some foreign law there is not even that system for classifying the rules with which we are familiar. But the reality must be faced that legal science has developed independently within each legal family, and that those categories and concepts which appear so elementary, so much a part of the natural order of things, to a jurist of one family may be wholly strange to another. This is true even as between those trained in a continental law and the common law, without going so far as to invoke Muslim law. Some matter of primary importance to one may mean nothing, or have only limited significance, to another. A question put by a European jurist, for example, to an African on a matter of family organisation or land law may well be totally incomprehensible if put to him in terms of European institutions (David and Brierley 1985:16).

1.4.1. Translation in plurilingual countries

Legal translation is especially important in plurilingual countries, i.e., countries with two or more official languages. As a rule, plurilingual countries have one legal system, as is the case in Belgium, Finland, Russia, Switzerland, and others. There is, however, a small number of plurilingual countries which are bilegal, i.e., they have two legal systems or a mixed legal system. Such countries include Canada, India, Israel, South Africa, Sri Lanka, and others (*see* Vanderlinden 1995:382). When Hong Kong is returned to China on July 1, 1997, it will retain its common law system at least 50 years, thus making the P.R. of China bilegal as well. In anticipation of the forthcoming change, Hong Kong became officially bilingual in 1986 and as of April 1989 all new principal Ordinances are enacted in both English and Chinese. Translation also began of existing legislation contained in the 31 volumes of the Laws of Hong Kong (*see* Mathews 1989:388; *also* Pasternak 1996:11–36). The conceptual, structural, and ideological differences between the Chinese socialist law and the English common law of Hong Kong make the difficulties of this enormous task formidable. In addition, translators must cope with linguistic problems caused by the distance between English and Chinese. Generally speaking, it can be said that the difficulty of a legal translation depends primarily on the affinity of the legal systems and only subsidiarily on the affinity of the source and target languages (*cf.* de Groot 1991:293; *also* de Groot 1987:5).

As a rule, the translation of legal instruments in plurilingual countries with one legal system is less complicated because the source and target legal systems are one and the same.[7] As a result, all the official languages share a common system of

---

7. Thus Didier makes a distinction between *transposition juridique*, which involves different legal systems, and *traduction juridique*, which he defines as: 'L'opération de transfert d'un message juridique, dans un seul système, d'une langue vers une autre langue' (1991:9). The distinction

reference, i.e., the signs in each language refer to the same objects and concepts (*see* Chapter 8, 8.2).[8] Furthermore, the system of classification is the same, as are the rules of interpretation and the socio-economic principles. In such plurilingual countries the main problem is often establishing and standardizing the terminology in the various official languages. This task should not be underestimated, particularly in federal states where there exist simultaneously a federal or central government (legislative and executive branch) and several state, provincial or cantonal legislatures and governments. When the same language is used in several states, provinces or cantons, this leads to terminological incongruency within the same language as each regional law has its own system of reference. This problem is especially acute in Switzerland where there are 16 German-speaking cantons and four plurilingual cantons in which one of the official languages is German (Weibel 1992:31). Since cantonal law is well developed, it is extremely difficult to agree on a uniform German nomenclature at the federal level. Once a nomenclature is established for federal law, the translation operations are greatly simplified (*see* Bocquet 1994:45–53). It is noteworthy that the terminological problems faced by Swiss translators during the formation of the plurilingual confederate state at the turn of the century were essentially the same as those now confronting Belgian translators in the new German-speaking region of Belgium (*see* Chapter 2, 2.9.3).

1.4.2. International and supranational law

The main bulk of legal translation is done at the international and supranational levels. Despite efforts to unify international law and harmonize supranational law such as European law, the translation of international and supranational law frequently involves two or more legal systems. In regard to translation in the European Union, Pascale Berteloot confirms that European law is still in the process of formation, thus forcing the parties to resort to municipal law as a supplementary legal order, for example, in non-contractual matters (law of torts) (1988:16). The situation is similar in international law where the core of uniform law is so sparse that it must be supplemented by institutions and concepts borrowed from various national legal systems. While Tabory remarks that the difficulty of translating international instruments increases with each additional language (1980:146), she fails to mention that translators also need to take account of the number of legal systems participating in the communication act. Generally speaking, the task of co-ordinating the parallel texts of a single instrument becomes more difficult as the

is important; however, assigning such a narrow definition to *traduction juridique* is unfortunate. Among other things, it implies that *transposition juridique* is not a form of legal translation. In his 1990 book Didier uses the expression *transcription* for the same concept (1990:207). This, however, is also an inadequate solution.

8. Crépeau (1995:53) uses the term *transposition linguistique 'simple'* to denote legal translation within the same legal system and *transposition linguistique 'complex'* or *transposition juridico-linguistique* to denote legal translation from one legal system into another.

15

number of languages and the participating legal systems increases (*see* Chapter 7, 7.5).

1.5. LEGAL TRANSLATION AND GENERAL TRANSLATION THEORY

Today, one of the main tasks of translation theorists is to define criteria to be used by the translator when selecting an adequate translation strategy (*see* Kussmaul 1995:55–72). This presupposes, of course, that the translator is at liberty to make such a decision. Legal translators have traditionally been bound by the principle of fidelity. Convinced that the main goal of legal translation is to reproduce the content of the source text as accurately as possible, both lawyers and linguists agreed that legal texts had to be translated literally. For the sake of preserving the letter of the law, the main guideline for legal translation was fidelity to the source text. Even after legal translators won the right to produce texts in the spirit of the target language, the general guideline remained fidelity to the source text. Today UN *Instructions for translators* appear to take a more liberal approach by admitting that 'there is always room for the exercise of stylistic judgment in the case of draft resolutions, treaties and other legal texts, or technical texts;' however, the final conclusion is that 'fidelity to the original text must be the first consideration' (1984:3). More recently, the traditional principle of fidelity has been challenged by the introduction of new bilingual drafting methods which have succeeded in revolutionizing legal translation (Chapter 4, 4.4.1). Contrary to freer forms of translation, legal translators are still guided by the principle of fidelity; however, their first consideration is no longer fidelity to the source text. Nonetheless, the question remains as to how translators can determine how much fidelity is required to guarantee the effectiveness of plurilingual communication in the law. Moreover, which criteria should be taken into account by legal translators when selecting a translation strategy. Seeking answers to these questions, lawyers began to differentiate between various types of legal texts.

1.5.1. Translation and text type

Emphasizing the constraints of legal translation, Didier generally concludes: 'La traduction juridique n'est pas libre, car le droit impose à la langue ses propres contraintes terminologiques et stylistiques' (1990:254). Elsewhere he remarks that judgments can be translated more freely than legislative texts; however, he provides no proof or arguments to support his statement (1990:280). For the most part, Didier focuses on translations of legislation which, in his opinion, require absolute literalness:

> Les textes d'arrivée reprennent donc les textes de départ mot pour mot, phrase pour phrase, et jusqu' à la ponctuation, sous réserve des transformation grammaticales absolument indispensables (1990:285).

Although Didier published his book in 1991, his comments are based primarily on translations of Canadian statutes made in the seventies prior to the legislative reform.

Another lawyer, W.E. Weisflog is more thorough in his differentiation of legal texts; however, in an attempt to draw upon translation theory, he refers to Nida's theory of formal and dynamic correspondence of the seventies. In regard to translations of national legislation and international treaties, he states that 'there is little or no room for free translation' and claims that 'it is desirable, if not imperative, to have the greatest possible degree of formal correspondence' (1987:191). In essence, formal correspondence is another expression for literal translation in which the translator reproduces the grammatical and stylistic patterns of the source language as closely as possible (*cf.* Nida 1974:201). Similarly, Weisflog advocates formal correspondence for translations 'of quasi legislation or recommendations such as the UN, UNCTAD, ILO, OECD, and EEC Codes of Conduct or Guidelines and OECD Model Conventions' as well as 'business contracts, license agreements, general conditions of supply and delivery (conditions of sale), Memoranda and Articles of Association (Articles of Incorporation), rules and regulations concerning share acquisition schemes' and other business documents (1987:194). In regard to textbooks, articles in legal journals, and lectures, Weisflog remarks that the translator's task is to 'get the author's message – meaning here his thoughts and ideas rather than his words – over to the receptor' (1987:195). Although he implies that such translations can be less literal, he does not go so far as to advocate dynamic correspondence, in which the message is conveyed in the spirit of the target language.

Finally, it should be noted that Weisflog also mentions legislation (constitutions, statutes, etc.) translated 'purely for information purposes, i.e., for the information of foreign lawyers, businessmen, and other foreign readers' (1987:193). This distinction is significant because it is one of the first signs of awareness by a lawyer that the function of a text might also play a role in determining translation strategy. In the end, however, he again recommends the method of formal correspondence or literal translation.

A linguist, Jean-Claude Gémar has devoted many years to the translation of legal texts and general translator training in Quebec. In the chapter on legal translation in his most recent work (1995–II:139–176), Gémar divides legal texts into three groups; however, his criterion for determining which texts belong to a particular group is not function but, in the case of the first two groups, subject-matter, i.e., whether the text regulates public or private affairs. As a result of this unorthodox approach based on categories of language (*see* 1.3 above), his first group of texts contains laws, regulations, judgments, and international treaties, while the second group consists of contracts, administrative and commercial forms, wills, etc. The third group contains scholarly works (doctrine) which, in his view, are the most difficult to translate.[9] In regard to translation techniques, Gémar mentions literal translation, functional equivalence, and interpretative translation; however, a clear distinction is not made between the latter two (1995–II:163–166). As a rule, functional equivalence is not a translation technique (*see* Chapter 2, 2.8.4), and it appears that he is not referring to what is known in modern translation theory as functional translation (*see* Nord 1993:8).

---

9. Since scholarly works are not normative texts and do not have the force of law, lawyers generally regard them as easier to translate than multilingual legislation and treaties (*see* Tallon 1995:342).

1.5.2. Translation strategy and function

After dominating translation for two thousand years, the traditional view that the translator's primary task is to transfer the meaning of the source text has been challenged. Of the few truly original ideas in translation theory, one of them is surely the 'discovery' that the same text can be translated in different ways for different receivers, as proposed, for example, by House in her notion of overt translation (1981:185). This idea liberated the translator, transforming him/her into a text producer whose task is to create a new text by selecting a translation strategy based on an analysis of the particular communicative situation. Above all, the translator should take account of pragmatic considerations: To whom is the target text addressed? Why is the target text being translated? What are the conventional rules in the target culture for producing texts for that particular purpose? Who wrote the source text? When and where was the source text written? (Hönig and Kussmaul 1982:23). At first it was believed that translation strategy is determined primarily by the type of audience to whom the target text is directed. For example, the translation of a medical report for laymen differs considerably from a translation of the same text for medical doctors. More recently, theorists have shifted the main emphasis to the function of a translation (why), which in turn also determines the target receivers (to whom) (Hönig and Kussmaul 1982:40).

Identifying the function of a translation as the main criterion for determining translation strategy, Hans J. Vermeer postulated his *skopos* theory which has modernized translation theory by offering an alternative to meaning-based translation (Chapter 3, 3.3.1). In traditional translation it is generally accepted that the primary task of the translator is to reconstruct the meaning of the source text in the target language (*cf.* Larson 1984:30). In such translations the function of the target text is always the same as that of the source text (*Funktionskonstanz*). Vermeer's *skopos* theory departs from tradition by recognizing translations in which the function of the target text differs from that of the source text (*Funktionsveränderung*). Pursuant to the *skopos* theory, the translator's main task is to produce a new text that satisfies the cultural expectations of the target receivers for a text with that particular function. Thus Vermeer shows that the same text can be translated in different ways depending on its function. For example, an advertising text will be translated differently depending on whether the intention is to sell the product to potential customers or to describe it at a marketing convention (Snell-Hornby 1990a:82).

Although Vermeer claims that the *skopos* theory applies to *all* translations (1982:99), he has had difficulty convincing LSP theorists that it is useful for special-purpose texts as well. This is because the function of special-purpose translations is usually the same as that of the source text. Thus theorists of specialized translation still tend to insist that the goal of LSP translators is to transfer the meaning or message of the source text as accurately as possible (Fluck 1985:136; Gémar 1995–II:115). Attempting to prove that function is also a key factor in specialized translation, Vermeer presents a hypothetical example of an insurance contract which, in his opinion, should be translated in different ways depending on the communicative function in each situation. As he puts it, target-language formulae are to be used in the translation of an insurance contract for use in practice, whereas source-language ones are to be imitated if the translation is to be used as court evidence (1986:34).

Vermeer is to be complimented for recognizing that all legal translation need not be literal; however, his example greatly oversimplifies the decision-making process of legal translators. By suggesting that the translation strategy of a legal translation can be determined solely on the basis of function, Vermeer disregards the fact that legal texts are subject to special rules governing their use in the mechanism of the law. Above all, legal translators must take account of legal criteria when selecting an appropriate translation strategy. For instance, in regard to contracts, the decision whether and to what extent target-language formulae should be used is determined primarily by the law governing the contract. This fact is essential because it determines whether the contract will be interpreted according to the source or the target legal system. In linguistic terms, it determines the system of reference, i.e., whether the signs in the target text refer to objects and concepts in the source or the target legal system.

Another theorist of general translation to comment on legal translation, Peter Newmark notes a difference in the translation of legal documents for information purposes and those which are 'concurrently valid in the TL community.' In regard to 'foreign laws, wills, conveyancing' translated for information purposes only, Newmark suggests that literal or semantic translation, as he refers to it, is necessary. In this respect, he appears to agree with Weisflog. On the other hand, he departs significantly from Weisflog's view when he stresses that 'the formal register of the TL must be respected in dealing with documents that are to be concurrently valid in the TL community (EEC law, contracts, international agreements, patents).' In Newmark's view, such translations require the so-called communicative approach that is target language-oriented (1982:47). Newmark is one of the few linguists to recognize that the status of a legal translation is instrumental in determining its use in practice (*cf. also* Sager 1986:341; *also* Sager 1993:179).

1.6. THE STATUS OF LEGAL TRANSLATIONS

The status of a legal translation is important because it determines which translations can be used in specific situations in legal communication. Thus it can be said that the communicative function of a legal translation is determined by its status., i.e., whether it is authoritative or non-authoritative. Legal instruments translated exclusively for information purposes are non-authoritative: they are not vested with the force of law and are non-binding. Translations of legal documents used as court evidence are also non-binding. Such translations are made by court translators who are required to swear to the accuracy and correctness of their translation. While they may be used for establishing or finding facts in court cases (Jessnitzer 1982:66–67), it is not admissible to use them for the purpose of interpreting statutes and other sources of the law. As a rule, only authoritative translations of constitutions, statutes, codes, treaties, and conventions may be used by the court for the purpose of interpretation.

19

1.6.1. Authoritative translations

Vested with the force of law, authoritative translations enable the mechanism of the law to function in more than one language. Translations of normative legal instruments constituting the sources of law of a particular legal system are regarded as authoritative only if they are approved and/or adopted in the manner prescribed by law. For instance, in order to be authoritative, the various language versions of a piece of legislation must be adopted by the competent lawmaking body of the particular country (*see* Chapter 4, 4.2.3). By virtue of the act of adoption, such texts are not mere translations of the law, they are the law itself. Today, the authoritative texts of a legal instrument are usually equally authentic. This means that no single text should prevail for the purpose of interpretation in the event an ambiguity or diversity in meaning is detected in the various language versions. In other words, the court should consult all language versions and attempt to resolve the conflict by ordinary methods of interpretation. If this is not possible, the court should determine which meaning best reconciles the texts (*see* Chapter 3, 3.3.2). Some plurilingual countries also publish the judicial decisions of their highest court(s) in the respective official languages. In private law, contracts are often drawn up and authenticated in various languages. Such contracts usually contain a language clause specifying which language version(s) is to prevail whenever a diversity or ambiguity is detected. In the absence of such a language clause, the source text usually prevails or the court declares all versions equally authentic. In international law numerous legal instruments are drawn up and authenticated in more than one language, particularly treaties and conventions. In European law, the Treaties establishing the European Communities, the Single European Act, and the Maastricht Treaty are equally authentic in all languages of the Member States (including Irish).

Legally binding instruments, including authoritative translations, are also referred to as authentic texts. A text becomes authentic only by reason of its adoption or other mode of authentication. Despite the advent of multilingualism in international law, the number of authentic texts of a single instrument is obviously limited. Therefore, in addition to authentic texts, there are also official texts, translations which are signed but not adopted by the member countries, and official translations, translations prepared by a government or international organization on its own responsibility (*see* Ivrakis 1954:216). In order to avoid confusion, the International Law Commission (ILC) has proposed that the term *text* be used to denote those language versions designated as authentic by the contracting parties or rules of procedure, whereas the term *version* be used to refer to all other language versions. As a result, international lawyers now differentiate between authentic texts and other versions. Today the term *version* covers 'mere translations into other languages possessing at most a certain "official" character' (Tabory 1980:171). Among other things, this distinction enables lawyers to avoid using the word *translation* when referring to authentic texts produced by translation. In their opinion, the term *translation* implies inferiority and is thus inconsistent with the principle of equally authentic texts. From the legal point of view, once a translation has been authenticated, it is vested with the force of law and is just as inviolate as the original text. In accordance with the theory of original texts, lawyers regard all authenticated texts as originals.

Equally authentic texts of the same instrument existing in two or more languages are sometimes referred to in legal discourse as parallel texts (Šarčević 1994:301).[10] It is particularly effective when parallel texts are published side by side in the same volume, thus facilitating their comparison. For example, the equally authentic English and French texts of Canadian federal statutes appear side by side in official publications of the *Statutes of Canada/Lois du Canada [SC]* and the *Revised Statutes of Canada/Lois révisées du Canada [RSC]*. Of course, this becomes unwieldy when several languages are involved, thus necessitating the publication of individual language volumes. Nevertheless, a high degree of systematization has even been achieved in the twelve parallel volumes of EU publications.[11] In order to facilitate their identification, each of the official languages of the European Union has been assigned a specific color and all texts in that language are published in the assigned color (either the pages themselves or the book cover). More important, care is taken to match the text and sometimes even the line numbers of text on each page in all volumes, thus assuring a uniform system of citation in all languages (*see*, e.g., the *Reports of Cases before the Court/Recueil de la Jurisprudence de la Cour/Sammlung der Rechtsprechung des Gerichtshofes*).

1.6.2. Institutional texts

This book deals primarily with the parallel texts of sources of law produced and used by national, supranational (EU), and international institutions. Curiously, such texts have rarely been mentioned in translation theory, let alone analyzed in detail. This is perhaps because they are institutional texts, thus implying off-limits for translation theorists. Since the communicative function of institutional texts is standardized, all the parallel texts of a single instrument always have the same communicative function. In other words, there is no shift of function as advocated under the *skopos* theory. In view of this, I was initially hopeful that it would be possible to identify a common translation strategy for parallel texts of the same type of instrument; however, my optimism soon faded. After visits to the Translation and Terminology Divisions of the UN Language Service in Geneva, the European Court of Justice in

10. This usage of the term *parallel texts* is not to be confused with its usage in general translation theory. For example, Snell-Hornby defines parallel texts as 'Originaltexte der gleichen Textsorte, die unabhängig voneinander zu demselben Thema mit identischer Funktion und in einer vergleichbaren Situation entstanden sind' (1990b:10; *cf.* Snell-Hornby 1988:86). Snell-Hornby's definition also differs from Thiel's. *See* Gisela Thiel's article 'Parallel text production. An alternative in pragmatically-oriented foreign language courses' in: C. Titford/A.E. Hieke (Hg.) *Translation in Foreign Language Teaching and Testing*, Tübingen 1985;117–133; *see also* Neubert and Shreve 1992:89.

11. At present, primary legislation of the EU (Treaties establishing the European Communities, the Single European Act, and the Maastricht Treaty are elaborated in twelve parallel texts (including Irish). Pursuant to an Agreement made in 1971 between Ireland and the Community, Irish (*Gaeilge*) is considered an official Community language; however, only primary legislation is drawn up in that language. Therefore, EU secondary legislation, regulations and directives are drawn up and published in eleven parallel texts.

Luxembourg, the Cour de cassation in Brussels, the Legislative Section of the Department of Justice in Ottawa, and the Central Language and Translation Service of the Federal Office of Justice in Berne, it became clear that, in addition to prescribing its own format and style for given text types, each institution has its own, usually unwritten guidelines for translators. As a result, the same text type may not only look very different but is frequently translated in a different manner at various institutions. Therefore, generalizations such as Didier's that legislation is translated literally and judgments more freely are definitely misleading. As for judgments, not only the format but also the methods of translation vary significantly from institution to institution. Generally speaking, the rigid form requirements of judgments of the Belgian Court of Cassation make it necessary for translators to follow the source text as closely as possible, whereas decisions of the European Court of Justice can be translated almost idiomatically. Even then, such statements are too general. Upon closer examination, one sees that certain parts of judgments of the European Court are less idiomatic than others, depending on whether they are descriptive or prescriptive. Thus function does play a role in legal translation; however, it is only one of the criteria to be taken into account when determining translation strategy.

2   History of Legal Translation

2.1. LITERAL VS. FREE TRANSLATION

Dating back to the wars between Egypt and Mesopotamia, the two dominant rivals
of the early Eurasian world, the oldest known recorded evidence of legal translation
is the Egyptian-Hittite Peace Treaty of 1271 B.C. Two versions of the Treaty were
discovered, one in hieroglyphic inscriptions in several Egyptian temples and the other
in cuneiform characters inscribed on tablets unearthed in the Hittite capital of
Bogazköy. Both are believed to be translations; however, the original was never
found (Hilf 1973:5).

Despite its long tradition which surpasses even that of Bible translation,[1] the
history of legal translation has remained more or less an enigma. To my knowledge,
there have been no previous attempts to make a comprehensive study of its
development. Nor are there any treatises on legal translation comparable to Martin
Luther's *Sendbrief vom Dolmetschen* (1530), Pierre Daniet Huet's *De optimo
genere interpretande* (expanded version of 1680) or to Alexander Fraser Tytler's
Essay on the Principles of Translation (1791). Pieced together from information
gathered from legal documents and statements made by legal translators, their critics,
and legal historians, this historical survey is by no means complete. For practical
reasons, it is based mainly on translations of statutes and codes, the primary sources
of written law (*cf.* Hattenhauer 1987:5).

For over 2000 years, general translation studies were dominated by the debate
whether a translation should be literal or free (*cf.* Steiner 1977:239). Due to the
sensitive nature of legal texts, this issue has been particularly controversial in legal
translation as it raises legal questions as well. Since both legal and religious texts
are normative, it is not surprising that the early history of legal translation is most
closely related to that of Bible translation, i.e., until the Middle Ages when the first
moderately literal translations of the Bible were made into vernacular languages.
Because of the authoritative status of legal texts, legal translation remained under
the grip of tradition much longer than other areas of translation. In fact, the first real
challenge to the literal translation of legal texts did not come until the twentieth
century when translators of lesser used official languages finally began to demand
equal language rights, thus setting the stage for the development from literal to near

---

1. When Nida (Nida and Taber 1974:vii) claims that Bible translation has a longer tradition than
    any comparable kind of translation, he fails to take account of legal translation. According to
    Nida, Bible translation dates back to the third century B.C.

idiomatic and idiomatic or 'linguistically pure' translation, as Beaupré calls it (1986:179). This development is illustrated on the continuum in figure 1 below. Commencing with strict literal translation, the development moves gradually towards idiomatic translation and, thanks to the new methods of bilingual drafting in Canada (Chapter 4 at 4.4.1), ends with co-drafting at the far right:

Figure 1: *Phases in the Development of Legal Translation*

strict literal	literal	moderately literal	near idiomatic	idiomatic	co-drafting

Although multilingualism is an outgrowth of the twentieth century, plurilingual communication in the law has a long and colorful history. Not only do the legal systems of the western world have their roots in Roman law, but the translation activities under Emperor Justinian also left their mark on the history of legal translation. Thus it is appropriate that this historical survey commences with Roman law.

2.2. JUSTINIAN'S DIRECTIVE: STRICT LITERAL TRANSLATION

Despite the authoritative status of translations of legal instruments, written guidelines or directives prescribing translation techniques for such texts are extremely rare. To my knowledge, the first known codified rule on the translation of legislative texts is Emperor Justinian's directive set forth in the *Corpus juris civilis*. After the fall of the Western Roman Empire in 476, the Empire continued in the East with its seat at Constantinople (Byzantium). It was there that Justinian ordered the great compilation, systematization, and consolidation of Roman law later known as the *Corpus juris civilis*. Justinian's codification consists of the Institutes, the Digest (or pandects) and the Code, promulgated between 533 and 534. Thereafter Justinian continued to legislate by a series of Novels (*Novellae constitutiones*), promulgated between 535 and 556 (von Mehren and Gordley 1977:6; Krüger 1912:400). As a Roman Emperor, Justinian upheld the rights of the Latin language, as a result of which the *Corpus juris* was basically written in Latin. This also included the *Digest*, a compilation of the writings of great Roman jurists (Liebs 1975:96–103). The *Digest* is the most important part of the *Corpus juris* for the history of western law and legal translation as well. After ordering revisions in the original texts comprising the *Digest*, Justinian attempted to prevent 'distortions' of his monumental codification by issuing a directive prohibiting all commentaries on his enactments. As an additional means of preserving the letter of the law, the directive explicitly permitted only translations into Greek that reproduced the Latin text word for word:

> Imperator Caesar Flavius Iustinianus... Augustus ad senatum et omnes populos... nemo neque eorum, qui in praesenti iuris peritiam habent, nec qui postea fuerint, audeat commentarios isdem legibus adnectere, nisi tantum si velit eas in Graecam vocem

transformare sub eodem ordine eaque consequentia, sub qua et voces Romanae positae sunt, hoc quod Graeci dicunt (§ 21 *Constitutio Tanta* [Introductory Act to the *Digest*]).

In word-for-word translation, the words of the source text are translated literally into the target language and even the grammatical forms and word order of the source text are retained. In essence, word-for-word translation is strict literal translation or 'primitive interlineal translation,' as it was called by early translation theorists, thus distinguishing it from 'refined interlineal translation' or literal translation (in Kloepfer 1967:42–43). In literal translation, the basic unit of translation is still the word; however, basic transformations (changes in syntax) are permitted to respect the rules of grammar in the target language, thus increasing comprehensibility while following the source text as closely as possible (*see* Wilss 1977:105).

As it turns out, Justinian's directive requiring word-for-word translation was modelled on the practice of the Church. This is not surprising in view of the close relations between Church and State. At Rome the Church was initially a branch of the State and *ius sacrum* a part of *ius publicum*. When Christianity was established as the official religion of the Roman State in 313 A.D., the State recognized the Church and its spiritual authority and the Church acknowledged the submission of Christians to the Emperor's sovereignty. The peaceful co-existence of spiritual and temporal powers was later disturbed by competing claims of Empire and Papacy for superiority, eventually resulting in a contest between civil law and canon law (*see* Walker 1980:214).

In early Christianity the Emperor had a claim to divine inspiration, as a result of which imperial enactments were deemed sacrosanct. Thus it followed that, like the word of God in the Scriptures, the letter of the law also demanded strict literal translation to protect it from heterodoxy. Moreover, both biblical and legislative texts were attributed the quality of mysteriousness, i.e., they conveyed an assumed truth, not to be comprehended by the human mind but accepted on faith alone (*cf.* Werk 1933:18). Thus it was believed that the 'word power' of such texts could be retained only by word-for-word translation. This follows from Hieronymus' warning in his letter to Pammachius: 'Absque Scripturis sanctis, ubi et veraborum ordo mysterium est' (*De optimo genere interpretandi*, cited in Kloepfer 1967:28; *also* Vermeer 1992b:93).

According to the nineteenth-century German lexicographer Wölfflin, early Bible translations from Greek into Latin were characterized by an overabundance of etymological equivalents of Greek words used without regard to context. This resulted in a large number of *faux amis* or, as Wölfflin put it, a large number of Latin words with the same stem as the Greek source words but with different meanings (1894:82–83). The same method of painstaking literalness was also found in Judaism, which had originally banned translation as blasphemy. In this context, Steiner refers to the belief recorded in the *Megillath Taanith* (Roll of Fasting) that 'three days of utter darkness fell on the world when the Law was translated into Greek' in the first century A.D. (1977:239). Even today translations of the Koran, the sacred book of Islam and primary source of Muslim law, are required to be as literal as possible (Preface to *The Quran*, Guildford and Surrey 1975:vii).

2.3. PRESERVING THE LETTER OF THE LAW IN THE MIDDLE AGES

Much of what is currently western Europe, including parts of England, had been romanized for some 400 years. After the shattering of the western Roman Empire by German tribes, the surviving elements of Roman law persisted mainly in memory or as custom and habit. Above all, it was the Roman Catholic Church that preserved in its canon law and culture much of Roman civilization, including the Latin language. In the early Middle Ages, national languages were still underdeveloped, as a result of which legal instruments and documents were recorded in Latin. In Germany, for example, there was no uniform spoken language and no written language. Since lawmakers and judges were not always versed in Latin, translation was essential in both the legislative and the judicial process. According to Philipp Heck, a legal historian, strict literal translation was the rule of the day for medieval translators of legislative texts. Convinced that historians could not objectively evaluate the sources of medieval law without taking account of the then practiced translation techniques, Heck took it upon himself to systematize the techniques used to translate legal instruments and documents in Germany in the early Middle Ages. His book *Übersetzungsprobleme im frühen Mittelalter* (1931)[2] is a noteworthy contribution not only to legal history but also to the history of translation.[3]

Heck speaks of *ad hoc* translation performed for the purpose of making or revising a particular law or deciding a court case. The translation operations were performed immediately without preparation, thus the designation *ad hoc*. Both written and oral discourse were involved, a process which Heck refers to as *Übersetzung zu Protokoll* and *Übersetzung nach Gehör* (1931:11). For example, between the fifth and ninth centuries, the laws of various German tribes (e.g., the *lex Salica, lex Alamanorum* and the *lex Baiuvariorum*) were formulated orally in vernacular German and recorded immediately by clerics in Latin. In order to avoid the necessity of convening for a second session, the lawmakers preferred to authenticate the Latin text with their signatures straight away, leaving the translator no time to revise his word-for-word translation. Moreover, from a technical point of view, revisions were practically impossible once the words had sunken into the papyrus (1931:7).

Since the written law was in Latin, it was necessary to translate relevant sections of the Latin text back into German during legal proceedings before the court. According to Heck, this process of 'back translation' was not so much for the benefit of the parties as for the judges. The translation was done orally much the same as court interpretation today. At the end of the proceedings, the decision was rendered orally in German and 'recorded' by the translator in Latin (Heck 1931:4–19).

Heck describes the Latin target texts as word-for-word translations in which the German source words were simply replaced by Latin 'equivalents' without regard to context and text coherency. Heck refers to this as the 'equivalent method'

---

2. Heck's first publication on translation problems was written in 1900; however, his articles were not published in book form until 1931.
3. Instead of giving Heck credit for his efforts to systematize early translation techniques, Vermeer (1992b:100) criticizes the terminology used by Heck to describe various translation procedures, such as *Grundübersetzung, Rückübersetzung*, and *Vorübersetzung*.

(*Äquivalentmethode*) and the relation between a source term and its equivalent as 'equivalence' (*Äquivalenz*).[4] Furthermore, he notes that the use of the equivalent method encouraged the use of etymological equivalents, thus resulting in a large number of errors due to polysemy, which he calls 'multiple equivalence.' Heck attributes the poor quality of the translations mainly to the fact that the translators were clerics without legal training. Unfamiliar with technical terms of the law, they tended to translate words in isolation. Since the translation operations had to be performed immediately, the clerics did not have time to think in the target language and formulate the text in good Latin.

Under such conditions Heck defends the use of word-for-word translation. As he put it, it was necessary to preserve the letter of the law in Latin so as to enable it to be reproduced correctly when back translated into German:

> Bei Rechtsaufzeichnungen war nun schon durch den Zweck der Aufzeichnungen eine gewisse Worttreue gegeben, die Äquivalentmethode in gewissem Grade notwendig. Der Wortlaut des Gesetzes war ja wichtig, er sollte so aufgezeichnet werden, daß er bei der Rückübersetzung wieder herauskam (1931:9).

Nonetheless, Heck admits that back translations made during court sessions were often erroneous, thus causing a discrepancy between the written law and its application (1931:7, note 1). Despite inevitable errors, Heck again emphasizes the importance of using the equivalent method. Since different clerics performed the various translation operations, he presumes that there would have been even greater inconsistency if freer methods of translation had been used. More important, however, is his comment that the equivalent method was used in glosses serving as translation aids. The original glosses were explanations of difficult words or phrases written in the margin or above individual words of the Latin text. Dating from the middle of the eleventh century,[5] the glosses mentioned by Heck contained passages from Latin texts with Old High German glosses in the margin to explain technical terms (Heck 1931:5, note 2, 146–151; *cf.* Kaufmann 1984:170). They also served as corpuses for medieval vocabularies (glossaries) which were essentially word lists of Latin terms and their equivalents extracted from glosses. As confirmed by Heck, word-for-word translation was the accepted method of producing such glosses and glossaries (Heck 1931:20, 149; *cf.* Vermeer 1992b:107).

The eleventh century marked the revival of the study of Roman law at universities in southern France and Italy (especially Bologna) where Justinian's *Corpus juris civilis* was taught by using monolingual glosses. Instead of explaining single words, these glosses were an exposition of the entire passage or principle concerned, in other words, a textual interpretation or commentary (von Mehren and Gordley 1977:9).

---

4. *See* 2.8.4 below on the equivalence discussion which dominated modern translation theory in the seventies and early eighties and has been revived in the nineties; on terminological equivalence, *see* Chapter 8 at 8.6.
5. The oldest known glosses – the Malberg Glosses – date from the middle of the eighth century. Among other things, they contained the original Latin text of the *Lex Salica* with explanatory glosses written in Frankish. *See* E.Erb, *Geschichte der deutschen Literatur von den Anfängen bis 1160*, Berlin Ost: Volk und Wissen (1965:230).

The period of the so-called glossators is said to have extended from 1015 to 1250. The most famous glossator, Accursius (1182–1260), made a fairly comprehensive collection and synthesis of earlier glosses, summaries, and other works. After Accursius the use of the gloss declined as a method of study because it had essentially become a substitute for the actual text (Walker 1980:528).

2.4. GRADUAL BREAKUP OF LATIN DOMINANCE

In England, the Latin monopoly in religion was weakened as early as the fourteenth century by Wycliff's translation of the Scriptures into English. Although the Reformation awakened popular interest in written English, the revolt against law Latin, as it was called, occurred long after England had cut herself off from the Church of Rome. This, however, was due to the presence of law French (Anglo-Norman law) and the argument that it was better to have Latin writs rather than unintelligible French ones (Mellinkoff 1963:82). Although the English courts never received Roman law, Latin had become the dominant written language for statutes, charters, and writs in England after the Norman conquest (1066). Even with the rise of law French, law Latin dominated the English statute books through the first half of the thirteenth century and some Latin could still be found in the statutes until 1461. With the advent of the printing press, the printing of statutes commenced in the 1480's, however, in Latin and French (Mellinkoff 1963:163). In 1527 the first glossary with a specialized vocabulary, a Latin/English glossary of law terms was published by John Rastell for the purpose of expounding 'certeyn obscure & derke termys concernynge the lawes of thys realme' (*New Encyclopedia Britannica* 1985 VII:719). At that time one of the goals of the language reform was to make the statutes and pleadings available in English. Nonetheless, Latin remained the favored language of the pleadings until being outlawed, along with law French, during the Commonwealth language reform (1649–1660). Although the reform met with resistance and had to be reinstated by a new English-for-lawyers law in 1731, the main bulk of translation was performed in the seventeenth century (Mellinkoff 1963:126–135; *also* Koschaker 1947:12).

Whereas the goal of the language reform had formally been achieved, the real intention of making the law intelligible to the common people had not been. This was due in part to the poor quality of the English texts which, in accordance with tradition, were strict literal translations. In the words of a legal historian, the word-for-word translations of law French documents were 'difficult and obscure' (Collas 1953:xiv). At the same time, those of law Latin documents were regarded as considerably more unintelligible. Today it is generally accepted that strict literal translation can be used only if the source and target languages are very closely related and even then real success is rare (Wilss 1977:104; Larson 1984:10). The following translation of a pleading from law Latin (1654) shows what happens when a highly inflected language is reproduced word for word in a language dependent on syntax instead of inflection for intelligibility:

> And so being thereof possessed, the sayd Beasts out of his hands and possession casually lost, which Beasts afterwards; that is to say, the 19th. day of December then

next following at C. aforesaid to the hands and possession of the foresaid Tho: by finding came, notwithstanding the sayd Tho: knowing the Beasts aforesaid to be the proper Beasts of the said Edw: and to the sayd Edw: of right to belong and appertain, craftily and fraudulently intending the sayd Edw: in that behalf craftily and subtley to deceive and defraud, the said sheep to the said Edward, though often thereunto requested, hath not delivered... (cited in Mellinkoff 1963:146).

Following Latin form proved not only to be clumsy but also wordy. Since English uses articles and prepositions to make up for what it lacks in inflection, the results were ostentatious wordiness and unclarity, or as a Scotchman put it in the eighteenth century:

> The luggage of particles, such as pronouns, prepositions, and auxiliary verbs, from which it is impossible for us entirely to disencumber ourselves, clogs the expression, and enervates the sentiment (*ibid.*).

As confirmed by Blackstone in his *Commentaries on the Laws of England* (1765–1769), such translations did little to achieve the goal of the reform:

> This was done, in order that the common people might have knowledge and under-standing of what was alleged or done for and against them in the process and pleadings, the judgment and entries in a cause. Which purpose I know not how well it has answered, but am apt to suspect that the people are now, after many years' experience, altogether as ignorant in matters of law as before (*ibid.*:135).

2.4.1. On the Continent

The final breakdown of Latin dominance occurred considerably later on the Continent as a result of the reception of Roman law. Not surprisingly, reception came about very early in Italy, where the *Corpus juris civilis* had a claim to direct authority as the law of the *imperius romanum*. In France, large-scale instruction in Roman law began in the thirteenth century (*see* von Mehren and Gordley 1977:10), and law was taught in Latin until the eighteenth century despite a declaration of 1680 requiring that ordinance law and customary law be taught in French. The movement to install French as the language of the legislature, the administration, and the judiciary was initiated in the sixteenth century, in particular by the Ordinances of Lyon (1510) and Villers-Cotterêts (1539) (*see* Didier 1990:7–8). As the major means of achieving the goals of the language reform, translation was deemed necessary to reduce the number and complexity of the glosses, to make the law accessible to the public, and to provide greater clarity, thereby reducing litigation and the number of interpretation errors by judges (Didier 1990:7).

In Germany the first serious challenge to law Latin dates back to the translation of the *Sachsenspiegel*, which was drafted in Latin in the thirteenth century but immediately translated and recorded in German as well (1220–1235). Thereafter, the *Landfriedengesetz* of Mainz (1235) was apparently drafted in both Latin and German (Hattenhauer 1987:5). Toward the middle of the thirteenth century private documents began to appear in German and instruments of city law were also germanized (Werk 1933:11). This development, however, succumbed with the advent of the Renaissance and, in particular, with the reception of Roman law. Latin was officially reinstated as the language of the law in Germany by the reception of the *jus commune (gemeines Recht* as Roman law was called) in a *Reichs-kammergerichtsordnung* of 1495.

Even the Reformation and Luther's monumental translations of the New and Old Testaments (1521, 1534) failed to threaten the dominance of law Latin in Germany. Recognizing the Bible, not Rome as the highest authority in religious matters, Luther was determined to make the Bible intelligible to the common people. In so doing, he was not only among the first to translate the Bible into vernacular German, but his efforts to imitate the language of the common people also resulted in a relatively free translation of the Bible. As Luther wrote in his *Sendbrief vom Dolmetschen* (1530):

> Denn man muß nicht die Buchstaben in der lateinischen Sprache fragen, wie man soll deutsch reden,... sondern man muß die Mutter im Hause, die Kinder auf der Gassen, den gemeinen Mann auf dem Markt drum fragen und demselbigen auf das Maul sehen, wie sie reden, und darnach dolmetschen, da verstehen sie es denn und merken, daß man deutsch mit ihnen redet (cited in Störing 1973:21).

Luther's translations marked the end of the parallel development of the translation of biblical and legislative texts. It is said that, in the spirit of the Reformation, Sebastian Brant had originally intended to produce a counterpart to Luther's translations in the field of law by translating the *Corpus juris civilis* into German. Apparently, Brant's plan was dismissed by others as legal dilettantism and a foolish undertaking for a lawyer. In Wieacker's words, this was the plan of a dilettante who failed to realize that, contrary to the Bible, the *Corpus juris* was not literature for the common people (Wieacker 1952:90). Thereafter, a century passed before a national language reform was initiated in Germany and another century before New High German was finally accepted as the uniform written language in the first half of the seventeenth century (Werk 1933:25). It was not until the Enlightenment that Brant's foolish project would be taken seriously.

2.5. THE INEVITABLE SHIFT TO LITERAL TRANSLATION

Latin survived the Middle Ages as the dominant language of international law and remained the principal diplomatic language until its supremacy was challenged by the national languages of the new prestigious western States, especially France. As a result of the success of the armies of Louis XIV (1647–1715) and the growing importance of French literature and the arts, the French language gained such prestige and widespread recognition 'that it was adopted by the courts of Europe and diplomats came to rely on it at international conferences and in treaties' (Hardy 1962:72).

The struggle for the identity of national languages resulted in a new language consciousness which was bound to have an impact on translation as well. In the seventeenth century Pierre-Daniel Huet raised his voice and rejected strict literal translation as 'primitive,' insisting that interlineal translation requires no intellect on the part of the translator. In his opinion, the translator must respect the basic rules of grammar and syntax in the target language, yet not 'adulterate' the source text by producing a free translation. Thus Huet advocated a 'refined' form of literal translation in which the words are translated in context, not in isolation (Kloepfer 1967:42–43). Although Huet was interested mainly in literary translation, the shift to literal translation was inevitable in the field of law as well.

The scientific knowledge of the seventeenth century bred new faith in reason and progress, ushering in the Enlightenment with its emphasis on the individual and the rights of man. Although the idea of codifying national laws dates back to Roman law, the codification movement in Europe did not commence until the Enlightenment. The first widely accepted legislative principles were established by Montesquieu in his work *L'Esprit des lois* (1748). Montesquieu did not explicitly state that legislation should be written in the national language(s) of a state; however, this followed from his emphasis on making the law intelligible to the public. To codify national legislation in Latin would not have been in keeping with the political policy of the Enlightenment.

Under Montesquieu's influence, Prussia's Frederick II ordered his chancellor (*Großkanzler*) Cocceji to abrogate the Roman codes in Latin and enact a new Prussian *Landrecht* in German. It appears, however, that his main motive in germanizing the law was not to produce a code which would be understood by the public but rather to facilitate the work of the judges and thus promote uniform interpretation (Hattenhauer 1987:40). In order to protect the codification from being misconstrued by false interpretations, Cocceji inserted a clause similar to Justinian's directive prohibiting scholars from writing commentaries on the law. Since much of the German text was itself a translation, the prohibitory clause contained no rule on translation as did Justinian's directive.[6]

Drafting a code in German which incorporated Roman concepts proved to be the Achilles heel of the legislative reform. Faced with the problem of expressing technical concepts in an underdeveloped language which was still 'concept deficient,' Cocceji had essentially three options: to borrow or naturalize the source terms into the target language, to use neutral terms to describe the concepts, or to create neologisms in the target language (*see* Chapter 8, 8.10). Instead of attempting to establish technical terms in German by creating neologisms, Cocceji resorted to the widespread use of Latin borrowings followed by an explanation in German. The term *de patria potestate*, for example, was recapitulated in a relative clause consisting of fourteen words, three of which were Latin. In Part I of the *Project des Corporis Juris Fridericiani* (1749), Cocceji argued that practitioners were accustomed to such

---

6. The prohibitory clause in the Preface to § 28.IX reads as follows: 'Und damit die Privati, insonderheit aber die Professores, keine Gelegenheit haben mögen, dieses Land-Recht durch eine eigenmächtige Interpretation zu corrumpiren, so haben Se. Königliche Majestät bei schwerer Strafe verboten, dass niemand, wer er auch sey, sich unterstehen solle, einen Commentarium über das gantze Land-Recht, oder einen Theil desselben zu schreiben; oder der Jugend Limitationes, Ampliationes oder Exceptiones *contra verba legis* an die Hand zu geben, oder dergleichen *ex ratione legis* zu formiren...' (cited in Koschaker 1947:453).

terms and that to introduce others would cause confusion among attorneys and judges. Obviously lacking the language skills needed for such a task, Cocceji had to admit his failure. As a result of these and other language problems (*see* Hattenhauer 1987:41–86), the *Allgemeines Landrecht für die Preußischen Staaten* was not completed until 1794, eighteen years after the death of Frederick the Great.

2.5.1. Signs of progress

The ideas of the Enlightenment were directly or indirectly responsible for the social and political upheaval in the late eighteenth century. Although the civil rights movement that led to the French Revolution (1789) was silenced under Napoleon's autocratic rule (1799–1814), Napoleon did not contest the right of a people to use their own national language. One of Napoleon's greatest achievements was the codification of civil law which created a lasting basis for France's civil institutions. As a result of Napoleon's insistence that the *Code civil* of 1804, later known as the *Code Napoléon*, be adopted by all the conquered and sister territories, translation remained in high gear for the duration of his rule.

The newly acquired German-speaking territories were permitted to produce and authenticate their own translations of the *Code Napoléon*, thus giving rise to a number of authentic texts in German, each of which was in force in a given jurisdiction. A comparison of the French source text and two German translations (one in force in the Grand Duchy of Berg and the other in Baden) shows that literal translation had finally become the accepted method of translation for legislative texts. Produced independently, both German texts make allowances to observe the basic rules of syntax of the target language, yet follow the source text as closely as possible. This is reflected in Article 1014 which reads as follows in the original *Code Napoléon* and the two German translations:

> De legs particuliers.
> Tout legs pur et simple donnera au légataire, du jour du décès du testateur, un droit à la chose léguée, droit transmissible á ses héritiers on ayant-cause. Néaumoins le légataire particulier ne pourra se mettre en possession de la chose léguée, ni en prétendre les fruits ou intérêts, qu'à compter du jour des sa demande en délivrance, formée suivant l'ordre établi par l'article 1011, ou du jour auquel cette déliverance lui auroit été volontairement consentie.

German Text A (Berg):

> Von den Particularvermächtnissen.
> Jedes unbedingte Vermächtniß gibt dem Legatar von dem Todestage des Testators an, auf die vermachte Sache ein auf seine Erben oder Nachfolger übergehendes Recht. Dessen ungeachtet kann der Particularlegatar nicht eher sich in den Besitz der vermachten Sache setzen, oder auf deren Früchte oder Zinsen Anspruch machen, also von dem Tage an, wo er entweder, nach der im 1011ten Artikel bestimmten Ordnung, das Gesuch um Auslieferung angebracht hat, oder wo ihm diese Auslieferung freyweillig zugesagt wurde.

German Text B (Baden):

> Von Stückvermächtnissen.
> Jedes unbedingte Vermächtnis gibt dem Vermächtnisnehmer von dem Tag an, da der Erblasser gestorben ist, ein Eigentum auf die vermachte Sache, das auf seine Erben oder Rechtsfolger übergeht. Der Erbstücknehmer kann jedoch weder den Besitz der vermachten Sache früher ergreifen, noch auf deren Früchte oder Zinsen Anspruch machen, also von dem Tag an, wo er das Gesuch um Auslieferung nach der Ordnung des 1011ten Satzes angebracht hat, oder wo ihm eine solche freiwillig zugesagt worden ist. (Texts cited in Kaufmann 1984:175–176).

Briefly it can be said that, as far as the syntax is concerned, both translations read like the source text, Text B somewhat more than Text A. The use of the compositum *Todestag des Testators* and the participial phrase *auf die vermachte Sache ein auf seine Erben oder Nachfolger übergehendes Recht* in text A (first sentence) make it more fluent than the wordy clauses in text B. Despite its awkwardness in German, the basic structure of the second sentence of the French text (negation + *que*) is retained in both translations. This is in keeping with the widespread belief that unnecessary syntactic transformations might endanger the thought pattern of the original. Similarly, both translators take care to reproduce all the words of the French text, thus acknowledging the importance of the letter of the law. The most notable difference between the two German texts concerns terminology. Whereas the term *droit* (first sentence) is translated literally as *Recht* in text A, the translator of text B uses the more precise term *Eigentum*. Furthermore, the *termini technici* of Roman law are germanized in text B, while text A imitates the French terms by using naturalizations. A comparison of the Roman law terminology is shown below:

French source text	German text A	German text B
legataire	Legatar	Vermächtnisnehmer
testateur	Testator	Erblasser
legataire particulier	Particularlegatar	Erbstücknehmer

By germanizing the Roman law terms, translator B attempts to establish corresponding technical terms in German, a task that the drafters of the Prussian *Allgemeines Landrecht* did not achieve with consistency. In fact, translator B avoids the use of borrowings and naturalizations throughout the entire text. This accomplishment is accredited double significance in that it contributes to the development of the German legal language and, perhaps more important, hides the embarrassing fact that the Code is a foreign legal instrument intended to implement the conqueror's will over the conquered (Künssberg 1930:18, note 44), thus foreshadowing a new national consciousness that was bound to influence the development of legal translation.

2.6. INCREASED CONCESSIONS TO THE TARGET LANGUAGE

Under the influence of German philosophers, hermeneutics was incorporated into translation theory in the nineteenth century. Above all it was Schleiermacher's essay *Über die verschiedenen Methoden des Übersetzens* (1813) that initiated the hermeneutic approach to translation, i.e., 'the investigation of what it means to understand a piece of oral or written speech, and the attempt to diagnose this process in terms of a general model of meaning' (Steiner 1977:237). In focusing the translator's attention on the dichotomy of word and sense, the hermeneutic approach raised the question whether the translator can convey the sense of a text by literal translation in which the basic unit of translation is the word.

Schleiermacher's hermeneutic considerations served as the basis for his distinction between the translation of works of art (literary translation) and worldly texts (later special-purpose or specialized translation). Legal texts belonged to Schleiermacher's group of worldly texts which could allegedly be translated by a mere mechanical process of interlingual substitution requiring neither hermeneutics nor creativity (*see* Chapter 1, 1.2). Schleiermacher's philosophical considerations about language and translation seemed irrelevant for legal translators, as did von Humboldt's beliefs that each language has its own structure and that no language can be a valid substitute for another. Most probably, legal translators were not even aware of such ideas. Under the firm grip of literal translation, translators of legislation continued to reproduce the words and syntax of the source text as closely as possible. The following statement by Künssberg confirms that literal translation still dominated the translation of legislative texts well into the twentieth century:

> Wenn man aus einer fremden Sprache überträgt, so such man ohnehin Wort für Wort die Entsprechungen in der Muttersprache (1930:18, note 44).

It was not philosophical considerations but rather national language consciousness that finally aroused the interest of legal translators in the quality of the target text. No longer satisfied to produce a text that was only generally understandable to their fellow countrymen, translators began to make a conscious effort to produce a text in good German, French, Italian or whatever the target language happened to be. Without openly rejecting the traditional method of literal translation, legal translators gradually began to make greater concessions to conform to the rules of the target language. This development can be shown by comparing corrected and revised texts with earlier versions of the same text.

2.6.1. Comprehension finally comes into play

After the defeat of Napoleon in 1815, Austria emerged as one of the great powers of Europe. Believing that any outbreaks of nationalism would be fatal to the Empire, Metternich imposed Austrian law in all the territories but permitted the various nationalities to retain their own official languages. As a result, legal translation continued to flourish in the nineteenth century. One of the greatest achievements was the translation of the Austrian Civil Code of 1811 (*Allgemeines Bürgerliches*

Gesetzbuch = ABGB) into ten languages: Bohemian, Croatian, Hungarian, Italian, Polish, Russian, Rumanian, Serbian, Slovenian, and even Latin. According to a rule adopted in 1849, all the texts were equally authentic. This meant that the national courts of the non-German-speaking territories were able to apply the authenticated translation in their own language, consulting the German text only in the event of a discrepancy or ambiguity. In an attempt to harmonize the legal terminology in the various official languages and encourage uniform interpretation and application of the parallel texts, a commission of legal and language experts compiled several multilingual law dictionaries. For example, the first edition of the *Juridisch-politische Terminologie für die slawischen Sprachen Österreichs* (German-Bohemian-Polish-Russian-Slovenian-Serbian) was published 1850 in Vienna. A separate edition of the Southern Slavic languages (German-Croatian-Serbian-Slovenian) followed in 1853, the year the Croatian text of the ABGB entered into force in the Kingdom of Croatia and Slavonia. Despite attempts to unify interpretation and application, the existence of eleven equally authentic parallel texts led to unsurmountable complications in practice, as a result of which the equal authenticity rule was repealed in 1869 (*see* Dölle 1961:6).

Although degraded to an official translation, the Croatian text, *Općí austrijanski gradanski zakonik*, was still used by the Croatian authorities. The text is of historical importance for the development of modern Croatian legal terminology as it represents the first attempt to express numerous civil law concepts in the Croatian language. This is because Latin remained the official language of the law in Croatia until 1847 (Mamić 1992:7, 15). It was hoped that the terms used in the Croatian version of the ABGB would set a precedence for judges and practicing lawyers in general; however, this was not always the case. Thus, by the end of the nineteenth century there were numerous discrepancies between the terms in the 1853 translation and those used in legal practice. In addition, after comparing the Croatian text with the original German text and the Czech (Bohemian) and Polish translations, F.J. Spevec, a practicing attorney, insisted that the number of discrepancies in the Croatian text was inexcusable and declared the text a threat to uniform interpretation. In his opinion, the quality of the Croatian text was at times so poor that it could be understood only by consulting the German source text. Maintaining that the translation could be written in correct Croatian and still be a precise rendering of the source text, Spevec and the Association of Croatian Lawyers requested the Croatian Government to prepare and adopt a new official translation. When the request was rejected, Spevec took it upon himself to correct and revise the old translation (Spevec 1899:iii). Although his text remained a private translation, Spevec's interventions and comments are relevant for this study.

Technically speaking, the majority of Spevec's interventions are not corrections of translation errors but rather revisions that improve the quality of the Croatian text, thus making it read more like natural Croatian. In particular, the translator took the liberty of improving the Croatian text by occasionally changing the word order and choosing more appropriate Croatian expressions. Although he notes that numerous expressions in the 1853 text were not used in the then current practice, he refrains from revising technical terms in the text itself, as this could be done only in an official text approved in due legislative process. Taking care not to overstep his authority, Spevec marks questionable technical terms with an asterisk and proposes corrections in footnotes that sometimes resemble a commentary. Other major revisions are made in the same way, thus enabling the reader to compare the old and new versions.

Emphasizing the importance of accuracy, the private translator carefully marks all places in the Croatian text where entire phrases and/or key terms were deleted or additional words added. Attributing such errors to carelessness (probably as a result of time pressure), he distinguishes between harmless and harmful deletions and additions, i.e., those which do and do not affect the sense. In regard to terminology, Spevec identifies terminological inconsistency as one of the major shortcomings of the official Croatian text: Different terms were used to express the same concept and sometimes the same term was used to express different concepts. For example, both *pogodba* and *ugovor* are used as equivalents for *Vertrag*. Adding to the inconsistency, *ugovor* is also used to express *Unterhandlungen, Verabredungen, Einverständnis, Pakt,* and *Bestimmung.* Although numerous German composita are rendered literally (e.g., *Grund-Eigenthum = zemljovlastništvo, Allein-Gesetz = samoposjed, Geschäftsführung = poslovodstvo*), Spevec warns that the overuse of literal translation can render the text incomprehensible, as in the following word-for-word translation: 'Verwahrungsmittel des Inhabers gegen mehrere zusammentreffende Besitzwerber / ohranjiva sredstva držaoca suprot više stičućih se tražilaca posjeda.' To facilitate comprehension, Spevec uses explanatory phrases which render the sense of the original in natural Croatian: 'Kako da se osigura drzalac, kad više njih traži stvar od njega' (1899:v).

Although Spevec did not directly challenge the use of literal translation, his emphasis on improving the quality of the target language as a means of increasing comprehension is definitely a move in this direction. Since language is the standard criterion of national identity, it is not surprising that legal translators began to insist that authenticated translations of legal texts be written in the spirit of the target language.

2.7. LETTER VS. SPIRIT: THE SWISS DEBATE

The debate on the dichotomy between 'letter' and 'spirit' was opened in legal translation long after the pendulum had already swung to the right, i.e., to idiomatic translation in other genres of translation. In the field of law it was practitioners who finally raised the question whether legal translations must follow the letter of the source text, as was traditionally believed, or whether they can be written in the spirit of the target language. One of the best documentations on this subject is the Swiss debate published in the *Schweizerischen Juristen-Zeitung* in the early twentieth century.

The occasion was the translation of the German text of the Swiss Civil Code (*Schweizerisches Zivilgesetzbuch* = ZGB) into French (*Code civil suisse*) and Italian (*Codice civile svizzero*).

After long years of preparatory work headed by Professor Huber, the father of the ZGB, and the two translators, Professor Rossel and Judge Bertoni, the three texts were promulgated in December 1907. Since all the language versions of the Code are equally authentic, it was agreed that the translator's task was to express the substance of the original text as accurately as possible. According to traditionalists, this meant that the French and Italian versions must follow the German text as closely as possible. In other words, fidelity to the source text was to be achieved by literal translation. On the other hand, the insistence on language equality awakened in Professor Rossel the desire to produce a translation in the spirit of the French language, not merely one that reproduced the letter of the German source text. As a result, Rossel produced a 'revolutionary' French translation which decidedly broke with the tradition of literal translation. His translation was severely criticized, in particular by G. Cesana, attorney in Zurich (later Lugano and Milan), who accused Rossel of nothing short of heresy for having altered the letter of the law. In his opinion, Rossel's free translation in idiomatic French was radically inaccurate because it failed to reproduce the 'individual words and syntax' of the German original. As such, Cesana claimed it posed a threat to the uniform interpretation of the three authentic texts.

2.7.1. Cesana's guidelines for translators

Advocating the traditional literal approach to legal translation, Cesana proposed three guidelines for the translation of legislative texts: literalism, no paraphrases, and no deletions. Firmly believing that the individual words of a legislative text are sacrosanct, Cesana regarded the literal translation of statutes and codes as essential. In regard to the choice of equivalents, he emphasized the importance of creating neologisms to render the new, progressive concepts expressed in German (*see also* Bocquet 1994:51). In his opinion, these should not be 'natural' French expressions but rather 'calques' or literal translations of the German original. In this sense, Cesana criticized Rossel's use of the French term *les autres droits réels* for *die beschränkten dinglichen Rechte* instead of the literal equivalent *les droits réels limités*, which was unknown in French law. Although the terms used by Rossel were already in use in the French-speaking part of Switzerland, Cesana proposed the literal equivalent *déclaration de majorité* as an equivalent for *Mündigerklärung* instead of *émancipation*, and *contrat successoral* as an equivalent for *Erbvertrag* instead of *pacte successoral*. Cesana's support of literalism was not confined to individual words but also included entire phrases and even idioms:

> Wenn also bei Gesetzesübertragungen schon der sinngetreuen, ganz deckenden Wiedergabe des *einzelnen* Wortes so hohe Bedeutung zukommt, wie viel mehr noch ist die Übereinstimmung und die wörtliche Reproduktion von Wendungen und ganzen Wortverbindungen nötig! (1910/10:151).

Although Cesana admitted that legal translation should not be mechanical or servile, he demanded strict observance of the syntax and grammar of the source language, allowing for exceptions only where absolutely necessary. As he put it, it is fidelity to the original which counts, not the beauty or elegance of the target language:

> Freilich klingt es so schöner und ist elegant ausgedrückt, aber hier kommt es nicht auf Schönheit und Eleganz an, sondern auf eine sich mit dem Urtext deckende sinngetreue Fassung (1910/12:188).

Cesana's second guideline is a negative rule which can be regarded as an extension of the first guideline in that it advises translators to achieve fidelity to the original text by avoiding the use of paraphrases. In Cesana's opinion, using paraphrases cannot help but distort the meaning of the source concept, thus causing *Begriffsverschiebungen*, as he called them. In this context, Cesana insisted that a translator who paraphrases legal concepts of the source text is overstepping his/her authority and assuming the difficult task of interpretation (in the sense of *Gesetzesauslegung*), which is reserved strictly for judges. Accordingly, Cesana concluded that the translator is not authorized to produce free translations of legislative texts as this would be an act of interpretation (*see* Chapter 4 at 4.2.2). It should be noted that the methods of interpretation differ in various legal systems (Chapter 3, 3.4). At that time, however, it appears that the so-called literal method of interpretation (i.e., grammatical interpretation, as it is called in continental systems) was used by Swiss judges. According to this method, the judge's duty is to interpret statutes according to the letter of the law, unless such interpretation would lead to unintended consequences. This was probably the strongest argument in favor of literal translation. Today, however, the literal method of interpretation is generally not used in multilingual interpretation, especially in Switzerland where judges tend to favor more liberal methods of interpretation.[7]

Cesana's third guideline requires that the source text be translated in full (*Vollständigkeit*). Whereas this guideline is generally acceptable as such, Cesana's explanation renders it unacceptable because he demands that each and every word be accounted for in the translation regardless of whether it is an information-carrying unit. As he put it, there should be no arbitrary deletion of words and phrases simply because they are difficult to translate or the translator considers them unimportant. Instead of leaving it to the discretion of the translator to delete any words that are superfluous in the target language, Cesana insists that the translator has no authority to make such deletions as he/she would be *de facto* altering the source text. As for the *Code civil suisse*, Rossel did make some deletions that affected the substance. For example, in Article 68, the German phrase *eine mit ihm in gerader Linie verwandten Person* was originally translated as *ses parents en ligne directe*. The deletion was obviously unintentional and the French text of the said article was corrected by the Swiss Federal Court in its decision of April 7, 1911 to read: *ses parents ou alliès en ligne directe* (*Recueil officiel des lois et ordonnances de la Confédération Suisse*, tome XXVII, 1911:200). Whereas this and a few other deletions were corrected by the Federal Court, the majority of Rossel's deletions were deemed acceptable because they had no effect on substance. The acceptable deletions included some of those singled out by Saleilles, the head French translator of the German Civil Code who joined Cesana in criticizing Rossel's idiomatic translation. For example, a good part of Saleilles' letter of December 22, 1910, to Cesana is

---

7. *See* von Overbeck (1984:980–988) on methods of multilingual interpretation applied by Swiss courts. In regard to multilingual interpretation at the European Court of Justice (EU), Volman comments: 'Dans le droit communautaire, la méthode littérale a une importance nettement moins grande que dans le droit international en général' (1988:35).

devoted to reprimanding Rossel for deleting the expletive *dabei* in Article 1(3) of the Code (cited in Cesana 1918:102), an omission that has no effect on substance.

In his conclusion, Cesana resolutely rejected Rossel's idiomatic translation, claiming that the translator had overstepped his authority by assuming responsibilities reserved exclusively for legislative drafters. According to Cesana, there was no legislative precedence for such action, i.e., producing two original texts of the same instrument in the same state:

> Nirgends treffen wir dieses legislative Unikum: *ein Gesetz für ein und dasselbe Land* bestimmt, mit zwei *ganz frei redigierten deutsch-französischen Gesetzestexten*! Denn der französische Text des ZGB darf füglich allen Anspruch erheben auf eine eigene redaktionelle Originalität, was gesetzgeberisch betrachtet selbstverständlich und ganz in der Ordnung wäre, wenn die französische Schweiz eben nicht auch zur Eidgenossenschaft gehörte. So aber büßt diese Originalität nicht nur alles Verdienst ein, sondern sie fordert ernstlichen Tadel heraus (12/1910:187).

2.7.2. Rossel's rebuttal

Rossel's rebuttal in the January 1911 issue of the *Schweizerischen Juristen-Zeitung* was brief but to the point. First and foremost he defended his idiomatic translation by arguing that the French-speaking population of Switzerland had the right to insist that their *Code civil suisse* be written neither in germanized French nor in gallicized German but rather in the spirit of the French language, thus upholding the principle of language equality:

> La Suisse romande avait le droit, selon moi, d'exiger que le texte français du Code civil suisse ne fût pas de l'allemand francisé avec une servile exactitude, ni même du français décalqué en quelque sorte sur l'allemand, mais du français suffisamment alerte et clair, pour qu'elle eût le sentiment de vivre sous l'empire d'une loi qui serait la sienne, et non pas d'une loi dans laquelle elle n'aurait retrouvé ni sa langue, ni son esprit (1911:201).

Rossel commented that he had attempted to convey the exact sense of the German text in idiomatic French, thus emphasizing the communicative aspect of translation. Defending his translation, he argued that the parallel texts of a single instrument do not have to correspond visually, nor do the terminology and syntax have to be modelled on the original; instead it is the virtuality that counts, i.e., the effect must be the same (1911:201). According to Rossel, upholding the principle of fidelity to the source text does not entail reproducing the source text word for word but rather producing a text that leads to the same results in practice. In Rossel's opinion, his own translation was by no means less precise than the literal translations of individual articles proposed by Cesana and, as far as the quality of the French language is concerned, his text was far superior to Cesana's.

In regard to terminology, Rossel rejected the literal equivalents proposed by Cesana as products of a mania for literal translation that only vulgarize the French language. Moreover, he claimed that mere substitution – the use of French words in German phrases – is no way to promote clarity. Long before Chomsky introduced the concept of native-speaker competence, Rossel made it clear that Cesana, a non-native speaker of French, was not fully competent to judge his French translation, let alone revise it. As Rossel put it, Cesana's translation is not French, he only uses French words (1911:203). Among other things, Cesana criticized Article 4 of Rossel's translation (*see* below). Insisting that the translation should follow the word formation of the German source text, Cesana 'corrected' the inversion preferred by Rossel. In addition, since *Ermessen* is a single word, he proposed the equivalent *appréciation* instead of *pouvoir d'appréciation*, the French term already in usage:

> Richterliches Ermessen.
> Wo das Gesetz den Richter auf sein Ermessen oder auf die Würdigung der Umstände oder auf wichtige Gründe verweist, hat er seine Entscheidung nach Recht und Billigkeit zu treffen.

Rossel's translation:

> Pouvoir d'appréciation du juge.
> Le juge applique les règles du droit et de l'équité, lorsque la loi réserve son pouvoir d'appréciation ou qu'elle le charge de prononcer en tenant compte soit des circonstances, soit de justes motifs.

Cesana's proposal:

> Appréciation du juge.
> Lorsque la loi s'en remet à l'appréciation du juge, ou qu'elle l'invite à décider en tenant compte soit des circonstances, soit de justes motifs, il prononcera selon les règles du droit et de l'équité.

Concluding with the words: 'La lettre tue, l'esprit vivifie,' Rossel regretted that he had not made his translation even more idiomatic (1911:203).

2.7.3. Authentic texts are living law

Although the debate continued, the basic issues had already been defined. Rossel conceded that in principle he had attempted to follow Cesana's guidelines; however, their views differed concerning the question of how closely a translation should follow the source text. According to Rossel, the translator's task is to convey the sense of the source text, not words in isolation. In his opinion, producing a literal translation is a craft, but it takes an artist to produce an idiomatic translation without altering the substance. As he sees it, the real challenge to the translator is to be an artist, not the master of a craft (1911:203).

Once again Rossel showed his *Feingefühl* for translation (years ahead of translation theorists) by recognizing that the same type of text can be translated differently depending on its communicative function. Emphasizing that his authentic translation was living law addressed to the people of the Suisse Romande, Rossel insisted that his translation had every right to be in idiomatic French, as opposed to non-authentic translations directed to a limited group of lawyers for information purposes

(1911:202). He was referring to the French translation of the German Civil Code prepared under Saleille's supervision in Paris, a non-authentic translation that upheld the tradition of literal translation. Years later Cesana continued to cite Saleilles' literal translation as a model of how to translate a piece of German legislation into French. He even went so far as to publish his correspondence with Saleilles in which he praises Saleilles as the greater authority of the two translators and, in return, receives support for his criticism of Rossel's idiomatic translation (1918:97–114).

The Rossel/Cesana debate aroused interest in other parts of Europe as well. For example, Cesana was praised by a law professor from Berlin who regarded all plurilingual legislation as a threat to the uniform interpretation and application of the law (Cesana 1918:114). On the other hand, the then head magistrate of the Belgian *Cour de cassation,* a bilingual institution since 1935, praised Rossel's translation as simple, clear and often elegant. As he put it, it was a commendable achievement in view of the difficulty of expressing the same thing in two languages as different as French and German (Terlinden 1912, in *Manuel de droit civil suisse* 1922:42).

In order to have the final word in the debate, Cesana published another article advocating literal translation. Defending the traditional belief that literal translation is the only acceptable method of translating legislative texts, Cesana insisted that form is essentially secondary to content and warned translators against taking on the role of drafters for the sake of elegance of form:

> Bei der Erstellung der dreisprachigen Texte muß also Hauptziel ins Auge gefaßt werden, nicht die Eleganz der Form, welche unwillkürlich und unbewußt zur Redaktions- und Ausschmückungsfreiheit führt, sondern die *klare, strenge sinngemässe* Wiedergabe des Urtextes, unter Befolgung möglichster *Wörtlichkeit.* Selbstverständlich hat das nicht die Meinung, es verdiene die Eleganz der Form überhaupt keine Berücksichtigung: sie soll nur zurücktreten und stets da weichen, wo sie nur auf Kosten der Übersetzungstreue erreicht werden kann (1918:98–99).

2.8. EQUAL LANGUAGE RIGHTS IN CANADA

Legal translators in Canada are in an even more precarious position than their Swiss colleagues: Canada is not only bilingual but also *bilegal,* i.e., it has two different systems – common law and civil law. At present, Canada consists of five English-speaking common law provinces, one bilingual civil law province (Quebec) and four common law provinces that are bilingual to varying degrees (New Brunswick, Manitoba, Ottawa, and Saskatchewan) (Reed 1993:79; Beaupré 1986:145, note 238; Richstone 1988:261, note 8). At the federal level, legislation follows the common law tradition and is officially bilingual as is that of the two territories under federal jurisdiction (the Northwest Territories and the Yukon). Under the political and social pressures of English dominance in North America, the campaign for idiomatic translation in law did not find resonance in Canada until the struggle for equal language rights was launched as an outgrowth of the silent revolution of the 1960s.

2.8.1. Preserving the status quo in translation

Prevailing for over two centuries, the tradition of literal translation in Canada dates back to the capitulation of New France (= Quebec) in 1760, which marked the unofficial beginning of legal translation in Canada. At that time the English governor appointed François-Joseph Cugnet as his bilingual secretary, entrusting him with the task of translating English proclamations into French for his fellow Québécois. Whereas Cugnet's translation of the Act of Quebec of 1774 is said to have been excellent, the quality of legal translation deteriorated after his death in 1789 (Gouin 1977:29). Cugnet's first successor, his son, was also a lawyer; however, thereafter Swiss officers of the British regiments took over the translation duties (Didier 1990:19). Respecting the authority of the English politicians, they produced strict literal translations, ushering in the so-called 'dark ages' of legal translation that contributed to the degradation of spoken and written French in Quebec (Gémar 1995–II:8; Gémar 1982:128; Horguelin 1977:21–25).

Under the Act of Quebec of 1774, private law based on the civil law of France remained in force; however, English public law was introduced. After initial efforts to completely anglicize the judicial system, a mixed system was finally accepted. Nominated by the governor and confirmed by England, the judges were predominantly anglophones, and even the francophone judges were in no position to play down the use of anglicizations. The mixed legal system resulted in a mixed legal terminology characterized by a large number of calques and borrowings. Generally speaking, it can be said that English terminology dominated the branches of law introduced from the common law: fiscal law, finance law, insurance law, maritime law, and commercial law. On the other hand, French terminology retained its priority in family law, contract law, property law, and other branches of private law (Didier 1990:20). As for the terminology of criminal law, it was anglicized to the point of being practically incomprehensible to a Frenchman (Gémar 1982:128). Criminal statutes were available only in English until 1841 when Black's laws on the reform of criminal law were adopted in Quebec and translated into French. As the following French translation of former Article 120 of the Criminal Code shows, the tradition of literal translation remained unshaken:

Everyone commits perjury who, being a witness in a judicial proceeding, with intent to mislead, gives false evidence, knowing that the evidence is false.	Commet un parjure quiconque, étant témoin dans une procédure judiciaire, avec l'intention de tromper rend un faux témoignage, sachant que le témoignage est faux. (cited in Didier 1990:20)

The abuse of the French language at the federal level did not begin to subside until 1854 when Antoine Gérin-Lajoie reorganized the translation bureaus working for Parliament. With the emergence of the Confederation in 1867, Canada officially became a bilingual country, as a result of which the translation of federal legislation and other legal instruments became a public service. Section 133 of the British North America Act of 1871, the basic text of the Canadian Constitution, required that federal legislation be published in both English and French and that either English or French be used in both Houses of Parliament and in any federal court of Canada.

This, however, did not alter the translation methods, nor did the establishment of the Bureau of Translation in 1934. Not only were the translators predominantly linguists without legal training, but it appears that for many years the translations were not even checked by a francophone lawyer with civil law training (Covacs 1980:3). According to Sussmann, the translators were so insecure that they refrained from making even slight language improvements, mostly out of fear that the intended meaning could be changed. Taking what they believed to be the safe way out, they resorted to literal translation although the results were sometimes misleading and potentially harmful:

> The difficulties (of the translation method used at the time) are very great, and lead to incongruous, not to say harmful, results. We may note generally that very often the insecure translator, no doubt for safety's sake, has clung to too literal a translation of the original version. This results, in the French version, in much clumsy and unFrench sentence structure and practically meaningless, sometimes misleading, French renditions of the English technical words or expressions.... (1968, cited in Covacs 1980:3).

2.8.2. Demands for equal language treatment lead to reform

In the 1960s a new wave of language consciousness triggered the so-called silent revolution in Quebec (*see* Gémar 1995–II:11;19). The Quebecers' demands for equal treatment of the French language had widespread effect not only in Quebec but also at the federal level and, in turn, in the common law provinces as well. Although bilingual interpretation at the federal level dates back to 1932 when the Supreme Court of Canada recognized the equal authenticity of the French text in *R. v. Dubois* (Beaupré 1986:17), the principle of equal authenticity did not become statute law until 1969. Among other things, the Canadian *Official Languages Act* of 1969 provided that English and French are to have 'equality of status and equal rights and privileges' for all purposes of the Parliament and Government of Canada. As Gémar put it, the Act ended two centuries of bilingualism dictated by the terms of colonialism (1982:130). Equal authenticity became a constitutional principle in the new *Constitution Act* of 1982, which not only provides that 'statutes, records and journals of Parliament shall be printed and published in English and French' but also that 'both language versions are equally authoritative' (section 18(1)).

The growing emphasis on official bilingualism in federal legislation encouraged francophones in some of the common law provinces to demand equal language rights in provincial institutions as well. In particular, precedence was set in the *Forest* Case of 1979, as a result of which Manitoba is constitutionally required to enact and publish its laws in both English and French. In *Attorney-General of Manitoba* v. *Forest,* the Supreme Court of Canada upheld the plaintiff's request to have the *Official Language Act of Manitoba* (1970) declared inoperative because of its English only clause. The Court ruled that the clause violated section 23 of the Manitoba Act of 1870 which provided that either English or French may be used in debates of the Houses of the Legislature, that either language may be used in any Court of Canada or any Court of the province, and that the Acts of the Legislature shall be published in both languages (101 *Dominion Law Reports* (3d) 1980,

387–390). The Court's ruling not only ended 90 years of unilingual legislation in Manitoba but also led to the development of what is now called 'Common law en français' (*see* Chapter 8 at 8.10.3). In New Brunswick, the only province that is officially bilingual (Reed 1993:79), legislation is legally required to be published in the two official languages and is authentic in both versions. The consolidated regulations were made available in March 1985. Ontario has also begun publishing some legislation in both languages, and as of 1987 Saskatchewan courts are obliged to hear cases in either language. The latter is in response to the decision of the Saskatchewan Court of Appeal in a criminal case which turned on the French language rights of the accused who invoked the equal language rights clause in the Canadian Charter of Rights of Freedoms of 1982 ([1987] 4 *W.W.R.* 577 (C.A. Sask.) 577–588; *see* Richstone 1988:261, note 8).

Emboldened by new guarantees of language equality, Quebecers launched a campaign to correct the historic injustice that had resulted in the 'raping' of their language in the form of forced anglicization. Initiating a linguistic evolution to purify the French language, they began the so-called process of 'refrancization' (Gémar 1995–II:26 note 39, 40, 70) of legal French: the language of the legislature, the judiciary, and the administration.[8] As mentioned above, many of Quebec's laws were originally translations from English containing a large number of borrowings and calques, some of which were *faux amis* used without regard to context (*see* Schwab 1984:19, 69–154). The most monumental achievement of the purification campaign was the total revision of the *Code civil*, which had been originally drafted in French and translated into English in 1866. In addition to modernizing the law, both the French and English language versions were refined. With the new emphasis on linguistic purity of their own language, the Quebecers were no longer in a position to force literal translation methods on their anglophone counterparts. Despite numerous revisions in the English text of the Code which had 'parroted the French original almost word for word,' Meredith blames his conservative colleagues for not having taken full advantage of the 'once-in-a-lifetime chance to get rid of those linguistic and terminological horrors which have plagued the English of [their] civil law for over one hundred years' (1979:55). While the traditionalists preferred to retain many of the neologisms that had been accepted by practitioners, they agreed more readily to changes in syntax. As Meredith points out, any translation should follow the syntax of the source text to a certain extent; however, 'this technique seems to be over-applied in legislation.' As an example he cites paragraph 1 of former Article 501 of the Civil Code:

8. Although the *Charter of the French Language* (1977) declared French the 'official' language of Quebec, this did not abolish the equal authenticity of English language versions of legislation, a rule that had been in place in Quebec since the codification of private law in 1866 (*Act concernant la Codifcation des Lois du Bas-Canada, qui se rapportent aux matières civiles et à la procédure*) (*see* Brierley 1987:16).

Les fonds inférieurs sont assujettis envers ceux qui sont plus élevés à recevoir les eaux qui en découlent naturellement sans que la main de l'homme y ait contribué.	Lands on a low level are subject towards those on a higher level to receive such waters as flow from the latter naturally and without the agency of man.

This example shows just how absurd a literal translation can be when the original word order is retained. Once it became clear that the thought sequence should be expressed logically in the target language, translators were permitted to revise the English text of the above provision as follows:

Water must be allowed to flow naturally from higher land to lower land.

In regard to legislative style, Meredith comments:

Style is in many cases sacrificed for accuracy whereas there is no reason at all why both cannot co-exist in any statute. Perhaps this exaggeration stems from a concern that other styles would leave open the door to *contresens*, however slight. While this concern is justified, what point is there in carrying it to extremes? (1979:60).

2.8.3. Federal reforms revolutionize translation methods

The explicit focus of the *Official Languages Act* of 1969 was the duty to serve the public in either language, subject to certain conditions. It was one thing, however, to declare English-French equality and another thing to achieve a more equal treatment of the two languages in practice. Moreover, there was disagreement among the parties as to the interpretation of the Act, thus resulting in a tension between 'a reductivist administrative reading of the Act' and 'a more generous projection of its political and philosophical assumptions' or, as Beaty concludes, 'between the letter and the spirit of the law' (1989:188). In 1973 a Parliamentary Resolution was adopted specifying measures 'to ensure the equitable use of English and French as federal languages of work and the full participation of members of both language groups in the federal service.' Moreover, the 1982 Canadian Constitution guarantees official language equality by recognizing 'the public's right to communicate with and be served by federal institutions in either language...' (Beaty 1989:186). Finally, a new *Official Languages Act* was adopted in 1988, bringing the Act into line with the new Constitution by taking a clearer and more proactive position on ways to achieve a more equal treatment of French in public service (*see* details in Beaty 1989:189–193).

Despite dissatisfaction with the *Official Languages Act* of 1969, it served as the impulse that finally set the wheels of reform into motion as far as translation techniques are concerned. Among other things, the Act created the position of Commissioner of Official Languages, a senior official independent of the Government who heads the Royal Commission on Bilingualism and Biculturalism. It is the Commissioner's duty to oversee implementation of the Act, to investigate complaints brought under the Act, to conduct special studies and to report to Parliament on progress (Covacs 1980:5).

In regard to the treatment of French in federal legislation, the Commissioner expressed 'extreme concern' in his 1971 report (Beaupré 1986:172). Although section 133 of the British North America Act had been observed, its compliance was essentially literal: all Acts of Parliament had been faithfully published in both English and French, however, without regard to quality. As the Commissioner saw it, the main problem was not in the legislative process itself but rather in the preparatory stage. Essentially the French texts were literal translations prepared by the Law Translation Branch of the Translation Bureau after the final English text had been approved by the Legislation Committee in the Department of Justice. Changes, however, did not come overnight. Dissatisfied with progress, the Commissioner made his point by condemning the federal drafting process in his *Special Study of the Department of Justice* in 1976. In his *Sixth Annual Report 1977*, the Commissioner acknowledged considerable improvement in the French versions of legislation. At the same time, however, he criticized the fact that they were 'still an embodiment of the Common Law approach,' making it clear that they should 'also reflect the intrinsic qualities of the French language' (Beaupré 1986:172).

Under pressure to improve the quality of the French version of legislation, the Legislative Section of the Department of Justice finally took a decisive step and broke with tradition. More than half a century after Rossel had produced his revolutionary version of the Swiss Civil Code in idiomatic French, the Department acknowledged that literal translation violates the principle of equal language rights. In order to implement the principle of equal treatment, a new approach was necessary: instead of requiring translators to reproduce the source text as closely as possible, they were finally granted freedom to produce a new text in the spirit of the French language. To achieve this objective, Alexandre Covacs, a jurilinguist in the French division of the Legislative Section, proposed five methods of bilingual drafting which gradually convert translators into co-drafters by incorporating them into the drafting process and entrusting them with greater drafting responsibilities (1982:92; *see* Chapter 4 at 4.4.1). The new methods of bilingual drafting have succeeded in modernizing legal translation by swinging the pendulum to idiomatic translation and even beyond to co-drafting.[9]

2.8.4. The new approach

While finally gaining the right to produce a text in the spirit of the French language, the translator's new freedom is not unrestricted. Accordingly, the new approach to legal translation is characterized by an inherent dualism: freedom and constraint. As Covacs puts it, the objective is to produce two versions which express the same message, each in its own way (1982:86). Supporting the new approach, Beaupré rejects the former 'slavishly literal French translations' as belonging to the 'dark ages' of translation and urges carefully selected teams of bilingual and, whenever possible, bilegal anglophones and francophones to formulate two 'equal' versions

---

9. Despite their importance for the development of legal translation in Canada and elsewhere, Gémar fails to mention the new bilingual drafting methods in his recent book (1995–II).

of the same instrument which strive not so much for 'verbal and grammatical parallelism' as for 'linguistic purity' within the confines of 'legal equivalence' (1986:179). When attempting to achieve a balance between 'linguistic purity' and 'legal equivalence,' the latter must always prevail. As a result, the translator must take account of legal criteria, even when making linguistic decisions. Hence, the decision-making process of the legal translator is based primarily on legal considerations.

Unfortunately, Beaupré does not define *legal equivalence*; nor does he explain how it can be achieved in translations of parallel legal texts.[10] This is reminiscent of the equivalence discussion that dominated translation theory during much of the seventies and eighties and has again experienced a revival of sorts in the nineties. At the offset it was generally agreed that the goal of all translation was to achieve equivalence by producing the closest possible equivalent text (Wilss 1977:72); yet theorists could not agree on what the term *equivalence* actually means. Convinced that *equivalence* represents an absolute that only needed to be qualified, theorists took it upon themselves to define the term by adding qualifying adjectives, such as dynamic, formal, communicative, stylistic, semantic, functional, etc. The result was a 'jungle of equivalence types,' as Snell-Hornby said in 1986, at which time she claimed to have accounted for as many as fifty-six equivalence types (1986:15). Most probably, legal equivalence was not on her list.

Despite the inflation of equivalence types, translators continued to be guided more or less by their own intuition. Without objective criteria, equivalence was whatever the translator wanted it to be (Wilss 1977:161). Agreeing that equivalence is a static absolute that cannot be attained in practice (Snell-Hornby 1986:15, *also* 1990a:80), theorists came to the conclusion that one should discard the term entirely or develop a new dynamic concept of equivalence. Opting for the second solution, Reiß attempted to explain equivalence in terms of adequacy. As she then put it, translators should strive to achieve adequacy, not equivalence. Nonetheless, Reiß admitted that equivalence is still relevant in translations in which there is no shift of function. In her words, two texts may be deemed equivalent if the target text is adequate to serve the same communicative function as the source text (Reiß and Vermeer 1984:140).

This, however, was by no means the final word on equivalence. Claiming that equivalence need not be conceived as a static absolute, Albrecht encourages translators to identify one or more factors which should remain constant in the target text, such as content, style, or receiver effect. The so-called mandatory invariants (*Invarianzforderungen*) differ in each case depending on the situational factors of production and reception. Not only do such invariants guide the translator in his/her selection of a translation strategy, they also serve as criteria for determining whether equivalence has been achieved in each particular situation. As for adequacy, Albrecht regards it as a pragmatic category describing the relation between the source text and the mandatory invariants in their order of priority. Like Reiß he regards adequacy as a dynamic relation subject to change depending on the invariants selected by the translator (1990:76–78). Still convinced that equivalence is the key to successful

---

10. In this context Beaupré merely mentions functional equivalence, referring the reader to an article by the late Justice Pigeon (1986:179).

translation, Koller takes up the subject again in the fourth edition of his book *Einführung in die Übersetzungswissenschaft*. Similar to Albrecht, he speaks of *Äquivalenzforderungen*, widening the list of potential invariants to include content, text, factual matter, style, norms of the target text, communicative value of the source text, receivers, scenes of the source text, etc. (1992:94–95).

On the other hand, not all translation theorists are enthusiastic about the revival of the equivalence discussion. Remarking that 'the celebration and the brain racking about translation equivalence goes on forever,' Newmark renounces all attempts to define translation equivalence. Convinced that equivalence cannot be defined, he insists that 'there are only degrees of translation equivalence.' Nonetheless, he admits that a notion of translation equivalence based on semantic aspects is an indispensable operational term. Without any explanation, he rejects the term 'adequacy,' claiming that it 'means different things in different languages' (1993:75).

Recognizing equivalence and adequacy as 'key terms' in the theory and practice of translation, Reiß insists that the terms cannot simply be discarded. Making it clear that equivalence and adequacy are not synonyms, as some theorists have claimed, she attempts to define each term and thus distinguish between them. According to Reiß, the adequacy of a translation depends on its function. Hence, adequacy is an operational term describing the relation between the means chosen by the translator and the function of the particular translation. For its part, equivalence describes the relation between two products: the source and target products, i.e., the source and target texts in their entirety or parts thereof (*see* Reiß 1995:106–123).[11]

The equivalence between individual lexical items of the source and target texts is known as terminological equivalence. Not surprisingly, terminological equivalence continues to play an important role in areas of specialized translation (*see* Arntz 1993:5–18) such as legal translation (*see* Chapter 8, 8.6). Lawyers also use the term 'legal equivalence' to describe a relationship at the level of the text. In such cases, one should note that it does not describe a quality of the translation but rather the relationship between the translation and the other parallel texts of that instrument. In accordance with the principle of equal authenticity, each of the authenticated texts of a single instrument has the force of law and can be used by courts for the purpose of interpretation. In order to be effective in the mechanism of the law, the principle of equal authenticity rests on the presumption that the authentic texts of the same instrument are equal not only in meaning but also in legal effect (Chapter 3, 3.3.3). Accordingly, legal equivalence is achieved if the parallel texts of a single instrument lead to the same legal effects. This is sometimes referred to as 'substantive equivalence' (Schroth 1986:57) or 'juridical concordance' (Rosenne 1983:784).

11. In her Vienna lectures Reiß acknowledges that equivalence can exist between the source and target texts. As she put it: 'Äquivalenz zwischen Ausgangs- und Zieltext besteht in der *gleichwertigen Relationierung von Inhalt(en) und Form(en) eines Textes in ihren Funktionen zur Erreichung des Textsinns*' [emphasis by author] (1995:123).

2.9. THE BELGIAN EXPERIENCE

In Belgium, a country where the linguistic boundary dividing the Flemish and Walloon communities dates back to the fifth century AD, it is the Dutch-speaking Flemish population that has had to exert its rights to equal treatment in areas of language and culture. Much of the legislation in Belgium and Holland dates back to French codes and statutes adopted at the beginning of the nineteenth century (van Dievoet 1987:18). At that time the territory of present day Belgium and Holland was under French rule until 1815 when it was declared a kingdom at the Vienna Congress. Following the Belgian Revolution in 1830, the provisional government adopted the first Belgian Constitution (1831). Although French, Dutch, and German were recognized as national languages, only French was declared an official language. In exchange for the recognition of its independence and neutrality in 1839, Belgium relinquished its territorial claims to some German-speaking regions (*see* Bergmans 1986:13). After World War I, the Versaille Peace Treaty placed the German-speaking regions of Eupen, Sankt-Vith and Moreset (now Kelmis) under Belgian sovereignty, thus raising the question of German language rights in Belgium.

Although the Flemish or Dutch-speaking population accounts for over fifty percent of the total population, the French language continued to dominate for almost a century after Belgian independence. This may be explained in part by the fact that the leaders of the revolution were homogeneously French-speaking. Moreover, the elite who retained political power were French-speaking, both in Wallonia and Flanders. Since French was the cultural and world language at the time, there was no resistance when French was declared the sole official language of Belgium in 1831. Even the language rights granted to the Flemish population were rarely practiced (Alen 1992:16). The first in a series of important victories for the Flemish Movement, the *Equal Treatment Law* of 1898 provided that legislation and regulations must be promulgated in Dutch as well as French and that both language versions are equally authentic. The introduction of Dutch into the judicial system was a slower process. While Dutch became optional as the language of criminal procedure in Dutch-speaking Flanders in 1873, it was not until 1935 that Dutch became the official language of procedure in all matters in Flanders. Moreover, Dutch did not gain complete control of the judiciary in Flanders until 1967 (Verrycken 1995:365). The slow evolution of legal Dutch in Belgium is probably due to the fact that Dutch-language secondary schools and universities did not open in Flanders until the 1920s.

Language rights in Belgium are based on the territorial principle adopted in linguistic legislation of 1931. The division of Belgium into four linguistic regions was enshrined in the 1970 Constitution: the French-speaking region, the Dutch-speaking region, the bilingual region of Brussels-Capital, and the German-speaking region. According to the 1990 census, 57.6 percent of the population lives in the Dutch-speaking region, 32.6 percent in the French-speaking region, and 9.8 percent in Brussels-Capital. There are about 70,000 German-speaking Belgians in the German region (Verrycken 1995:364).

2.9.1. Development of legal Dutch

From the offset, legal Dutch in Belgium was a language of translation in the literal tradition. As a result, the terminology, style and syntax of legal Dutch were more French than Dutch for many years. As Verrycken put it, legal Dutch was 'contaminated' by French:

> L'influence du français a été telle que la langue juridique néerlandaise est littéralement 'contaminée' par le français non seulement quant au vocabulaire, mais également en ce qui concerne le style et la structure des phrases (1995:370).

Since the translation and authentication of legislation in Dutch did not begin until 1898, in most cases there were not even Dutch translations of legislation prior to that date. To fill this gap, the Van Dievoet Committee was established in 1923 to translate the Constitution, the Civil Code, the Penal Code, and other principal legislation. The translations, however, were never authenticated. Therefore, in 1954 the Van Dievoet Committee II began to prepare new Dutch translations that would be acceptable for authentication. Since then, most of the translations have been submitted as draft bills for approval by Parliament, thus completing the process of authentication. In 1967 the Flemish Community finally received the first authentic Dutch text of the Constitution (*see* van Dievoet 1980/81:2361–2368; 1987:94–98).

Unlike Canada and Switzerland, there is no central translation bureau for federal legislation in Belgium, as a result of which translations into Dutch are frequently plagued by terminological inconsistency. In order to promote the use of uniform terminology at the federal level, the Central Committee for the Dutch Legal and Administration Language was established in 1954, followed by a special terminology committee. Nonetheless, translators still honored literal translation by resorting to a large number of literal equivalents and borrowings. The real 'purification' of legal Dutch in Belgium did not get underway until much later. In particular, the Van Dievoet Committee II made conscious attempts to 'purify' the Dutch text by following, whenever possible, Dutch terminology in the laws of the Netherlands (*see* Dievoet 1987:95–98). Concerned about the poor quality of translations, the Minister of Justice mentioned the possibility of co-drafting legislative texts in both French and Dutch as early as 1961; however, no action was taken. In fact, until recently all legislation has been drafted exclusively in French and translated into Dutch. Although Verrycken currently recognizes the advantages of co-drafting legislation in plurilingual countries (1995:368), it appears that Belgium is still not ready to experiment with methods of bilingual drafting.

2.9.2. Translation at the Court of Cassation

Commenting on translation, Herbots remarks that legal translators should strive to produce a text that respects the genius of the target language (1987:814). Unfortunately, this approach to legal translation is very new in Belgium; for years both legislation and judgments were translated in the literal tradition. Although bilingualism was officially introduced into the judiciary in all matters in 1935, the language of judges, attorneys and other lawyers remained French until the late 1950s. As a result, the translation of judgments at the Court of Cassation, the highest court of the land, was strictly one way: from French into Dutch. While lawyers sometimes blamed the poor quality of translations on the fact that the translators were linguists (Herbots 1987:817), today the majority of legal translators at the Court of Cassation are still linguists. Nonetheless, the quality of the translations has improved immensely. Translators at the Belgian Court of Cassation have generally been required to adhere to the original text as closely as possible in respect of both form and substance. Although this unwritten in-house rule still prevails, it is no longer interpreted to mean that all translations must be literal.

According to Leo Vande Velde,[12] translator at the Court of Cassation, legal Dutch in Belgium was still undeveloped in the fifties. In the absence of Dutch terms, translators frequently created gallicisms such as *Verantwoordelijkheid (buiten overeenkomst ontstaan)* for *responsabilité (hors contrat)* (Judgment No. 87 of December 11, 1950). Moreover, translations of judgments were often literal reproductions of the French to the extent that rules of Dutch grammar were ignored. Strict adherence to French word order was common place and often resulted in French-sounding sentences like the following: *'Dat, wijl hij het niet gedaan heeft, het middle niet ontvankelijk is'* (Judgment of March 17, 1952). Whereas French is known for its frequent use of participles, Dutch is not. Nevertheless, *dommages et intérêts dus* is translated as *schadevergoeding verschuldigd* and *juge du fond déduisant des éléments de la cause* as *rechter over de grond uit de elementen van de zaak afleidend* (Judgment of December 11, 1950).

According to Vande Velde, the quality of Dutch translations of judgments has improved considerably at the Court over the past twenty years. As the use of Dutch by the judiciary steadily increased, language consciousness gradually developed among Dutch-speaking judges, some of whom were also active in the Van Dievoet Committee II. Insisting that translations of cassation judgments can read like Dutch and still be faithful to the substance and standard form, translators began producing moderately literal and even near idiomatic translations. Despite the rigid form requirements of cassation judgments, which are formulated in a single sentence with each part indicated by an introductory conjunction (*see* Chapter 5, 5.3.1), the word order is now more or less natural Dutch. Compare, for example, the position of the subject *cour d'appel / het hof van beroep* in the following excerpt from judgment No. 87 of October 15, 1986:

Attendu que, d'une part, par les con-sidérations de l'arrêt reproduites dans le moyen, *la cour d'appel...*	Overwegende dat enerzijds *het hof van beroep*, door de in het middel weergegeven overwegingen van het arrest,...

Similar to the process of 'refrancization' in Quebec, legal Dutch finally freed itself of the many gallicisms that had cluttered the language for years. Thus, in later

---

12. Information on translation at the Belgian Court of Cassation in Brussels is based mainly on my interview and subsequent correspondence with Leo Vande Velde, who has been in the translation department for uniformity since 1974 and is currently head of that department.

judgments one finds natural Dutch terms, such as *aansprakelijkheid buiten over-eenkomst* for *responsabilité hors contrat* (Judgment No. 87 of October 15, 1986) and *vordering tot het instellen van een gerechtelijk onderzoek* for *réquisitoire d'informer* (Judgment No. 58 of September 30, 1986). Today judgments at the Court of Cassation are also rendered in Dutch and translated into French. Dutch judgments observe the abrupt style of French cassation judgments, which are known for their technical refinement and concision. As far as drafting cassation judgments is concerned, true craftsmanship is required to arrange the substance within the framework of a single sentence, grouping the reasons for each particular argument in a series of subordinate clauses so as to lead to the conclusion in a more con-centrated fashion (Mimin 1978:185; Lashöfer 1992:42). In the same token, the hand of a true master is required to express the substance of the original while honoring the form requirements and respecting the genius of the Dutch language.

2.9.3. Legal German in Belgium

The constitutional revisions of 1970 resulted in the recognition of the German-speaking minority as a German-speaking region and a German Community. Although this raised German to an official language, by no means was it put on equal footing with French and Dutch. In accordance with the territorial principle, German became an official language only in the Eastern parts of Belgium constituting the German Community (Alen 1992:219). Founded in 1973, the Council of the German-speaking Community adopts regional laws and regulations in German, which are then translated into French. The *Ausschuß für die offizielle deutsche Übersetzung der Gesetze und Erlasse* was created in the seventies to translate national legislation; however, its work focused on translating the Constitution. After the Ausschuß was transferred to Brussels, the Central German Translation Service was established in Malmedy. Translations of national legislation are not authenticated and are frequently of inferior quality. As Bergmans puts it: 'Man sieht ein, daß die Qualität der Rechtstexte in deutscher Sprache oft zu wünschen übrig läßt' (1986:87).

An important step in the development of legal German in Belgium came in 1985 with the creation of a German-speaking judicial district (Kremer 1994:93). This set the translation mechanism in high gear to meet the demands of local courts which cannot administer justice effectively without German translations of national legislation. Currently the district commissioner is being allotted an annual budget for the translation of national legislation into German. Progress is slow and the translations have not yet been authenticated; hence, they do not have the force of law.[13] The German text of the Constitution was finally authenticated in 1991 (Alen 1992:219).

The small German-speaking Community of Belgium has made considerable progress over the past twenty years (*see* Kremer 1994:86–95). In fact, today it is regarded as one of the best protected minorities in Europe (Bergmans 1986:105).

---

13. As a rule, subsequent translations can be authenticated by Royal Decree in Belgium; however, Dutch and French are the sole official languages for statutes, codes, and Royal Decrees.

Having learned from the past mistakes of their older Flemish colleagues, German-speaking translators of Belgium attempt to produce translations that read like German. Legal German in Belgium, however, is still in the phase of development, thus making this task extremely difficult. Since most areas of Belgian law have not yet been translated into German, the Belgian German legal lexicon is still small. Moreover, the existing terminology has not been unified in the few areas of Belgian law where translations have been made. Therefore, the main task facing Belgian lawyers of the German Community is to create a uniform German legal lexicon. Whenever a new legal lexicon is created for concepts which already exist, terminologists must agree on a strategy for naming the concepts. Realizing the importance of creating a uniform terminology, German-speaking lawyers founded the *Belgisch-Deutsche Juristenvereinigung* which held its first meeting in October of 1986 to discuss, among other things, a strategy for creating a German legal lexicon for Belgium. While the members regard this as a unique opportunity, they are also aware of the great responsibility involved. Since corresponding terms already exist in French and Dutch, they viewed the task essentially as one of translation, i.e., translating the existing terms into German. In a report on translation strategy, Bergmans proposed two possibilities: to use borrowings and literal equivalents, preferably of French terms of Belgian law, or to borrow existing German terms from German or Swiss law. In the latter case, one would follow either the German or Swiss model and borrow only terms whose content approximately corresponds with the Belgian concepts (Bergmans 1987b:15) (*see* Chapter 8, 8.10).

When selecting a translation strategy for terminology, the text as a whole, or parts thereof, the translator must keep in mind that translation techniques developed in one jurisdiction are not necessarily adequate elsewhere (*cf.* Šarčević 1990:156–163). In other words, techniques used in Switzerland or Canada might not be adequate in Belgium and vice versa. As in other areas of translation, legal translators must always take account of the situational factors of the particular communication process or, as Vermeer would say, the text-in-situation (1986:38). In regard to the translation of institutional texts, it is safe to say that the situational factors of production vary from institution to institution. But what about the situational factors of reception? In the end, it is these considerations which often have the greatest impact on the translator's decision-making process. The next Chapter deals with the communicative aspects of legal translation.

3 Legal Translation – An Act of Communication within the Mechanism of the Law

3.1. FROM A PROCESS OF TRANSCODING TO AN ACT OF COMMUNICATION

Special-purpose communication involves the transfer of a message from a sender to a receiver, both of whom are specialists in the same discipline. In written communication the message is encoded in a system of signs (text) which is decoded by the receiver (Sager 1993:96; Cornu 1990:212). Since communication can be successful only if the receiver is able to decode the message, translation theorists originally regarded the translator as a mediator whose primary task was to transcode the message into a linguistic code that could be understood by the receiver. Thus translation was largely regarded as a process of transcoding a message from one language into another, whereby the primary goal was to preserve the meaning of the message. Although LSP theorists now acknowledge that a message consists of both text and intent, they still tend to regard translation as a means of transferring meaning by linguistic transcoding.[1] This also includes lawyers who view translation as a mechanical process of linguistic transcoding or *transposition linguistique*, as they sometimes refer to it (Tallon 1995:342; Crépeau 1995:51–53).

In this study, legal translation is no longer regarded as a process of linguistic transcoding but as an act of communication in the mechanism of the law. As such, one must take account of the situational factors constituting the production and reception of the parallel texts of legal instruments. This unique communication process has largely been ignored in translation studies, perhaps because it seems to defy the categories established by theorists of both general and special-purpose translation.[2] Moreover, scholars who focus their attention primarily on language and the linguistic elements of the text tend to ignore the fact that, like other areas of translation, legal translation is also receiver-oriented. Yet previous studies on legal translation by both linguists and lawyers fail to take account of the receivers. This

---

1. For example, Gémar defines translation as a process of transcoding a message into the target language (1995–I:12).
2. Earlier Sager briefly mentions translations which are dependent and parallel but have either an autonomous or interdependent status (1986:341). Coming back to this subject, he later identifies two types of interdependent documents: 'parallel' and 'full equal documents,' the latter of which are equally authentic (1993:180). As in his earlier works, he does not analyze the translation process involving such documents.

is all the more surprising because legal communication can be effective only if interaction is achieved between text producers and receivers.

Analyzing the communicative aspects of legal translation, this Chapter first identifies the text producers and receivers participating in plurilingual communication in the law. Only then is it possible to define the goal of legal translation as an act of communication in the law. Encouraging translators to establish a dynamic relationship with the actual receivers, this Chapter focuses on the interpretation of legal texts as primary sources of the law. While some authors doubt the value of translation theory for legal translators (Weston 1991:1), others agree that, in order for legal translation to be professional, it is necessary to create a theory of legal translation (Bocquet 1994:i). Like the law itself, a theory of legal translation needs to be practice oriented in order to be useful for translators.

3.1.1. Text producers in legal communication

Regardless whether it is an original or a translation, a legal text is deemed authoritative if it has been authenticated in the manner prescribed by law for that particular instrument. Contracts, for instance, are authenticated by the act of signature when the final document is signed by the parties or their authorized representatives. In international law, it has traditionally been presumed that, in order for the text of a treaty to be authoritative, it has to be adopted by the treaty-adopting body itself (*see* Chapter 7, 7.4.3). Similarly, in municipal law, the various language versions of legislation and other texts must be adopted by the competent lawmaking authority in order to be authoritative. Accordingly, it is commonly said that the text producers of legislation are the lawmakers themselves. But who are the lawmakers? When continental lawyers say that legislation is made by the legislator, they are not referring to a single person as in the days of royal decrees but rather to the legislature as a collective body, i.e., to the parliament (Larenz 1983:314).

As a rule, the legislative process consists of a preliminary and a parliamentary procedure. In most countries the parliamentarians debate, revise, approve, and enact legislature; however, they neither make the policy nor draw up the bills themselves. In Canada, for example, the majority of proposals are public bills initiated by government policymakers. Public bills may also be proposed by members of Parliament but only during special sessions limited to several hours weekly. Private bills may be initiated by individuals or groups of persons; however, they are limited in scope. Public bills initiated by the government are drawn up by professional drafters from the Legislation Section of the Department of Justice after the policy has been approved by Cabinet. At the close of the preparatory stage, the draft bill is printed and submitted to Cabinet for approval before being introduced in Parliament. In Canada all bills must pass through nine parliamentary stages before becoming law: notice of introduction, introduction and first reading, second reading, committee study, report state, third reading, consideration by the other House, royal assent, and proclamation (*The Federal Legislative Process in Canada* 1987:14).

In this study the term *lawmaker* is not used in its restrictive sense. Thus it refers not only to parliamentarians who 'make' and 'enact' laws but also to policymakers and drafters. In Canada, legislative drafters (frequently called legislative counsel) are professionals who have had special training in legislative techniques. While postgraduate courses on the drafting of common law legislation are offered at various law schools, the first parallel program on civil law drafting techniques for franco-phones was introduced by the Civil Law Section of the Law Faculty of the University of Ottawa in 1980 (Beaupré 1986:173, note 38). Although drafters do not make policy themselves, they are responsible for critically examining the approved policy and determining how that policy can be expressed in appropriate legal language so as to achieve the desired effect (*The Federal Legislative Process in Canada* 1987:10). In legal parlance, the term *drafter* is used in general to designate a professional who drafts or draws up legal texts such as laws, treaties, conventions, contracts, and others (Dick 1985:1).

The legislative process in Switzerland differs considerably from that in Canada (*see* Gesetzgebungsleitfaden 1995:16–32). The preliminary proceedings, which consist mainly of policymaking, hearings, and the preparation of a preliminary draft, are followed by polling proceedings (*Vernehmlassungsverfahren*) in which the cantons are invited to submit their opinions. If the results are favorable, the actual drafting process begins. In Switzerland bills are not drawn up by professional drafters but by experts of the federal department sponsoring the bill, or in the case of more important legislation, by a committee of experts consisting not only of departmental experts but also of prominent professors and judges. The draft bill is then submitted to the In-House Administrative Drafting Committee, which was established in 1975 to control and improve the linguistic and technical quality of legislative texts. At the offset, a three-member committee was assigned to each bill: a linguist from the Central Language and Translation Service of the federal government, a lawyer from the main legislative department of the Ministry of Justice, and the subject expert from the department concerned. The constitution and working methods of the In-House Administrative Drafting Committee have changed rather significantly since the introduction of co-drafting in the early 1990s (Schneider 1992:85; *see* Chapter 4, 4.3.2). At the conclusion of the drafting procedure, the draft bill is printed and distributed to the deputies of both Houses and other interested parties.

The parliamentary procedure commences with the debate in the National Council (Upper House). Thereafter a parliamentary drafting committee is in charge of revising the bill before it is submitted to the Council of States (Lower House) for debate. A general revision of the bill is carried out jointly by the parliamentary drafting committee and the administrative drafting committee (*see* Hauck, Moos, Keller & Schweizer 1982:94–99). A bill becomes law when it has been passed by both Houses and promulgated. In accordance with the Swiss Law on Official Publications, federal legislation as well as decisions of the federal government, international treaties, intercantonal agreements, and regulations issued by inter-cantonal institutions must be promulgated in German, French, and Italian (Articles 6 and 7).

3.1.2. Text receivers in legal communication

In legal communication it is far easier to identify the text producers than the re-ceivers. As paradoxical as it may sound, a dispute has been waged in legal circles for years in an attempt to reach consensus on the identity of the receivers or addressees of legal texts (*see* Kindermann 1979:40–46). While some authors believe that the addressees of legal texts are exclusively the persons on whom an obligation is imposed or on whom a right, privilege or power is conferred (Krüger 1969:42), others broaden the group of addressess to include not only the legal subjects named in the text but also all persons affected by the piece of legislation (*cf.* Noll 1973:180–183). One distinguishes between collective and individual addresses. While the party/ies named in contracts, wills, and judgments are individual addressees, legislative texts have collective addresses, including the general public. Rossel, for example, regarded the French-speaking community of Switzerland as the collective addressee of his translation of the Swiss Civil Code (Chapter 2, 2.7). Codes, criminal statutes, and traffic regulations are examples of legislative texts of universal description that affect the general public. In addition, there are also legislative texts of class description which apply to a specific class of persons (e.g., taxpayers, directors, divorcees) or to different classes of persons affected by the same relations (e.g., banks, creditors, debtors, insolvent persons, trustees) (*see* Driedger 1976:19).

The view that the addressees of legislative texts are those affected by the particular instrument was challenged by lawyers who insisted that the 'man on the street' does not read the statute books and in any case he usually cannot understand them (Baden 1977:65–68).[3] The reasoning that such persons cannot be the actual text receivers is reinforced by the linguistic principle that successful communication presupposes interaction between producers and receivers (de Beaugrande and Dressler 1981:3, 113). From the linguistic point of view, interaction presupposes that the receiver 'accept' the text. Acceptance does not necessarily mean that the receiver must act or refrain from acting as intended by the text producer but rather that he/she acknowledges the text as a cohesive and coherent instrument for attaining a specific goal (de Beaugrande and Dressler 1981:7, 130–135). Convinced that the majority of those affected by a legislative text do not 'accept' the text in this manner, some linguists argued that there is no interaction with such addressees, thus coming to the conclusion that legislative texts are monologues (Sandig 1972:118). This idea may have been prompted by a well-known German lawyer years ago when he commented that legislative texts have no receivers at all (Forsthof 1940:8). Such conclusion, however, is misleading because it contradicts the basic presumption that a legal text is a 'communicative occurrence.'

Insisting that legislation is addressed to the general public, other linguists maintained that the lawmakers were at fault for failing to communicate effectively with the addressees. Believing that the problem could be corrected by simplifying legislative language, they joined forces with a group of lawyers who had revived a campaign to make legislation intelligible to the common man (e.g., Hauck 1985:193–195). Although history shows that such reforms have generally failed or

---

3. Most lawyers do not agree with Gémar's statement that legislative texts are more readable and easier to understand than other legal texts (1995–II:117).

were merely a pretense to achieve another goal,[4] efforts of individuals such as Eugen Huber, father of the Swiss ZGB, and, more recently, Fritz Schönherr (1985:35–49) have produced some concrete results. Today legislative guidelines throughout the world encourage drafters to make legislation 'clear' and 'intelligible to the common man' (e.g., Kindermann 1979:31–46; Thornton 1989:48; Gesetzgebungsleitfaden 1995:298). In North America the parallel movement for 'plain English' has resulted in the adoption of a number of Plain English Laws in the US which require documents produced by state agencies to be written in 'plain, straightforward language, avoiding technical terms as much as possible, and using a coherent and easily readable style' (California Govt. Code & 6212, West 1984 Supp.; see Wydick 1985:73). It should be noted that such laws are state laws and are restricted to 'some kinds of consumer documents' (Wydick 1985:4).

Although the campaign to simplify legislative texts succeeded in bringing about some visible improvements in the quality of legislation, numerous lawyers warned drafters against making unnecessary compromises that could endanger the effectiveness of legislative texts. In their opinion, legislative texts are a means of specialized communication and must remain so in order to be effective as instruments of the law. Hence, simplification is acceptable but not popularization. One of the few lawyers to analyze the communication process in the law, Baden claims that the main problem is not for drafters to make legislative texts intelligible to the general public but rather to improve the efficiency of legal communication by achieving interaction with the actual receivers (1977:85). But who are the actual receivers in legal communication?

As in general communication, a distinction can be made in legal communication between actual and intended receivers (Lyons 1977:34), or to use Kelsen's terminology, between direct and indirect addressees (1979:40).[5] Since legal communication is first and foremost a form of specialized communication, it follows that the actual or direct addressees of legislative texts must also be specialists. This is in keeping with Sager's principle that the knowledge base of the producers and receivers is presumed to be on the same level in specialized communication (Sager 1990:102, also 1993:40). Accordingly, the direct addressees of legislative texts are also lawyers, as confirmed by Kelsen in his *Allgemeine Theorie der Normen*

---

4. For example, it is said that Frederick the Great's main motive in having the Prussian *Landrecht* codified in German was not to make the law intelligible to the general public but to judges who were not fluent in Latin (*see* Chapter 2 at 2.5). Similarly, the argument that the general public did not read the statute books because they were not available proved to be ill founded. The reading of legislative texts by the general public did not seem to increase even after they were made accessible through obligatory promulgation (Baden 1977:71). Nor did the marked improvement in the literacy level during the twentieth century seem to broaden the readership of legislative texts.

5. In Chapter 14 of his *Allgemeine Theorie der Normen* Kelsen writes: 'Die unmittelbaren Adressaten der generallen hypothetischen Rechtsnormen sind somit die Individuen, die die – als Sanktionen fungierenden – Zwangsakte in concreto anzuordnen und zu vollstrecken ermächtigt und unter Umständen auch verpflichtet sind. Die nur mittelbaren Adressaten der generellen Rechtsnormen sind die Individuen, deren Verhalten die Bedingung der in diesen Normen statuierten Zwangsakte ist' (1979:40).

(1979:40). Regarding legal norms as coercive acts (*see* Chapter 5 of this book, 5.7), Kelsen maintained that the direct addressees of general legal norms are the specialists empowered to interpret and apply such norms, i.e., the competent law-applying organ. As for the persons affected by the particular norms, Kelsen refers to them as indirect addressees (1979:41). Although the idea that legal texts can have more than one group of receivers is by no means new (*cf.* Rehbinder 1972:25), it has been overlooked by most linguists (Kurzon is an exception, 1986:26–29) and even some lawyers (Cornu 1990:217).

Concerned with specialized communication, the main emphasis in this study is on direct addressees. Following Kelsen's lead, Baden identifies the direct addressees of a law as its 'potential users,' i.e., lawyers who apply the law:

> Als Adressat des Gesetzes sei daher der potentielle Benutzer des Gesetzes angesehen, welcher auch *Gesetzesanwender* genannt werden soll (Baden 1977:69).

Generally speaking, legal texts have more than one group of direct addresses (*see* Driedger 1982a:6; *also* Baumann 1991:62, note 83). To a large extent, the text type (contract, will, legislative text etc.) and subject-matter are decisive in determining the direct addressees. In regard to legislative texts, a non-specialist who needs to be informed about his statutory rights and duties arising from a particular text may consult his attorney or seek the advice of a legal specialist such as a tax consultant, corporate lawyer, patent lawyer, trust lawyer, etc. Moreover, persons trained to administer the law, i.e., public officers in government and administrative agencies, are also direct addressees of some legislative texts. The role of such direct addressees, however, is minor in comparison with that of the major group of direct addressees – those responsible for the administration of justice, i.e., the judiciary (*see* Kelsen 1979:41). Since most legal disputes are ultimately adjudicated by a court, it follows that the primary direct addressees of normative legal texts are judges. As Legault put it:

> Le droit pose des normes qui s'adressent premièrement aux juges (1977:21).

The judiciary constitutes the main group of direct addressees who are responsible for interpreting and applying all types of normative legal texts, including codes and statutes, international treaties and conventions, contracts, and even judgments. In regard to judgments, the direct addressees include law enforcement officers and ultimately other judges, whereas the indirect addressees are the parties or party named in the instrument. This is especially true in the case of precedents which are binding on the same and lower courts. Thus case law is appropriately referred to as judge-made law (*see* Walker 1980:190).

Summing up, it can be said that communication in the legislative process occurs primarily between two main groups of specialists: lawmakers who make the laws (policymakers, drafters, legislators) and lawyers who interpret and apply the laws (attorneys, administrators, judges). In the remainder of this Chapter the emphasis is on text reception, i.e., the interpretation and application of legal texts by courts of law. In an attempt to present a receiver-oriented approach to legal translation, this study presupposes that, in order to be an effective text producer, the translator must be thoroughly familiar with legal hermeneutics, in particular with the methods of interpretation used by the courts having jurisdiction over matters governed by the legal instrument in question (*cf.* Tallon 1995:341). In regard to the translation of legislative texts, lawyers generally acknowledge that 'linguistics must play second fiddle to jurisprudence, since legislative drafting and judicial interpretation are so inextricably linked' (Beaupré 1987:738). This, however, does not mean that legal translators have discretionary power to interpret or construe the source text as judges do.

3.2. LEGAL HERMENEUTICS

A branch of jurisprudence commonly known as judicial method, legal hermeneutics involves the interpretation or construction of texts, as it is technically called. The primary task of the judge is to construe the text by ascertaining its meaning as intended by the legislature or by the contracting parties or States and to apply the law, treaty, convention, or contract accordingly. In legal circles it has long been debated to what extent judges are permitted to use hermeneutical techniques to construe legal texts, particularly legislation. It is not our purpose here to take sides in the debate nor to provide a detailed analysis of the methods of interpretation commonly used. It should, however, be noted that the methods of interpretation vary for different types of legal texts.[6] Moreover, the methods of interpreting legislative texts differ from jurisdiction to jurisdiction. The following is a brief summary of the most common methods of legislative interpretation.

3.2.1. Interpretation of legislative texts

Generally speaking, there are two broad approaches in the traditional interpretation of legislative texts: the literal and liberal methods. In early British history judges wrote the statutes themselves. Knowing what the King intended, they gave effect to that intention irrespective of the actual text of the law. Even when judges no longer wrote the statutes, the approach remained more or less the same. Equitable construction, as it was called, was based primarily on the principle of fairness. In essence, the statutes were short statements of policy and the judges 'put things into the statutes that were not there, they took out things that were there, and they filled in gaps' (Driedger 1982b:9). The change came when Parliament firmly established its supremacy at the end of the seventeenth century. To confine the judges to the text, parliamentarians began writing statutes that were 'particular rather than general, an enumeration of instances rather than a broad statement of principle... and the law was only what Parliament had said – no more and no less' (Driedger 1982b:12). Accordingly, the accepted method of interpretation became the literal method which focuses on the words of the text. Literal interpretation was described in the *Sussex Peerage Case* (1857) by Chief Justice Tindal as follows:

---

6.   On the interpretation of contracts, *see* Lewison 1989:1–7.

> If the words of the statute are in themselves precise and unambiguous, then no more can be necessary than to expound those words in their natural and ordinary sense. The words themselves alone do, in such case, best declare the intention of the lawgiver (cited in Driedger 1982a:67).

Since literal interpretation sometimes led to inconsistencies or even absurd results, modifications eventually had to be made. As a result, more liberal methods of interpretation are generally preferred today, with some jurisdictions being more liberal than others, i.e., they tolerate a greater degree of judicial discretion. As for common law judges, they are generally permitted to determine the sense of the words in the context of the sentence, paragraph, section, and entire text. Moreover, they are also allowed to take account of the purpose of a piece of legislation, however, strictly as a supplementary means to enable them to understand the words of the statute (*Reigate Rural District Council v. Sutton District Water Co.*).

As a rule, continental legislation is a statement of general principles and thus lacks much of the detail characteristic of common law statutes. Nonetheless, civil law judges must also take account of the words of the text and their grammatical meaning. However, grammatical interpretation, as it is called, serves only as a starting point in civil law circles (Larenz 1983:305). As friends of the liberal method, continental judges take account of the sense of the disputed words, sentence, or paragraph in the context of the entire text (contextual interpretation) and ascertain the meaning in the light of the purpose of the particular piece of legislation (teleological interpretation). For example, § 133 of the German BGB explicitly authorizes judges to construe statutes on the basis of their *Sinn* and *Zweck*. Contrary to their common law colleagues, civil law judges are not bound to the text when ascertaining the purpose of a statute but may consult preparatory materials as well. Known as the historical method of interpretation, the use of preparatory materials is not restricted to determining the purpose of a legislative text. Furthermore, civil law judges are not restricted to the particular text when determining the sense of a provision but are encouraged to take account of its position within the context of the entire legal system (Baumann 1984:107–109). The emphasis on systematic interpretation occasioned judges of the German Federal Constitutional Court to declare that German judges are servants of the law, not slaves of its letters:

> Am Wortlaut einer Norm braucht der Richter aber nicht haltzumachen. Seine Bindung an das Gesetz (Art. 20 Abs. 3, Art. 97 Abs. 1 GG) bedeutet nicht Bindung an dessen Buchstaben mit dem Zwang zu wörtlicher Auslegung, sondern Gebundensein an Sinn und Zweck des Gesetzes. Die Interpretation ist Methode und Weg, auf dem der Richter den Inhalt einer Gesetzesbestimmung unter Berücksichtigung ihrer Einordnung in die gesamte Rechtsordnung erforscht, ohne durch den formalen Wortlaut des Gesetzes begrenzt zu sein (BVerfGe 35:278; cited in Hegenbarth 1982:19, note 10).

Contrary to their common law colleagues, civil law judges are usually permitted to supplement statutory and customary law by filling in gaps. In this sense, Article 1 of the Swiss ZGB allows judges practically unlimited discretion by providing that, in the absence of a statutory provision or customary rule of law, the judge should decide in accordance with the rule that he would establish as legislator. In disapproval, some common law lawyers refer to this approach as the 'transfer of legislative power to the judiciary' (Driedger 1982a:72).

3.2.2. The application of legal texts

From what has been said thus far, one might get the false impression that legal hermeneutics does not differ significantly from general hermeneutics. As emphasized earlier, legal texts differ from other texts by virtue of their normative function (Chapter 1, 1.3.1). This was recognized in particular by Emilio Betti (1890–1968) who made a distinction between cognitive, normative, and reproductive hermeneutics in his monumental work *Teoria generale della interpretatione*, in which he discusses the normative interpretation of law within the larger framework of general hermeneutics (English translation in *American Journal of Jurisprudence* 1987:245–268). Thanks to studies such as Betti's, legal hermeneutics has become an independent discipline. A lawyer by profession with a substantial background in classical studies, Betti was particularly interested in the responsibility of legal practitioners in shaping social conduct through their application of rules of law (*see* Wright 1987:191). Although all interpretation involves application to a certain extent, in normative interpretation the main emphasis is on application. In fact, interpretation and application are regarded as a single act in which interpretation is only a means of achieving the end, i.e., application (*cf.* Gadamer 1975:293). Accordingly, the goal of legal hermeneutics is not merely to ascertain the meaning of a rule of law but to determine whether the fact situation of a concrete case can be subsumed under the framework of the abstract rule. Mayer-Maly summarized the difference between general hermeneutics and legal hermeneutics as follows:

> Bei der allgemeinen Hermeneutik zielt das Verstehen auf alles, was der Text bedeutet. Der juristischen Auslegung dagegen geht es zumeist bloß darum, ob ein Text so zu verstehen ist, daß er für einen bestimmten Sachverhalt erheblich ist (1969:414).

In greatly simplified terms, it can be said that judges resolve disputes by establishing the facts of the case and applying the law to the facts so found. The techniques used by a judge in deciding a case vary from jurisdiction to jurisdiction, depending on the sources of law authoritative in that jurisdiction. Generally speaking, judges may proceed from the facts in order to determine whether they can be subsumed under the abstract fact situation of a normative text or the general principle of a decision (deduction), or they may formulate a rule applicable to the particular case by proceeding from the abstract fact situation of a normative text or general principle of a decision (induction). A third method commonly used is analogy or decision-making based on similarity: If rule A applies to case X, and case Y is similar in all substantive aspects to case X, rule A should apply to case Y as well (*see* Walker 1980:674, 53).

63

3.2.3. Plurilingual communication in the mechanism of the law

Despite the tendency for lawyers to avoid using the term *translation* when referring to the authentic texts of a legal instrument (*see* Chapter 1, 1.6.1),[7] they cannot deny the fact that parallel texts of bilingual and multilingual legislation, treaties, conventions, contracts, and judgments have traditionally been produced primarily by translation. In the past it has been common practice to draft one or, in exceptional cases, two originals and to produce the other texts by translation. In the eyes of lawyers, all texts are authentic and thus 'originals' as long as they have been authenticated in the prescribed manner. Accordingly, from the legal point of view, it is improper to use the terms *source* and *target texts* when referring to authentic legal texts. In an attempt to strike a balance, the term *authenticated translation* is used here, although it too is only reluctantly accepted by lawyers.

As legally binding texts, all the authentic texts of a particular legal instrument have the same communicative function. Vested with the force of law, authenticated translations are authoritative sources of law used by the courts for the purpose of interpretation. Thus it follows that the direct addressees of authenticated translations are the judges authorized to interpret and apply the particular law, treaty, convention, or contract. Today the parallel texts of legal instruments are deemed equally authentic unless specified otherwise. In regard to treaties, Article 33(1) of the Convention of the Law on Treaties provides that 'when a treaty has been authenticated in two or more languages, the text is equally authoritative in each language, unless the treaty provides or the parties agree that, in the case of divergence, a particular text shall prevail.' In regard to plurilingual national legislation, the constitution or other act of authorization usually contains a clause declaring legislation equally authentic in all official languages. For example, Article 9(1) of the Swiss Law on Official Publications reads as follows:

> Les trois versions des actes législatifs de droit interne, publiées dans le Recueil officiel, font également foi....

The principle of equal authenticity has been a major factor in eliminating the traditional subordination of authenticated translations by placing them on equal footing with the 'original' texts. Theoretically, the court is no longer permitted to give priority to the original text when ascertaining the meaning of a plurilingual legal instrument. Although each authentic text of an instrument is deemed independent for the purpose of interpretation by the courts, all of the authentic texts of that instrument are mutually dependent on each other in the sense that they all contribute to the common meaning of the single instrument.

---

7. In regard to international practice, *see* Tabory (1980:171) on Sir Humphrey Waldock's discussion in his Sixth Report on the Law of Treaties.

3.3. THE GOAL OF LEGAL TRANSLATION

Lawyers are aware that, in order for plurilingual communication to be effective in the law, one must preserve the unity of the single instrument, as it is called in international law (Tabory 1980:195). This has long been taken to mean that the goal of legal translation is to preserve the meaning of the original. Such approach, however, automatically places legal translation on the same level with other subject areas of special-purpose translation. In the tradition of meaning-based translation, the goal of special-purpose translation has long consisted in reproducing, transferring, or reconstructing the meaning or content of the message of the source text as accurately as possible.

3.3.1. Special-purpose translation

During the debate on form vs. content in the fifties, Casagrande made it clear that content has priority in specialized translation:

> The emphasis is on the content of the message as such rather than on its aesthetic form, grammatical form or the cultural context, all of which are subsidiary to the practical, matter-of-fact goal (1954:335).

Following in Casagrande's footsteps, Jumpelt proclaimed that translators of special-purpose texts must strive to convey the information content of the source text as accurately as possible. In his opinion, the extent to which a translator succeeds in conveying the information content serves as an objective criterion for judging the success of a special-purpose translation (Jumpelt 1961:18). This idea was later promoted by O. Kade in his notion of *inhaltliche Invarianz* which celebrates content as the invariable element for measuring equivalence in translation. Claiming that the conditions for achieving semantic equivalence, as it was called, are optimal in special-purpose texts, O. Kade encouraged LSP translators to make an exact reproduction of the content of the source text (1968:75). LSP translation scholars later admitted that exact reproduction is impossible; however, they still insisted that the translator's task is to preserve the information content. Fluck, for example, continued to cite Kade as an authority and called on translators to convey the content as accurately and clearly as possible:

> Der Inhalt bildet das invariante Element der Übersetzung. Er muß präzise und deutlich wiedergegeben werden (1985:136).

Thus it is not surprising that LSP theorists were not ready to embrace the ideas in Vermeer's *skopos* theory, which allegedly applies to all texts (Vermeer 1982:99, *also* 1988:127). According to the *skopos* theory, the most important element in translation is not content but function. By showing that the same text can be translated in different ways if there is a shift in communicative function, Vermeer created an alternative to meaning-based translation. Although the *skopos* theory is best suited for translations whose function differs from that of the source text, Vermeer and his supporters have insisted that it also applies to traditional translations in which there is no shift in function, as is the case in regard to LSP translations (Vermeer 1986:38; Reiß 1988:70–72). Today Sager acknowledges that the function of the target text may differ from that of the source text; however, as an LSP expert, he regards such texts as the exception, not the rule (1993:183; similarly Albrecht 1990:78; opposite view in Vermeer 1992a:100).

In particular, LSP translation scholars have remained critical of the *skopos* theory because of its emphasis on the shortcomings of translation as a means of communication. In Vermeer's opinion, the meaning of a text depends on its cultural context and other situational factors. This is what he refers to as text-in-situation (*cf.* Snell-Hornby 1988:47). Presuming that all translation is a cross-cultural event, he believes that the translator is bound to interpret the source text differently than intended by the original sender (*see* Chapter 4, 4.2.1). Insisting that the information contained in a translation is inevitably tainted by the translator's subjectivity, Vermeer concludes that all translation is at best approximation, thus denying that it is possible to preserve or transfer the information content of the source text:

> Ein Translator bietet nicht mehr oder weniger Information als ein Ausgangstextproduzent; ein Translator bietet andere Information auf andere Weise an (Reiß and Vermeer 1984:123).

Emphasizing the objectivity of special-purpose translation, LSP scholars argue that the information content of special-purpose texts is widely independent of cultural context (*cf.* Casagrande's statement above.) Not only do they maintain that it is possible to transfer the information content of the source text, they also insist that the conditions in specialized translation are optimal for perfect communication, i.e., that the receiver's state of knowledge after reception of the translation corresponds to the sender's intention in originating the message (*cf.* Sager 1990:100; *also* Needham 1958:87). Although Wilss also speaks about ideal relations between text producers and receivers in specialized translation, he is careful to qualify his statement, acknowledging that it does not apply to all subject areas. As Wilss correctly remarks, texts of the humanities and the social sciences are exceptions (1992:129). As for texts of the exact sciences, their content consists of factual information describing some state of affairs, i.e., referential meaning. More important, the referential meaning of such texts is based largely on a universal system of knowledge interpreted according to a common system of reference (*cf.* Sager, Dungworth and McDonald 1980:70–81; Wilss 1992:129). Greatly simplified, the system of reference can be explained as follows. In mathematics, chemistry, computer science, mechanical engineering, and other fields, the referents of the extralinguistic realia (objects of reference) are largely uniform throughout the world. Consequently, it has been possible to achieve a high degree of international standardization of the concepts (definitions) constituting the knowledge base of such disciplines and, in turn, the terms (signs) used to express them (Lerat 1995:114–118; *see* Chapter 8, 8.2 on reference). Although the participants in the communication process use different languages, the signs refer to a common conceptual system and consequently a common knowledge system. Accordingly, the chances are optimal that the receivers will attach the same meaning to the linguistic signs regardless of the language and cultural context.

As a note of caution, this simplified explanation does not mean that texts of the exact sciences can be translated simply by interlingual substitution (*cf.* Fluck 1985:136). Authors such as Arntz (1993:6) and Schmitt (1986:252) have convincingly shown that such assertion is a 'fiction' and that some concepts of the exact sciences have been standardized at the national but not at the international level, thus resulting in unavoidable conceptual incongruency. Although Schmitt hints that the terms used to denote such concepts are 'cultural specific,' it is generally agreed that the role of cultural context is greatly reduced in texts of the exact sciences. Moreover, the specialized terminology of the exact sciences is predominantly monosemic (one term for each concept). Therefore, as Steiner once put it, texts of the exact sciences tend to have a 'single agreed meaning independent of local context' (1977:309). Sorry to say, this is not the case in the field of law.

3.3.2. Determining the meaning of plurilingual legal texts

In legal translation, in which accuracy is of utmost importance, it is presumed that all the authentic texts of a single instrument have the same meaning. Regarding treaties, Article 33(3) of the Convention on the Law of Treaties states that the terms 'are presumed to have the same meaning in each authentic text.' Lawyers, however, are the first to admit that the presumption of equal meaning can rarely be achieved in practice (Hardy 1962:82). Some are even more emphatic, insisting that diversity of meaning is inevitable in the parallel texts of a single instrument (Kuner 1991:958).[8] As such, the presumption of equal meaning is reduced to a mere rule of convenience allowing judges to consult only one language version unless a divergence or ambiguity is actually detected (*see* Kuner 1991:958, 962). Nonetheless, the presumption of equal meaning stands until refuted. In other words, the authentic texts of a single instrument are presumed to have the same meaning until proven otherwise.

Unlike texts of the exact sciences, the meaning of legal texts is usually dependent on local context, thus raising the question to what extent the actual receivers, i.e., the judiciary, can be expected to attach the same meaning to each of the parallel texts of a plurilingual instrument. While Vermeer and other contemporary translation theorists regard local context as being synonymous with cultural context (Hönig and Kussmaul 1982:58; exceptions in Kussmaul 1995:74), the meaning of legal texts is determined primarily by legal context. When dealing with legal texts, it is always necessary to determine according to which legal system the text, parts thereof, or even individual institutions and concepts are to be interpreted. Particularly in

---

8. The Sixth Report on the Law of Treaties states: 'Few plurilingual treaties containing more than one or two articles are without some discrepancy between the texts. The different genius of the language, the absence of a complete *consensus ad idem*, or lack of sufficient time to co-ordinate the texts may result in minor and even major discrepancies in the meaning of the texts' (in *Yearbook of the International Law Commission* 1966, 2:225).

plurilingual communication it is important to note that the legal system according to which a text or parts thereof are to be interpreted is usually not determined by language. Contracts, for example, are interpreted according to the law governing the contract regardless of the language in which they are written. Accordingly, if a contract is governed by Chinese law, all the parallel texts of that contract will be interpreted according to Chinese law. Sometimes a contract contains elements of foreign law. In some cases, the receiver may interpret those elements according to the particular foreign legal system and not according to the law governing the contract. As a result, the receiver may sometimes need to use several systems of reference to interpret parts of the same text. The situation is similar in instruments of international law, as well as instruments of European law containing technical terms that derive their meaning from a particular municipal law.

The chances that the receivers will attach the same meaning to the parallel texts of a plurilingual instrument are greatest when all the texts derive their meaning from the same legal system irrespective of language. The fact that the receivers share the same knowledge base means that they also use a common system of reference, thus greatly simplifying the interpretation process. This is the case when receivers interpret the parallel texts of the legislation of plurilingual countries with one legal system, such as Switzerland, Belgium, and Finland. Swiss federal law, for example, is based on one legal system and thus the receivers of all three language versions of federal legislation share essentially the same knowledge base. Consequently, they use a common system of reference in which the linguistic signs in each of the authentic texts signify the same concepts and, in turn, the same objects (*see* Chapter 8, 8.2). The following diagram illustrates how the common system of reference[9] operates when interpreting the parallel texts of Swiss federal legislation:

Figure 2: *Common System of Reference in Swiss Federal Legislation*

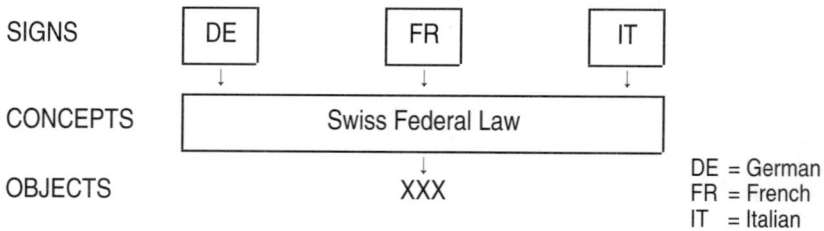

SIGNS	DE	FR	IT	
CONCEPTS		Swiss Federal Law		
OBJECTS		XXX		DE = German FR = French IT = Italian

Although Canada has 'only' two official languages, the process of interpretation is more complex. This is because Canada has two legal systems and thus conflicting systems of reference come into play in the interpretation of the parallel texts of

9. This greatly simplifies the situation. Above all, it disregards the fact that cantonal law cannot be completely neglected. Since cantonal law varies from jurisdiction to jurisdiction, conflicting systems of reference come into play whenever reference is made to cantonal law in federal legislation. Although each canton has its own system of reference for cantonal law, all are based on the civil law, thus making the conflicts more manageable (*see* Chapter 1, at 1.4.1).

federal legislation. Canadian federal law (both private and public) is modelled primarily on the common law and common law concepts (Didier 1990:243–226); however, it must also be applied in Quebec, thus causing confusion when the English text is interpreted in a common law context and the French text in a civil law context. This occurs especially in texts relating to private law which depend to a large extent on concepts of provincial law. In such instances the receivers are bound to attach different meanings to the same text if they are interpreted according to different systems of reference. This is also a constant problem in the interpretation of bilingual instruments of provincial law in which civil law is translated into English and common law into French. The diagram below shows basically what happens when federal legislation in private law matters is interpreted according to different systems of reference.

Figure 3: *Conflicting Systems of Reference used to Interpret Canadian Federal Legislation*

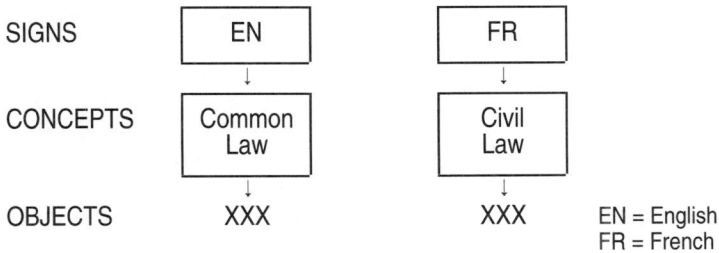

SIGNS	EN	FR	
	↓	↓	
CONCEPTS	Common Law	Civil Law	
	↓	↓	
OBJECTS	XXX	XXX	EN = English FR = French

Even if receivers use the same system of reference when interpreting a text or parts thereof, there is no guarantee that their interpretations will reflect the intended meaning. If a receiver is from a different legal system, this may be due to his/her lack of knowledge about the foreign legal system or simply because of the dominating influence of his/her own legal system. Moreover, legal context serves only a starting point for interpretation. Although normative legal texts usually consist of abstract rules of behavior, Hegenbarth maintains that pragmatic considerations should also be taken into account when interpreting such texts:

> Wer wissen will, was ein [normativer] Text bedeutet, muß danach fragen, von wem er stammt, in welcher Situation er entstanden ist, von welchem Wirklichkeitsmodell der Sprecher ausgeht, welche Intentionen realisiert werden sollen, usw. (1982:165).

As a social science, law is a regime of adjusting relations and ordering human behavior through the force of a socially organized group. Although lawyers are frequently interested only in the practical meaning of a legal text and its implications for what one can or cannot do, a legal text also has a social meaning that can be understood only by examining the social context in which the text is produced (Sumner 1979:277). The most important factor constituting social context is the social order of the state or region in question, i.e., how that society is organized. In its broad sense, the social order of a state or region is determined not only by social but also by economic, political, and ideological principles. According to David and Brierley, the social order of a state is important as it 'determines the way in which the law is applied and shapes the very function of law in that society' (1985:19). Particularly in countries with socialist legal systems, legal rules are regarded as a superstructure of the social and economic conditions of society. As an instrument of the ruling class, the primary purpose of law is not to establish a rule of order by providing principles for the solution of disputes but to transform society in accordance with the Marxist doctrine. As a result, Marxist legislation contains a high ideological content. In regard to the People's Republic of China, von Senger shows how three types of party norms (*zhengzhi luxian, fangzhen* and *zhengce*) have permeated national legislation, even foreign investment laws, giving the texts a connotational meaning that is difficult or almost impossible for foreign lawyers to grasp (1985:177, 184). In this context it should be noted that all legal texts have ideological implications to a greater or lesser degree. In particular, Kelsen reminds us that legal terminology contains a high ideological intensity regardless of the social order involved (de Torres Carballal 1988:447).

In some countries and regions, religion is an important and sometimes the dominant factor shaping the law of that society. This is especially true in Muslim and Hindu law which propound a view of the world based on spirituality and morality (*see* Zweigert and Kötz (1984, Bd.I:420, 431; *also* Gräf 1974:66). The cultural aspects of law are important in every society, as a result of which customary law is recognized as one of the formal sources of law. Nonetheless, customs have a different role in developed, developing, and primitive societies (Vanderlinden 1995:338). Parts of Africa, for example, were ruled for centuries by their own ancestral customary laws. Linked to a mythical order of the universe, ancestral customs are based on notions 'entirely different from those which have dictated modern western thinking' (David and Brierley 1985:549). As a result, the symbolic and connotational meanings of cultural-specific legal concepts cannot be translated and thus tend to remain a mystery even when extensive explanations are used (*see* examples in Möhlig 1973:239; *also* Vanderlinden 1995:412; on the translation of cultural-specific items in legal texts, *see* Šarčević 1985:127–133). As Hegenbarth concludes, concepts with a very high level of cultural context are frequently untranslatable:

> So hat z.B. die Rechtsethnologie aufgezeigt, daß rechtliche Verfahren traditionaler Gesellschaften in kulturspezifischen symbolischen Sinnwelten so sehr verankert sind, daß die Übertragung dieser Verfahren in andere gesellschaftliche Wirklichkeiten von vornherein ausgeschlossen ist (1982:60, note 55).

3.3.3. Redefining the goal of legal translation

Since the meaning of legal texts is determined primarily by legal context, lawyers now admit that the presumption of the equal meaning of parallel texts is an illusion that cannot be achieved in practice (Didier 1990:235). Therefore, unlike other areas of special-purpose translation, the main goal of legal translators cannot be to produce a text with the same meaning as the message of the source text. Although lawyers have been forced to acknowledge that legal translation is also approximation (*cf.*

Gémar 1995–II:154),[10] they are still unable to accept Vermeer's basic presumption that all translation is only an attempt to present information about the source text:

> Entscheidend ist nun, daß *jede* Translation als Informationsangebot in einer Zielkultur und deren Sprache (IAz) über ein Informationsangebot aus einer Ausgangskultur und deren Sprache (IAa) aufgefaßt werden kann. Damit is eine einheitliche Translationstheorie erreicht. Ein Translat bietet ein Informationsangebot über einen A-Text (Vermeer 1982:99).

Although Vermeer claims that his basic presumption applies to all translations, authentic legal texts are an exception. Authenticated translations of parallel texts could never retain their unique status as equally authentic texts if they were deemed merely to present information about the source text. As emphasized in Chapter 1 (1.3.2), it is their normative function and authority that makes authentic legal texts special. In particular, statutes, codes, treaties, conventions, and contracts prescribe commands and prohibitions, grant permission and power, create obligations and rights, all of which are enforceable by law (Cornu 1990:267). Thus authenticated translations of legal texts do not simply contain information about a law; they are the law. In regard to translations of legislation, Legault remarks:

> On ne peut pas se permettre de traduire une loi comme on traduit un autre texte, car la traduction est aussi loi (1977:19).

As equally authentic instruments of the law, parallel legal texts can be effective only if all indirect addressees are guaranteed equality before the law, regardless of the language of the text. This brings us to the second presumption of parallel legal texts: the presumption of equal effect (*see* Didier 1990:221). While lawyers cannot expect translators to produce parallel texts which are equal in meaning, they do expect them to produce parallel texts which are equal in legal effect.[11] Thus the translator's main task is to produce a text that will lead to the same legal effects in practice. As confirmed by Louis-Phillipe Pigeon, late Justice of the Supreme Court of Canada with an impressive record in legal bilingualism, it is the results that count in legal translation (1982:281). In essence, this is what Beaupré means when he mentions legal equivalence, but fails to define the term (*see* Chapter 2, 2.8.4). Similarly, when Herbots remarks that the translator must produce a translation with the 'same legal signification,' he makes it clear that he is referring to legal consequences:

---

10.   Gémar quotes Lazar Focsaneanu's statement: '... la traduction juridique ne saurait jamais être rigoureusement exacte. C'est une opération approximative, dont il convient d'apprécier la marge d'erreur. En somme, une traduction juridique constitue une simple présomption, que les intéressés doivent toujours pouvoir contester en se référant au texte authentique' ('Les langues comme moyen d'expression du droit international' dans *Annuaire français de droit international*, vol. XVI, 1970:262; cited in Gémar 1995–II:154).

11.   In regard to the situation in Canada, the Law Reform Commission confirms that the legislator's intent is to express the message of the single instrument in two linguistic codes and still achieve the same effects: 'Cela signifie qu'on a l'intention d'obtenir, par le biais de la traduction, un effet équivalent de la règle exprimée en anglais et de la règle exprimée en français' (Didier 1990:221).

> Le text d'arrivée doit avoir la même signification juridique (c'est-à-dire qu'il aura les
> mêmes conséquences en droit) que le texte de départ (1987:822).

To produce a text that leads to the same results in practice, the translator must be able 'to understand not only what the words mean and what a sentence means, but also what legal effect it is supposed to have, and how to achieve that legal effect in the other language' (Schroth 1986:55–56; *cf.* Šarčević 1989:286–297; *also* Lehto 1985:156). As emphasized by Koutsivitis, this is undoubtedly the most serious matter to be considered by translators in their decision-making process (1988:49).

In an attempt to redefine the goal of legal translation, it can thus be said that the translator should strive to produce a text that is equal in meaning and effect with the other parallel texts, whereby the main emphasis is on effect. This, however, is not the ultimate goal in a receiver-oriented approach to legal translation. Since the success of an authenticated translation is measured by its interpretation and application in practice, it follows that the translator can best preserve the unity of the single instrument by striving to produce a text that will be interpreted and applied by the courts in the same manner as the other parallel texts of that instrument, particularly the original. This is known as uniform interpretation and application. Thus it can be said that the goal of legal translation is to produce a text that will preserve the unity of the single instrument by guaranteeing uniform interpretation and application.

To this end, the translator must produce a text that has the same normative intensity as the other parallel texts. For example, in penal provisions, it must be clear whether a sanction (e.g., fine or imprisonment) is intended to be mandatory or discretionary (*see* Chapter 5, 5.8). Similarly, legal translators should be able to predict how the courts will apply the text to concrete fact situations. As mentioned above, normative legal texts contain general rules of conduct prescribing how parties are to act or refrain from acting in certain situations. The judge's task is to determine whether the facts established in a concrete case can be subsumed under the fact-situation of the abstract rule. Therefore, the translator should strive to produce a text in which the elements of the abstract fact-situation are interpreted and applied the same regardless of language. For example, if X commits an act in Ontario that qualifies as crime Z under the Criminal Code of Canada and Y commits the same act in Quebec, Y should also be accused of crime Z under the Code penal du Canada, providing the circumstances of the case are the same or similar and judicial discretion is not permitted. It requires considerable skill to produce plurilingual provisions that will be interpreted and applied uniformly in all languages. One of the main obstacles is the varying scope of application of corresponding legal terms of different legal systems (*see* Chapter 8, 8.8.2).

3.3.4. The presumption of equal intent

Promoting uniform interpretation and application of the parallel texts of a plurilingual instrument requires interaction between the translator and the legislator, on the one hand, and the translator and the judiciary, on the other. Above all, such interaction is necessary in order to assure that the second element of the message is realized, i.e., intent.[12] While the presumption of equal effect has priority over that of equal meaning, both are subordinate to the presumption of equal intent. Basically there are two forms of intent: macro and micro. While the macro intent of a text is commonly identified as its general communicative function (Chapter 1, at 1.2. and 1.3), the micro intent is the specific purpose of the particular text, i.e., what the author is specifically attempting to achieve. This is sometimes referred to as author intent (Neubert and Shreve 1992:72). Whereas LSP scholars maintain that special-purpose texts consist of purely factual information, the meaning of which is not influenced by author intent (Wilss 1988a:113; Bühler 1988:281), this is not true of legal texts. On the contrary, legal translators must strive to produce a text which expresses the meaning and achieves the legal effects intended by the 'author.'[13] In legislative texts this is known as the legislative intent, in treaties between states as the intent of the States parties or signatory States, in contracts as the intent or will of the parties, etc. Generally speaking, author intent is often referred to in legal texts as the true or original intent.

In plurilingual communication it is presumed that all the authentic texts of a plurilingual instrument are equal in intent, i.e., that they all express the intent of the single instrument, the so-called uniform intent, and that this is the original intent (cf. Didier 1990:221). Accordingly, the translator's primary task is to produce a text that expresses the uniform intent of the single instrument, in other words, a text that will be interpreted and applied as intended by the legislator. From this point of view, perfect communication can be said to occur in the mechanism of the law when the authentic texts of a single instrument are interpreted and applied uniformly as intended by the legislator, States parties, or contracting parties. Unfortunately, perfect communication is extremely difficult to achieve in the parallel texts of a single instrument. In fact, Hans Dölle once remarked that the uniform intent may ultimately prove to be a fiction:

> The whole exercise in construing a bilingual statute is to uncover a single and uniform legislative intent that has been expressed in two equal but sometimes incongruous language versions, and such uniform intent may in the end be highly fictional (cited in Beaupré 1986:6, note 12).

While this problem is dealt with in Chapter 4, the remainder of this Chapter focuses on the interpretation and application of plurilingual texts by the courts. To compensate for the shortcomings of translation, judges have developed special methods of interpretation to reconcile divergences between the parallel texts of a single instrument. In an attempt to promote uniform interpretation and application, it is

12. Today LSP scholars recognize that the message consists of two main elements: text and intent, either explicit or implicit (Sager 1990:99). Nonetheless, Sager insists that the element of intent plays a subordinate role in *most* areas of specialized translation (1993:183). One of the few LSP experts to mention parallel legal texts ('full equal documents'), Sager stresses the importance of 'identity of content' and 'identity of effect' but fails to mention intent (1993:180).

13. The legal debate on subjective vs. objective intent is not dealt with in this study. *See* Baden 1977:124; Hegenbarth 1982:170–178; on legal vs. literary interpretation, *see* Hegenbarth 1982:185–194.

essential for translators to interact with the judiciary by taking account of the methods of interpretation used in jurisdiction(s) where the parallel texts of that instrument are to be interpreted and applied. Recognizing the importance of such interaction, Tallon remarks: 'La traduction doit toujours avoir présentes à l'esprit les règles d'interprétation du pays vers lequel il traduit' (1995:341).

3.4. PLURILINGUALISM IN ACTION: INTERPRETATION BY RECONCILIATION

Since textual inconsistencies are bound to occur in the parallel texts of a single instrument, it is ultimately up to the judiciary to reconcile any differences by ascertaining the common meaning of all the parallel texts and ensuring that each text is interpreted and applied in accordance with the uniform intent. As in ordinary interpretation, the judiciary must ascertain the common meaning objectively. As a means of limiting judicial discretion, common law lawyers require judges to be bound to the text when ascertaining the legislative intent. To confine judges to the text, drafters have made common law legislation detailed rather than general which, in turn, has had an impact on the common law rules of construction (Driedger 1982b:12). Nonetheless, some drafting specialists are of the opinion that 'judges are more likely to be controlled by clear statements of purpose' rather than by 'rigid grammatical constructions' (Thornton 1987:48). Although Thornton is not referring to plurilingual legislation, lawmakers could certainly promote uniform interpretation and application by defining the purpose clearly and precisely in all parallel texts, thus leaving no doubt as to the uniform intent of the single instrument. As a rule, the legislative intent is set forth in general terms in a purpose clause or preamble that serves as a guideline for judges (*see* Chapter 5, 5.4).

3.4.1. Reconciliation not subordination

In the interpretation of equally authentic texts, each text of a single instrument is independent for the purpose of interpretation, yet all the texts should be consulted in order to determine the common meaning. In this respect, Rosenne emphasizes that 'a good practitioner would almost automatically compare the different language versions before starting any interpretation process' (cited in Tabory 1980:196). This, however, is not always the case in practice. On the contrary, judges frequently consult the other language version(s) only in the event of alleged textual inconsistencies and/or an ambiguity or unclarity in the text of the language of the proceedings. Although this practice is widely criticized, particularly in international law (*see* Kuner 1991:954), it is a matter that must be resolved in each plurilingual jurisdiction. For example, it is an unwritten rule that justices of the Swiss Federal Court should consistently compare the provision(s) of all three authenticated texts when ascertaining the legislative intent, even though the text in the language of the proceedings is clear and unambiguous.

Before the principle of equal authenticity had achieved general recognition, judges tended to resolve textual inconsistencies and ambiguities by giving priority to the original text, which, as the reasoning went, was more likely to express the true intent (*cf.* Tabory 1980:193). Today it may sometimes be necessary to establish a hierarchy between the various language versions; however, the emphasis is no longer on subordination but reconciliation. For example, Article 33(4) of the Convention on the Law of Treaties provides that, when a comparison of the authentic texts discloses a difference of meaning which is not removed by the ordinary rules of interpretation, 'the meaning which best reconciles the texts, having regard to the object and purpose of the treaty, shall be adopted.' Although this provision is instructive, it has been criticized for failing to provide sufficiently firm guidelines. According to Tabory, it does not specify which methods should be used to determine 'the meaning which best reconciles the texts.' The only guidance is a reminder to take account of the 'object and purpose of the treaty,' a general reference to the teleological method of interpretation (1980:213). This occasioned Tabory to raise the following questions:

> Is the meaning 'which best reconciles the texts' to be arrived at by pushing or stretching the meaning in one text as far as possible towards the other; or by finding the midpoint between them; or by reducing the meaning in both texts to the lowest possible common denominator (the latter clearly rejected as an all-encompassing rule of interpretation)? (1980:213).

Since the Convention is silent on this matter, it is left to the courts to determine how the parallel texts of treaties and conventions can best be reconciled in each individual case. The high degree of judicial discretion in resolving disputes arising from treaties and conventions can be viewed as a direct threat to the uniform interpretation and application of parallel texts, thus placing greater pressure on translators. This is all the more true because such disputes are frequently resolved by national courts, the majority of which have no or little experience in interpreting plurilingual texts (*see* Chapter 7, 7.6.2), with the exception of the national courts of plurilingual countries.

In Switzerland, there are no special statutory rules on the interpretation of plurilingual instruments; however, in its long practice the Federal Court has developed a variety of practical methods of trilingual interpretation. The most logical method is to reconcile the three texts by using the principle of the majority: if one text differs, then the common meaning of the other two is the true intent. If all three texts differ, the Court usually gives one text priority. This may be the clearest text or the text that in the Court's opinion best expresses the true intent of the legislator. In criminal cases it is common to give priority to the text most favorable to the defendant (*see* cases in von Overbeck 1984:985).

The interpretation of plurilingual legislation is a complex and sensitive matter in Canada where the courts have the task of applying two equally authentic texts uniformly within the context of two legal systems. Although the principle of equal authenticity was not statute law until 1969, bilingual interpretation began in the federal courts in 1935 by virtue of the Supreme Court's ruling in *The King v. Dubois* (*see* 3.4.2 below). Sometimes taking its cue from Quebec courts, the Supreme Court of Canada gradually developed a pragmatic and sophisticated, bilingual approach to interpretation known as *interprétation croisée* (bilingual cross-construction) (Beaupré 1986:4–11). It is not our purpose here to analyze the case law on the basis of which the Supreme Court developed its principles of bilingual interpretation. This has already been done by Michael Beaupré in his excellent book *Interpreting Bilingual Legislation* (1986). The following summary of the main principles of bilingual cross-construction should suffice to demonstrate that, despite inevitable textual divergences, the federal courts in Canada are committed to achieving uniform interpretation and application to the greatest extent possible.

3.4.2. Resolving ambiguities and textual inconsistencies

In its landmark decision in *The King v. Dubois* ([1935] S.C.R. 378 at 382)), the Supreme Court of Canada resolved the ambiguous provision in the English version by reference to the French version, thus acknowledging for the first time that 'the French version must... be read with the statute in the English version' (Beaupré 1986:18). Stressing the necessity of construing federal legislation in light of both authentic texts, the Court postulated the principle that an ambiguity in one authentic text can be resolved by reference to the other text, provided that the wording in that text is clear and the result can be regarded as a 'reasonable' construction of the ambiguous version. To prevent unwarranted subjectivity, the Court later found it necessary to prove the 'reasonableness' of a construction by reference to context. Similar problems arise in the event of textual inconsistency, especially when each text is clear but tends to say something different or one text is clear but its meaning conflicts with the purpose of the section or Act as a whole. For example, in *Food Machinery Corp. v. Registrar of Trade Marks* ([1946] 2 D.L.R. 258 (Ex.Ct)), the Court found that the wording of the French text was clear and that it coincided with one possible construction of the ambiguous English text. Nonetheless, the French construction was rejected because it was found to be repugnant to the section as a whole. Disqualifying the French construction as unreasonable, the Court favored the only other possible construction of the English text on the ground that it was in harmony with the section as a whole. While the disqualification of a clear version as unreasonable should be used only as a last resort (Driedger 1983:33), the Court's reference to the rule in *Grey v. Pearson* made its reasoning 'more compelling.' As stated in *Grey v. Pearson* ([1857], 6 H.L. Cas.61, 10 E.R. 1216), a reasonable interpretation must conform not only to the intent of the disputed section but also to the declared purpose of the law as a whole (Beaupré 1986:18–24).

These and other principles were later codified in section 8 of the *Official Languages Act* of 1969 which, in essence, can be regarded as an attempt by lawmakers to control the judiciary. Although section 8 has since been repealed (*see* Chapter 8, 8.8.4), the principles therein still constitute the most commonly observed guidelines for construing bilingual legislation in Canada. With the aim of promoting uniform interpretation and application of federal legislation in all parts of Canada, the general rule in paragraph 8(2)(a) provides that, whenever there are differences in the meaning of the two versions of an enactment, the courts should strive to give 'the like effect' to the enactment in all parts of Canada where the enactment is applicable, 'unless a contrary intent is explicitly or implicitly evident.' While this general rule places priority on using methods of reconciliation to achieve 'the like effect' in all parts of Canada, it does not necessarily override the other canons of construction, in particular paragraph 8(2)(d) which allows judges to favor the version that, 'according to the true spirit, intent and meaning of the enactment, best ensures the attainment of its objects.' While the Court of Appeal implied in its ruling in *Dep. M.N.R. for Customs & Excise* v. *Film Technique Ltd.* ([1973] F.C. (C.A.)) that paragraph 8(2)(d) should be invoked only when the conflict cannot be resolved by other means of reconciliation (*see* Beaupré 1986:50, 54), the Supreme Court rejected this view, arguing that the test of *ratio legis*, the underlying purpose of the statute, should not be restricted to special cases falling under paragraph 8(2)(d) (Beaupré 1986:50, 54). As a result the Court has effectively retained a significant amount of discretion when resolving such conflicts.

3.4.3. Determining the highest common meaning

Judges are encouraged to reconcile terminological conflicts by reading both texts to determine their highest common meaning, i.e., the meaning that is 'apt' to both texts within the context of both legal systems (Beaupré 1986:45, note 7). In this sense, paragraph 8(2)(b) provides that 'a reference to a concept, matter or thing' shall 'be construed as a reference to the concept, matter or thing to which in its expression in both versions of the enactment the reference is apt.' For example, in *Gravel v. St-Léonard* ([1978)] 1 S.C.R. 660), the appellant maintained that the English text of section 25 of the *Quebec Municipal Commission Act* which reads 'every agreement whatsoever affecting its credit' should be construed as applicable only to agreements that have an effect on the credit of the municipality in the sense of affecting its solvency. Whereas such a construction was possible under the English text, the word *engager* in the French version 'toute convention quelconque engageant son crédit' clearly does not include the sense of prejudicing the city's credit. Referring to the French text, the Supreme Court construed the English text in its narrow sense, thus rejecting the appellant's claim. In the Court's opinion, this was the only sense that was 'apt' in the context of the relevant provision in both texts (Beaupré 1986:90).

As the Supreme Court cautions, the highest common meaning of a concept, matter, or thing in both texts must be consistent with the purpose of the instrument as a whole. In *The Queen* v. *Compagnie Immobilière BCN Ltée* ([1979] 1.S.C.R. 865), the Federal Court of Appeal reconciled the two divergent texts by interpreting the word *disposed of* 'in the sole relevant sense that the expression has in common with the French word *aliénés.*' In this case, however, the Supreme Court reversed the decision because, as the Court reasoned, one cannot insist on using the principle of the highest common meaning if 'the meaning clearly runs contrary to the intent of the legislation and thus tends to defeat rather than assist the attainment of its objects' (in Beaupré 1986:54). Thus the Supreme Court made it clear that the courts should always attempt to reconcile divergent language versions; however, in so doing they cannot disregard the ordinary rules of interpretation. Moreover, reconciliation is not always possible and in some cases it is clearly not intended.

3.4.4. Priority of one legal system

Although the primary goal of bilingual interpretation at the federal level is to reconcile the two language versions by ascertaining their common meaning, this is usually impossible when technical terms of the civil law and common law are used. Due to their incompatibility, the court should no longer search for a common meaning but, pursuant to paragraph 8(2)(c), construe the concept, matter, or thing that is incompatible with the legal system where the enactment is intended to apply as a reference to the concept, matter, or thing in that version of the enactment that is compatible therewith. This clause authorizes the courts to ascertain which legal system Parliament intended to apply in each individual case and to construe the particular term or institution according to that legal system. In essence, it permits the courts of Quebec to interpret federal statutes within the framework of civil law institutions and principles despite the obvious risk that such practice poses to uniform interpretation and application. For example, in *Gulf Oil Can. Ltd. v. Canadien Pacifique Ltée* (*see* Chapter 8, 8.8.2), the Superior Court of Quebec upheld Quebec law by favoring the French version which used the term *cas fortuit*, whereas the English version used the expression *act of God*. As a result, the defendant railway company was exonerated from liability although the same fact situation would not have qualified as an act of God in the common law (Beaupré 1986:133–134).

Problems arise particularly in federal legislation on private law matters where the legislative intent is to have the English text apply exclusively in common law provinces and the French text in Quebec. To discourage parties from attempting to evade the law by insisting on using the other language version, it was proposed that two sets of parallel texts of federal legislation be enacted: one set in English and French for the common law provinces, the Northwest Territories, and the Yukon, and a different set in French and English for the civil law province of Quebec. This idea was largely dismissed as impractical (Didier 1990:234). To leave no discretion to the courts, drafters and translators of private law statutes of federal legislation sometimes incorporated both civil law and common law concepts into the same provision. For example, in Article 53 of the *Loi sur la faillité* of 1970, the English text reads 'mortgage, charge or hypothec' and the corresponding French text 'mortgage, privilège ou hypothèque.' When parties insisted on applying the English text in Quebec, the court used the term *hypothec* which derives its meaning from the concept of *hypothèque*; while *hypothec* and *hypothèque* apply only in cases in Quebec, *mortgage* applies only in common law jurisdictions (*see* Didier 1990:227; on *mortgage* and *hypothèque see* Chapter 8, 8.8.1, 8.8.3, 8.9.1).

With the introduction of paragraph 8(2)(c) it was no longer necessary to duplicate concepts. In essence, paragraph 8(2)(c) permits federal courts in Quebec to exclude the common law system by interpreting common law terms in the English text as references to civil law institutions. From the linguistic point of view, it enables courts to manipulate the system of reference to obtain the desired result by deriving the meaning of the target term from the source instead of the target legal system. This is also done in the bilingual interpretation of parallel texts of provincial law. Although now repealed, the rule of paragraph 8(2)(c) is still practiced. Accordingly, the courts can use their discretion to ascertain whether Parliament's intent is to override or alter the institutions of one of the legal systems (Beaupré 1986:120–121, 136–140).

3.5. ROLE OF THE RECEIVER IN MODERN TRANSLATION THEORY

The era of modern translation began when the translator was released from his/her commitment to reproduce the source text, thus ending the predominance of retrospective translation. No longer bound by the principle of fidelity to the source text, the translator became a text producer with the responsibility of selecting a translation strategy based on the communicative situation of reception. Thus translation became receiver oriented, marking the beginning of perspective translation, as modern translation is sometimes called (*cf.* Snell-Hornby 1988:44). In translation theory it is presumed that the target text is received at a different time and place than the source text, the only exception being in interpretation (*cf.* Steiner 1977:334). Thus it became common to distinguish between source and target text receivers. At first, the translator was expected to produce a text that evokes nearly the same response in the target text receivers as the source text in the source text receivers. This is what Nida referred to as functional or dynamic equivalence (Nida and Taber 1974:22–28), Koller as pragmatic equivalence (1979:187), and Newmark as communicative translation (1982:38–56). Then came the discovery that the target text can be addressed to an audience that is basically different from that of the source text (Newmark 1982:10), for instance, when Bible stories are translated for children.

With this in mind, House differentiated between two basic types of translation strategies: *overt translation* in which the target text receivers are 'overtly' not the same as the source text receivers, and *covert translation* in which the target text receivers are basically the same as the source text receivers. According to House, the latter group includes texts that are not addressed exclusively to the source text receivers, such as commercial texts, scientific texts, journalistic articles, and tourist information booklets (House 1981:188–194). Although House did not mention parallel legal texts, they would also belong to this group. In fact, since special-purpose communication is strictly between specialists from the same subject-area, it is safe to generalize that all special-purpose texts would fall under her category of covert translation. On the other hand, Vermeer clearly favored House's notion of overt translation, which he modified and developed further in his *skopos* theory. From Vermeer's point of view, the decisive element determining translation strategy is communicative function which, in turn, determines to whom the text is addressed in the target culture. In situations where the function of the target text differs from that of the source text, the source and target receivers may represent very different types of audiences (*see* Chapter 1, 1.5.2).

Regardless whether there is a shift in function, the translator always bases his/her translation strategy on the expectations and conventions of the receivers in the target culture. According to Vermeer, the source and target receivers always differ because they inevitably belong to a different linguistic and cultural community (Vermeer 1988:126; *cf.* Nord 1988:49). Thus it is presumed that the situation of reception of the target text always differs from that of the source text, just as the situation of production of the target text differs from that of the source text. This led translation theorists to regard the production and reception of the target text as an act of communication that is largely independent from the production and reception of the source text. As the translator increasingly disregards the source text, the degree of independence of the communication acts reaches the point that they can be regarded as two separate acts of communication (Holz-Mänttäri 1986:363).

Such approach is obviously incompatible with the production and reception of parallel legal texts, which in ideal situations should constitute one and the same act of communication (*see* Chapter 4, 4.5). Recognizing that the chances of achieving uniform interpretation and application of parallel texts depend largely on the situational factors of reception, lawyers have made conscious attempts to institute controls over the judiciary process. Aware that the same text can be interpreted differently in different situations of reception, lawyers realized at an early date that one of the best ways to promote uniform interpretation and application is to require that disputes relating to the parallel texts of a particular instrument be decided by a special court (international and supranational law) (*see* Chapter 7, 7.7) or a hierarchy of courts subject to certain checks and balances (municipal law). Before examining the hierarchy of courts in Switzerland and Canada, it is necessary to present some background information on plurilingualism in the administration of justice in the two countries.

3.5.1. Plurilingualism in the courts

In Canada, section 133 of the *British North American Act* 1867 also guaranteed that any person could use either English or French in any pleading or process in or issuing from any court of Canada or any of the courts of Quebec. For over a century, however, this constitutional right was little more than dead letter. It was not until after the *Official Languages Act* of 1969 declared the French and English texts of federal legislation equally authentic that citizens began to exercise their language rights in the federal courts of common law provinces. Even then, the courts interpreted section 133 restrictively, permitting citizens to use the official language of their choice; however, this did not include the right to trial in the language of their choice. An exception is the *Jones* case ([1975] 2 R.C.S. 182) where the Supreme Court regarded the literal interpretation of section 133 as a minimum (Low 1989:196). Despite progress in language rights, Article 19(1) of the *Canadian Charter of Rights and Freedoms* of 1982 merely confirms the wording of section 133. In *McDonald* ([1986] 1 R.C.S. 460) and *Société des Acadiens* ([1986] 1 R.C.S. 549), the Supreme Court continued to interpret the provision literally. Moreover, bilingualism in the courts was not regarded as a universal right, as a result of which some federal courts were not even required to provide facilities for simultaneous interpretation (*see* Low 1989:197).

It is the new *Official Languages Act* of 1988 that finally guarantees citizens the right to trial in the official language of their choice in Canadian federal courts. Section 16 makes it clear that the parties have the right to determine the language of the proceedings. Furthermore, for the first time it requires that every judge or other officer who hears the proceedings must be able to understand the language of the proceedings without the assistance of an interpreter, thus implying that the judge(s) assigned to a case must also be able to interpret and apply the relevant legislation and other texts in the language chosen by the parties (*see* Low 1989:198). While lower federal courts hear only civil cases involving federal law, criminal cases based on the federal Criminal Code are heard by provincial courts. To avoid accusations that the accused is the victim of language discrimination, Part XIV.1 of the Criminal Code, as amended in 1978, provides that the language of proceedings issuing from the Criminal Code is the language of the accused. Amended again in 1985, Part XIV.1 now requires that judges speak the official language of the accused and, as amended in 1990, the jury must also speak the official language of the accused. As of 1990, Part XIV.1 is in force in all common law provinces. This can perhaps be regarded as a first step towards bilingualism in all common law provinces. Currently, parties to civil disputes before provincial courts can choose the language of the proceedings only in bilingual provinces. As mentioned in Chapter 2, precedence was set in the *Forest* case (1979), as a result of which Manitoba was the first common law province to become partially bilingual (*see* 2.8.2).

In Switzerland the regulation of language rights falls in the jurisdiction of the cantons. At the level of the Confederation, Article 116 of the Federal Constitution has long made a strict distinction between national and official languages, recognizing German, French, Italian, and Rhaeto-Romanic as national languages, but only German, French, and Italian as official languages. As part of the recent constitutional reform, Article 116 has now been revised and approved on March 10, 1996. While the distinction still remains, paragraph 4 provides that Rhaeto-Romanic is also an official language in relations between the Confederation and a person who speaks Rhaeto-Romanic. It remains to be seen how farreaching the effects will be; however, the first results are already visible (*see* 3.5.2 below). Language rights in the cantons are based on the territorial principle, i.e., the linguistic constituency of the population in that area (Weibel 1992:29; *cf.* the situation in Belgium in Chapter 2, at 2.9). Originally created along language borders, the majority of cantons have a relatively homogenous population. As a result, twenty-two cantons are monolingual, three bilingual, and only one trilingual (Dessemontet 1984:111). In monolingual cantons the courts hear civil and criminal cases only in the official language of the canton; simultaneous interpretation in the other official languages is provided if necessary. Application of the territorial principle in the plurilingual cantons has sometimes resulted in a diverse language network, in which the official language varies not only from region to region but also from town to town. To ensure equality, the plurilingual cantons are encouraged to follow the language policy of the Confederation. Although Article 9(1) of the Swiss Law on Official Publications guarantees that the three versions of national legislation published in the respective official gazettes are equally authentic, the rule of equal authenticity is not always practiced in plurilingual cantons. Whereas civil and criminal proceedings are conducted in either German or French and both texts are equally authentic in cantons Berne and Wallis, the proceedings in canton Fribourg are in either French or German but the French text prevails in the event of a divergence. In the trilingual canton of Grisson proceedings are held in German, Italian, or Rhaeto-Romanic with the German text prevailing in the event of a divergence (Voyame 1989:349; von Overbeck 1984:976).

3.5.2. The hierarchy of courts

The goal of plurilingual communication in the administration of justice is equality: not only the right to trial in one's language but, more importantly, the guarantee that all the parallel texts of a plurilingual instrument will be interpreted and applied uniformly, irrespective of the court having jurisdiction to hear a particular case. In legal communication a conscious attempt is made to promote the uniform interpretation and application of parallel texts by controlling the judiciary. Despite attempts to introduce special rules of plurilingual interpretation, courts generally exercise a considerable amount of discretion. Thus the most effective method of controlling the interpretation process is to limit the number of courts having competence to hear cases in disputes arising from the parallel texts of a given instrument. The ideal solution, of course, is to relegate exclusive jurisdiction to one court, making it competent to resolve all disputes arising under a particular instrument. This, however, is not possible in municipal law where the administration of justice is exercised by a hierarchy of courts. There are, however, various checks and balances which have been built into the judicial systems of plurilingual countries to promote uniform interpretation and application.

Generally speaking, the judicial process in plurilingual countries functions in one of the following ways. The lower and higher courts either hear cases only in the official language(s) of the particular province, canton, or republic, or in all the official languages of that country, or there may be a mixed system as in the federal and provincial courts of Canada. In either case, the highest court of the land is responsible for promoting the uniform interpretation and application of plurilingual instruments by all courts, itself included. In the majority of the Swiss cantons, cases are heard before cantonal courts in the official language of the particular canton, either German, French, or Italian. At the top of the hierarchy, the Federal Court hears cases in all three official languages. Whether it will now add Rhaeto-Romanic is a matter to be regulated in forthcoming revisions of the federal Law on Organization. Nonetheless, the Federal Court has already responded to the recent revision of Article 116 of the Federal Constitution by writing its first judgment in Rhaeto-Romanic, thus setting a precedent even before the new Constitutional revisions have entered into force (*Bundesgerichtsentscheidungen* 1996: 122 I 93).[14] As a rule, justices of the highest court are proficient in the three official languages. When appointing new justices, the Federal Assembly takes account of their native language so as to ensure that all three official languages are duly represented in the Court's composition.

---

14. In its reasons the Federal Court writes: 'Ein Urteil des Bundesgerichts in einer Beschwerde einer romanischen Gemeinde oder Person gegen den Entscheid einer Instanz des Kantons Graubünden ist auf Rumantsch Grischun zu verfassen' (BGE 1996: 122 I 93).

Figure 4: *Plurilingualism in the Swiss Court System*

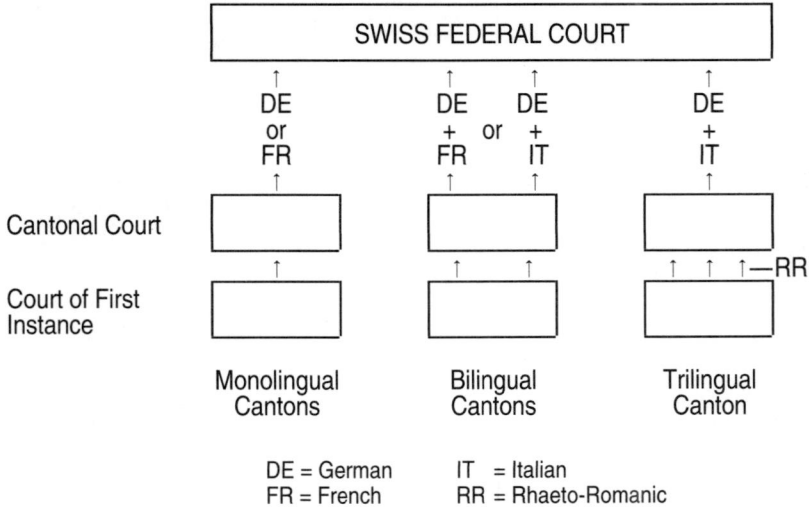

```
                    ┌─────────────────────────────────────────────┐
                    │          SWISS FEDERAL COURT                │
                    └─────────────────────────────────────────────┘
                        ↑           ↑     ↑              ↑
                        DE          DE    DE             DE
                        or          +  or +              +
                        FR          FR    IT             IT
                        ↑           ↑     ↑              ↑
Cantonal Court       ┌──────┐    ┌──────────┐      ┌──────────┐
                     └──────┘    └──────────┘      └──────────┘
                        ↑           ↑     ↑          ↑  ↑  ↑—RR
Court of First       ┌──────┐    ┌──────────┐      ┌──────────┐
Instance             └──────┘    └──────────┘      └──────────┘

                     Monolingual    Bilingual        Trilingual
                      Cantons        Cantons            Canton
```

DE = German   IT = Italian
FR = French   RR = Rhaeto-Romanic

In Canada, all federal courts are bilingual (at least on paper). Although this obligation is still not practiced universally, federal courts are at least expected to provide facilities for simultaneous interpretation if requested. Section 16 of the new *Official Languages Act* of 1988 does not require federal judges to be bilingual; however, federal courts should be comprised of sufficient judges who understand either French or English or both languages (*see* Low 1989:198). In criminal matters, all provincial courts are now required to hear cases in the official language of the accused. To date, parties to civil disputes before provincial courts can choose the language of the proceedings only in bilingual provinces. The Supreme Court of Canada hears cases in both official languages. All nine justices of the Court must be bilingual to the extent that they are able to follow proceedings and construe texts in both languages. The following diagram shows how bilingualism functions in civil disputes before Canadian federal and provincial courts:

83

Figure 5: *Bilingualism in Canadian Courts in Civil Disputes*

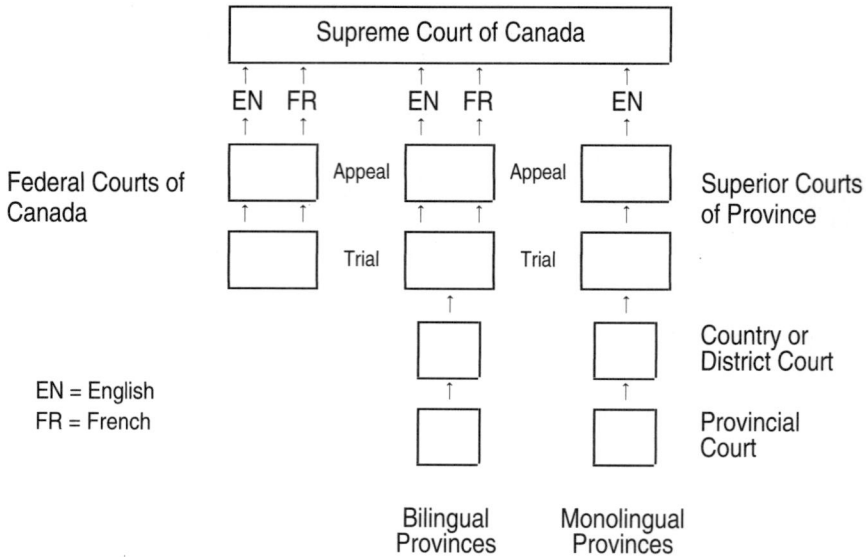

3.5.3. Special role of the highest court

Although the organization and composition of municipal courts varies from country to country, the role of the highest court in plurilingual countries in respect of language questions is practically the same worldwide. Above all, it is the justices of the highest court (and in Canada judges of the superior courts of bilingual provinces, especially Quebec) who promote uniform interpretation and application by handing down precedents that are binding or serve as guidelines for their peers and especially for judges of lower courts. Such rulings occasionally contain instructions on preferred methods of interpretation to be used when reconciling ambiguities and textual inconsistencies. If the highest court maintains that the methods of interpretation used by a lower court lead to an unreasonable result, the court can overturn the lower court's ruling in that case, as the Supreme Court of Canada did in *The Queen v. Compagnie Immobilière BCN Ltée* (*see* 3.4.3 above). Moreover, the highest court (and in Canada the superior courts) may rule that a disputed provision contains a translation error and in some cases even correct the error. This authority was exercised by the Superior Court of Quebec in *Rémillard v. Couture* ([1955] C.S.162) concerning the question whether Article 758 of the Civil Code of Quebec is to be construed as being intended to void gifts made 'so as to take effect only after death,' as in the English version, or 'à cause de mort,' as in the French version. Favoring the French version, the Superior Court of Quebec ruled that the English version of Article 758 was a mistranslation and should read 'in contemplation of death.' In its reasons the Superior Court pointed out that the French phrase *à cause de mort* was translated by the expression *in contemplation of death* in other articles of the Code (Beaupré 1986:124). While it is not unusual for the highest court to correct a single translation error in a disputed provision, correcting an entire piece of legislation in a decision is highly unusual. In this context, we are reminded of the Swiss Federal Court's decision of April 7, 1911, in which it authorized a list of translation corrections of the French version of the Civil Code, thus bypassing the usual legislative procedure required for approving revisions and corrections of authenticated texts (*see* Chapter 2, 2.7.1).

Finally, it can be said that the communicative situation of reception is truly unique in the highest court of plurilingual jurisdictions. This is because the very same justices or judges are responsible for the interpretation and application of all texts, regardless of language. By virtue of their authority, they promote uniform interpretation and application by consulting and comparing all the language versions of a given instrument when ascertaining the common meaning in accordance with the uniform intent. From the point of view of translation theory, such a communicative situation of reception is truly unique because the source and target text receivers are identical, a situation that defies both traditional and modern definitions of translation. Presuming that the situations of reception always differ in acts of communication involving the source and target texts, Nord comments: 'insofern kann eine Übersetzung sich niemals an denselben Empfänger richten wie das Original' (1988:58).

Having focused their attention primarily on the interpretation and application of the parallel texts of legal instruments, lawyers later realized that they could not simply ignore the situational factors of text production. To improve the reliability of authenticated translations, urgent changes were required in the production of parallel texts. Attempts to coordinate the situational factors of the production of parallel texts gradually led to innovations which have radically changed the role of the translator. The next Chapter deals with text production.

4 The Changing Role of the Legal Translator

4.1. THE TRANSITION TO TEXT PRODUCER

Isolated from both producers and receivers, the legal translator traditionally acted as a mediator between text producers and receivers in a sterile triadic relationship (*see* figure 6A). It was not until the twentieth century that the legal translator succeeded in converting his/her passive role in the communication process into an active one, finally emerging as a text producer with new authority and responsibility. Today legal translators are encouraged to strive for linguistic purity, however, not at the expense of substantive equality (*cf.* Beaupré 1986:179). In keeping with the principle of equal authenticity, translators must attempt to preserve the unity of the single instrument by producing a text that expresses the uniform intent (*see* Chapter 3, 3.3.4). Focusing on matters relating to legal hermeneutics and text production, this Chapter sheds light on the translator's decision-making process, raising the question to what extent it is possible to produce a text that expresses the uniform . intent.

While legal translators must understand the source text in order to be effective text producers, it is generally agreed that they should not overstep their authority and interpret the text in the legal sense. Above all, they must avoid making value judgments when determining the uniform intent of the single instrument. To promote objectivity in translation operations, institutions now attempt to coordinate the situative factors (time and place) of the production of parallel texts. In the late seventies legislative reforms in Canada led to the introduction of new bilingual drafting methods which have revolutionized the role of the legal translator by transforming him/her into a co-drafter with broad decision-making authority. As a result, the translator's relationship with the other text producers is now a dynamic one, in which there is mutual cooperation between producers, all of whom are encouraged to interact with the actual receivers (*see* figure 6B). The goal is to coordinate the situational factors of production to the point that all text producers of the parallel texts of a legal instrument participate in the same act of communication. To promote the uniform interpretation and application of parallel texts, the ultimate goal is to coordinate the situational factors of both production and reception, thus resulting in a unique communication process previously unknown in translation theory.

Figure 6: *Roles of the Legal Translator*

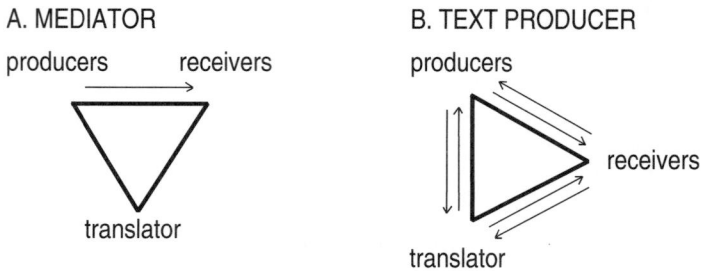

A. MEDIATOR

producers   receivers

translator

B. TEXT PRODUCER

producers

receivers

translator

4.2. THE UNIFORM INTENT OF THE SINGLE INSTRUMENT

Although the translator does not interpret the text as the judge does, he/she is expected to preserve the unity of the single instrument by producing a text that expresses the uniform intent, i.e., the original intent of the lawmakers (legislation), States parties (treaties), or contracting parties (contracts). As stated in Chapter 3 (3.3.4), the presumptions of equal meaning and effect are subordinate to the presumption of equal intent. In other words, a reliable translation is one that expresses the *intended* meaning and leads to the *intended* results. Furthermore, it is presumed that all the parallel texts of a plurilingual instrument express the same intent and that this is the original or true intent.

In this Chapter the emphasis is on micro intent, i.e., what the authors specifically intend to achieve in a particular text. Author intent is frequently referred to in special-purpose communication as the purpose of the text (*see* Sager 1993:67). One of the best methods of making the purpose of a text known is to use an informative title (*see* Nord 1993:15). Thus drafters sometimes state the general purpose of a piece of legislation in a long title (*see* Thornton 1987:151), as in the following example from the *Statutes of Canada* [1993]:

An Act to facilitate compromises and arrangements between companies and their creditors

Loi facilitant les transactions et arrangements entre les compagnies et leurs créanciers

Like other text types (Nord 1993:9, note 2), legislative texts often have several principal purposes, especially if the Act is more complex. In such cases, the long title should describe each of them in the same order of reference. The following Act from the *Statutes of Canada* [1986] has two principal purposes:

An Act respecting corrections and the conditional release and detention of offenders and to establish the office of Correctional Investigator

Loi régissant le système correctionnel, la mise en liberté sous condition et le maintien en incarcération, et portant création du bureau de l'enquêteur correctionnel

Whereas legislative drafters previously used a preamble to explain 'the object of [the] Act or... the reasons why its enactment is considered desirable' (Thornton 1987:154), this practice has largely been discontinued.[1] In view of its usefulness in making the intention of Parliament known, the discontinued use of the preamble has been lamented by some lawyers. As Lord MacDermott once put it:

> The Legislature should make greater efforts to state its mind more clearly. The time was when Statutes set out by way of preamble and recital the intention of Parliament more fully than is now the practice; sometimes, indeed, individual sections had their own introductory preambles. It is a pity that this practice should have fallen into comparative disuse for it is a valuable way of declaring the essential aim of any important piece of legislation (cited in Thornton 1987:154).

Whereas a preamble is still widely used in treaties and agreements, it has been generally replaced in statutes and other legislative texts by a purpose clause which summarizes the problems addressed by the piece of legislation and the remedy prescribed therein. As mentioned in Chapter 3 (3.4), drafters are encouraged to write clear and precise purpose clauses as a means of controlling the judiciary. Purpose clauses are particularly useful in plurilingual texts if they are specific. As a rule, greater efforts are made in the common law to define the purpose of a piece of legislation in the instrument itself. This is because common law judges are generally precluded from using preparatory materials to ascertain the legislative intent. But what about translators? How do they determine the legislative intent? Moreover, to what extent are translators able to determine the true intent of a legal instrument? These are matters of hermeneutics.

4.2.1.   Hermeneutics and legal translation

As a result of the increasing emphasis on hermeneutics in modern translation theory, it is generally agreed that the translator must understand the source text in order to produce an adequate translation (Paepcke 1986:104; Gémar 1995–I:152; Dancette 1995:22). Thus the translator is generally viewed as having a double role as receiver of the source text and producer of the target text (*cf.* Stolze, 1992:21; Wilss 1988:47; Vermeer 1992a:55). Since the reception of the source text by the translator is bound to have an impact on translation operations, it is essential for legal translators to determine the intent of the single instrument objectively. This, however, is precisely where the problem begins. As a rule, theorists of general translation cast serious doubts on the translator's ability to ascertain the intended meaning of the source text objectively (Holz-Mänttäri 1984:36, 72; Holz-Mänttäri 1990:62). In particular, Vermeer regards the reception of the source text by the translator as an act of

---

1.   In Canada the use of a preamble in legislative texts is optional (*see* Chapter 5, at 5.4). As a rule, a preamble is used when the subject matter of the legislation is of constitutional or international importance, as is the case, for example, in the *Official Languages Act*.

interpretation which is a creative act involving the translator's own hermeneutical situation (1986:34; *also* Vermeer 1992a:52, 78). Similarly, Reiß views the target text as a product shaped by the translator's knowledge of the text, reality in which he/she lives, his/her past experiences, capabilities, and even personal disposition (Reiß and Vermeer 1984:68; *also* Reiß 1995:50–51). Thus Vermeer concludes that there is no guarantee that the translator will understand the source text as intended by the author. In this sense, some German translation theorists make a distinction between what is actually said in a text (*das Gesagte*) and what the author intended to say (*das Gemeinte*) (*see* Stolze 1992:49). Going a step further, Vermeer postulates his basic presumption that all translation can be regarded only as an attempt to present information about the source text (*see* Chapter 3, 3.3.3). In other words, a translation inevitably contains 'different information' or a 'different meaning.'

This is reminiscent of Gadamer's notion of *Anders-Verstehen*. Under Heidigger's influence, Gadamer denied the possibility of any objective interpretation independent of the existential conditions of the receiver. Maintaining that all interpretation presupposes participation on the part of the receiver, Gadamer regarded interpretation as a creative act, not in the usual sense of *Besser-Verstehen* (the receiver understands the text better than the author himself), a notion that dates back to Kant, but rather in the sense of the notion of *Anders-Verstehen*: the receiver understands the text differently than the author had intended; in other words, he/she creates a new meaning (1975:280).

Whereas Gadamer was referring strictly to texts of the arts and social sciences as opposed to those of the exact sciences (1975:267), Vermeer makes no such distinction. In his attempt to create a universal translation theory, he disregards the fact that texts containing primarily factual information can be understood independent of local context. Later Vermeer is forced to acknowledge that such texts do exist; however, he simply notes that they are the exception rather than the rule. Referring to texts which can be understood independent of local context as *Zéro-Setzungen*, he defends his own theory by insisting that theories are based on general rules, not exceptions (1992a:49, 57).

As early as the nineteenth century Dilthey had recognized the high level of factuality of special-purpose texts (*see* Orth 1984:50–54). Similarly, Wilss emphasizes that the aim of special-purpose texts is not to make the 'unknown known' but to present scientific and technological knowledge that can be understood by analytic explanation (1988:113). Unfortunately, Wilss' general conclusion that the interpretation of special-purpose texts does not involve the 'personal participation' of the translator in the hermeneutic sense (1992:129) applies only to texts of the exact sciences. As for legal texts, translators must constantly be on their guard to avoid relying on value judgments when determining the author intent, i.e., the intent of the legislature, parties, or States parties. In this respect, one of the Dutch translators of the EC Rome Treaty acknowledged that he was constantly conscious of the danger of passing off his own ideas as those of the parties (cited in Ginsbergen 1970:14). Therefore, as a precautionary measure, lawyers discourage translators from using legal methods to interpret the source text. This applies particularly to non-lawyers who, as Herbots warns, are bound to arrive at a different interpretation than lawyers, thus threatening to distort the original intent:

Le traducteur non juriste doit se rendre compte qu'il interprète nécessairement un text en le traduisant, et que son interprétation – donc sa traduction – n'est peut être pas celle auquel arriverait un juriste interprétant le texte de départ (1987:831).

4.2.2.   No double role for legal translators

The fear that the original intent will be tainted by the translator's subjectivity is undoubtedly one of the main reasons for the highly restricted role of legal translators in the past. For this reason it has taken much longer for legal translators to gain even limited authority to make decisions concerning linguistic questions. In the debate on the translation of the Swiss Civil Code in the early 1900s, Cesana represented the traditional view that the legal translator's task is to faithfully reproduce the source text, allowing concessions for linguistic divergencies only when absolutely necessary (*see* Chapter 2, 2.7.1). In his view, the translator is overstepping his/her authority merely by using descriptive paraphrases for German composita. As he put it, by making such decisions the translator assumes the difficult task of interpretation that is reserved strictly for the courts:

> Sodann hat jeder Umschreibung eine eigentliche Gesetzesauslegung voranzugehen. Wenn je, so muß der umschreibende Übersetzer sich aufs genaueste Rechenschaft geben und an der Wurzel erfassen, was der Gesetzgeber gedacht und gewollt hat – er verwickelt sich da in die äußerst schwierige Tätigkeit der Interpretation, was ja Sache der Gerichte ist... (10/1910:151).

Legal translators are now permitted to make linguistic decisions; however, they should always be aware that even minor linguistic changes can sometimes unintentionally alter the substance, thereby changing the meaning and/or effect (*see* the example of UN Security Council Resolution 242 in Chapter 7 at 7.4.2). Generally speaking, most translators are barred from making legal decisions, although translators trained in law are now an exception (*see* 4.7.2 below). As a rule, lawyers agree that legal translators must understand the source text in order to produce an adequate translation; however, they are not permitted to interpret the source text(s) as judges do (Pigeon 1978:37). In view of this clear stand taken by lawyers, it is surprising that Gémar encourages translators to interpret legal texts by using methods of interpretation normally reserved for judges:

> Les systèmes juridiques sont ainsi faits qu'ils ne laissent à personne d'autre qu'au juge le soin de 'dire le droit'. Mais rien n'interdit au traducteur de... *dire le texte* [author's emphasis] (Gémar 1995–II:166).

Gémar's further remark that one of the main tasks of legal translators is to 'interpret the law' (1995–II:167) reflects his view that the translator's interpetation of the source text constitutes the crucial phase of all translation, including legal translation. As the common title of his recent works implies, Gémar regards all translation as 'l'art d'interpréter' (1995–I:151). While it is essential for legal translators to be familiar with the methods of interpretation used by judges participating in the communication process, they themselves should refrain from interpreting the text in the legal sense. As Beaupré's puts it, any act of interpretation by the translator threatens to 'scuttle' the original intent (1986:197; *cf.* Rossini Favretti 1994:337–339).

In legal hermeneutics a distinction is made between understanding and interpretation. Whereas understanding is an act of cognition that occurs automatically without reflection, the receiver begins to interpret or construe the text as soon as he/she is forced to reflect about the meaning as a result of an ambiguity or other textual unclarity (Larenz 1983:195). Sometimes it is difficult to make a clearcut distinction between understanding and interpretation; however, the view prevails that the translator's duty is to express what is said in the source text and not what he/she thinks ought to have been said. The latter is clearly an act of interpretation involving the personal participation of the translator.

One of the few legal translators to address this problem is Michael Akehurst, a member of the team that translated the English version of the Treaty establishing the EEC. By the time work commenced on the English text of the Treaty,[2] the European Court had already developed a sizeable case law that was bound to influence the Working Party's view of the intent expressed in the 'original' French, German, Dutch, and Italian texts adopted in 1957. Reading the 'original' texts in the light of relevant case law, Akehurst doubted at times whether the sense conveyed by the words of the text reflected the true intent of the States parties. As in Kant's notion of *Besser-Verstehen*, he believed to have understood the intention of the founding States better than the original drafters/translators. Raising the question to what extent one can disregard the literal meaning of the source texts if it appears not to reflect the author intent, Akehurst concluded that the translator's job is to translate 'what is actually said, not what he thinks ought to have been said.' Although he admits of having 'stretched' the literal meaning at times, Akehurst acknowledges that his task 'was to translate the Treaty, not to improve it' (1972:25–26).

In regard to ambiguities, it is generally agreed that the translator has no authority to resolve an ambiguity in the source text as this would be an act of interpretation. This is especially true in the case of treaties which are often the product of political compromises where clarity must be sacrificed for the sake of obtaining consensus, thus resulting in ambiguous or vague formulations. As emphasized in Chapter 7 (7.4.2), one of the biggest fears of treatymakers is that translators will clarify an intentional ambiguity or unclarity, thus upsetting the delicately achieved balance and inviting adverse interpretations. Sometimes, however, translators are forced to make such decisions, especially when there is more than one source text. In Akehurst's case, the English translation of the EEC Treaty is a subsequent translation made and adopted after the authentication of the 'original' authentic texts in French, German, Dutch, and Italian. This put Akehurst in the unusual situation of having four source texts (although the Dutch, Italian, and most of the German texts are authenticated

---

2. The Working Party for the authentic English translation of the Treaty establishing the EEC was set up in the winter of 1970–71 and completed its work in April 1971. A translation made by the British Foreign Office in 1967 was used as a starting point. *See* Akehurst 1972: 20–22.

translations).[3] In the event of an ambiguity, Akehurst consistently compared all the existing authentic texts regardless of whether they were originals or authenticated translations. If the ambiguity was present in all the texts, he was obliged to retain it in the English text as well. On the other hand, if there was a discrepancy among the four texts, he was forced to decide which text to favor. To assist in his decision-making process, Akehurst developed a set of rules similar to those used by judges in plurilingual interpretation. First of all, he favored the text in which the disputed provision was originally drafted, secondly, the text(s) expressing the common meaning of the majority of the parallel texts and thirdly, the clearest text (Akehurst 1972:25). Since such decisions can sometimes affect the substance rather significantly, Akehurst was criticized for having overstepped his authority as a translator. Although he did not make the decisions alone and without prior consultation, the unusual circumstances in which this and other translations were produced occasioned lawyers to examine the authentication process and the situational factors of text production.

4.2.3.   Authentication and the situational factors of production

The Danish, English, Irish, Greek, Spanish, and Portuguese, as well as the recent Swedish and Finish versions of the Rome Treaties establishing the EC are examples of subsequent translations made and authenticated after the authentication process was formally closed for the particular instrument. Although subsequent translations are justified in this case as a necessary means of expanding EC/EU membership, the ominous practice of authenticating translations under irregular conditions has threatened to undermine the very principle of equal authenticity. Insisting that there is no guarantee that such texts reflect the uniform intent of the single instrument, lawyers began to cast doubt on the interpretative value of subsequent translations and other texts authenticated in irregular proceedings (Rosenne 1983:783; Tabory 1980:229).

From the legal point of view, a text is considered authentic if it has been adopted by the competent lawmaking or treatymaking body. In the past the most important factor in the authentication procedure has been the time element. Traditionally, it was held that, at the latest, all the parallel texts of a single instrument should be submitted for scrutinization prior to adoption, allowing the lawmakers ample time to examine the text(s) before granting their approval. This is important because, once approved, the text becomes law and is legally binding. Moreover, the texts are definite upon approval and usually cannot be corrected or revised without subsequent approval in newly initiated proceedings. Despite the seemingly simplicity of this basic rule, it is not always honored in practice. Due to technical difficulties, it sometimes occurs that a text cannot be submitted in one of the official languages prior to adoption and is approved in absentia (on treaties *see* Chapter 7, 7.4.3).

---

3.   *See* Tabory on the translation of the original Rome Treaties establishing the European Communities (1980:114–116).

For example, when Switzerland granted Italian the status of an official language in 1902, it was technically impossible to prepare Italian texts of legislation in time for adoption by the Federal Assembly. Due to the lack of qualified translators,[4] it became common practice to commence the Italian translation after the German and French texts had been adopted by both Houses. As a result, the Italian texts were usually not completed until the deadline for promulgation. Tolerated for over 70 years, this deficient practice was finally banned in 1974 by a revision of the Federal Act of March 23, 1962 on the Procedure of the Federal Assembly and the Promulgation and Entry into Force of Legislation. The revised provision of Article 31 requires that the Italian text be presented to the Federal Assembly prior to adoption (Brühlmeier 1989:123, note 32, *cf.* the apparently contradictory provision of Article 66).

The former practice in Canada was even more deficient, though not unconstitutional. Prior to the legislative reform, the French text was prepared by the Law Translation Branch of the Translation Bureau after completion and approval of the final English text. This procedure was in keeping with the letter of section 133 of the *British North American Act* which merely required that all Acts of Parliament be printed and published in both official languages (Covacs 1982:85). Although the Supreme Court of Canada had recognized the equal authenticity of the French and English versions of federal statutes in *The King v. Dubois* (1935), this rule did not become statute law until the *Official Languages Act* of 1969 (*see* Chapter 3, 3.4.2). Mistrusting translations prepared and authenticated in irregular circumstances, Canadian judges reserve the right to dispute the interpretative value of a translation if it appears that a provision does not reflect the original intent of Parliament, thus justifying their decision to give priority to the original text when resolving textual inconsistencies in the authentic texts of federal legislation, especially texts enacted prior to the legislative reform. When determining which text reflects the true intent, they sometimes examine the legislative history of the disputed provision, including the translation operations and subsequent revisions. One of the most famous cases in this regard is *R. v. Popovic and Askov* (1976) 2 S.C.R. 308), in which Justice Pigeon dismantled 'a century of awkward revisions, redrafting, rearrangements and retranslations' to finally conclude that the French expression *vol avec effraction* does not describe any offense in the Criminal Code in force and is thus 'imprecise and ambiguous.' Retracing the revisions and retranslations of the disputed provision over the century, Pigeon also rejected the expressions *effraction nocturne* and *effraction,* which appeared in earlier translations of the Code. Insisting that Parliament's intention was not to widen the scope of the original Code, Pigeon gave priority to the English text and the term *burglary* which, in his opinion, clearly relates back to the definition in the constructive murder section of the original Code of 1892. According to Pigeon, the English text best ensures 'the attainment of the objects of the enactment according to its true spirit, intent and meaning' (Beaupré 1986:70).

Providing an escape mechanism for judges to 'discriminate' against authenticated translations, this practice is incompatible with the principle of equal authenticity. Its continued usage shed light on growing concerns about the fiction of authentic texts,

---

4. Italian is the native language of only 7.6 percent of the Swiss population (Caussignac 1995:71).

finally forcing lawyers to acknowledge that mere satisfaction of the requirements for authentication does not guarantee reliability. In other words, the fact that a text has been authenticated does not necessarily mean that it reflects the uniform intent of the single instrument. In addition to the time element, there has been increasing concern about the place where the translation is made, as well as the qualifications of the translators. In particular, lawyers tend to mistrust texts that are produced by a translation service outside the lawmaking or treatymaking process. At the offset, they did not question the technical skills of translators but rather the fact that they were often isolated from the parliamentary process or negotiations, as a result of which they did not have first-hand knowledge of the true intent (*cf.* Chapter 7, 7.4.3). In such cases it is feared that the decisions of translators are more likely to be influenced by value judgments. For this very reason, Tabory questions the interpretative value of translations not made at the place where the 'original' instrument is prepared:

> Under these circumstances, perhaps a more relevant distinction as regards interpretation may be drawn between language versions originally produced by persons responsible for drafting an instrument who have first-hand knowledge of the intentions and purpose to be expressed, and those versions which are translated by staff who are linguistically and technically competent, but otherwise removed from the actual preparation of the document (1980:193–94).

The realization that the interpretative value of an authenticated translation is directly related to the situational factors of its production finally opened the door to long-awaited reform. Motivated in particular by the need to preserve the intent of the single instrument, reformers made a radical move to improve the reliability of authenticated translations by incorporating the translator into the legislative process. While the immediate goal was to encourage interaction between translators and source text producers, the long-term goal was to coordinate the production of parallel texts by controlling the time and place of their production.

4.3. INCORPORATING THE TRANSLATOR INTO THE LEGISLATIVE PROCESS

In translation theory it is traditionally presumed that the target text is prepared at a different time and place than the source text. In regard to the time factor, it is presumed that the target text is commenced after completion of the source text. According to Gadamer, the so-called temporal distance is the critical factor in translation, i.e., the period of time that lapses between the production of the source and target texts (1975:280). His implication that the ability to express the original intent decreases as the temporal distance increases applies to legal translation as well. On the other hand, Gadamer's notion of historic distance is not relevant for this study as we are dealing exclusively with translations of living law, not historical texts.[5]

---

5. Referring to the 'hermeneutic consciousness of translation,' Habermas regards difficulties of comprehension as 'the result of cultural, temporal, or social distance' (1970:205). Holz-Mänttäri mentions cultural, spatial, temporal, knowledge, or ability distances (1990:65).

Nonetheless, as emphasized above, the time element is extremely important in the production of parallel texts from the legal, as well as the linguistic point of view. Above all, changes in the role of the translator have come about as a result of attempts to bridge the time lag between the production of the source and target texts of living laws. Such attempts have been coupled with efforts to bring the producers of the source and target texts under the same roof, thus defying the traditional presumption that the translator works in isolation and has no contact with the source text producer(s).

Recognizing the absence of interaction between the translator and source text producer(s) as a potential danger, Wilss once warned that without such interaction there can be no assurance that the target text reflects the intention of the author. As such, translation can be regarded as a monologue, an act of one-way communication:

> Dabei sieht eich der Übersetzer auf sich selbst verwiesen; aus der ihm von seiner Funktion aufgezwungenen Isolation tastet er sich ohne Netz und doppelten Boden an den zu übersetzenden Text heran. Ob und in welchem Umfang die Übersetzung eines Textes geglückt ist, ob der Übersetzer das ausgangssprachlich Gemeinte beim Transfer in die Zielsprache inhaltlich und stilistisch richtig getroffen hat, läßt sich meist nicht mit letzter Sicherheit sagen, weil in der Regel keine Rückfragemöglichkeit zwischen Übersetzer und Autor des ausgangssprachlichen Textes besteht, der Transfer also nicht in einem Sender/Empfänger-Rückmeldekreis eingebettet ist. Jede Übersetzung ist daher ihrem Wesen nach ein interaktionsfreier, monologischer Akt, eine *Ein-Weg-Kommunikation* (1977:74).

Traditionally, legal translation was also an act of one-way communication. For that matter, it still is in numerous countries where the translation operations are performed in isolation by a translation service attached to the Ministry of Justice or other government department. This was the case in Canada as well, i.e., until the decisive legislative reform of the 1970's. It is well known that one of the best ways of making translators aware of the original intent is to have them consult with the source text producer(s).[6] Although this is rarely done in general translation, legislative reformers in the Canadian Federal Department of Justice broke with tradition in the early seventies and invited francophone translators to attend the advisory sessions held prior to the drafting of the English text. By giving translators a passive role in the initial drafting process, reformers hoped, among other things, to improve reliability by curtailing translator subjectivity (*cf.* Beaupré 1986:170). The sessions, however, were in English only and thus it is questionable to what extent the translators were able to grasp the details of the policy and drafting initiatives. Moreover, it appears that the translators did not take advantage of the opportunity to consult with the drafter(s) of the source text. Although the presence of the translator at the sessions was deemed to have a positive effect, it brought about little visible improvement in the French texts.

6. Holz-Mänttäri maintains that there is no guarantee that the translator will grasp the author's intent even in situations where the translator has direct contact with the author (1990:65).

4.3.1.   Consultation in both directions

After writing another negative report in 1976, the Commissioner of Official Languages proposed that francophone translators be given an active role in the drafting and revision operations (Beaupré 1986:168, note 29). This was a bold move because it incorporated the translator into the legislative process, entrusting him/her with new authority and responsibility. The first step was to require the francophone translator to consult the drafter(s) of the source text on matters of content, effect, and intent. As the extent of the consultations increased, the source text drafter(s) became not only an advisor to the translator during the production of the target text but also an active participant in the revision and coordination phases. Thus it became important for the drafter(s) of the source text to have a reasonable command of the target language and preferably the target legal system as well. The next logical step was to encourage mutual cooperation between the translator and the drafter(s) of the source text or, as Beaupré calls it, consultation in both directions (1986:171). In other words, the drafter(s) of the source text would also consult the translator on matters pertaining to the source text. This development is significant because, for the first time, the translator was given limited authority to take part in the production of the source text.

Experience has shown that permitting the translator to participate in the production of the source text frequently results in improvements in both the source and target texts (Gesetzgebungsleitfaden 1995:321). Forced to analyze every detail of the source text, a critical translator tends to detect unclear or ambiguous formulations, misleading logical connectors, and other linguistic defects that obstruct comprehension of the source text (*cf.* Didier 1990:308). If detected before the text is definite (i.e., prior to adoption), such defects can be corrected, thus improving the source text and in the end the target text as well. As the late Justice Pigeon put it:

> C'est pourquoi, dans une bonne rédaction législative, il faut que le traducteur ait accès au rédacteur de façon à pouvoir lui signaler toutes les ambiguïtés que le texte peut recéler car, ces ambiguïtés, elles doivent disparaître (1978:37).

The idea of revising the source text through translation is by no means new. The history of plurilingual legislation in Switzerland shows that both texts are often improved if the translator cooperates closely with the source text producer in all phases of production – drafting, revision, coordination, and final scrutinization. Such cooperation sometimes results in a reconciliation of both texts that would otherwise be impossible. For example, the final German and French texts of the Swiss Civil Code are said to have been the result of a 'mutual giving and taking' between the drafter of the German text and the French translator, both of whom were legal experts (Brühlmeier 1989:131). In an attempt to coordinate the texts as closely as possible, concessions were made on both sides. Since French syntax is often more concise than German, Huber agreed to change some German phrases to follow the French text. For his part, Rossel relented and created some neologisms to express new ideas proposed by Huber, especially in property law which was more developed in the German-speaking cantons. In the end, Huber also approved numerous idiomatic expressions and stylistic divergencies in Rossel's translation. While some critics disapproved of Huber's compromises (notably Cesana 1910a:151), others claimed that without such cooperation it would have been impossible to unify civil law at the federal level (*see* Brühlmeier 1989:131). It appears that language issues constituted one of the greatest obstacles to the adoption of federal legislation in Switzerland.

Although the translator's decision-making ability in his/her capacity as reviser of the source text was normally limited to linguistic questions, Brühlmeier already refers to the translator as a type of co-drafter:

> Die Erfahrung zeigt, daß der Entwurf in mehreren Sprachen für jede Fassung meistens die Verständlichkeit verbessert, weil ein guter *Mitredaktor* der anderen Sprache sich jeweils außerstande erklärt, unklare Texte in seiner Sprache zu formulieren [emphasis added] (1989:128).

This, however, was only the beginning. New emphasis on equal rights for lesser used languages gradually modernized the role of the legal translator.

4.3.2. Transforming the translator into a text producer and ultimately a co-drafter

Incorporating the translator into the drafting process enabled maximum cooperation between the translator and drafter(s) of the source text. Ironically this had the reverse effect of making the translator more independent from the source text. With increased decision-making authority, the translator gradually assumed the responsibilities of a text producer, even gaining the right to help determine what the text ought to say in order to achieve the effect desired by the legislator, States parties, or contracting parties, as the case may be. Such decisions were traditionally reserved strictly for drafters of the original text.

In Switzerland rising concern about the predominance of the German language resulted in a parliamentary initiative to guarantee the linguistic and cultural identity of the Swiss minorities. On April 20, 1978, the National Council (Upper House of Parliament) forwarded the so-called Delamuraz Postulate to the Federal Council (collegial executive body). Claiming that German was gradually becoming the sole official language, the postulate called for amends to be made in the federal administration in order to guarantee equal rights for the lesser used official languages. In its reply the Federal Council stated that the main problem was not so much the translation procedures as the fact that 'original' texts were not drafted in French or Italian. In other words, there should be some French and even Italian source texts that would then be translated into German and the other official language. To appease the francophone population, which constitutes 19.2 percent of the total population, the government took steps to recruit more French-speaking experts, thus enabling some original drafting to be done in French. Progress, however, has been slow. Estimates show that only about 10 percent of federal legislation (primary and subordinate) is originally drafted in French (Brühlmeier 1989:120).

Unable to increase the number of original drafts in French, the administration proposed a compromise solution for the production of more important bills. Instead of drafting the bill entirely in one language and translating it into the other, the Expert Drafting Committee is encouraged to have at least some parts of the bill drafted originally in French and translated into German. As a result, both the German and French drafts consist of some original and some translated parts. Although the original parts drafted in French are considerably smaller, the results have been encouraging. This method was successfully used *inter alia* in the preparation of the preliminary draft of the Swiss Act on Private International Law of 1982 (*see* von Overbeck 1984:977). Today attempts are made to use alternate drafting, as it is called by Canadian jurilinguists, in the most important federal laws.

In Switzerland bills are drafted by an Expert Drafting Committee or the Drafting Section of the Department of Justice, translated by the Translation Section of the department involved, and submitted to the In-House Administrative Drafting Committee for revision. At first the In-House Administrative Drafting Committee was responsible only for the German text; however, a francophone team was later formed to improve the quality of the French text as well. Each team, which consisted of three members (*see* Chapter 3, 3.1.1), worked independently, frequently without consulting the other team. In the early nineties an important step was taken to coordinate the work of the German and French teams of the In-House Administrative Drafting Committee by introducing co-drafting. As a means of ensuring that the authentic texts enjoy the same precision and quality of language, it was decided that the German and French texts of all federal laws and important regulations should be scrutinized, revised, and coordinated simultaneously; hence the name co-drafting (*see* Gesetzgebungsleitfaden 1995:323).[7] As provided by the Regulation concerning the In-House Administrative Drafting Committee, approved on June 19, 1993, a co-drafting team consisting of two linguists (French and German), at least one lawyer from the Department of Justice, and subject expert(s) from the department concerned is constituted for each federal law and important regulation. The co-drafting team follows the German and French drafts through all phases of the preliminary procedure until their publication in the *Botschaft* and *Message*. The Italian draft, which is a translation prepared by the Italian section of the Central Language and Translation Service (Gesetzgebungsleitfaden 1995:322), is not included in the co-drafting process. It appears that the federal administration does not have sufficient qualified Italian-speaking personnel to participate in co-drafting teams (*see* Schneider 1992:86; *also* Caussignac 1995:84).

The next step in the lawmaking process is the parliamentary procedure (*see* Chapter 3, 3.1.1). Here all language versions (including the Italian translation) are presented and discussed by both Houses of Parliament. The Parliamentary Drafting Committee, which consists of six members from each House (two for each language), examines the texts to detect any divergencies, ambiguities, and/or inconsistencies and coordinates all three language versions. After meeting with government officials of the Federal Council and occasionally with deputies of the National Council, the Committee divides into three subcommittees (German, French, and Italian), each

---

7. '*Koredaktion*' is defined in the Swiss *Gesetzgebungsleitfaden* as 'die gleichzeitige Überprüfung durch Juristinnen und Juristen sowie Sprachwissenschaftlerinnen und -wissenschaftler von in verschiedenen Sprachen erarbeiteten Texten (in der Praxis der Bundesverwaltung: deutsch und französisch) auf ihre sprachlich-stilistische Übereinstimmung, unter besonderer Berücksichtigung der Mehrsprachigkeit' (1995:323).

of which checks its text against the others and then prepares the final drafts together with the In-House Administrative Drafting Committee. The final texts are presented individually for adoption by each House and then promulgated (*see* Hauck et al. 1982:94). As Schneider put it, co-drafting has the advantage that the texts are 'original' from both the legal and linguistic standpoints:

> Es entstehen zwei Fassungen, die nicht nur vom rechtlichen, sondern auch vom sprachlichen Anspruch her als Originalversionen zu betrachten sind. Zwei Fassungen, die sprachlich unter Umständen ein verstärktes Eigenleben haben, sich äusserlich vielleicht nicht mehr gleichen wie die sklavische Übersetzung einem Original, die aber inhaltlich zwei gleichwertige, authentische Ausformulierungen eines Gedankens darstellen (1992:84).

4.4. TEXT PRODUCTION, TRANSLATION, CO-DRAFTING

The demand for greater equality of the official languages has been particularly strong and effective in Canada (Crépeau 1995:54, 59). After the Commissioner of Official Languages recommended that the translator be given an active role in the drafting of federal legislation, francophone jurilinguists in the French division of the Legislation Section of the Department of Justice in Ottawa proposed a methodology of five bilingual drafting techniques which has since revolutionized legal translation (*see* Covacs 1982:92–93). Since all the techniques require the anglophone and francophone counterparts to cooperate in all phases of text production, the methodology is generally referred to as co-drafting, thus making it necessary to distinguish between co-drafting in Switzerland (the specific method described above) and the co-drafting techniques developed by francophone jurilinguists in Canada. The Canadian co-drafting techniques coordinate the time and place of the production of parallel texts to varying degrees, thus making it increasingly difficult to distinguish between the source and target texts. As this process advances, the translator assumes greater drafting responsibilities, ultimately becoming a co-drafter in his/her own right.

In Canada there is no expert drafting committee as in Switzerland. Instead all bills are drafted at the federal level by professional drafters called legislative counsel (*see* Chapter 3, 3.1.1). Previously all bills had been drafted exclusively in English by professional drafters who were common law lawyers with special training in legislative techniques. The French version was a translation prepared by a jurilinguist from the French division of the Legislation Section and vetted by a francophone lawyer (Beaupré 1986:172, note 35). Having learned from past mistakes, the Department of Justice decided that, in order to assure the success of the new co-drafting techniques, it was necessary to upgrade the position of the legal translator. Basically it was reasoned that, if translators take on drafting responsibilities, they should be qualified to make both legal and linguistic decisions. Thus it was decided that such translators also need training in law, in this case the civil law of Quebec. In addition, francophone translators who aspire to become legislative counsel are now required to complete specialized courses in legislative drafting (Beaupré 1986:173) (*see* 4.6.2 below).

Today a bilingual drafting team consisting of one anglophone and one francophone legislative counsel is assigned to each new (i.e., non-amending) statute (Levert 1995:258). The key to the success of the new bilingual drafting techniques often lies in the interaction between the co-drafters and their active participation in the preliminary advisory sessions convened by the policymakers.[8] After the informative briefings, the anglophone and francophone co-drafters hold their own consultations to map out a strategy for the production of both texts. The co-drafters cooperate closely at all times during preparation of the texts. Thereafter they attend the Cabinet Committee meeting at which the draft bills are examined before being approved by Cabinet. The same team that draws up the bill for the first reading also revises the drafts and prepares the final texts, following the draft bill until it is passed by both Houses of Parliament and promulgated (*The Federal Legislative Process in Canada* 1987:10–18).

4.4.1. New methods of bilingual legal drafting

The initial phase of bilingual drafting is usually alternate drafting, the method commonly used to draft important legislative texts in Switzerland. As described above, alternate drafting is a combination of drafting and translation. At the preliminary consultations the co-drafters designate which parts of the bill are to be drawn up in English and which in French. They then retire to their respective offices and draft the designated parts. Thereafter, these parts are exchanged and translated into the other language by the same co-drafter or a legal translator. In the latter case, the translation is revised by the responsible co-drafter and then by a special revisory committee (Covacs 1982:93). The term *alternate* does not refer to the alternate process of drafting and translation but rather to the fact that the source text is not always the same, i.e., one part of the bill is drafted in English, the next in French and so on. Alternating the source text is truly a unique innovation in parallel text production. At this stage it is still possible to distinguish between the principal source and target texts. This, however, is no longer the case in shared drafting. Shared drafting is essentially the same as alternate drafting with the exception that each co-drafter draws up half of the text, then translates or has the other half translated (Covacs 1982:93). As a result, neither language version can be designated as the principal source or target text.

The third method of bilingual drafting – double entry drafting – is named after the accounting method. As the name suggests, the same person drafts both texts, preferably part by part in tandem (Covacs 1982:93). Although it is questionable to what extent the second text is actually a translation, it appears that one text serves as the source text for the other. Theoretically, this method should be ideal because it guarantees unity of thought; however, experience has shown that bilinguals often tend to favor one language, thus running the risk that the target text will not be

8. The Swiss *Gesetzgebungsleitfaden* also advise translators to participate in the policymaking sessions and cooperate with the drafters of the 'original' draft bill, thus encouraging co-drafting from the very beginning of the project (1995:320).

linguistically pure. Since it is extremely difficult to find a bilingual legislative counsel who writes in the genius of both languages and is trained in both common law and civil law, this method can be used only in exceptional cases.

The method of parallel drafting has a brighter future. As in simultaneous interpretation, the drafting is done simultaneously; however, the comparison ends here because the texts are drafted independently. In other words, one text does not serve as the source text for the other. After preparing a detailed outline of the draft bill, the co-drafters retire and draw up large parts or even the entire bill in their own departments (Covacs 1982:93). This method enables each co-drafter to preserve the original intent by producing a text that expresses what the parties meant to say instead of reconstructing what is said in a source text. Such freedom requires maximum cooperation between the text producers and puts greater pressure on them to modify and coordinate the drafts before passing them on to the revision committee. The ultimate goal is to achieve joint drafting. The difference between parallel and joint drafting is significant because the co-drafters not only prepare the outline jointly but also do the drafting jointly. Working together, they proceed section by section, comparing and revising both texts as they write. Though time consuming, this method is considered ideal because the co-drafters are required to collaborate to the utmost, thus guaranteeing unity of thought, yet assuring that each text is formulated in the genius of that language. The success of joint drafting depends on the ability of the co-drafters to work as a team, their interest in producing two reliable texts which are equal in quality, and their willingness to make concessions. In order to enable maximum cooperation between the two co-drafters, the anglophone co-drafter should be bilingual as well (Covacs 1982:93).

The new bilingual drafting methods are currently being used successfully at the federal level in Canada (*see* Chapter 6, 6.8) and also in the province of New Brunswick.[9] In Switzerland, in addition to the preference for alternate drafting at the federal level, methods of bilingual drafting have been used several times in canton Berne, a German and French bilingual canton (Caussignac 1995:72). In 1991, a germanophone and a francophone lawyer prepared the cantonal bill on Official Publications using the method of parallel drafting (*see* Caussignac and Kettinger 1991:79–81). After discussing the purpose and scope of application of the proposed bill, as well as matters relating to substance and procedure, the drafting team drew up a detailed outline before sitting down to draft, revise, and coordinate the two texts. Caussignac describes the actual drafting process as follows:

> Ils ont travaillé dans le même bureau, à la même table. Chaque unité de l'acte législatif, à savoir chaque phrase, chaque alinéa, chaque article ont été écrits de concert, d'un côté en allemand, de l'autre en français. Chaque pas de l'élaboration du texte était précédé d'une discussion au cours de laquelle des rédacteurs décidaient ce qu'ils allaient écrire. Les deux versions du projet ont été conçues simultanément mais séparément dans deux langues différentes... Chacun d'eux a ensuite mis son texte en page, l'a imprimé et

---

9. Despite the difficulty of using co-drafting methods in a common law province where English and common law drafting methods dominate, Keating is convinced that this is the only way to achieve equality and produce French texts of high quality in New Brunswick (1995:206–217).

transmis à son collèque pour contrôle. Chacun a ainsi pu vérifier la concordance des deux textes (1995:78).

More significant is the effort that went into the revision of the Constitution of Canton Berne that entered into force in January of 1995. It is a bold undertaking to make a total revision of a constitution and even more so to draft the text in two languages at the same time. From August 1989 to April 1990, the Drafting Committee discussed substantive issues in four parallel work sections, each consisting of approximately eight members. One section was chaired by a francophone lawyer. On the basis of a detailed plan drawn up by the Drafting Committee, a secretariat consisting of a germanophone and a francophone lawyer produced the draft texts by alternate drafting.[10] Working separately, each drafted assigned portions of the instrument in his own language, revised his own text and then passed it on to the other co-drafter who translated that part into the other language. The original author then examined both drafts with a critical eye. During the discussion period that followed the co-drafters exchanged ideas, made proposals and counterproposals before agreeing on the final wording of both texts. Despite joint efforts to produce two draft texts in the genius of each language, only the German draft text was formally adopted. All revisions made in that text were later made in the French draft text which was then published for presentation to Parliament together with the German text in January 1992 (Caussignac 1995:81; Gerber 1992:76–82). Although the French text of the new Constitution was not adopted, it is significant that francophone lawyers were able to influence the content of the single instrument during the preparatory sessions as well as the actual drafting process. Produced by alternate drafting, the original draft proposals are truly products of reconciliation.

4.4.2.   The changing nature of translation

Recent developments in translation theory have succeeded in changing the very notion of translation and the traditional view of the acceptability of a translation. The traditional approach to translation is represented in Mildred Larson's book *Meaning-based Translation*, which was published the same year Vermeer presented his comprehensive work on the *skopos* theory in his joint book with Katharina Reiß. In

---

10.   The terminology used by Swiss authors to describe bilingual drafting methods does not necessarily correspond to the Canadian terminology. Moreover, since there is no authoritative catalogue of bilingual drafting techniques in Switzerland, the terminology used by Swiss authors to describe domestic methods is not uniform. For example, Gerber says that the Constitution of Canton Berne was revised by parallel drafting (*rédaction parallèle*). From his description we learn only that the co-drafters worked on the same text at the same time (1992:78, note 10). Caussignac also uses the term *rédaction parallèle* when referring to the experimental methods used in Canton Berne. Kettiger translates this with the more general term *Koredaktion* (co-drafting) in the German text of the same article (Caussignac and Kettiger 1991:77). In a later report presented at a colloquium in Canada, Caussignac uses the general term *rédaction bilingue* (bilingual drafting) to describe the same procedure; however, from his article one can conclude that he is talking about what the Canadians call alternate drafting (1995:80–82).

the tradition of the linguistic theories of the fifties, sixties, and seventies, Larson views translation as a process of transcoding languages. As she puts it, translation is a process 'of transferring the meaning of the source language into the receptor language' (1984:3). Claiming that the translator's goal is to achieve idiomatic translation, Larson rejects 'unduly free' translations, unless the intent is to evoke humor or other special response in the target receivers. According to Larson:

> Translations are unduly free if they add extraneous information not in the source text, if they change the meaning of the source language, or if they distort the facts of the historical and cultural setting of the source language text (1984:17).

Larson's definition of unduly free translation includes adaptation, one of the most disputed forms of text production in modern translation theory. In Vinay and Darbelnet's classic book, which Didier (1990:254, 293) and Gémar (1995–I:93) still cite as an authority on translation, *adaptation* is listed as one of the translation techniques resulting in semantic distortions (1968:52). For his part, Koller welcomed the emergence of the translator as a text producer; however, he refused to recognize all forms of text production as translation, especially paraphrases, commentaries, and adaptations. *Adaptation* is the English term for *Textbearbeitung,* i.e., the adaptation of a text to meet the expectations of a different type of audience, for example, adapting Bible stories for children. While admitting that the dividing line between translation and adaptation is not always clearcut, Koller insisted that adaptation is not an accepted method of translation (1979:89).

At the same time proponents of linguistic theories of translation were discrediting adaptation, Vermeer began advocating its use as an alternative to meaning-based translation (1982:98). Today adaptation is generally recognized as a legitimate form of translation for texts whose communicative function differs from that of the source text (*cf.* Reiß in Reiß and Vermeer 1984:137; Holz-Mänttäri 1986:350; Reiß 1995:22; *cf.* Bastin 1990:215–229).[11] In translations with a shift in function, the translator has practically unlimited freedom to adapt the new text to meet the expectations of the target receivers for a text with that particular function. Encouraging the translator to take advantage of this freedom, Vermeer goes so far as to authorize him/her to 'dethrone' the source text by producing a new text that has very little or even nothing in common with the source text (1986:42). Threatening the very definition of translation, Vermeer's comment about dethroning the source text set off a heated debate among translation theorists. Even Reiß reprimands Vermeer, insisting that the translator cannot completely disregard the source text as this would no longer be translation (1988:68, *also* 74, note 6). Similarly, Nord maintains that a text produced by methods resembling translation cannot be regarded as translation if the target text is not 'bound' to an existing source text (1988:31).

---

11. In her Vienna lectures Reiß defines adaptation as follows: 'Wenn ich einen Typ "bearbeitende Übersetzung" eigens herausstelle, so meine ich damit alle jene Übersetzungen, die – aus welchen Gründen auch immer – den Ausgangstext in der sprachlichen Gestaltung, vor allem aber inhaltlich und/oder in der Mitteilungsintention nicht aus übersetzungstechnisch notwendigen Erfordernissen, sondern bewußt zu einem bestimmten Zweck verändern' (1995:22).

More radical in her methods, Holz-Mänttäri not only defends Vermeer but goes a step further by declaring the existence of a source text an unnecessary precondition in modern translation: 'In vielen Translationsfällen der modernen Praxis existiert nicht einmal ein Ausgangstext' (Holz-Mänttäri 1988:380). In her own theory of translatory action (*translatorisches Handeln*), Holz-Mänttäri regards the translator as an expert who creates a new text by means of a whole complex of actions based on external factors independent of a source text (1990:67). As such, she views translation as 'professional text production for foreign need' (1988:380).

Unable to remain silent, Koller speaks about a modern notion of translation in the fourth edition of his classic book *Einführung in die Übersetzungswissenschaft* (1992:80–89). A traditionalist, Koller is forced to acknowledge that some forms of adaptation can be regarded as translation; however, he continues to insist that all forms of text production are not translation. Warning against stretching the notion of translation too far, he stresses the need to identify a criterion for distinguishing translation from other forms of text production. He himself comes to the conclusion that the translator's freedom cannot be unlimited because he/she is necessarily bound to a source text (1992:88). In this sense, Reiß maintains that an adaptation can be regarded as a translation as long as the operations are dependent on a source text, even though it sometimes serves only as 'raw material' (1995:22). Calling the source text the *sine qua non* of translation, she maintains that the translator's decisions are always related to factors linked to the source text or to the relation between the source and target texts (1990:37; *cf.* 1995:23). Most theorists tend to agree that there can be no translation without a source text (*cf.* Snell-Hornby 1990b:10; *also* Sager 1993:177).

4.4.3. Are the new bilingual drafting methods forms of translation?

Whereas it is traditionally presumed that the source and target texts are produced at a different time and place (*cf.* Vermeer's definition of translation),[12] the goal of bilingual drafting (co-drafting) is to coordinate the time and place of the production of parallel texts to the greatest extent possible. Thus the question arises as to whether the new bilingual drafting methods can be regarded as forms of translation. Clearly they do not qualify as traditional translation, and it is questionable whether some of them can be regarded as translation in the modern sense.

In regard to the time element, the view is generally held that work on the target text commences only after the source text has been completed. In this context Vermeer remarks: 'Der Translator geht von einem vorgegebenen, von ihm verstandenen und interpretierten Text aus' (Reiß and Vermeer 1984:84). The only previously recognized exception to this chronology is interpretation, which Steiner referred to earlier as 'simultaneous translation':

---

12. Vermeer defines translation as an attempt to present information in language z of culture Z that imitates a message in language a of culture A, while observing the textual conventions dictated by the function of the new text (1986:33; *see* Chapter 3, at 3.3.1).

> Every act of translation except simultaneous translation as between earphones, is a transfer from a past to a present (1977:334).

As far as the time and place of production is concerned, the bilingual drafting techniques resemble what is now called simultaneous and alternate interpretation. There are, however, major differences which make it clear that the new techniques are not forms of interpretation. Above all, translations are written texts while interpretation operations are oral, at least in their final form (*see* Reiß 1995:48; *also* Sager 1993:125). The consequence of this basic difference is more significant than might appear at first glance. As Vermeer points out, the fact that translations are in written form means that they can be revised (Reiß and Vermeer 1984:13; Reiß 1995:48). Thus translation operations usually include one or more revisions after the new text is completely written. Revisions are especially important in the case of parallel texts produced by the new bilingual drafting techniques (*see* 4.3.2 above).

Obviously the new bilingual drafting techniques are not forms of interpretation; however, this does not necessarily mean that they are forms of translation. To determine whether the new methods qualify as translation, it is necessary to examine the relationship between the target and source texts or at least to confirm the existence of a source text. As a rule, it is agreed that the source text must serve as the 'source' for the target text; in other words, the target text must be bound to the source text in some way. At present, however, theorists have still not reached consensus on how or to what extent the target text must be bound to the source text. More recently, the conventional views on the relationship between the source and target texts and even the form of the source text have come under attack, thus making it possible to introduce new forms of translation. For example, it was initially believed that the target text should convey the same message as the source text; however, with the introduction of the *skopos* theory and its emphasis on producing texts with a shift in function, texts such as adaptations are now widely recognized as translations, although they do not convey the same message as the source text. Furthermore, the traditional notion of translation has been broadened to include forms of text production in which the source and target texts are written in the same language. Thus a distinction is now made between interlingual and intralingual translation.[13]

As in the traditional notion of translation, the new methods of co-drafting involve at least two languages, hence the name bilingual drafting. Moreover, there is no shift in function so that all the parallel texts of a single instrument always convey the same message. On the other hand, the new methods depart from tradition by coordinating the time and place of production to the extent that it is sometimes difficult, if not

---

13. Koller refers to adaptations of texts which are written in the same language but represent different text types as forms of intralingual translation (1992:83); Sager uses the term *intralingual translation* when speaking about texts which are written in the same language but are from different historical periods (1993:124). Snell-Hornby refers to parallel texts (*see* note 10 in Chapter 1 of this study) consisting of the same text types but written in regional variations of the same language as forms of translation; she does not use the term *intralingual translation* (Snell-Hornby 1990b:11).

impossible to identify a source and target text. Although it is generally presumed that the source and target texts are different texts, one of which serves as the source for the other, this presumption says nothing about the time and place of text production; nor does it require that the source text exist in its entirety before work on the target text commences. From this point of view, the method of alternate drafting can be regarded as a legitimate form of translation, even though the idea of alternating the source and target texts is new. Furthermore, since there is no requirement that there be a principal source and target text, the method of shared drafting can also be regarded as translation. Although the method of double entry drafting is unorthodox, it is not the first time that the source text producer is also the translator. Though highly unusual as a practice, it can still be regarded as translation as long as parts of one text are used as the source for the other, as is presumably the case.

What happens, however, when the production of the various language versions is coordinated to the point that one can actually speak of simultaneous text production? For example, in parallel drafting, both texts are drafted simultaneously and independently. Since neither text is used as a source for the other, it follows that parallel drafting cannot be regarded as translation in the traditional sense. In regard to the texts of the Law on Official Publications of Canton Berne, Caussignac confirms that neither text is a translation of the other:

> Les deux versions du projet ont été conçues simultanément mais séparément dans deux langues différentes. L'un n'était donc pas la traduction de l'autre... (1995:78)

In joint drafting the texts are drafted simultaneously but jointly. Instead of completing each text independently, the text producers draft, compare, and modify the texts as they proceed, presumably section by section. Although time consuming, this method is considered ideal because the text producers cooperate to the utmost. Again, however, one text does not serve as a source for the other, thus suggesting that we are dealing with text production, not translation. This, however, is not the final word on co-drafting and translation.

While claiming that texts which are not bound to an existing source text cannot qualify as translation, Nord also acknowledges that her statement represents the view at that time (1988:310), thus implying that change is not inevitable. The ink had barely dried on Nord's manuscript when Holz-Mänttäri broke with tradition by rejecting the conventional source text. Earlier Holz-Mänttäri had declared that it is the 'message' (*Botschaft*) that counts, not the text, thus reducing the role of the text to the 'carrier of a message' (*Botschaftsträger 'Text'*) (1986:366; *also* 1990:66). Convinced that the text is not the only valid 'carrier of a message,' Holz-Mänttäri then proposed that the traditional source text be replaced by new forms. As she put it, translations can also be based on source materials such as briefings and agreements specifying the characteristics of the new product(s) (1988:380). Although Holz-Mänttäri does not mention the production of legal texts, the methods of parallel and joint drafting would both qualify as translation from her point of view. As mentioned above, in both parallel and joint drafting, the texts are created on the basis of policy briefings and a common outline prepared by the text producers themselves. Accordingly, the new texts can be regarded as target texts, while the briefings and outline take the place of the traditional source text. Although it is not clear whether the outline is drafted in one or two languages and whether the briefings are mono-lingual or bilingual (*see* Covacs 1982:93), such questions seem to be of minor importance.

To date, theorists have not yet reached consensus on which forms are acceptable as source materials. Speaking in general terms, Sager mentions an 'input text' which can be either a 'text' or 'message' (1993:177). For her part, Reiß maintains that producing an independent text on the basis of 'presented facts' is no longer trans-lation (1990:37). On the other hand, she does not hesitate to regard forms of adaptation as translation although the source text serves only as 'raw material' (1995:22). Thus it appears that she too is ready to reject the traditional role of the source text. This is further reflected in her use of the neutral terms 'text$_1$' and 'text$_2$' instead of source and target texts (1990:33–34). For that matter, the terms 'text$_1$' and 'text$_2$' can also be used to designate the parallel texts of a legal instrument. In this instance, however, all the parallel texts of a single instrument express the same message. Moreover, all the bilingual drafting methods – especially parallel and joint drafting – rely heavily on the traditional translation operations of revision and coordination. The fact that these operations are not used in adaptation seems to suggest that parallel and joint drafting have more in common with traditional translation than do forms of adaptation. Nonetheless, by way of analogy it can be said that the new co-drafting methods assume a position in the development of legal translation which corresponds to that of adaptation in general translation. More liberal than idomatic translation, the new bilingual drafting methods can be placed at the far right on the continuum depicting the development of legal translation (*see* figure 1 in Chapter 2, at 2.1). Despite certain similarities, co-drafting and adaptation clearly represent opposite trends in modern translation.

4.5. A Unique Communication Process

Like Vermeer and other advocates of the *skopos* theory, Holz-Mänttäri views translation as an act of communication across cultures (1988:380). In this study legal translation is also regarded as an act of communication; however, the communication process involving parallel legal texts differs considerably from the one proposed by Holz-Mänttäri. No longer regarding translation strictly as a process of transcoding texts from one language into another, translation theorists began to view translation as an act of communication in a two-step communication process (*cf.* Bühler 1988:289). Since the first step involved the reception of the source text by the translator, it seemed only natural to regard the act of translation as a continuation of the communication act involving the source text. While Vermeer rejects both the traditional view of translation as a transcoding process (1986:33) and the notion of a two-step communication process (1982:97), it is again Holz-Mänttäri who makes the final break with tradition: By reducing the role of the source text to part of the preparatory materials, she frees the translator from his/her role as receiver of the source text. Going a step further, she reasons: If the translator is not the receiver of the source text, then the production and reception of the target text is not a continu-ation of the communication process involving the source text. Furthermore, if the two-step communication process is ruled out, then this in itself eliminates the possibility that translation is a transcoding process because transcoding is a two-step communication process (1988:381). Insisting that the translator acts independently of the source text in a new communicative situation (1986:362), Holz-Mänttäri concludes that the production and reception of the target text constitute a new communication process. Therefore, in Holz-Mänttäri's theory of translatory action, the production and reception of the source text are viewed as constituting one act of communication and the production and reception of the target text a separate act of communication (*cf.* Chapter 3, 3.5).

In an earlier innovative step, Holz-Mänttäri had stripped the translator of his/her role as sender of the target text. According to Holz-Mänttäri, the translator is an outsider who acts in a role resembling that of a ghost writer commissioned by a third party to produce a new text. This idea resulted in the introduction of the commissioner as a major participant in the communication process (*Initiator,* Holz-Mänttäri 1984:111; *Bedarfsträger,* Holz-Mänttäri 1988:380; *Auftraggeber,* Vermeer 1992a:33). Now considered a permanent member of the communication process by translation theorists (*cf.* Nord 1988:9; Sager 1993:94), the commissioner is the new sender who initiates the translation operations by commissioning the translator to produce a text. Depending on his/her professional profile, the commissioner may propose that a particular translation strategy be used to produce the target text; however, in most cases he/she merely specifies the function of the translation, leaving it up to the translator to select an adequate strategy. As in the *skopos* theory, the translator mainly takes account of the function of the new text and the conditions of its reception when choosing a translation strategy. Often a member of a translation team, the translator is a professional text producer who cooperates with the other team members. As a decision-making expert, the translator keeps his/her distance from both the commissioner and the target receivers. This is what Holz-Mäntäri refers to as 'expert distance' (1986:363).

As shown in this Chapter, the trend in contemporary legal translation is the very opposite: the goal is to overcome the distance by incorporating the translator into the drafting process, as a result of which he/she becomes an insider who consults and cooperates with the other text producers and interacts with the target receivers as well (*see* 4.3.1 above). Since the translation operations are automatically initiated as part of the legislative, treaty-making or judicial process, there is no need for a commissioner, unless the policymaker, contracting parties, or organization convening a conference would be considered a type of commissioner. This, however, is unlikely because the communicative function of parallel legal texts is always identical and cannot be altered by an outside party, thus eliminating one of the primary tasks of the commissioner. Without a commissioner, the attention is again focused on the triadic relationship between the translator, the source text producer(s), and the receivers. The relationship, however, is now a dynamic one characterized by interaction is both directions (*see* figure 6B, at 4.1).

Attempts to coordinate the situational factors of the production of parallel legal texts have resulted in a unique communication process which also defies the traditional notion of translation. No longer are the production and reception of the target text considered a continuation of the communicative act involving the source text. At the same time, however, it is the very opposite of the communication process proposed by Holz-Mänttäri. Whereas Holz-Mänttäri and Vermeer maintain that the target text is always produced and received in a new situation and culture (Holz-Mänttäri 1988:379; Vermeer 1992a:55), the goal of the new bilingual drafting techniques is to coordinate the time and place of production to the point that all producers of the parallel texts of a single instrument can be regarded as participating in the same communication process. In ideal situations the situational factors of reception are also coordinated to a certain extent by building controls into the judicial system, for example, by establishing a hierarchy of courts (municipal law) or a special court to resolve disputes arising from texts of the same instrument (international law) (*see* Chapter 3 at 3.5.2; *also* Chapter 7 at 7.7). The end result is a unique communication process in which the production and reception of all the parallel texts of a single instrument can be regarded as constituting one basic act of communication, as illustrated below.

Figure 7: *The Communication Process involving the Production and Reception of Parallel Texts*

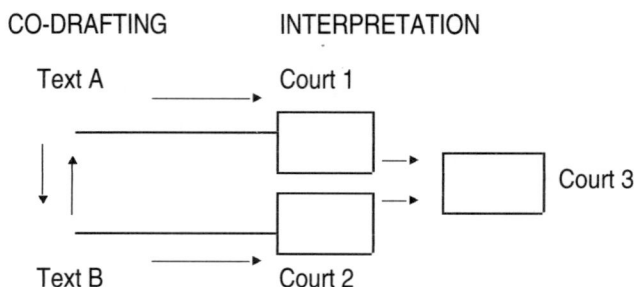

CO-DRAFTING   INTERPRETATION

Text A ————————→ Court 1

Text B ————————→ Court 2

Court 3

4.6. IMPORTANCE OF CENTRALISM IN TEXT PRODUCTION

Technically speaking, if all text producers are expected to participate in the same act of communication, they should be accommodated under the same roof. This, of course, is easier to achieve in municipal law, as the experiments with the new bilingual drafting techniques in Canada and Switzerland have shown. The fact that the Canadians refer to the new methods as 'bilingual' does not mean that they are restricted to communication in two languages. With the emergence of multilingualism in the twentieth century, international organizations attempted to coordinate the production of parallel texts by inviting the translators to the site of the negotiations. This, however, often proved to be technically impossible. As a precautionary measure to preserve the original intent, delegates participating in the negotiations are encouraged to assist the translation teams, regardless where the texts are produced. In some cases the delegates assume the translation duties themselves (Tabory 1980:96–101). The most remarkable example of multilingual drafting in international law took place at the third UN Conference on the Law of the Sea (1973–82), where the six authentic texts of the Convention were drafted in tandem (parallel drafting) by special language groups of the drafting committee (*see* Chapter 7, 7.5).

Aware of the importance of exercising control over the production of parallel texts, the founding fathers of the European Communities took steps to coordinate text production by establishing central language services at each of the four main institutions (the Commission in Brussels, the Council in Brussels, the Parliament in Strassbourg, and the Court of Justice in Luxembourg). The decision to have the translators under the same roof instead of using national translation staffs encourages direct consultation among them, thus making the translation process more expedient. Moreover, the approximat to the source text producers makes it possible for translators to consult with the authors. In order to increase cooperation between translators and source text producers in the Commission, specialized sections have been established in which translators and subject specialists work side by side (Brackeniers 1991:7).

With every expansion of the EC/EU come new fears that the translation mechanism will become unmanageable and too costly. When the EC expanded into a nine-language body, Kusterer argued in favor of decentralizing the translation operations as a means of improving efficiency and cutting costs (1981:49–51). Kusterer's proposal to have all translation done by national translation staffs was strongly opposed by Van der Haegen, then chairman of the EC board of translators. Reminding Kusterer that EC instruments have the force of law without ratification at the national level, Van der Haegen warned that the uniform intent of the single instrument could be falsified in the hands of national translation staffs:

> Die Gefahr der Verfälschung europäischer Rechtsakte durch nationale Übersetzungs-
> dienste ist nicht von der Hand zu weisen (1982:13).

Brackeniers, head of the Translation Service of the Commission, has continued to support centralization, emphasizing that its advantages still outweigh the disadvantages (1991:5). Nonetheless, the future of multilingualism in the EC was again at stake in the early nineties. In anticipation of a large increase in membership, Jacques Delors, then president of the European Commission, went so far as to question the feasibility of retaining the principle of absolute language equality in an expanded EC (*The Economist*, April 11, 1992:32). Despite initial fears by Delors and others, the principle of language equality has been retained and the centralized translation mechanism enlarged to accommodate for the new Member States.[14] As of January 1995, the EU has fifteen Member States and is currently a twelve-language body (*see* Chapter 1, note 15). The decision to retain the centralized translation operations is important because it guarantees that the production of all the language versions of each instrument will be coordinated at the respective EU institutions. This means, in effect, that all text producers of the parallel texts of a single instrument will be participating in the same communication process.

---

14. In the event of another expansion of the European Union, Brackeniers fears that it will become impossible to retain the principle of language equality. In view of its importance for European integration, he suggests that three or four communities of European States be established within the framework of a United Europe. Each community would have its own official languages and they would communicate with each other in one or two languages (1991:5).

4.7. EMANCIPATION OF THE LEGAL TRANSLATOR

Despite major differences between the new legal drafting methods and the theory of translatory action, there are also similarities which should not be overlooked. Although some theorists refer to legal translation as the 'most restricted form of translation' (Newmark 1982:47), modern legal translation can also be regarded as a process of complex actions in which translators exercise new decision-making power. During the transition from literal to idiomatic translation (*see* Chapter 2), decisions made by legal translators were primarily linguistic in nature. Aware, however, that linguistic decisions can also affect the substance, translators have never been completely free to create new texts in the genius of the target language. Without specific guidelines on 'how to' or 'how not' to translate, they were generally advised to honor the principle of fidelity to the original text. At first, the principle of fidelity was interpreted restrictively, as a result of which translators tended to follow the syntax, terminology, and style of the source text as closely as possible, making only limited concessions to the target language. In the interest of preserving the unity of the single instrument, they had no authority to question the intent. Since the source text was deemed to express the true intent, the translator's primary task was to reconstruct what was said in the source text and, to a certain extent, how it was said.

4.7.1. New principle of fidelity

Since the eighties legal translators have gradually become text producers with drafting responsibilities, thus decreasing their dependence on the source text. As active members of the drafting process, they are now widely permitted to make legal as well as linguistic decisions. Possessing first-hand knowledge of the legislative intent, they are no longer bound to the source text to determine the true intent. This has broadened their decision-making power considerably, enabling them to help determine what ought to be said – not only in the target text but also in the source text. Moreover, they are encouraged to cooperate with the other drafter(s) to determine how the original intent can be best expressed. Thus it can be said that the translator's first consideration is no longer fidelity to the source text but rather fidelity to the *uniform intent* of the single instrument, i.e., what the legislator or negotiators intended to say.

The declining role of the source text in plurilingual communication is a paradoxical development that initially came about as a result of the principle of equal authenticity. From the legal point of view, the source text suddenly lost its status as the prevailing instrument in matters of interpretation. In turn, authenticated translations have become increasingly independent as instruments of plurilingual communication. With the introduction of the new bilingual drafting methods, it is even becoming difficult to distinguish between source and target texts, a development which threatens to 'dethrone' the traditional source text altogether. The new independence of the parallel texts of authentic legal instruments has raised doubts among some lawyers, occasioning them to question whether a single instrument actually exists in modern plurilingual communication (Kuner 1991:955). Although this question is particularly sensitive for lawyers, it appears that they have come to terms with it and now admit that, as such, the single instrument exists only in theory. This, however, also has implications for translators. For example, doubts about the unity of the single treaty were raised by international lawyers in regard to Article 33(3) of the 1969 Vienna Convention on the Law of Treaties, which provides that the terms of a treaty are presumed to have the same meaning in each authentic text. In response, the ILC (International Law Commission) recognized in its commentary that the treaty remains a single treaty despite the fact that it is plurilingual in expression and some diversity is inevitable. As they put it:

> In law there is only one treaty – one set of terms accepted by the parties and one common intention with respect to those terms – even when two authentic texts appear to diverge (Tabory 1980:195, note 24).

On the one hand, the principle of the unity of the single instrument places the final burden on judges to find a uniform intent for all the language versions of the same instrument. At the same time, it also places translators under greater pressure to produce texts which express the uniform intent. The fear that the uniform intent of parallel texts could be reduced to a fiction[15] by the negligence and errors of translators raised serious concern about the qualifications of legal translators. Realizing that a higher degree of professionalism is required if legal translators are expected to preserve the unity of the single instrument, administrators finally began to upgrade the status of legal translators participating in plurilingual communication in the law (*see* Beaupré 1986:180).

4.7.2. Profile of the legal translator

Generally speaking, all LSP translation is interdisciplinary in nature. Thus it follows that, in addition to translation skills, specialized translators also need a certain amount of expertise in the particular subject matter or *Sachwissen,* as Snell-Hornby calls it (1986:18; *cf.* Fluck 1992:221; *also* Lerat 1995:94). Accordingly it follows that, if translators are to make legal as well as linguistic decisions, they must be competent in both translation and law (*see* Šarčević 1994:303). Legal competence presupposes not only in-depth knowledge of legal terminology, but also a thorough understanding of legal reasoning and the ability to solve legal problems, to analyze legal texts, and to foresee how a text will be interpreted and applied by the courts.[16] In addition to these basic legal skills, translators should also possess extensive

---

15. *Cf.* Dölle's implication that the uniform intent of the parallel texts of a single instrument could be a fiction, Chapter 3, at 3.3.4.
16. Regarding all translation as a process of interpretation, Gémar proposes that future legal translators be taught to construe texts using legal methods of interpretation. In fact, he goes so far as to designate this as one of the main priorities of a training program for legal translators (1995–II:154). As emphasized earlier, legal translators need to be thoroughly familiar with legal rules of interpretation; however, this is to enable them to predict how texts will be interpreted by the courts. Lawyers generally agree that translators should refrain from construing the source text (*see* 4.2.2 above).

knowledge of the target legal system and preferably the source legal system as well (Šarčević 1989:281). Moreover, drafting skills are required and a basic knowledge of comparative law and comparative methods (*see* de Groot 1987:3 and 1992:310; *also* Moreau 1995:272–274; Forti and Vesco 1991:269).[17] Not surprisingly, such ideal translators simply do not exist, thus raising the question: What are the qualifications of translators of authentic legal texts?

Legal translators have various titles, some of which indicate a greater degree of specialization. For example, legal translators at the International Court of Justice at The Hague are called legal secretaries because they are actually involved in the administration of justice (Frame 1985:1). In Canada, specialists in legislative drafting are referred to as legislative counsel, thus distinguishing them from revisers and other legal translators. In the European Union, legal translators are interdisciplinary specialists called *lawyer-linguists* (French: *juristes-linguistes*). Teams of lawyer-linguists are also responsible for revising, harmonizing, and coordinating all language versions (*see* Koutsivitis 1994:345) so as to ensure that each text expresses the uniform intent. As Morgan put it, the Jurist/Linguists Service (as it was first called) was created in 1966 'to compare the language versions of a legal text, to arrive at a uniform interpretation and to ensure that each version faithfully reflected that interpretation' (1982:109, 112). Lawyer-linguists at the EU usually have a law degree in their own country and may have studied law in other countries as well. They are expected to have a good knowledge of their own national law, European law, and some knowledge of public international law. Their first foreign language must be French, the main working language of the EU, and they are expected to have a good command of several other Community languages as well. In accordance with Chomsky's notion of native-speaker competence, they translate only into their native language (Morgan 1982:113; *cf.* Koutsivitis 1988:77).

In Canada interdisciplinary specialists in linguistics of the law and translation are frequently referred to as *jurilinguists* or *jurilinguistes*, the French term originally coined by francophone Canadians.[18] In the absence of an official definition of the term, the question remains unresolved as to whether the main accent is on the lawyer or the linguist (Gémar 1995–II:3, 81; *cf.* Cornu 1990:16). Whereas this is the view commonly held by linguists, lawyers tend to insist that jurilinguists must be lawyers like their counterparts in the EU (Moreau 1995:272). This is in keeping with the widely held belief that lawyers are 'natural' legal translators (*cf.* Keating 1995:206).

---

17. Following Gutteridge (1946), de Groot regards all legal translation as an act of comparative law (1987:3). The act of comparing the corresponding concepts of the source and target legal systems is so important that Bocquet (1994:7) regards it as the second step in a three-step translation process (*see* note 7 in Chapter 8).

18. The term *jurilinguiste* is derived from *jurilinguistique* which Jean-Claude Gémar (University of Montreal) first used in the title of his collection of essays: *Langage du droit et traduction. Essais de jurilinguistique / The Language of the Law and Translation. Essays on Jurilinguistics* (1982). While the term *jurilinguistique* is used in Canada, Gérard Cornu (Professor of Civil Law at Paris II) prefers the expression *linguistique juridique*, the title of his book (1990). According to Cornu, the term *jurilinguistique* refers only to the linguistic study of legal language, whereas *linguistique juridique* includes not only jurilinguistics but also legal linguistics, i.e., the operation of language in the service of the law (1990:17, *also* 211).

This belief, however, is misleading. Above all, it disregards the fact that, in addition to legal and language competence, legal translators also require translation skills that can be acquired only through special training in translation. Aware of this fact, Brackeniers recommends that lawyer-linguists in the EU attend special courses in translation, preferably at the postgraduate level (1991:8).[19] This is important because a higher degree of professionalism can be attained only if legal translators have professional training in both law and translation (Gémar 1995–II:155; Šarčević 1994:304).

Although the greatest volume of legal translation is done in the European Union, Canadians are credited with being the first to offer postgraduate courses in legislative drafting for common law and civil law lawyers, as well as a postgraduate program in legal translation for both linguists and lawyers. In order to implement the new bilingual drafting methods proposed by the Francophone Division of the Legislative Section of the Ministry of Justice, francophone jurilinguists were needed with special training in legislative drafting. As a counterpart to postgraduate courses on the drafting of common law legislation, the first parallel program on civil law drafting techniques was introduced for francophone lawyers by the Civil Law Section of the Law Faculty of the University of Ottawa in 1980 (Beaupré 1986:173, note 38). As part of the legislative reform in Canada, the Department of Justice also increased its staff of francophone translators, most of whom were linguists with training in translation. The results, however, were unsatisfactory, mainly because the translators had no basic training in law. Thus, when a symposium on legal translation was held in Ottawa in 1985, it was strongly recommended that specialized training courses be offered in legal translation for both linguists and lawyers.

In response, the Ottawa Faculty of Law and the School of Translation and Interpreting introduced a postgraduate program in legal translation for candidates already holding a degree in either law or translation (*see* Šarčević 1994:305). The first part of the program is designed to bring the law and translation students to the same level of proficiency by offering intensive training in the other discipline. In order to acquire language and translation skills, the law students begin by taking twenty-four credits in language, translation, and terminology, while the translation students are introduced to the basic concepts of law by taking twenty-four credits in law. The students are then brought together for twelve credits of courses in legal translation and terminology. This is followed by a practicum of six credits (eight weeks full time) in a legal translation unit in a non-academic setting. The program can be completed in twelve months on a full-time basis or in two or three years on a part-time basis (*see* Roberts 1987:9).

19.   While lawyer-linguists are part of the Legal Service, there are also 'ordinary' translators in the Translation Service who do much of the routine translation work, especially at the Commission in Brussels. These translators are not subject experts but usually have degrees from Schools of Translation and Interpretation. Sensing the need to motivate such translators, Brackeniers suggests that they should have the opportunity to become specialists by doing postgraduate work in fields such as law and economics (1991:8).

4.8. CREATIVITY DESPITE CONSTRAINTS IN LEGAL TRANSLATION

In the history of legal translation linguists were frequently blamed for defects in the quality and reliability of authenticated translations. In Canada, for example, the majority of translators were linguists working in large translation departments isolated from the legislative or treatymaking process. According to Sussmann, they were often too insecure to make even linguistic decisions. Fearing that linguistic improvements could affect the substance, they usually took the easy way out and simply reproduced the source text by literal translation (in Covacs 1980:3). Today this situation has changed significantly in Canada and elsewhere as teams of legal translators with interdisciplinary training are encouraged to produce parallel texts in the genius of the target language. Despite numerous restrictions in legal translation, legal translators have recently won new freedom, as a result of which one can even speak of a certain degree of creativity. Of course, creativity in legal translation is manifested much differently than in other areas of translation, especially literary translation.

Without mentioning legal translation, Wilss was among the first to acknowledge that creativity is possible in translations of special-purpose texts (1988:112). Durieux is more specific and even encourages technical translators to use their imagination and creativity when formulating the target text:

> Conscient de la mission fondamentale du texte à traduire, le traducteur peut ne retenir du texte original que son contenu informatif et faire appel à ses resources imaginatives et créatives pour le reformuler dans la langue d'arrivée, sous une forme qui soit de nature à produire l'impact recherché (1991:19).

Claiming that technical translators need not be bound to the source text, she believes that any constraints placed on them do not arise from the source text but are dictated by the communicative function of the target text (Durieux 1991:19). While Durieux talks about technical translation, she goes beyond the accepted notion of LSP translation as communication between specialists. For example, translating economic texts for marketing purposes cannot be regarded as special-purpose translation in the strict sense. Nonetheless, her appeal for creativity in technical translation is a welcome change. This also applies to Poulsen's (1990:33) and Fluck's (1992:227) pleas that instructors of specialized translation reject conventional teaching methods which discourage individuality and creativity (on LSP didactics, *see* Lerat 1995:185–192).

4.8.1. Traditional constraints

Vested with greater authority, legal translators with interdisciplinary training have won the right to exercise creativity in their new role as text producers and co-drafters. Despite this trend, some theorists of general translation still regard the production of parallel legal texts as a mechanical process (*see* Holz-Mänttäri's comments on bilateral agreements at 1986:350). This is undoubtedly because these are institutional texts and, as such, are relatively standardized in respect of their communicative function, content, and format (*cf.* Rothkegel 1984:239). As a result, parallel legal texts are often placed into the linguistic category of 'frozen' texts (*see* Sager 1993:78–79; *also* Trosborg 1991:69). This is unfortunate because it implies that the production of parallel texts is a mechanical process. Despite the traditional constraints imposed by mandatory standardization, skilled legal translators know exactly when and where they can be creative. This is confirmed by Koutsivitis, lawyer-linguist at the EU Commission, who makes a general distinction between standardized and non-standardized or 'free' parts of EU legislative texts. In his words: 'Le texte législatif communautaire est composé de deux parties: une partie normalisée et une partie libre'. In regard to the standardized parts, Koutsivitis notes that they are a necessity but also a source of irritation because they limit the translator's freedom:

> La normalisation du discours législatif communautaire et, partant, de la traduction législative au sein des Communautés européennes, est une nécessité qui découle du caractère contraignant de ces textes. Cette normalisation conduit à la création de correspondances types, à des traductions préétablies et répétitives qui limitent la créativité du traducteur et constituent pour lui une source d'un certain agacement (1990:145).

In order to minimize misinterpretation and ambiguity, institutions prescribe a standard format for each type of parallel text. A standard format includes not only the organizational plan and division of a text into parts but also the layout on the page, including spacing, paragraphing, punctuation, and even typographic characteristics such as capitalization, typeface, boldface, and underlining. As a rule, institutions request strict adherence to the standard format, requiring the visual appearance of parallel texts of a given instrument to be identical. This is especially true of texts printed side by side; however, it is not uncommon for parallel texts printed in individual volumes also to be 'mirror images' of each other.

Undoubtedly the greatest constraint imposed on legal translators is the mandatory use of standard formulae. The use of standard formulae in legal documents is a practice with a long tradition dating back to ancient times. Largely illiterate, the populace believed that only word-for-word repetition of the formulae would produce the desired effect. Contractual relations, for example, were concluded orally by reciting the pledge of faith with oath and surety. Similarly, oral pleadings consisted mainly of standard formulae recited by both plaintiff and defendant (Mellinkoff 1963:41). Today standard formulae are used to express repetitive actions, many of which are procedural formalities required as a condition of the validity of the text. To facilitate the application of parallel texts, entire clauses have been standardized for some repetitive actions, particularly in the preliminary and closing provisions. An example is the enactment formula which guarantees the legality of the Act by declaring that it has been enacted by the lawfully authorized person or body (*see also* Chapter 5, 5.4.2). For instance, the *Interpretation Act* of Canada recommends the following enactment formula for federal legislation:

Her Majesty, by and with the advice and consent of the Senate and House of Commons of Canada, enacts as follows:	Sa Majesté, sur l'avis et avec le consentement du Sénat et de la Chambre des communes du Canada, édicte:

Some texts have been standardized to the point that even the principal provisions contain repetitive actions which are expressed largely by standard formulae. Bilateral agreements based on a so-called 'broiler-plate text' fall into this category (*see* Harwood Cline and Mazza 1992:5). Other texts used to conclude basic transactions in fields such as transport, banking, and sales of goods have been almost completely standardized and are now available as standard forms. Standard forms are frozen documents in which only limited items need be inserted, for example, the names of the parties, the price, date of the transaction, etc. The texts are stored in computers in various languages and can be reproduced in minutes. This, however, is not translation and is not dealt with in this study.

Although legal translators are now generally permitted to be creative with language in the non-standardized parts of legal texts, there are restrictions in these parts as well. Above all, translators must honor the principle of language consistency. As far as technical terminology is concerned, once an equivalent has been selected, the same term must be repeated over and over again instead of using synonyms. The use of synonyms is discouraged in legal texts because the user might think that reference is being made to a different concept (Gesetzgebungsleitfaden 1995:307; *cf.* Weston 1991: 32–33). In order for the law to function, the principle of language consistency applies not only to the text at hand but to all related instruments. Therefore, when selecting equivalents, translators must always take account of the terminology used in other instruments already in force. Since authenticated texts are considered final and definite, the language therein has the status of a precedent. This means that once an equivalent has been used for a particular concept in any authentic text, other translators are obliged to use the same equivalent, even if they consider it inadequate (*cf.* Šarčević 1990:163). Thus one of the first questions of translators of authentic texts is: 'Are there any precedents?' (Morgan 1982:113). Authentic instruments on the same and related subject matters are obligatory preparatory materials for all legal translators. As normative instruments of the law, they also have the authority of precedents whenever reference is made to the particular instrument or its provisions are cited. As a result, translators are required to cite the exact wording in all references and/or quotations from authentic texts. Thus it has become a golden rule of legal translation that translators must refrain from correcting any errors and improving the language of authenticated translations having the force of law. This occasioned a translator at the European Court of Justice to describe authenticated translations as texts 'engraved in stone' because once published they are 'often quoted and referred to again and again' (Frame 1985:6). More recently, Bocquet refers to the use of citations from authenticated translations as 'la traduction bloquée' (1994:40). Since authenticated translations are sources of the law, this automatically puts greater pressure on translators to get it right the first time.

4.8.2. Encouraging creativity

According to Koutsivitis, the translator's creativity is limited to those parts of legislative texts which he refers to as 'free.' Using a negative definition, Koutsivitis defines 'le text libre' as 'la partie du texte qui n'obéit pas aux règles qui régissent la terminologie technique et les formules standardisées.' In his words, this is 'le discours courant, l'énonciation spontanée, qui peut se matérialiser par des phrases libres "pures" ou mélangées avec des termes et des formules' (1990:146). In such instances Koutsivitis encourages translators to select words, expressions, and grammatical constructions of the target language which best express the sense of the original. In closing he proposes two guidelines for the translation of non-standardized parts of legislative texts: transfer the sense of the original and respect the genius of the target language (1990:146).

Unfortunately, Koutsivitis' guidelines are too general to be of much use for translators. In particular, a detailed analysis of the so-called free parts of legal texts is needed to shift the emphasis from isolated specimens of language to language in action. Today legal translators are encouraged to be creative with language, not for the sake of language itself but to achieve the intended legal effects. Making reliable decisions requires not only legal competence but also considerable intuition on the part of translators. In legal translation intuition is not a natural ability but is acquired through interdisciplinary training in law and translation. The Chapters in Part II of this book are designed to help translators develop the competence and intuition necessary to make reliable decisions. Above all, they show how translators put legal language into action to achieve the desired results in legal communication.

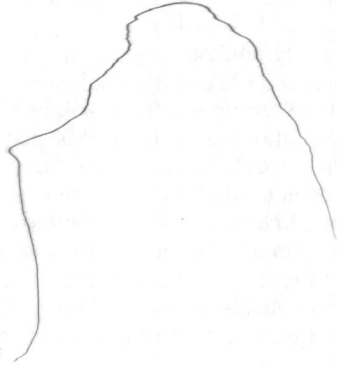

5 What All Translators Should Know about Legal Texts

5.1. BASICS OF LEGAL TRANSLATION

While legal translators are now encouraged to strive for linguistic purity, their primary task is to produce a text that promotes uniform interpretation and application of the single instrument. Above all, the new text must preserve the intent of the single instrument by leading to the desired results in practice. Like legal drafters, translators need to be thoroughly acquainted with the format of a legal text and understand the function of each of its parts in order to be effective text producers. After a brief introduction to the basic structure of judgments, legislative texts, and treaties, this Chapter analyzes the basic elements of legal rules which are characteristic of normative texts in general. Just as the structure of a legal text reflects the underlying process of legal analysis, legal rules must express the proper logical relations in order to create the intended legal effects. Most legal rules consist of a prescriptive and a descriptive part.

The prescriptive or operational part of a legal rule contains the normative content which is concerned mainly with expressing legal actions. Thus it should not come as a surprise that lawyers analyzed legal speech acts long before John Searle's (*Speech Acts*, 1969) and J.L. Austin's (*How to do Things with Words*, 1962).[1] Some of the major decisions made by legal translators involve regulatory speech acts. In particular, translators must be able to recognize and formulate commands, prohibitions, permissions, and authorizations. The descriptive part contains the propositional content of a legal rule which specifies the conditions under which a rule becomes operative. In order to ensure uniform interpretation and application of the elements constituting the so-called fact-situation of legal rules, translators must learn to compensate for conceptual incongruency. This is also essential when translating legal definitions which are vital to the operation of legal instruments. Generally speaking, in order to make reliable decisions, translators must be able to analyze legal texts, recognize potential pitfalls, and send the proper signals to the judiciary by using language

---

1. In his monumental work *How to do things with Words* J.L. Austin acknowledges 'that writers on jurisprudence have constantly shown themselves aware of the varieties of infelicity and even at times of the peculiarities of the performative utterance.' On the other hand, he maintains that the 'widespread obsession' of lawyers that 'utterances used in "acts in the law" *must* somehow be statements true or false' has prevented them 'from getting this whole matter much straighter than we are likely to.' Finally he remarks: 'I would not even claim to know whether some of them have not already done so' (1962:19).

effectively. The examples cited in this Chapter are from the principal provisions of Canadian, Swiss, and Belgian legislation. Some examples are also cited from treaties and conventions.

5.2. INSTITUTIONAL DRAFTING GUIDELINES

Despite Driedger's insistence that legal drafters should not be shackled by artificial rules or forms (1982a:4), it is common practice for institutions (ministries, parliaments, courts) to adopt drafting guidelines to coordinate the production of the parallel texts of a particular instrument. For example, in September 1976 the Swiss Federal Office and the Federal Department of Justice published the *Richtlinien der Gesetzestechnik / Directives sur la technique législative* to coordinate the drafting of federal legislation in German and French. The Guidelines, as they are referred to here, were supplemented in 1995 by the *Leitfaden für die Ausarbeitung von Erlassen des Bundes* or *Gesetzgebungsleitfaden,* which is more general and covers such areas as legislative procedure and methods, administrative and parliamentary procedure, language, etc. In 1996 the Federal Department of Justice updated the Guidelines with the *Gesetzestechnische Richtlinien* (Guidelines 1996) which, however, are pending revision. In Canada, francophone jurilinguists in the Department of Justice (Ottawa) completed the second edition of the *Guide Canadien de rédaction législative française* in June 1984. Intended as an aid for francophone drafters and translators of federal legislation, the *Guide Canadien* provides recommendations for translating common law provisions by presenting model provisions in both English and French. It also deals with specific problems relating to common law drafting practices and style, as well as specific terminological questions. Published in looseleaf form, the *Guide Canadien* is continually supplemented and updated.

In the European Communities one of the first drafting guidelines for coordinating texts in the official languages was the *Manual of Precedents drawn up by the Legal/Linguistic Experts of the Council of the European Communities* (1977). To ensure a greater degree of standardization in the structure and formulation of Council regulations, directives, and decisions, the *Formulaire des actes mis au point par les groupes juristes/linguistes du Conseil des Communautés Européennes* was published in October 1983. Revised in 1989, the third edition of the *Formulaire des actes établis dans le cadre du Conseil des Communautés Européennes* was published in French and in French/Greek, French/Italian, French/Spanish, etc. The third edition of the English *Manual of Precedents for Acts established within the Council of the European Communities* was published in 1990. For the purpose of promoting uniformity between legal instruments of the Council and the Commission, the *Règles de technique législative à l'usage des services de la Commission* were revised and expanded to include all the official languages of the EC. General guidelines on the Quality of Drafting of Community Legislation were adopted in a Resolution of the Council of the European Communities of June 8, 1993.

Drafting guidelines usually prescribe the standard format for specific instruments produced by an institution for use in a particular jurisdiction. Among other things, the format of a text includes the organizational plan and division into parts, i.e., its structure (*see* Chapter 4, 4.8.1). Despite variations from jurisdiction to jurisdiction, the basic structure of a legal text usually reflects the underlying process of legal reasoning and thus tends to be similar for the same type of instrument. Judgments are largely an exception. The fact that some institutions specify stricter form requirements for judgments is bound to have an effect on translation as well. As mentioned in Chapter 4 (4.8.1), translators must follow the standard format prescribed by the particular institution.

5.3. STRUCTURE OF JUDGMENTS

Didier's remark that judgments can be translated 'freely' (1990:285) refers to Canadian judgments in the common law style. Written like a dissertation, they lack the formal restraints of civil law judgments, many of which still follow the French tradition of formulating the entire judgment in a single sentence. Regardless of style, the parts of a judgment are more or less organized in the form of a syllogism which reflects the basic rationale of judicial decision (Bocquet 1994:34). As shown in the well-known example below, a syllogism consists of three major steps: a major premise, a minor premise, and the conclusion:

All human beings are mortal.	(major premise)
Socrates is a human being.	(minor premise)
Socrates is mortal.	(conclusion)

Greatly simplified, the process of judicial decision can be described as follows: After identifying the issues or questions of law (major premise) and establishing the facts of the case (minor premise), the judge applies the law to the facts, reaching a conclusion of law (conclusion) on which the final decision is based (*cf.* Walker 1980:673; *see* Chapter 3, 3.2.2).

5.3.1. Judgments at the Belgian Court of Cassation

The most rigid form requirements in legal drafting and translation can be found in judgments following the traditional French style (Lashöfer 1992:44). Formulated in one sentence with each point of the reasons introduced by the conjunction *attendu que* in the higher courts and *considérant que* in the lower courts, such judgments are particularly suitable for expressing rigid, Latin logic (Wetter 1960:28; Mimin 1978:185). The French tradition of formulating judgments in one sentence was adopted by some German courts during the reception of French law in the nineteenth century (Daubenspeck 1893:42, cited in Dölle 1949:6, note 4) but was later replaced by the more flexible method of presenting the judgment in the form of a dissertation with headings for each section. In Europe, the French style of judgments is still used in France, Belgium, Luxembourg, Finland, Portugal, and Spain (*cf.* David and Brierley 1985:142). In the seventies it was replaced by a more flexible style in Sweden and the Netherlands.

123

The highest court of civil and criminal appeal in Belgium, the Court of Cassation (Cour de Cassation) has the power to quash (*casser*) the decisions of inferior courts. Following the tradition of cassation courts, it considers only questions of law concerning the legality of proceedings in inferior courts. Accordingly, it does not consider facts and appeals on fact, nor does it have the power to review legislation. This, in turn, enables cassation judgments to be relatively short, concise, and impersonal. Judgments at the Belgian Court of Cassation consist of five parts: introduction, arguments, reasons, conclusion, and decision. Their chronology strictly follows the structure of a syllogism. The question of law under consideration is cited in the introduction (major premise), followed by the arguments containing excerpts from the challenged decision which prove or disprove the legality of the proceedings (minor premise). This leads to the conclusion of law (conclusion) and the final decision whether the attacked decision of the inferior court is to be quashed (Lashöfer 1992:51). Since there are neither headings nor explanations, only translators who are familiar with the structure and rigid form requirements can follow the process of judicial reasoning without difficulty (*cf.* Soetaert 1980:366). Experienced translators are not intimidated by the high degree of subordination and complexity, nor by the fact that, irrespective of their length, cassation judgments are always formulated in one sentence. Knowing that the subject of the main clause is at the very beginning and the main verbs and objects at the end, they do not even bother to hunt the subject as it is always *La Cour.* Before reading the entire judgment, they often turn to the decision at the end introduced by the standard phrase: *Par ces motifs* (Soetaert 1980:366). The other four parts are arranged within this frame in a series of subordinate clauses introduced by standard conjunctions or phrases. The unorthodox system of punctuation and capitalization also signalizes the end or beginning of a certain part. A simplified version of the standard format of judgments at the Belgian Cour de Cassation is reproduced below in French and Dutch:

Arrêt	Arrest
LA COUR; – Vu l'arrêt attaqué,...;	HET HOF; – Gelet op het bestreden arrest,...;
Sur le moyen,...:	Over het middel...:
Attendu que...; Attendu que...; Attendu que...;	Overwegende dat...; Overwegende dat...; Overwegende dat...;
Que le moyen...;	Dat het middel...;
Par ces motifs,....	Om die redenen,....

As a rule, translators at the Court of Cassation are required to follow the original text as closely as possible in respect of both form and substance (*see* Chapter 2, 2.9.2). Above all, it is the rigid form requirements of cassation judgments in the French tradition that make them inordinately difficult to translate, especially into a language with relatively strict rules of syntax such as Dutch. As confirmed by Leo Vande Velde, translator at the Court of Cassation (*see* Chapter 2, note 12), it is a considerable challenge to respect the rigid format and still produce a text that reads like natural Dutch. As if translating in a straight jacket, the formal constraints give the translator very little room to be creative with language. In addition, cassation judgments are extremely concise, thus forcing the translator to carefully weigh each and every word. Although the reasons are much shorter than in other types of judgments, utmost care must be taken to translate them correctly as even a slight change in emphasis could detract from the force of the argument, possibly rendering both the reasons and the decision inconclusive. To be able to follow the court's arguments, the translator must understand the implicit meaning of the arguments of counsel and be thoroughly familiar with the technique of cassation. According to Soetaert, president of the Court of Cassation from 1990 to 1992, the whole technique of cassation is reflected in the reasons: First the Court tests the arguments of counsel in light of the rules of admissibility and then the rules of law. Only the most important arguments are taken into account because one argument suffices to quash the attacked decision (Soetaert 1980:369).

5.3.2. Judgments at the European Court of Justice

As of May 1979, judgments of the European Court of Justice at Luxembourg have a uniform format and style that can be described as a hybrid of the French technique and the more flexible dissertation method (Berteloot 1988:13). This, however, was not always the case. In fact, the Court learned the hard way that, for the sake of preserving the unity of the single instrument, all parallel texts should follow the same format and have the same style. Whereas Article 63 of the Court's Rules of Procedure specifies the constituent parts of the judgment and supplementary materials, the Court can use its discretion to structure the judgment as it deems appropriate (Klinke 1989:63). Since the end of 1984, the body of the judgment consists of only two parts: the recital of the parties and the decision (reasons + operative part), while the introductory materials include the summary (key words + synopsis), report for the hearing (facts and issues), and the non-binding opinion of the advocate general.[2]

While the Court's decision to streamline the body of the judgment has not significantly affected translation, the decision to adopt a uniform style has facilitated translation. When the Court was established in 1952, the various language divisions were permitted to use stylistic variations as long as they followed the basic format and structure which was based on judgments in the French tradition. While some

2. The introductory materials originally included only the summary (key words + synopsis), whereas the body of the judgment consisted of the recital of the parties, facts and issues, and the decision (reasons + operative part). The opinion of the advocate general was published after the judgment in the *Court Reports*. Since the facts and issues were already recorded in the report for the hearing, it was decided to omit the facts and issues from the body of the judgment and to publish the report for the hearing in introductory materials together with the summary and opinion of the advocate general (*see* Pescatore 1985:22).

departments preferred strict adherence to French style, including the use of *attendu* clauses in the reasons, others favored a looser style resembling the dissertation method. Perhaps the non-uniform style would not have created problems were it not for the unusual communicative situation at the Court. Due to the large number of official languages, the working language at the Court is French As a result, the judgment is usually written in French for deliberation. Regardless of the language of the case, the French judgment always serves as the source text for all translations (Berteloot 1988:13). Unlike Community legislation, only the judgment in the language of the case is authentic. Thus it occurs that the authentic judgment is a translation whenever the language of the case is not French (Lashöfer 1992:140).

Since the French division strictly adhered to traditional French style, the critical factor for translators of other language divisions was often understanding the French source text. As in all judgments, the most important part of judgments at the European Court is the *ratio decidendi*, the Court's 'reasons for deciding' which are binding on future courts (Golding 1984:101). Any mistakes in conveying the reasons of the Court may have serious repercussions, especially in preliminary rulings which are binding on future cases. Although it is essential for translators to recognize and reproduce the logical structure of the reasons correctly, translation mistakes were not infrequent (Pescatore 1985:44). Above all, the French technique of introducing each reason by the conjunction *attendu* and expressing the constituent points in a string of subordinate *que* clauses sometimes made it difficult to identify the logical function of each point of the reasons. While some logical connectors were poorly marked, others were ambiguous or had been omitted from the source text altogether. Another source of potential confusion was the use of the conditional in the French text to formulate arguments of the parties in the reasons. This can perhaps be attributed to the influence of German grammar which requires indirect speech to be written in the subjunctive (Berteloot 1988:14). Accordingly, the arguments of the parties in the reasons of German judgments are presented in the subjunctive, those of the Court in the indicative. This difference is important because it is essential to make a clear distinction between the arguments of the parties and those of the Court when formulating the reasons.

Failure to make this distinction led to a costly error in the authentic German judgment of June 16, 1966, in case 57/65. The issue turned on the question whether Article 97 of the Treaty establishing the EEC applies in cases where average rates of internal taxes have been established for import products subject to a turnover tax calculated on a cumulative multi-stage tax system. Based on the negative arguments in points 1 and 2 of the reasons, which appeared in the subjunctive and were thus taken to be arguments of the parties, it appeared that Article 95 was to be applied although its application led to complications in practice. While this judgment was made available to German finance courts immediately after pronouncement, a different text was published in the *Sammlung der Rechtsprechung des Gerichthofes*.[3]

---

3. In the German judgment distributed following pronouncement, the use of the subjunctive (*erlaube, stelle, könne*) and the paragraphing suggest that these are arguments of the parties, while the point that follows states the Court's conclusion. In the published German judgment, the use of the indicative makes it clear that the Court is speaking in all points. For this reason,

In the published text (RsprGH XII S. 257), the negative arguments in points 1 and 2 are no longer in the subjunctive and thus are clearly statements made by the Court. As a result, German national courts were inclined to reject the application of Article 95.

Although the error was discovered and corrected prior to publication, it caused considerable confusion and damage. Due to the conflicting reasons in the two German texts, some 200 000 appellate proceedings were initiated before German national courts (Everling 1967:184). In this case it is difficult to detect the source of the error. Fortunately, the French text published in the *Recueil de la Jurisprudence de la Cour* is correct. Since it served as the source text for all other translations, needless litigation was at least avoided in other Member States. Most probably, the erroneous German text was a translation of the French text used for deliberation. In this case, the error could have been in the source text or the German text could have been mistranslated. Whatever the source, errors in an authentic text disrupt the communication process considerably.

5.4. STRUCTURE OF LEGISLATIVE TEXTS

Despite fundamental differences in the styles of national legislation, the formal elements and even their arrangement are strikingly similar in legislative texts from different jurisdictions. Generally speaking, legislative texts (statutes, Acts, codes) contain preliminary, principal, and final provisions. The main emphasis in this study is on principal provisions, substantive as well as administrative. While the substantive provisions set forth the obligations and rights of the legal actors, the

---

the final sentence containing the Court's conclusion is included in the same paragraph (*see* Everling 1967:182). The disputed points of the reasons read as follows in the two authentic German texts:

A. *Judgment distributed following pronouncement:*

Drei Regierungen haben in ihren schriftlichen und mündlichen Erklärungen unter Berufung auf Artikel 97 eine andere Auslegung des Artikels 95 vertreten. Artikel 97 erlaube den Mitgliedstaaten, welche die Umsatzsteuer nach dem System der kumulativen Mehrphasensteuer erheben, Durchschnittssätze für Waren oder Gruppen von Waren festzulegen, und stelle somit eine spezielle Anpassungsvorschrift zu Artikel 95 dar; diese Norm könne aber ihrem Wesen nach keine unmittelbaren Wirkungen in den Rechtsbeziehungen zwischen den Mitgliedstaaten und ihren Rechtsunterworfenen erzeugen.

Dieser Sonderfall des Artikels 97 kann jedoch keinesfalls die Auslegung von Artikel 95 beeinflussen.

B. *Judgment published in the Court Reports:*

Drei Regierungen haben in ihren schriftlichen und mündlichen Erklärungen unter Berufung auf Artikel 97 eine andere Auslegung des Artikels vertreten.

Artikel 97 erlaubt indessen den Mitgliedstaaten, welche die Umsatzsteuer nach dem System der kumulativen Mehrphasensteuer erheben, Durchschnittssätze für Waren oder Gruppen von Waren festzulegen, und stellt somit eine spezielle Anpassungsvorschrift zu Artikel 95 dar, die ihrem Wesen nach keine unmittelbaren Wirkungen in den Rechtsbeziehungen zwischen den Mitgliedstaaten und ihrem Rechtsunterworfenen erzeugen kann. Dieser Sonderfall des Artikels 97 kann jedoch keinesfalls die Auslegung von Artikel 95 beeinflussen.

administrative provisions regulate the legal machinery by means of which those obligations and rights are declared and enforced. The final provisions are primarily procedural and are widely expressed by standard formulae. To illustrate similarities and differences in the structure of common law and civil law legislation, the main elements of Canadian and Swiss federal legislation are cited below:

CANADIAN LEGISLATION

Preliminary provisions
– Long title
– Preamble (optional)
– Short title
– Enacting clause
– Application provisions
– Interpretation provisions

Principal provisions
– Substantive provisions
– Administrative provisions

Supplementary provisions
– Offenses and penalties
– Provisions on the making of subsidiary legislation, indemnities, etc.

Final provisions
– Savings
– Repeals, consequential amendments
– Transitional provisions
– Commencement provisions
– Schedules (annexes)

SWISS LEGISLATION

– Title
– Short title
– Enacting clause

Preliminary provisions
– Purpose clause
– Application provisions
– Interpretation provisions

Principal provisions
– Substantive provisions
– Administrative provisions
– Offenses, penalties, remedies
– Special measures
– Measures in criminal proceedings
– Costs and fees

Final provisions
– Execution provisions
– Repeals, consequential provisions
– Transitional provisions
– Referendum provisions
– Commencement provisions
– Schedules (annexes)

At this point one notable difference should be mentioned. Contrary to Canadian legislation, the title, short title, and enacting clause do not belong to the preliminary provisions in Swiss legislation. In common law jurisdictions, the function of the long title is to indicate the general purpose(s) of the piece of legislation (*see* Chapter 4, 4.2). Having been enacted, it belongs to the preliminary provisions and is subject to amendment by the legislature. More important, it may be used to interpret the Act as a whole and to ascertain its scope (Thornton 1987:150). In view of its importance for interpretation, the translator should proceed with caution and produce a title that contains the same information content as the source title, as in the following Act from the *Statutes of Canada* [1986]:

An Act to impose reporting requirements with respect to public pension plans and to amend certain Acts in consequence thereof

Loi imposant certaines exigences en matière de rapports sur les régimes publics de pensions et modifiant certaines lois en conséquence

Serving merely as a means of identification, the short title has the characteristics of a label. Nonetheless, the translation must be precise so as to avoid confusion in identifying the proper Act. The short titles of the above Act are *The Public Pensions Report Act* and *Loi sur les rapports relatifs aux pensions publiques*. As mentioned above, the titles of Swiss legislation do not belong to the body of the Act itself. Since the purpose of the Act is defined in a purpose clause in the preliminary part, the title is regarded strictly as a means of identifying the Act and distinguishing it from existing legislation. Nonetheless, the title should describe the contents in clear, concise language and all language versions should be coordinated to the point that they are easily recognized as the same legislative act. In modern Swiss legislation, the short title is commonly reduced to an abbreviation cited in parenthesis following the title:

Bundesgesetz über die Förderung der ausserschulerischen Jugendarbeit (Jugendförderungsgesetz, JFG)	*Loi fédérale concernant l'encouragement des activités de jeunesse extrascholaires (Loi sur les activités de jeunesse, LAJ)*

5.4.1. Division and arrangement of legal provisions

Lawyers usually turn directly to the provisions governing a particular matter instead of reading a legislative text from beginning to end. Nonetheless, legal drafters must always take account of principles of textuality such as cohesion and coherency. Accordingly, the arrangement of provisions should be logical and clear language should be used to mark the transitions (Fleiner-Gerster 1985:6–12). Due to differences in legislative style, each jurisdiction determines the constituent units of a provision and the arrangement of provisions into parts. As a result, the divisions and their designations vary from jurisdiction to jurisdiction. Frequently they do not even correspond with those of other jurisdictions within the same legal family. For the sake of guaranteeing uniform citation, the various divisions of provisions must be carefully preserved in all the parallel texts of a single instrument. This is absolutely essential; otherwise plurilingual communication could not function in the mechanism of the law. The provisions of Swiss and Canadian federal legislation are divided as follows:

SWISS LEGISLATION

Buch	Livre	Libro
1. Teil	Partie 1	Parte 1
1. Titel	Titre 1	Titolo 1
1. Kapitel	Chapitre 1	Capitolo 1
1. Abschnitt	Section 1	Capo 1
* Artikel 1	* Article 1	* Articolo 1
Absatz (1)	Alinéa (1)	alinea (1)
Buchstabe (a)	Lettre (a)	lettera (a)

CANADIAN LEGISLATION

Part I	Partie I
Division I	Section I
Subdivision a	Sous-section a
* Section 1	* Article 1
Subsection (1)	Paragraphe (1)
Paragraph (a)	Alinéa (a)
Subparagraph (i)	Sous-alinéa (i)

As indicated by the asterisk, the basic unit in Swiss legislation is the article, in Canadian legislation the section. The paragraph (§) is also a common designation for the basic unit of legislation, especially in German-speaking jurisdictions and others influenced by the German BGB and/or the Austrian ABGB.[4] Despite its relative independence, each section (article or §) should be read and interpreted within the context of the whole statute, Act, or code so as to ensure unity of purpose. The arrangement of sections (articles or §§) should be logical. In civil law jurisdictions, the thought progression is usually from general to specific. Thus general provisions precede specific provisions and exceptions follow the general rule (Gesetzgebungsleitfaden 1995:295). As for translators, they usually proceed section by section in chronological order, taking care to preserve the logical connectors and harmonize the text as a whole, i.e., ensure internal consistency of presentation and terminology.[5]

5.4.2. The one-sentence rule

Traditionally, the entire text of a statute was formulated as one sentence. Dating back to antiquity, this practice may be attributed at least in part to the former lack of punctuation. When punctuation was finally introduced in statutes of the ancient Greeks and Romans, a system of oral dotting was used in which the breathing stops were marked by commas and half stops, and the document was formally ended by a period (Mellinkoff 1963:170). Following this practice, early British statutes were formulated as a single sentence consisting of the enactment clause ('Be it enacted') and the enactment. As statutes became more complicated, it became necessary to divide the text into sections. Regarded as a separate enactment, each section began with an abbreviated enactment clause: 'And be it further enacted That...' (*see* Kurzon 1986:11). Regardless of its length, each section was drafted as a single sentence.

---

4. When translating municipal legislation into another language for information purposes, the designations of the various divisions of the source text must be retained. For instance, the basic unit of German legislation remains the §, of French legislation the article, etc. *See*, e.g., Forrester, Ilgen, and Goren's translation of the BGB into English: The German Civil Code, Amsterdam: North Holland (1975); and Crabb's translation of the Code civil into English: The French Civil Code, South Hackensack, New Jersey: Fred B. Rothman & Co. (1977).

5. On the difference between harmonization and correspondence or concordance of parallel texts in plurilingual communication *see* Chapter 7, at 7.4.1.

Today the enactment clause is no longer repeated; however, the practice of formulating each section or subsection as a single sentence has been retained in common law jurisdictions despite protests by reformers (*cf.* Driedger 1976:77). Whereas the reformers regard complex sentences as an obstacle to comprehension, supporters of the one-sentence rule insist that a legislative sentence consisting of three or more main clauses, each modified by a number of subordinate clauses, is easier to understand because the reader need not identify the relationship between the individual sentences (Driedger 1976:77). Moreover, the view is held that communication is likely to be hindered by a series of sentences because 'the inevitable result will be either needless repetition or tiresome and confusing cross-references or both' (Thornton 1987:61). In defense of the one-sentence rule, Thornton concludes that sentence length is not a valid criterion for intelligibility (1987:61). A plea for reasonableness, however, is in order. We are reminded of the critical works of Jeremy Bentham, one of the reformers of English law during the American revolutionary days who attacked the verbosity of an English statute that was thirteen pages long and formulated as a single sentence (Mellinkoff 1963:265).

On the other hand, Swiss drafting principles advise drafters to make legislation as concise and simple as possible so as to promote intelligibility. To this end, it is recommended that drafters follow the so-called Eugen Huber-rule, named after the father of the Swiss Civil Code of 1907. Pursuant to this rule, each article should contain no more than three paragraphs (*Absätze*); each paragraph should consist of one sentence, and each sentence should express a single thought (Gesetz-gebungsleitfaden 1995:288). Swiss drafters are advised to use simple sentences and to avoid complex sentences with a series of subordinate clauses (Gesetz-gebungsleitfaden 1995:300).

5.5. STRUCTURE OF TREATIES

Treaty is a generic term denoting all types of international agreements, some of which are more like contracts (treaties of peace, alliance, neutrality, arbitration) while newer forms resemble legislation (conventions, declarations, protocols, acts, final acts and general acts) (*see* Chapter 7, 7.1). The fact that a treaty (in the narrow sense) is not only a law but also a contract between the signatory States is reflected in the traditional format. As developed in the late Middle Ages, a treaty usually contains a title, preamble, main part, and final clauses. While the title of a multilateral instrument serves mainly as a means of identification, the preamble specifies the purpose of the treaty, often mentioning the international obligations set forth or explaining the reasons for adopting the particular treaty. The preamble of traditional treaties consists of the following parts: names of the High Contracting Parties, the reasons (*considérants*), the designated Plenipotentiaries, the exchange and review of powers, the agreement clause. The entire preamble is formulated as a single sentence and usually ends with an agreement clause (*...have agreed as*

131

follows.).[6] Each reason appears in a recital introduced by a standard formula such as *CONSIDERING, RECOGNIZING, DESIRING...* The following is an excerpt from the preamble of the Treaty on European Union / Traité sur l'Union européenne:

HIS MAJESTY THE KING OF THE BELGIANS, HER MAJESTY THE QUEEN OF DENMARK, THE PRESIDENT OF THE...	SA MAJESTÉ LE ROI DES BELGES, SA MAJESTÉ LA REINE DE DANEMARK, LE PRÉSIDENT DE LA...
RESOLVED to mark a new stage in the process of European integration undertaken with the establishment of the European Communities,	RÉSOLUS à franchir une nouvelle étape dans le processus d'intégration européenne engagé par la création des Communautés européennes,
RECALLING the historic importance of the ending of the division of the European continent and the need to create firm bases for the construction of the future Europe,...	RAPPELANT l'importance historique de la fin de la division du continent européen et la nécessité d'établir des bases solides pour l'architecture de l'Europe future,...
RESOLVED to achieve the strengthening and the convergence of their economies and to establish an economic and monetary union,...	RÉSOLUS à renforcer leurs économies ainsi qu'à en assurer la convergence, et à établir une Union économique et monétaire,...
HAVE DECIDED to establish a European Union and to this end have designated as their Plenipotentiaries:	ONT DÉCIDÉ d'instituer une Union européenne et ont désigné à cet effet comme plénipotentiaires:
...	...
WHO, having exchanged their full powers, found in good and due form have agreed as follows.	LESQUELS, après avoir échangé leurs pleins pouvoirs reconnus en bonne et due forme, sont convenus des dispositions qui suivent.

The substantive provisions constituting the main body of a treaty contain legal rules setting forth the legal obligations, prohibitions, and rights of the parties. At this point it suffices to note that these provisions are generally formulated in the same way as legal rules of municipal legislation. The final provisions of treaties include, *inter alia*, provisions on ratification, depositary, amendments, revisions, repeals, reservations, the period of validity, entry into force, language, the place and date of signature. Consisting mainly of procedural formalities, they are commonly expressed in standard formulae (*see* Chapter 4, 4.8.1). For instance, the final provision of the

---

6. Sometimes the preamble closes with an agreement clause followed by a semicolon. For example, the agreement clause in the UN Convention on Contracts for International Sale of Goods reads: '*Have agreed* as follows: / *Sont convenus* de ce qui suit:'. Instead of citing all the States parties, preambles to conventions usually commence with a general statement, such as: *The States parties to this convention / Les États parties à la présente Convention*. Also, the plenipotentiaries are not named in the preamble.

Treaty on European Union containing the language clause and place and date of signature reads as follows in the English and French texts:

This Treaty, drawn up in a single original in the Danish, Dutch, English, French, German, Greek, Irish, Italian, Portuguese and Spanish languages, the texts in each of these languages being equally authentic, shall be deposited in the archives of the government of the Italian Republic, which will transmit a certified copy to each of the governments of the other signatory States.

IN WITNESS WHEREOF the undersigned Plenipotentiaries have signed this Treaty.

Done at Maastricht on the seventh day of February in the year one thousand nine hundred and ninety-two.

Le présent traité rédigé en un exemplaire unique, en langues allemande, anglaise, danoise, espagnole, française, grecque, irlandaise, italienne, néerlandaise et portugaise, les textes établis dans chacune de ces langues faisant également foi, sera dèposé dans les archives du gouvernement de la République italienne, qui remettra une copie certifiée conforme à chacun des gouvernements des autres États signataires.

EN FOI DE QUOI, les plénipotentiaires soussignés ont apposé leurs signatures au bas du présent traité.

Fait à Maastricht, le sept février mil neuf cent quatre-vingt-douze.

5.6. PRIMARY ROLE OF LANGUAGE IN LEGAL TEXTS

The language of the law is concerned primarily with 'parole' (how language affects behavior) as opposed to 'langue' (the language system). Recognizing that 'la parole juridique' is inseparable from 'les actes juridiques,' Sourioux and Lerat described the language of the law as 'un langage d'action' (1975:50). Today it is generally agreed that the primary role of language in normative legal texts is to prescribe legal actions, the performance of which is intended to achieve a specific goal (Weinberger 1988:52). For example, legislative texts are intended to modify social behavior by laying down rules of conduct prescribing how one shall act or refrain from acting in certain situations. Similarly, treaties are agreements in which States parties agree to perform or refrain from performing certain acts as a means of attaining a specific goal. Contracts are agreements between two or more parties to exchange performances in a given situation for a specific purpose, e.g., sales contracts, loan contracts, service contracts, agency contracts, etc.[7] In all three types of instruments, the legal actions to be performed or not performed are set forth in the substantive provisions in the form of obligations, permissions, authorizations, and/or prohibitions,

---

7. In the common law, *contract* is sometimes defined as a promise made by the promisor and promisee to exchange performances. *See* Farnsworth (1991) *United States Contract Law*, Ardsley-on-Hudson, New York: Transnational Juris, 1. According to Tallon, the notion of a contract as a promise is 'baffling' to civil law lawyers, who regard contracts as creating obligations (*see* Tallon 1990:283–290).

133

all of which are enforceable by law. Legal disputes arising as a result of the performance of illegal acts or the failure of a party to perform its obligations are resolved by courts of law which pronounce their decisions in the form of a judgment. The operative part of judgments (the decision) also expresses a legal action.

In view of the actional nature of legal texts, lawyers were quick to recognize the relevance of the speech act theory for legal discourse (Sourioux and Lerat 1975:50; later Weinberger 1988:52; Cornu 1990:44). Sourioux even includes a brief introductory chapter on signs in the language of the law in his textbook *Introduction au droit* (1990:15–20). In the speech act theory, language is viewed as a system of actual or potential speech acts. As Searle put it: 'Speaking a language is engaging in a rule-governed form of behavior. To put it more briskly, talking is performing acts according to rules' (1969:22). Among other things, J.L. Austin distinguished between 'constative utterances,' which describe or report things and events, and 'performative utterances,' which perform actions merely by virtue of being made. While constative utterances may be true or false (e.g., It is raining), performance utterances may not (e.g.: I pronounce you man and wife). Depending on the success or actual performance of the act (felicity), performative utterances are either felicitous or infelicitous (Austin 1962:14–16). For example, a marriage ceremony performed by an unauthorized person is not 'happy.' Austin distinguishes between locutionary acts, the 'performance of an act of saying something,' and illocutionary acts, 'the performance of an act in saying something' (1962:99), a distinction not accepted by Searle although he also uses the expression *illocutionary act* (1969:23, note 1).

Illocutionary acts (performatives) are particularly important in legal discourse (Weinberger 1988:53; Bocquet 1994:3) because something is not merely said but is actually done:

   a) X is hereby sentenced to five years in prison.
   b) I hereby bequeath all my property to my wife.

Generally speaking, illocutionary acts which produce legal effects are referred to as legal speech acts. Thus it is appropriate when Cornu calls legal speech acts the 'generator' of the law: 'Le droit attache au langage certains effets de droit. Plus précisément, il dote les actes de langage de conséquences juridiques. Le prononcé d'une parole devient, en vertu du droit, générateur de droit' (1990:33–34). As Cornu correctly remarks, the verb is 'la parole' of legal discourse (1990:44). According to Austin, illocutionary acts are expressed by performative verbs which are either explicit or implicit (1962:99). While explicit performatives express the action directly: 'I permit you to go,' 'I order you to deliver the merchandise in two weeks,' implicit performatives express the same action indirectly: 'You may go,' 'You shall deliver the merchandise in two weeks' (*cf.* Kurzon 1986:7). Austin divided explicit performatives into five classes of speech acts, of which commissives, verdictives, and exercitives express various forms of legal actions. While commissives (*promise, pledge, offer, agree*) commit the party in varying degrees to some future course of action, verdictives (*find guilty/not guilty*) are used by jurors in the delivery of their finding on a matter submitted to their judgment (1962:42, 153). Most important are exercitive verbs (e.g., *order, command, demand, permit, allow*) which express 'that something is to be' as a result of some decision, the consequence being that 'others are compelled, allowed or not allowed to do certain acts' (Austin 1962:154).

The philosopher who developed Austin's theory furtherst, Searle found it necessary to reclassify Austin's categories of speech acts. For our purpose it is important to note that Searle placed many of Austin's exercitive verbs (including *order, command, demand, permit* and *allow*) in a class he refers to as directives (1975:355). Other verbs belonging to Austin's class of exercitives (e.g., *enact, nominate, declare open, declare closed*) are placed in a class of their own which Searle calls declarations (*see* Trosborg 1991:72). In addition, Searle's classification of speech acts also includes representatiaves, commissives, and expressives (*see* Searle 1975:354–361). While Searle succeeded in improving Austin's classification from the linguistic point of view, both Austin's and Searle's classifications of speech acts have been criticized as inadequate for legal purposes. As Habermas points out, Austin's and Searle's classifications fail to take account of the normative aspect of legal speech acts (1981:428–429). In particular, he criticizes Searle's class of directives which includes orders, petitions, directions, requests, summons, questions, etc. As far as legal criteria are concerned, Searle does not make a distinction between legally binding normative acts and simple imperatives, i.e., acts of volition without the force of law. Searle himself made it clear that he does not regard requests as legally binding acts: 'The point of a request is to try to get the hearer to do something (and not necessarily to commit or obligate him to do it)' (Searle 1975:356). Similarly, Searle fails to make a clearcut distinction between his classes of directives and declarations. According to Habermas, declarative acts such as appointments, abdications, declarations of war, and notices of dismissal all produce legal effects and have a normative content similar to orders and requests. While Austin's and Searle's class of commissive acts 'commits the speaker to do something,' it does 'not necessarily try to get himself to do it' (Searle 1975:356). Again, this is not acceptable for legal texts because normative texts are legally binding and nonperformance of the acts specified therein can result in litigation. In view of these shortcomings, Habermas proposes his own classification of speech acts, in which legal performatives are placed in one general class called regulatives. Habermas' tripartite classification of speech acts consists of regulatives, expressives, and constatives (1981:427).

This is not the place to present a detailed analysis of the classification of speech acts. Instead, the above remarks are intended to serve as a warning to linguists who classify legal speech acts according to linguistic categories without taking account of legal criteria.[8] In particular, one should refrain from using the class of directives for legal purposes. Ignoring legal criteria can prove dangerous for translators who are required to put language into action to achieve the desired legal results. Since some of the major decisions of translators concern legal speech acts, they must understand how illocutionary acts operate in legal rules.

8. Using Searle's system of classification, Trosborg speaks about directive acts in contracts (1991:74–83). Later she acknowledges the regulative function of legal speech acts in contracts; however, she still classifies legal actions therein as directive, constitutive, and commissive acts (1994:311–312).

5.7. BASIC ELEMENTS OF LEGAL RULES

One of the first analyses of legislative texts was written in 1843 by an English barrister named George Coode. Acknowledged as 'a major breakthrough in the drafting of legislation' (Driedger 1982b:3), Coode's analysis is a rudimentary attempt to show how language is used to achieve certain effects in legal rules. Although it focuses on common law legislation, Coode's analysis sheds light on the basic elements of legal rules in general. From Coode's point of view, a piece of legislation is a means of securing a benefit to some person(s) by creating an obligation or conferring a right, privilege or power. Thus he concluded that all legal rules contain the following four elements: legal subject, legal action, case, and conditions. According to Coode, the legal subject is the person on whom the obligation is imposed or on whom the right, privilege, or power is conferred. The obligation itself or the right, privilege, or power and all that the law brings about is the legal action. The case expresses the circumstances or situation(s) in which the legal action is intended to take place, and the conditions specify what must have been done before the legal action is performed (*cf.* Dick 1985:57–58); Driedger 1982b:2–3). The following is a simplified example of Coode's showing the four elements in their mandatory order:

(Case)	Where any Quaker refuses to pay any church rates,
(Condition)	if any churchwarden complains thereof,
(Subject)	one of the next Justices of the peace,
(Action)	may summon such Quaker.

Theorists later came to the conclusion that Coode's elements and his prescribed order are not of universal application. Today, for example, both theorists and practitioners are of the opinion that there is no grammatical difference between Coode's case and condition (*see* Driedger 1982b:3) and, more important, both have essentially the same function. Therefore, the two elements are now combined in what jurisprudents refer to as the fact-situation (*Tatbestand*) which specifies the conditions under which the particular rule operates. As for the legal subject and legal action, these two elements constitute the so-called statement of law (*Tatfolge*) prescribing the action to be taken and by whom in the event the conditions constituting the fact-situation are fulfilled. Most frequently, the fact-situation is formulated in the subordinate clause of a conditional sentence and the statement of law in the main clause so as to express the logical relation: If P1 + P2, then Q (*cf.* Bocquet 1994:17). According to this formula, Coode's example can be reformulated as follows without altering the content of the fact-situation:

Fact-situation	*Statement of law*
Where a churchwarden files a complaint against a Quaker for refusing to pay any church rates	one of the next Justices of the peace may summon such Quaker.

Coode's definition of the legal subject has also been criticized as being too rigid. First of all, there are numerous legal rules in which the grammatical subject is not a legal person and secondly, the person upon whom the obligation is imposed or the right, power, or privilege is conferred need not be the grammatical subject. This occurs frequently in passive sentences, the use of which Coode explicitly opposed. For the sake of language concision and emphasizing the impersonal, legal rules are sometimes expressed in the passive voice today (*see* Chapter 6, 6.6). Despite criticism of Coode's work, it is significant that he singled out the legal action as the most important element of a legal rule. As Coode put it, the legal action (obligation, right, privilege, or power) is the element on which 'the whole function of legislation exercises and exhausts itself' (cited in Dodova 1989:75).

Possibly the most influential jurisprudent of the twentieth century, Hans Kelsen (1881–1973) and his followers in the Austrian School of Jurisprudence analyzed the prescriptive and descriptive elements of legal rules or norms, as they call them (1991:163–165). Legal norms are not limited to legislation but can be found in other normative instruments, including treaties, conventions, contracts, and even wills. Most legal norms consist of a descriptive fact-situation (propositional content) and a prescriptive statement of law (normative content) (Weinberger 1988:62). While the propositional content of the fact-situation describes the conditions under which the norm operates, the normative content of the statement of law prescribes the legal action to be taken. It is the principal verb in the statement of law which determines whether the legal action has the illocutionary force of ordering, prohibiting, permitting, or empowering. To lessen the degree of directness of legal norms, implicit performatives (*shall, may,* and their negatives) are used instead of explicit performatives (*order, forbid, permit*). Whereas earlier legal decrees, especially those of emperors, were written in the first person, legal norms are now written almost exclusively in the impersonal third person, as in Coode's example.

Legal translators must be able to identify the normative content expressed in the statement of law of the source norm and formulate a legal norm in the target text that leads to the same results. Translation problems arise because legal speech acts cannot be translated literally, thus preventing the translator from simply using the same form of the verb in the target text. Recognizing this as one of the greatest pitfalls in legal translation, Pigeon repeatedly warned francophone translators of Canadian legislation against using the future tense in French to translate the English imperative *shall:* 'C'est évident une erreur à éviter' (cited in Dick 1988:91).[9] The forms used to express legal speech acts are determined by drafting practices, not by rules of grammar. Accordingly, in order to formulate legal norms that express the intended normative content, legal translators cannot rely on contrastive linguistics but must be well versed in the drafting practices of both the source and target jurisdictions.[10]

9.   According to Bocquet, the use of the indicative future to express commands in French provisions is archaic. Although he remarks that some authors recommend the use of the indicative future in French commands in which the subject is a public authority, he notes that such distinction is not made in practice (1994:14).

10. The question of how to interpret the modal *shall* in legal speech acts is not a question of grammar, as Gémar suggests (1995–II:111), but rather a question of language usage in drafting practices. As a result, contrastive linguistic studies are sometimes more harmful than helpful for translators. For instance, Didier's table of correspondences (1990:292) is misleading when it says that obligations are expressed in English by the present or future indicative, and in French by the present or future indicative and the imperative.

Moreover, it is necessary for translators to determine whether the source provision is mandatory or directory and to formulate a legal norm with the same normative intensity, as it is called. Failure to distinguish between mandatory and directory provisions can have serious repercussions on the application of a legal rule in practice. Mandatory provisions are compulsory and non-compliance is punishable by sanction or may render the instrument or procedure invalid. On the other hand, directory provisions should be complied with; however, the court may rule that non-compliance is a mere error without invalidating the instrument or procedure (Walker 1980:802).

5.8. LEGAL COMMANDS AND REQUIREMENTS

A legal command imposes a duty upon the legal subject to act in a certain manner under given circumstances. Legal commands are mandatory provisions; hence failure to act accordingly is a violation of the law punishable by sanction. The English practice of imposing legal duties by the legal imperative *shall* is a longstanding practice dating back to English translations of Roman law texts. The first extant translation of *Magna Carta,* originally in Latin, has been called 'an exercise in *shall*' (Dodova 1989:72). One of the articles of the 1534 text published in Redman, *The Boke of Magna Carta, with divers other statutes translated into Englyshe*, reads as follows:

> No free man shall be taken or imprisoned or be disseised of his freehold or liberties, or free customs, or be outlawed or exiled or otherwise destroyed, nor we shall not pass upon him nor condem him but by lawful judgement or his peers or by the law of the land, we shall sell to noman we shall deny nor deferr to noman neither justice nor right.

In legal discourse a distinction is commonly made between commands and require-ments, the latter of which are expressed in English by the implicit performative *must* or by the present indicative of the principal predicate:

> *The application must be signed by the candidate.*
> *The candidate signs the application.*

Requirements indicate the existence of a duty that is usually procedural in nature; they may be either mandatory or directory. Failure to comply with a mandatory requirement may affect the validity of the instrument or procedure (Driedger 1976:14). Whereas the use of *must* makes it clear that the requirement is mandatory, the use of the present indicative is ambiguous. In such cases it is up to the judge to decide from the context whether the particular requirement is mandatory or directory.

5.8.1. Use of the imperative vs. normative indicative

The generalization that strong verbs such as *shall* and *must* are used in mandatory, and weak indicative verbs in directory provisions is only a half truth. The case against this generalization is even stronger in other jurisdictions where the use of the imperative is considered too direct, as a result of which the present indicative is preferred in mandatory provisions as well. Thus, as mentioned above, legal speech acts cannot be translated literally. In Canada it took the Silent Revolution to make lawmakers finally recognize and accept the fallacy of literal translation. In keeping with the tradition of literal translation in Canada (*see* Chapter 2, 2.8), the federal *Interpretation Act* in the Revised Statutes of Canada of 1970 prescribed the use of *doit* or *devra* (literally *will have to*) to express a duty in French as an equivalent to the imperative *shall* in English. Nonetheless, francophone translators and drafters became increasingly reluctant to use the prescribed forms. Desiring to write in 'natural French,' they favored using indicative forms to express both legal commands and requirements, a drafting practice dating back to the *Code civil de Napoléon* (*see* Villay 1974:39). During the drafting reform of the eighties, lawmakers finally relented and revised section 11 of the *Interpretation Act* [RSC 1985] to read as follows:

> L'obligation s'exprime essentiellement par l'indicatif présent du verbe porteur de sens principal et, à l'occasion, par des verbes ou expressions comportant cette notion.

Pursuant to section 11, legal commands as well as requirements are commonly expressed in French by the indicative present of the principal predicate and occasionally by special verbs (*est tenu, est obligé*) and indicative expressions (*il faut, est à* + *infinitive*) (on the practice in France, *see* Bocquet 1994:14). The following examples are from the *Criminal Code* of 1993:

An application *must be made* in writing	La demande *est formulée* par écrit	(276.1(2))
The jury and the public *shall be excluded*	Le jury et le public *sont exclus*	(276.2(1))
The jury *shall determine*	Le juge *est tenu de motiver* la décision	(276.2(3))
The reasons *shall be entered* in the record of the proceedings	Les motifs *sont à porter* dans le procès-verbal des débats	(297.2(4))

The *Règles de technique législative* of the EU prescribe the use of the present indicative to express mandatory provisions in French, confirm the exclusive use of the imperative *shall* in English, and warn against using the future tense:

> Les verbes exprimant des dispositions impératives s'emploient au présent indicatif... La formule utilisée en anglais étant toutefois *shall* plus l'infinitif. Le temps futur est à éviter (1985:23).

The use of the indicative present and special verbs to express legal obligations, a drafting practice also common in Russian legislation, is sometimes referred to as the

139

normative indicative. The use of the normative indicative is a commonly accepted practice not because the particular language is 'weak in future tenses,' as an American lawyer once implied in regard to the Soviet Criminal Code (*see* Dodova 1989:77, note 22), but because it is a method of expressing commands and requirements less directly (*see* Cornu 1990:270). On the other hand, the use of the normative indicative has the disadvantage of making it more difficult for translators to recognize commands and requirements as such. Although it can be argued that translators should be able to identify the intended normative intensity from the context, in many cases the text is ambiguous, thus forcing the translator to decide whether an indicative form in the source text is intended to express a command or a requirement and, in the case of requirements, whether the provision is mandatory or directory. Conversely, if translators use an indicative form in the target text to express a mandatory provision, they should make it clear that the provision is mandatory. Otherwise, if the intended normative intensity is ambiguous, judges are encouraged to use their discretion in interpreting it, thus endangering uniform interpretation and application.

This problem arose in *R. v. Voisine* (1984, 57 N.B.R. 2d 38 T.D.) which turned on an inconsistency in the English and French versions of subsection 104(2) of the New Brunswick *Fish and Wildlife Act*. At stake was the question whether the penalty provision expressed a mandatory minimum/maximum or whether it permitted sentencing discretion. While the English 'shall be imprisoned for a term of seven days for the first offence' left no sentencing discretion, the French version appeared to allow some discretion by stipulating that a person convicted of a named offense 'est passible d'une peine d'emprisonnement de sept jours pour une première infraction.' After consulting a dictionary and discovering that 'est passible' could mean either 'who must suffer' or 'who incurs a punishment,' the trial judge resolved the ambiguity by applying the less onerous alternative that permits discretionary sentencing. This decision, however, was reversed by the appeals judge who insisted that the obligatory sentencing of the English text could not be simply ignored. Investigating the legislative history of the provision, he traced the English source provision back to the *Game Act* of 1927 where it read: ' *shall... be liable* to imprisonment for a term of *not less than...*' [emphasis added]. Since the French translation was not enacted until the bilingual revision in 1973, the court concluded that the real intention of the legislator was expressed in the English text which clearly indicates that the penalty is meant to be a mandatory minimum (*see* Beaupré 1986:150–152).

5.8.2. Linguistic conformity reduces judicial discretion

Whereas francophone translators in Canada prefer to follow French drafting guidelines when formulating legal speech acts, this is not necessarily the case in Switzerland where francophone translators generally tend to favor linguistic conformity for the sake of reducing judicial discretion. In an attempt to avoid textual ambiguities and inconsistencies that allow judicial discretion and encourage litigation, Swiss drafting practices are more restrictive in regard to the formulation of legal speech acts in legal rules. Like their Anglo-Saxon colleagues, German-speaking drafters favor the use of imperatives to express commands and mandatory requirements. Accordingly, Swiss drafters use the imperative modal *muß* or special verbs for expressing the imperative such as *verpflichtet sein, haben* and *zu* plus infinitive (active), and *sein* and *zu* plus infinitive (passive). On the other hand, they are advised to avoid using the modal *soll* as it is generally interpreted as a warning or requirement that is to be fulfilled in normal cases, thus allowing discretion in borderline cases to decide whether and under which conditions exceptions are permitted (Gesetzgebungsleitfaden 1995:312). For the sake of uniformity, French and Italian translators and drafters are encouraged to follow Swiss German drafting techniques, a practice that is still honored today. As a result, the modals *doit* and *deve* or special forms that express the imperative are used in the French and Italian versions of Swiss legislation to express commands and mandatory requirements. There is clearly no doubt that the following provisions from the 1989 revisions of the Swiss *Obligations Act* are mandatory:

Art. 257f
DE: Der Mieter *muss* die Sache sorgfältig gebrauchen.
FR: Le locataire *est tenu* d'user de la chose avec le soin nécessaire.
IT: Il conduttore *è tenuto* alla diligneza nell'uso della cosa locata.

Art. 267(1)
DE: Der Mieter *muss* die Sache in dem Zustand zurückgeben, der sich aus dem vertragsgemässen Gebrauch ergibt.
FR: A la fin du bail, le locataire *doit* restituer la chose dans l'état qui résulte d'un usage conforme au contrat.
IT: Il conduttore *deve* restituire la cosa nello stato risultante da un uso conforme al contratto.

In regard to administrative sanctions, the Swiss Guidelines of 1976 recommended that mandatory provisions be explicitly designated as such, thus leaving no discretionary power to the administrative authority in question. As explained in the Guidelines (1976:25), this is a precautionary measure guaranteeing that all sanctions are imposed in accordance with the principle of administrative legality. On the other hand, in Swiss criminal legislation it is not uncommon to find mandatory provisions in the indicative present in the French, Italian, and even German texts. To be less direct, the indicative future is commonly used in the French and Italian versions of sentencing provisions (*sera puni, è punito*)[11] and indicative passive present in German (*wird bestraft*). As a means of avoiding ambiguity, a mandatory minimum penalty is indicated by the words *nicht unter,* a discretionary minimum and maximum

---

11. In the French text of Swiss criminal provisions it is common to use the indicative future in the statement of law expressing the sentence and indicative future anterior in the fact-situation listing the elements constituting the particular crime. This practice follows the old drafting principles of the French Penal Code of 1810. In an attempt to emphasize the abstract and timeless nature of acts prescribed by criminal provisions, the future tense has recently been replaced by the indicative present in the new French Penal Code of 1994 (*see* Bocquet 1994:16–17).

penalty by *von... bis zu,* a discretionary maximum penalty by *bis zu,* and the corresponding expressions in French and Italian. The following sentencing provision from Article 122 of the Swiss Criminal Code on intentional physical harm prescribes a discretionary maximum penalty up to 10 years in solitary confinement or a discretionary minimum/maximum prison sentence from six months to five years:

DE: Wer vorsätzlich einen Menschen lebensgefährlich verletzt,... *wird* mit Zuchthaus *bis zu* zehn Jahren oder mit Gefängnis *von* sechs Monaten *bis zu* fünf Jahren *bestraft.*

FR: Celui qui, intentionnellement, aura blessé une personne de façon à mettre sa vie en danger,... *sera puni* de la réclusion pour dix ans *au plus* ou de l'emprisonnement pour six mois *à* cinq ans.

IT: Chiunque intenzionalmente ferisce una persona mettendone in pericolo la vita,... *è punito* con la reclusione *sino a* dieci anni o con la detenzione *di* sei mesi *a* cinque anni.

5.9. PERMISSIONS AND AUTHORIZATIONS

In addition to imposing duties, legislative texts also confer rights, privileges, and powers on legal subjects in the form of permissions and authorizations (*cf.* Cornu 1990:269). Although their function differs, the same modals are used to express both permissions and authorizations: *may* (English), *kann/darf* (German), *peut* (French), *può* (Italian), and *podrá* (Spanish). While it is agreed that a permission expresses a facultative operation, there are cases where the courts have interpreted a permissive *may* as *shall,* thus turning it into a mandatory provision. Although authorizations can be construed as a duty, such provisions are usually ambiguous as to whether the performance of an authorized act is mandatory.

5.9.1. Permissions

Lawyers often say that an act that is not expressly prohibited is permitted. Yet there are a number of explicit permissions. By granting permissions, the legislature limits the number of potential prohibitions. More important, the granting of a permission is a means of cancelling a command, requirement, or prohibition or making an exception to a command, requirement, or prohibition. For example, there might be a provision that a corporation *may* perform an act that would otherwise be unlawful. In such provisions the granting of a permission can be regarded as an instrument of change (Weinberger 1988:62). Theoretically, a permission cannot be violated. In other words, it permits the performance of a specific action, but at the same time the non-performance of that action is also permitted. In this sense, a permission expresses a facultative operation which a person or institution is free to do if he/she/it choses to do so. For example, the following provision from the Swiss Civil Code permits the general assembly of a joint-stock company to dismiss at any time any liquidator it has appointed. The permission, however, is not violated if the general assembly does not dismiss a liquidator:

Art. 740(4)
DE: Die Generalversammlung *kann* die von ihr ernannten Liquidatoren jederzeit abberufen.
FR: L'assemblée générale *peut* en tout temps révoquer les liquidateurs qu'elle a nommés.
IT: L'assemblea generale *può* sempre revocare i liquidatori da essa nominati.

In view of the discretionary nature of permissions, the Swiss Guidelines of 1976 recommended that they be used in provisions with administrative sanctions only in borderline cases. As emphasized, the goal is to guarantee equal treatment of all citizens by eliminating discretion:

> Kann-Formeln räumen der zum Verwaltungszwang zuständigen Behörde ein gewisses Ermessen ein. Sie sind für Grenzfälle am Platz, im übrigen aber aus Gründen der Rechtsgleichheit zu vermeiden (1976:25).

The problem of guaranteeing equal treatment is even greater in the parallel texts of multilingual, multilateral treaties and conventions. To promote uniform interpretation and application of the single instrument, drafters and translators need to be particularly cautious when formulating the illocutionary force of speech acts in the legal rules of such instruments. In particular, the normative content of legal rules should be formulated clearly and consistently in the parallel texts of conventions whose purpose is to establish uniform laws in the jurisdictions of the signatory States. When interpreting treaties and conventions, the courts are supposed to consult each text and reconcile the meaning in the event of any textual inconsistency or ambiguity. Too often, however, they rely on a single text, thus jeopardizing uniform interpretation (*see* Chapter 7, 7.6.2). One of the purposes of the New York Convention on the Recognition and Enforcement of Foreign Arbitral Awards (1958) is to make the law more predictable in regard to the recognition and enforcement of foreign awards. Yet the normative content is inconsistent in the statement of law of Article V(1), which prescribes the action to be taken by the court when one of the grounds for refusing enforcement is proven. As a rule, recognition and enforcement is not refused unless the defendant proves the existence of one of the specified grounds for refusal. This is expressed in the French text of Article V(1) as follows:

> La reconnaissance et l'exécution de la sentence *ne seront refusées*, sur requète de la partie contre laquelle elle est invoquée, *que si cette partie fournit* à l'autorité compétente du pays où la reconnaissance et l'exécution sont demandées, la preuve:...

In the English text, however, the use of the permissive *may* implies that the court can use its discretion to determine whether to enforce an award even when one of the grounds contained in Article V is proved (Dicey & Morris 1980:1150).

> Recognition and enforcement of the award *may be refused,* at the request of the party against whom it is invoked, *only if that party furnishes* to the competent authority where the recognition and enforcement is sought, proof that:...

143

This raises the question as to the real legislative intent. Despite the use of a permissive in the English text, relative case law shows that the courts have refused to execute an award in the vast majority of cases where it is clear that one of the grounds for refusal exists. Nonetheless, it appears that the real legislative intent was not to express a command. This view is supported by the fact that the delegates to the Convention refused a West German proposal to formulate the opening words of the English text of Article V as a command: 'Recognition and enforcement of the award *shall be refused* if...' (*see* van den Berg 1996:80).

Although drafting experts of common law legislation insist that '*may* never means *shall* and that *shall* never means *may*' (Driedger 1983:13), judges admit that in certain circumstances the word *may* is interpreted to mean *shall*. This appears to be common practice in the construction of legal rules in Spanish legislative texts. According to Dahl, the term *podrá* in Spanish legislation means *may*; however, it may be interpreted as *shall*, 'when the principal aim or purpose of the statute is that the thing permitted be done' (1992:240). The fact that a permissive is also used in the Spanish text of Article V(1) suggests that the real legislative intent was to express a permission:

> *Sólo se podrá denegar* el reconocimiento y la ejecución de la sentencia, a instancia de la parte contra la cual es invocada, *si esta parte prueba* ante la autoridad competente del pais en que se pide el reconocimiento y la ejecución:...

By using a permissive, the legislators have left the door open for the courts to base their ruling on the circumstances of the particular case. On the other hand, the French text does not favor such discretion.

To prevent unintended discretion in the interpretation of legal rules containing *may* and *shall*, drafters and translators need to make a clear distinction between commands and permissions. While there have been cases in Canada where the courts have interpreted *shall* as *may*, the Supreme Court of Canada took a clear stand in *Attorney General of Manitoba* v. *Forest* ([1979] 2 S.C.R. 1032) by maintaining that the use of *shall* and *may* in section 133 of the *Constitution Act, 1867* and in section 23 of the *Manitoba Act, 1870* was deliberate and thus obliges the province to print and publish all legislation in both languages. In the French text of section 133 *shall* appears as *sera obligatoire* at one point and as *devront être* at another, while *may* is first expressed as *sera facultatif* and later as *pourra être... à faculté*. The wording in section 23 is almost identical, thus leaving no room for discretion.[12] In this landmark decision the Supreme Court struck down the English only clause of Manitoba's *Official Language Act, 1890* as unconstitutional.

---

12. The following provision of section 133 is clearly mandatory: 'The Acts of the Parliament of Canada and of the Legislature of Quebec shall be printed and published in both of those languages. / Les actes du parlement du Canada et de la législature de Québec devront être imprimés et publiés dans ces deux langues.' The same is true of section 23 of the *Manitoba Act, 1870*: 'The Acts of the Legislature shall be printed and published in both of those languages. / Les actes de la législature seront imprimés et publiés dans des deux langues.'

5.9.2. Authorizations

An authorization is a special type of legal speech act in which the permissives *may, kann, peut,* and *puo* can be construed as expressing a duty. Technically speaking, authorizations confer power upon some person or authority to perform an act which otherwise that person or authority would be without power to perform. Whereas it is not surprising that linguists often fail to recognize authorizations as a special type of legal speech act (e.g., Trosborg 1991:82), the same cannot be said of lawyers. Although Coode recognized power-conferring acts as one of the basic legal actions, it appears that authorizations have received little attention in studies by jurisprudents (*see* Weinberger 1988:64). In regard to the interpretation of authorizations, the question arises as to how one can determine when performance of an authorized act is mandatory. As mentioned above, the modal *may* and its equivalents do not express a duty. Therefore, if there is a duty to perform the authorized act, it usually arises 'out of the purpose and text of the statute and the facts of the particular case' (Driedger 1983:13). In Canada there have been a number of cases in which the courts have had to decide whether an empowering *may* is mandatory. In *Re Falconbridge Nickel Mines and Minister of Revenue* ((1979), 100 D.L.R.(3d) 570), the statute invoked provided that an overpayment of tax *may* be refunded. Against the plaintiff's argument that *may* ought to be interpreted as being mandatory, the court maintained that the intention was to allow the Minister discretion in the matter. On the other hand, in *Clarkson Co. Ltd. v. White* (1979), 32 C.B.R. (N.S. 25), the relevant authorization ('the court *may* give judgment to the trustee against the other party to the transaction') was construed as being obligatory. Hart J.A. summarized the court's reasoning as follows:

> Normally when the power to be conferred may be exercised upon the establishment of legal rights in favour of some person there is a duty to exercise the power when the rights have been established (cited in Driedger 1983:11).

Following Sourioux and Lerat, Didier refers to authorizations as *le facultatif,* thus stressing that the authorized person or authority has the option to decide whether to perform the act or not. The French verbs used to express authorizations also do not make it clear whether an authorization is intended to be construed as a duty: *peut, a la possiblité, est autorisé, est habilité, est reçu* (Sourioux and Lerat 1975:50; Didier 1990:86). This is the case in regard to the inspector's authorization in section 251.(1) of the *Canada Labour Code* (1993) which reads as follows:

Where an inspector finds that an employer has failed to pay an employee any wages or other amounts to which the employee is entitled under this Part, *the inspector may determine the difference...*	S'il constate que l'employeur n'a pas versé à l'employé le salaire ou une autre indemnité auxquels celui-ci a droit sous le régime de cette partie, *l'inspecteur peut déterminer lui-même la différence...*

5.10. PROHIBITIONS

Prohibitions are legal speech acts with the illocutionary force of forbidding. The most common type of prohibitions are acts that persons and/or an authority are explicitly forbidden to perform and whose performance is punishable by sanction. In view of their obligatory nature, Weinberger regards such prohibitions as negative commands: X is obliged to refrain from performing act A; if X performs act A, he/she/it is subject to punishment (1988:61). As the very opposite of commands, prohibitions are expressed in English with the negation *shall not* and in German with *darf nicht.* The German term *kann nicht* is also used to express prohibitions, as are the Dutch, French, and Italian terms *kann niet, ne peut,* and *non puo.* Universal prohibitions apply to all persons; they are commonly expressed by negating the subject, as in the following example from Article 13 of the Belgian Constitution:

NL: *Niemand kan* tegen zijn wil worden afgetrokken van de rechter die de wet hem toekent.
FR: *Nul ne peut* être distrait, contre son gré, du juge que la loi lui assigne.
DE: *Niemand darf* gegen seinen Willen seinem gesetzlichen Richter entzogen werden.

Some prohibitions are negations of permissions or authorizations. Such prohibitions come about as a result of the withdrawal of a permission or authorization, thus prohibiting an act that was once explicitly permitted or authorized, or as a result of an exception to a permission or authorization. Thus it is common practice for a general permission to be followed by a prohibition withdrawing the permission in specific situations. For example, Article 128(1) of the Swiss Civil Code permits a marriage entered into by a person who does not fulfill the marriage requirements, is not of age or who has been deprived of his/her legal capacity to be annulled by the person's mother, father, or guardian. Exceptions to the general permission, i.e., situations in which the permission cannot be exercized, are specified in paragraph 2 of the same Article as follows:

DE: Eine Ungültigerklärung *darf* jedoch *nicht* mehr erfolgen, wenn inzwischen der Ehegatte ehefähig oder mündig oder...
FR: La nullité *ne peut* plus être déclarée lorsque les époux ont dans l'intervalle atteint l'âge requis, obtenu ou recouvré l'exercice des droits civils...
IT: La nullità *non può* tuttavia essere pronunciata se nel frattempo il coniuge è diventato capace o maggiorenne...

As a rule, the performance of an act that is explicitly prohibited invalidates the underlying procedure or transaction; however, the court may choose to rule otherwise if the circumstances of the case warrant such decision, as in cases where the prohibited action qualifies as the restriction of a right. For example, in *Gema* v. *Gerber* (1934), the Swiss Federal Court had to decide whether the fact that the joint stock company Gema had purchased its own shares, an act prohibited under Article 659 of the Obligations Act, rendered the transaction invalid. This, in turn, would make the plaintiff's claim unfounded and release the defendant from the obligation to pay the purchase price of the stocks. From the wording of the three texts, *ne peut acquérir, non puo acquistare* and *darf nicht erwerben*, it is clear that the act is prohibited, thus suggesting that the underlying transaction should be declared invalid. On the other hand, the language of the proceedings was German, and the German text used the form *darf nicht erwerben* instead of *kann nicht erwerben*. Since *darf nicht erwerben* was regarded at that time as the weaker form, the Court reasoned:

> Der Wortlaut *darf nicht erwerben* ist jedoch nicht eindeutig. Immerhin läßt er eher eine blosse Einschränkung der Handlungsfreiheit vermuten, im Gegensatz zum Ausdruck *Nichtkönnen*, der auch die Möglichkeit ausschliesst, die gewollte rechtliche Wirkung hervorzubringen. Aus dem Wort *darf* ist somit zum mindesten nichts gegen die Rechtsbeständigkeit des Erwerbsaktes herzuleiten (BGE 60 II:315).

Conceding that the wording *darf nicht erwerben* is ambiguous, the Court chose to interpret the prohibition as the restriction of a right. In view of the circumstances of the case, the Court ruled that the performance of the particular prohibition did not affect the validity of the underlying transaction, thus upholding the decision of the lower court. As for the French and Italian texts, the Court contended that the forms *ne peut* and *non puo* are used as equivalents for both *kann nicht* and *darf nicht* (BGE 60 II:313–321).[13]

Such issues are of importance for translators because they must understand how legal speech acts are construed by the courts. In order to produce an unambiguous text that will promote uniform interpretation, translators must be able to recognize the normative content of a statement of law in the source text and produce a text that leads to the same legal effects. If the linguistic forms in the source text are ambiguous, translators should be able to identify the intended normative content from the context. As a note of caution, however, translators must guard against overstepping their authority when resolving such ambiguities. Whereas it is legitimate for judges to use their discretion to construe the normative content of an ambiguous statement of law in light of the purpose and object of the text as a whole, translators have no such decision-making authority. Consultation with the drafter of the original is the best way to resolve such ambiguities (*see* Chapter 4, 4.3).

5.11. UNCONDITIONAL COMMANDS, PERMISSIONS, AUTHORIZATIONS, AND PROHIBITIONS

As emphasized earlier, the most common form of the legal rule is the conditional sentence with the statement of law prescribing the legal action to be taken in the main clause and the fact-situation describing the conditions under which the rule operates in the subordinate clause. There are, however, some legal rules which consist exclusively of a statement of law. In such cases, the legal action is unconditional, i.e., not subject to any conditions whatsoever (*see* Koch and Rüßmann 1982:20),

---

13. Today the Swiss *Gesetzgebungsleitfaden* (1995:313) recommends the use of '*dürfen nicht*' to express prohibitions.

thus making a fact-situation unnecessary. Commonly used to express the civil rights of citizens in constitutions and other instruments, such legal rules have the illocutionary force of ordering, permitting, or prohibiting. The following example in Dutch, French, and German is an unconditional prohibition from the Belgian Constitution which officially became trilingual in 1991:

Art. 17
NL: De straf van verbeurdverklaring der goederen kan niet worden ingevoerd.
FR: La peine de la confiscation des biens ne peut être établie.
DE: Die Strafe der Vermögenskonfiskation darf nicht eingeführt werden.

Unlike criminal law provisions, constitutional provisions usually prescribe no punishment for violators. Instead, any act by a person or authority that violates a citizen's civil rights will be declared unconstitutional by the constitutional or other competent court and adequate compensation awarded to the violated citizen. Civil rights are usually universal in that they apply to all persons on the territory of the particular state. Thus if the subject of an unconditional norm is a person, it is often *all persons, everyone* or the negation *no person*. The following example from the Belgian Constitution is an unconditional, universal right. Rights are a special form of permission often expressed with *have a right* (EN), *hat ein Recht, ist berechtigt* (DE), *a le droit, il est loisible* (FR), *heeft het recht* (NL):

Art. 22(3)
NL: Ieder *heeft recht* op onderwijs, met eerbiediging van de fundamentele rechten en vrijheden.
FR: Chacun *a droit* à l'enseignement dans le respect des libertés et droits fondamentaux.
DE: Jeder *hat ein Recht* auf Unterricht unter Berücksichtigung der Grundfreiheiten und Grundrechte.

Authorizations are frequently unconditional, especially those which empower a lawmaking or other body to enact rules and regulations. The following example is from the Swiss Code of Obligations:

Art. 257e(4)
DE: Die Kantone *können* ergänzende Bestimmungen erlassen.
FR: Les cantons *peuvent* édicter des dispositions complémentaires.
IT: I Cantoni *possono* emanare disposizioni complementari.

5.12. PROPOSITIONAL CONTENT OF THE FACT-SITUATION

Although translators should concentrate first and foremost on translating the statement of law correctly, the propositional content of the fact-situation must also be translated as accurately as possible. In a rare statement about translation, Weinberger remarks that the translation of a fact-situation is exact if it expresses the same propositional content as the source text (1988:54). While Weinberger's comment is correct, he does not say how one can determine whether the propositional content is the same in the source and target texts. Since the success of a legal translation is measured by the results in practice, the propositional content of a legal norm can be deemed to be the same in parallel texts if the fact-situation is interpreted and applied uniformly by the courts regardless of language. Accordingly, the propositional content of a legal norm is the same in texts A and B if the established facts of a particular case that can be subsumed under text A can also be subsumed under text B and vice versa. Although translators do not interpret and apply the text like a judge, they should be able to foresee in which situations the abstract fact-situation of a legal rule will be declared operative and formulate the elements of the fact-situation in the target norm accordingly. The difficulty of this task should not be underestimated. Due to the conceptual incongruency between legal systems, it is sometimes extremely difficult to select equivalents that will guarantee uniform interpretation and application of the propositional content of a legal norm. Thus, in the so-called search for equivalents (*see* Chapter 8, 8.5), it no longer suffices for translators to merely identify the closest corresponding equivalents in the source and target legal systems. They must also be able to analyze their conceptual similarities and differences (*cf.* Bocquet 1994:7) and, if possible, compensate for any conceptual differences that might endanger uniform interpretation and application of the propositional content.

5.12.1. Compensating for conceptual incongruency

Undoubtedly the translator's greatest challenge when translating the fact-situation of a legal rule is to find suitable ways of compensating for conceptual incongruency (*see* details in Chapter 8, at 8.9). As illustrated by the Warsaw Convention of 1929, the fate of an instrument may be determined by the translator's ability to compensate for conceptual incongruency, especially in the case of treaties and conventions authenticated in more than one language. Since such instruments must be interpreted and applied in all jurisdictions of the signatory States, the use of national or system-bound terms as constituents of a fact-situation is particularly problematic. This includes the use of common law and civil law terms for which there are no close equivalents. In the case of the Warsaw Convention for the Unification of Certain Rules relating to International Carriage by Air, the use of incongruent terms in the fact-situation of a key provision ultimately led to the failure of the Convention.

Instead of promoting uniform interpretation and application, the disputed fact-situation of Article 25(1) resulted in conflicting decisions, thus defeating the very purpose of the Convention, i.e., to protect international carriers by placing universally accepted caps on compensation claims. The fact-situation of the said provision is of particular importance because it specifies the conditions describing situations in which the provisions of the Convention excluding or limiting the carrier's liability do not apply, thus permitting victims to evade application of the Convention and invoke unlimited liability. The problem hinges on the use of the term *dol* in the French original, a concept unknown in the common law. Article 25(1) originally read as follows:

Statement of law	*Fact-situation*
Le transporteur n'aura pas le droit de se prévaloir des dispositions de la présente convention qui excluent ou limitent sa responsabilité,	si le dommage provient *de son dol* ou d'une autre faute qui, d'après la loi du tribunal saisi, est considérée *comme équivalente au dol.*

In the absence of an exact equivalent, the closest equivalent of *dol* in the common law, i.e., *wilful misconduct*, was proposed for the English translation. Despite warning by the English delegate that *wilful misconduct* includes not only acts performed with intention but also acts performed carelessly without regard for the consequences (Mankiewicz 1962:466), the delegation approved the following translation:

Statement of law	*Fact-situation*
The carrier shall not be entitled to avail himself of the provisions of this Convention which exclude or limit his liability,	if the damage is caused *by his wilful misconduct* or by such default on his part as, in accordance with the law of the Court seized of the case, is considered to be *equivalent to wilful misconduct.*

As a result, it is not surprising that there were conflicting decisions in similar cases. Since an act that qualifies as wilful misconduct under Anglo-American law is not necessarily done with intent and vice versa, in cases where a continental court would rule in favor of limited liability, American and English courts are inclined to declare the carrier to have unlimited liability (Mankiewicz 1962:467). This occurs particularly in cases involving deaths and bodily injuries resulting from acts not caused with intention. By characterizing such acts as wilful misconduct, the courts are no longer required to apply the provisions of the Convention excluding or limiting compensation, thus providing a loophole to evade the Convention altogether.

It appears that lawyers learned a lesson from the mistakes of the delegates who approved the defective translation of Article 25 of the Warsaw Convention. Above all, the failure of the Warsaw Convention showed the need for drafters and translators to cooperate in overcoming conceptual incongruency. While the blame was first placed entirely on the translators, lawyers later admitted that the drafters were also at fault for using a civil law term that has no adequate counterpart in the common law. In translation theory it is often argued that a translation can be no better than the source text if the translator has no authority to improve or alter the text. Since drafters are not always aware of the potential pitfalls resulting from conceptual incongruency, they should consult translators and other experts on particularly sensitive matters.

One way to compensate for conceptual incongruency is to avoid the use of technical and other system-bound terms that have no close equivalent in the other jurisdiction(s). Instead, elements of the fact-situation can be explained by using descriptive paraphrases. This method was used in the revised formulation of the disputed fact-situation of Article 25 of the Warsaw Convention. As amended by the Hague Protocol of 1955, Article 25 reads as follows in both authentic texts:

Les limites de responsabilité prévues à l'article 22 ne s'appliquent pas s'il est prouvé que le dommage résulte d'un acte ou d'une omission du transporteur ou de ses préposés fait, *soit avec l'intention de provoquer un dommage, soit témérairement et avec conscience qu'un dommage en résultera probablement,* pour autant que, dans le cas d'un acte ou d'une omission de préposés, la preuve soit également apportée que ceux-ci ont agi dans l'exercice de leurs fonctions.

The limits of liability specified in Article 22 shall not apply if it is proved that the damage resulted from an act or omission of the carrier, his servants or agents *done with intent to cause damage or recklessly and with the knowledge that damage would probably result*; provided that, in the case of such an act or omission of a servant or agent, it is also proved that he was acting in the scope of his employment.
[Emphasis added in both texts].

For the sake of coordination, the concept of *dol* is explained not only in the English but also in the French text (in italics). The explanation of *dol* in the English text prevents common law courts from applying Article 25 in all situations that qualify as *wilful misconduct* in the common law, thus promoting uniform interpretation and application. Unfortunately, by the time the amendment was proposed, there were already so many conflicting court decisions that it was deemed too late to salvage the Convention. Although descriptive paraphrases can be useful in overcoming conceptual incongruency in legal translation, theorists of general translation often disapprove of the use of paraphrases, which Newmark calls 'the translator's last resort' (1982:130; *see* Reiß 1990:41–53).

5.12.2. The importance of logical connectors

In legal texts it is particularly important to express the intended logical relations correctly in each language version. A potential pitfall when translating the fact-situation of legal norms is presented by the logical connectors *and / or,* which are so beguilingly simple that drafters and translators sometimes overlook their important function. As in ordinary language, the connector *and* is conjunctive, whereas *or* is disjunctive. In legal texts, the function of these connectors takes on added significance as it may be decisive in determining whether a person has committed a crime, whether a contracting party has fulfilled its obligations and so forth. If the conditions specified in the fact-situation are connected by *and,* this signifies that they are to be applied cumulatively. Conversely, the use of the connector *or* means that the stipulated conditions are to be applied alternatively. This can be illustrated by the following examples:

A: If X does A, B and C, X shall be liable to punishment.
B: If X does A, B or C, X shall be liable to punishment.

In the first example, X is liable to punishment only if he/she performs all three acts (A + B + C). If the disjunctive connector is used, he/she is liable to punishment if he/she performs any of the three acts (A or B or C).

151

Thus it follows that a translation error involving these logical connectors endangers uniform application and can have farreaching legal implications. Assuming that the source text is unambiguous, the use of the wrong logical connector can usually be attributed to inaccuracy, often because of time pressure to meet a deadline. Translators need to be especially cautious when using logical connectors as such mistakes frequently go unnoticed during scrutinization of the texts. If the source text is ambiguous, the translator should have the ambiguity clarified and revised by the drafter immediately. If this is not possible, the translator should determine the legislative intent by consulting other competent experts, preferably prior to authentication. The lack of cooperation between drafters and translators frequently results in inconsistencies that could otherwise have been avoided. For example, prior to the 1970 revision of the Swiss Criminal Code, Article 42 of the French text provided that a recidivist was liable to indefinite confinement if any of three conditions was fulfilled, i.e., if he was 'penchant au crime ou au délit, à l'inconduite *ou* à la fainéantise.' On the contrary, pursuant to the Italian text, all three conditions had to be fulfilled cumulatively in order for a recidivist to be sentenced to indefinite confinement. Since the German source text was ambiguous, the Federal Court could not base its decision on the principle of the majority (two out of three texts), as it frequently does. Construing the provision in the light of the scheme and spirit of the law, the Federal Court relied on the French text and applied the conditions alternatively (von Overbeck 1984:982, 984).

Particularly in common law jurisdictions, drafters often prefer to place a series of conditions in a column, thus making them easier to understand by virtue of their being set apart. When tabular enumeration is used, the question arises as to how drafters and translators are to indicate whether the conditions are to be applied cumulatively or alternatively. Whereas it is common to insert the appropriate logical connector before the final condition in the English text, the authors of the *Guide Canadien de rédaction législative française* now insist that the French text need not follow the English practice. In their opinion, it suffices to make the distinction by inserting explanatory words in the introductory text such as *dans le cas suivant* (cumulative) or *selon le cas* (alternative) (*Guide Canadien* 1991: énumération verticale). In the following example from section 58(4) of the *Official Languages Act,* the French phrase 'dans l'un ou l'autre des cas suivants' makes it clear that the conditions apply alternatively:

The Commissioner may refuse to investigate or cease to investigate any complaint if in the opinion of the Commissioner
(a) the subject-matter of the complaint is trivial;
(b) the complaint is frivolous or vexatious or is not made in good faith; *or*
(c) the subject-matter of the complaint does not involve a contravention or failure to comply with the spirit and intent of this Act, or does not for any other reason come within

Le commissaire peut, à son appréciation, refuser ou cesser d'instruire une plainte *dans l'un ou l'autre des cas suivants*:
a) elle est sans importance;

b) elle est futile ou vexatoire ou n'est pas faite de bonne foi;
c) son objet ne constitue pas une contravention à la présente loi ou une violation de son esprit et de l'intention du législateur ou, pour toute autre raison, ne relève pas de la com-

152

the authority of the Commissioner   pétence du commissaire.
under this Act.

5.13. THE ROLE OF LEGAL DEFINITIONS

While some legal definitions are formulated by judges and legal scholars, the majority are set forth in normative legal instruments, especially legislation. Such definitions are referred to as statutory definitions. Vested with the force of law, statutory definitions are widely regarded as being prescriptive (*cf.* Wank 1985:65). This may be the reason for the older practice of formulating definitions in English with *shall mean* rather than with the indicative *means* which is used in English texts today in accordance with the notion that the law is always speaking. Although Bowers admits that this change is 'justifiable on all grounds,' he feels that it has left definitions 'in an illocutionary and interpretive twilight zone, with the result that courts do not regard them as being of the same status as other provisions.' While Bowers maintains that this reduces the effectiveness of definitions considerably (1989:177), his remarks seem rather misguided. As Driedger points out, the *shall* in older definitions did not impose an obligation to be obeyed or disobeyed but merely expressed the authoritative power of the lawmaker to create rules of law (Driedger 1976:13).

Today, legal definitions are generally regarded as aids for interpretation that promote clarity by reducing indeterminacy and help achieve consistency. Above all, they promote uniform interpretation and application by enabling courts to know with some degree of certainty 'whether a particular set of facts amount to a particular category for the purposes of legal consequences, e.g., whether an association is a "partnership" or a building a "factory" or a death in particular circumstances "manslaughter"' (Walker 1980:346). According to Bowers, legal definitions are either explanatory or stipulative. While explanatory definitions 'provide a necessary degree of definiteness' without altering conventional significations (Thornton 1987:54), stipulative definitions alter 'the ordinary meaning of words by narrowing or enlarging their sense or by creating a wholly new meaning for them' (Bowers 1989:173). For the most part, the formulation of a definition is determined by its position in the instrument. For example, in Canadian legislation both explanatory and stipulative definitions are placed in the definition section of the preliminary provisions or, if they apply to a particular Part of an Act, in the principal provisions at the beginning of that Part. Generally speaking, there are more definitions in common law than civil law legislation.[14] In civil law legislation, definitions of ordinary terms are usually placed in a definition section in the preliminary provisions or following the general provisions, while definitions of technical terms are in-

---

14.   Wank views the abundance of statutory definitions in common law jurisdictions as a means of deliberately limiting judicial discretion, while civil law jurisdictions tend to encourage judges to use their own discretion: 'Der kontinentaleuropäische Gesetzgeber sieht den Richter hingegen als "denkenden Diener", der das Gesetz vernünftig im Sinne des Gesetzgebers interpretieren wird. Er verzichtet daher weitgehend auf Legaldefinitionen' (1985:64).

153

corporated into the principal provisions. In both common law and civil law legislation, definitions in the definition section are formulated as definitions, whereas
those appearing in the main body of the instrument usually take the form of 'real'
provisions. Although they do not impose obligations or grant rights, definitions in
the substantive provisions can be regarded as having a lawmaking function (Lampe
1970:41).

5.13.1. Definitions in the definition section

Like ordinary definitions, legal definitions can be either intensional or extensional.
While intensional definitions cite the essential features constituting the core sense
of the *definiendum*, extensional definitions list the objects denoted and/or not denoted
by the *definiendum*. Whereas dictionary definitions of ordinary terms are primarily
intensional, a large number of statutory definitions are extensional. Without giving
assistance on the meaning of the *definiendum*, extensional definitions define its scope
of application by enumerating those objects to which it applies or does not apply in
that instrument, as in the following example:

> 'Securities' includes bonds, debentures and obligations, secured or unsecured, whether
> issued within or outside Canada, and rights in respect of such bonds, debentures and
> obligations, but does not include shares of capital stock of corporations or rights in
> respect of such shares (cited in Driedger 1976:46).

When translating legal definitions it is essential to express the proper logical
relations. Generally speaking, legal definitions set the limits of the *definiendum* by
expressing logical relations of equivalence (X means Y), inclusion (X includes Y),
and exclusion (X does not include Y) as well as combinations of equivalence and
inclusion (X means Y and includes Z) or equivalence and exclusion (X means Y but
does not include Z). Without differentiating between intensional and extensional
definitions, Driedger divides legal definitions into six groups (1976:45–47). These
are explained below and illustrated by examples which, unless indicated otherwise,
are taken from the Canadian *Trust and Loan Companies Act* [SC 1991]:

1) Definitions which delimit meaning by expressing equivalence; they may but need
   not alter the ordinary meaning:

'person' *means* a natural person, an entity or a personal representative;	'personne' Personne physique, entité ou représentant personnel.

2) Definitions which restrict a term to a particular thing without changing its
   ordinary meaning:

'company' *means* a body corporate to which this Act applies;	'société' Toute personne morale régie par la présente loi.

3) Definitions which narrow the ordinary meaning by exclusion; things ordinarily included are excluded either by setting limits or by expressly excluding:

'earth' does not include topsoil and peat;	'terre' Exclut le sol arable et la tourbe.[15]
'grain' includes wheat, oats, barley and rye;	'grains' Compris parmi les grains le blé, l'avoine, l'orge et le seigle.[16]

4) Definitions which enlarge the ordinary meaning by adding a meaning it does not

normally have:

'real property' *includes* a lease-hold interest in real property;	'biens immeubles' *Sont assimilés aux* biens immeubles les droits découlant des baux immobiliers.
'guarantee' *includes* a letter of credit;	'garantie' S'entend *notamment* d'une lettre de crédit.

5) Definitions which delimit the ordinary meaning and then expressly include or exclude a meaning for the purpose of emphasis:

'fiduciary' *means* any person acting in a fiduciary capacity and includes a personal representative of a deceased person;	'représentant' Toute personne agissant à ce titre, *notamment* le représentant personnel d'une personne décédée.
'affairs' with respect to a company, *means* the relationships among the company and its affiliates and the shareholders, directors and officers of the company and its affiliates, *but does not include* the business of the company or any of its affiliates;	'affaires internes' Les relations entre une société, les entités de son groupe et leurs actionnaires, administrateurs et dirigeants, *à l'exclusion* de leur activité commerciale.

6) Definitions which are used to abbreviate, particularly names of corporations, officials, bodies, etc.:

'Minister' *means* the Minister of Finance;	'ministre' Le ministre des Finances.

The French texts of the above examples show to what extent Canadian francophone drafters and translators have succeeded in adopting their own style of formulating definitions. Such stylistic differences are acceptable as long as the intended logical

---

15. Source: *Aggregate Resources Act of Ontario* [*Revised Statutes of Ontario* 1990].
16. Source: *Canadian Wheat Board Act* [*RSC* 1985].

155

relations are expressed correctly and the information content remains unchanged. The most notable difference in the above examples is the absence of a verb in the French text to express equivalence (*means*). In English definitions, *includes* is sometimes used not to express inclusion but rather to 'settle doubt' as to whether the word means a particular thing (Driedger 1976:46). In such cases it is used instead of *means* to express equivalence and should be translated as such. According to the *Guide Canadien*, no verb is used in the French text in such cases. Otherwise, inclusion is expressed in French definitions by *est assimilé, est compris parmi, notamment, en outre,* and *y compris* (depending on context), and exclusion by *à l'exclusion de* (*see* examples in *Guide Canadien* 1991: définitions). In Canada the two texts must no longer be exact images of each other. Moreover, each text lists definitions according to its own alphabetical order, as a result of which corresponding definitions are not necessarily side by side in the definition section. Sometimes it occurs in Canadian legislation that the definition of a term appears in one text but not in the other. This occurs, for example, if the meaning of a term is unclear in one language only, thus making a definition in the other language superfluous. The omission of a definition in one of the texts is indicated in a marginal note next to the definition in the other text, as in the following example from the *Trust and Loan Companies Act*:

'prescribed' *Version anglaise seule-ment*   'prescribed' means prescribed by regulation.

5.13.2. Definitions in principal provisions

As a rule, legal definitions incorporated into the principal provisions of legislative texts are formulated like 'real' provisions. Accordingly, inverted commas or italics are no longer used and the *definiendum* is not referred to as a term. In English texts, instead of *means* or *includes,* expressions such as *is* or *is deemed to be* are commonly used (*cf.* Bowers 1989:177). The following example cited by Bowers shows how the same definition would be formulated in the definition section and as a provision in the main body of the instrument:

In the definition section:
'pensionable age' means –
(a) in the case of a man, the age of 65
(b) in the case of a woman, the age of 60

In the principal provisions of the instrument:
The pensionable age of a man is the age of 65, and of a woman, the age of 60.

Definitions in the principal provisions contain descriptive material but have a lawmaking function in that they establish the legal criteria of terms. Although drafters are discouraged from placing lengthy definitions in the main body of an instrument, this cannot always be avoided. Definitions which define individual elements of the fact-situation of a legal rule can be regarded as constituting an extended fact-situation. In criminal provisions of common law legislation, it is common to define an offense or a crime by enumerating its constituent elements and situational components in an extended fact-situation. For example, to determine in which situation the death of a newly-born child qualifies as infanticide pursuant to the *Canadian Criminal Code*, the judge relies on the extensional definition of *infanticide* in the extended fact-situation in section 233:

<table>
<tr><td>

A female person commits infanticide when by a wilful act or omission she causes the death of her newly-born child, if at the time of the act or omission she is not fully recovered from the effects of giving birth to the child and by reason thereof or of the effect of lactation consequent on the birth of the child her mind is then disturbed.

</td><td>

Une personne du sexe féminin commet un infanticide lorsque par un acte ou une omission volontaire, elle cause la mort de son enfant nouveau-né, si au moment de l'acte ou de l'omission elle n'est pas complète-ment remise d'avoir donné naissance à l'enfant et si, de ce fait ou par suite de la lactation consécutive à la naissance de l'enfant, son esprit est alors déséquilibré.

</td></tr>
</table>

The legal rule on infanticide is set forth in section 237 which reads as follows:

<table>
<tr><td>

Every female person who commits infanticide is guilty of an indictable offence and liable to imprisonment for a term not exceeding five years.

</td><td>

Toute personne de sexe féminin qui commet un infanticide est coupable d'un acte criminel et passible d'un emprisonnement maximal de cinq ans.

</td></tr>
</table>

Accuracy is the top priority in the translation of definitions. For the sake of promoting equality in the administration of justice, translations of definitions must contain all the elements of the source definition and express the same logical relations. This is particularly important in criminal provisions which define the kinds of conduct, the circumstances, and the concomitant mental or other factors which amount to crimes. Since such acts are subject to punishment by fine, imprisonment, or even death (in some jurisdictions), stylistic creativity is discouraged. This can be seen in the example of the definition of infanticide above; here the French text follows the original English as closely as possible.

Contrary to ordinary definitions, legal definitions are often negative, i.e., they define terms by specifying what they are not instead of what they are (e.g.: X is non-Y). For example, section 234 of the *Canadian Criminal Code* defines manslaughter as follows: 'Culpable homicide that is not murder or infanticide is manslaughter.' In other words, manslaughter is an act of culpable homicide that does not qualify as murder or infanticide pursuant to sections 231–233. Accordingly, to prove that a defendant has committed manslaughter, prosecution must present facts establishing that the accused has committed culpable homicide but not murder or infanticide. Generally speaking, translators are warned against tampering with the wording of definitions as even the slightest change may affect the logical relations and the facts to be established. In some cases, the burden of proof could be affected as well. It is absolutely essential that all authentic texts express the intended burden of proof (*see* Chapter 6, 6.5.1).

157

5.13.3. Definitions in instruments of international law

Legal definitions are extremely important in instruments of international law. Since there is only a small number of international legal terms with a universally accepted signification (de Groot 1991:283), it is essential that the parties agree on the signification and scope of terms and incorporate the definitions into the treaty or convention. In view of the large number of courts involved in the communication process, this is undoubtedly the most effective method of promoting the uniform interpretation and application of international instruments (*see* Chapter 8, 8.9.2). This presupposes, of course, that the definitions contain no technical or other system-bound terms unknown in the legal systems of the signatory states. As a rule, an attempt should be made to formulate definitions of international law in general terms that are understood by all and can be translated without altering the substance. Definitions are abundant, especially in long and complicated instruments. While definitions pertaining to the whole instrument are usually placed in the definition section following the preamble, definitions pertaining to a specific Part are placed at the beginning of that Part among the substantive provisions. Explanatory definitions in the main body of the instrument are usually formulated with *means* and the term is placed in italics or inverted commas. The example below is from Article 18 of the UN Convention on the Law of the Sea of 1982:

Article 18

Signification du terme 'passage'
1. On entend par 'passage' le fait de naviguer dans la mer territoriale aux fins de:
a) la traverser sans entrer les eaux intérieures ni faire escale dans une rade ou une installation portuaire située en dehors des eaux intérieures; ou...

Meaning of passage
1. Passage means navigation through the territorial sea for the purpose of:
a) traversing that sea without entering internal waters or calling at a roadstead or port facility outside internal waters; or...

Stipulative definitions in the main body of an instrument are usually formulated like provisions. As the following example shows, it is not uncommon for international lawyers to borrow terms from other specialized fields and assign them a new meaning. A geographic term adopted by the International Law Commission (Tabory 1980:133), the legal criteria of *continental shelf* are currently laid down in the Convention on the Law of the Sea (1982). Whereas the first legal definition of *continental shelf* in the Convention on the Continental Shelf (1958) completely disregarded the physical features of the actual shelf (*see* Chapter 8, 8.10.4), a conscious attempt has been made to recognize the features of the actual shelf in the new legal definition:

Article 76

Définition du plateau continental
1. Le plateau continental d'un Etat côtier comprend les fonds marins et

Definition of continental shelf
1. The continental shelf of a coastal State comprises the sea-bed and

leur sous-sol au-delà de sa mer territoriale, sur toute l'étendue du prolongement naturel du territoire terrestre de cet Etat jusqu'au rebord externe de la marge continentale, ou jusqu'à 200 milles marins des lignes de base à partir desquelles est mesurée la largeur de la mer territoriale, lorsque le rebord externe de la marge continentale se trouve à une distance inférieure.

subsoil of the submarine areas that extend beyond its territorial sea throughout the natural prolongation of its land territory to the outer edge of the continental margin, or to a distance of 200 nautical miles from the baselines from which the breadth of the territorial sea is measured where the outer edge of the continental margin does not extend up to that distance.

Having learned from past mistakes in the Warsaw Convention, lawyers generally require that the parallel texts of international instruments be coordinated as closely as possible (*see* Chapter 7, 7.4.1). In view of the decisive role of definitions in promoting the uniform interpretation and application of international instruments, translators have little room to be creative when formulating definitions. This can be seen in the above examples from the Convention on the Law of the Sea, a multilateral instrument enacted in six equally authentic texts (*see* Chapter 7, 7.5). Although all the parallel texts of this Convention were drafted simultaneously, a truly unique drafting experiment in international law, the first priority was to preserve the unity of the single instrument.

6 Creativity in Legal Translation

6.1. BEING CREATIVE WITH LANGUAGE

In their new role as text producers, legal translators are increasingly assuming tasks previously reserved strictly for drafters. While both translators and drafters are frequently snubbed as 'mechanical word polishers,' Elmer Driedger strongly denies such accusation. In his opinion, 'a good draftsman is more than a mechanical word polisher; he is one of the creative participants in the legislative process' (1976:1). Driedger's words also hold true for the modern translator who, as 'a writer of laws must have the freedom of an artist,' i.e., 'the freedom to use to the fullest extent everything that language permits' (Driedger 1982b:4). While some may deny that this is creativity, they are reminded that creativity manifests itself differently in different areas of translation (*cf.* Wilss 1988:112; *see* Chapter 4, 4.8).

This Chapter raises the question to what extent legal translators can be creative with language in parallel texts and still preserve the unity of the single instrument. Since even slight changes in language may affect the substance, translators must always take account of legal factors when making linguistic decisions. As Newmark once remarked: 'Differences in terminology and function [must be] noted and as much attention paid to the content as to the intention and all possible interpretations and misinterpretations of the text' (1982:47). While such considerations caused Newmark to conclude that legal translation is 'more restricted than any other form,' they also shed light on the decision-making process of legal translators who must decide when, where, why, how, and to what extent they can be creative.

In this Chapter examples are cited from Swiss, Canadian, and Belgian legislation illustrating how translators can make basic alterations in syntax without affecting the substance of legal rules and consequently their operation. In particular, translators should be creative with syntax not for the sake of creativity itself but to achieve greater clarity, emphasis, and effect. In addition to changes in syntax, translators sometimes make stylistic changes as well. Since drafting styles can differ considerably from jurisdiction to jurisdiction, the question arises to what extent stylistic diversity should be permitted in legal translation. Examples from Canadian federal legislation illustrate how far the co-drafting experiment in Canada has gone in an attempt to accommodate two drafting styles in the parallel texts of legal instruments. Among other things, the revolutionary Canadian experiment raises a basic question which is of concern to all legal translators: What determines how much creativity can be tolerated in parallel texts without posing a threat to uniform interpretation and application?

6.2. SYNTAX AND THE THOUGHT PROCESS

For centuries legal translators faithfully followed the syntax of the source text as closely as possible, mainly out of fear that any changes might disturb the thought process. This fear disappears when translators understand how legal rules operate and are able to express the intended logical relations. Some translators claim that translating legal rules is not difficult because the same syntactic structures are repeated over and over again (Rothkegel 1984:255). This is because there is essentially one basic underlying thought pattern. As shown in the previous Chapter, the basic logical structure of legal rules is expressed by the formula: if P, then Q, which means that Q shall be performed only in cases where the conditions constituting P are fulfilled. Thus it is only natural that legal rules are most frequently formulated in conditional sentences (*cf.* Bocquet 1994:17; Cornu 1990:284). In Coode's analysis of the conditional sentence, he identified four elements of legal rules: case, condition, legal subject, and legal action. The first two elements constitute the fact-situation (P), the latter two, the statement of law (Q) (*see* Chapter 5, 5.7). Since P is a precondition to Q, Coode insisted that the fact-situation precede the statement of law, and that each of the four elements appear in the order indicated above. Today Coode's prescribed arrangement of elements is no longer considered mandatory. Instead, drafting experts believe it is possible to formulate the same provision in different ways without altering the substance and disturbing the thought process. To prove this point, Driedger experimented with a sample provision, formulating the same provision in nine different ways (1976:xxvi). Although Driedger's exercise is in English only, it has valuable implications for translators as well. In the examples below the elements of the fact-situation are in italics.

Driedger's sample provision contains the four essential elements designated by Coode. Not by chance, the first example lists the four elements in the order prescribed by Coode:

1)   *Where an applicant has passed the test,* / *if he pays the fee,* / the Minister / shall grant him a licence.

Elsewhere Driedger argued that Coode's case and condition can frequently be interchanged because they have the same basic function and are both adverbial modifiers (1982b:3).[1] This is done in his second example of the sample provision:

---

1.   Bocquet also concludes that the case and conditions of a fact-situation express the same idea. Moreover, as he points out, this has important consequences for French drafting practices: unlike in ordinary French, the conjunctions *lorsque, quand* and *si* have exactly the same meaning when used to introduce elements of the fact-situation of a legal rule (1994:19). Compared with English and German drafting practices, francophone drafters are more restricted in their use of conjunctions to introduce clauses expressing elements of the fact-situation. Bocquet cites examples showing how French drafters alternate the above conjunctions when formulating a fact-situation consisting of two or more subordinate clauses (*see* Bocquet 1994:19–23; *also* Cornu 1990:284–287). In general rules in which the fact-situation is formulated in a single clause, Bocquet recommends using the conjunction *si* (1994:21).

2) *Where an applicant pays the fee, / if he has passed the test, /* the Minister / shall grant him a licence.

The original condition is again converted into an element of case in the third example. This time, however, both are expressed as cumulative circumstances in the same *where* clause:

3) *Where an applicant has passed the test / and paid the fee /* the Minister / shall grant him a licence.

Driedger then defies Coode's basic rule on word order by reversing the statement of law and the fact-situation. The elements of the fact-situation are expressed as cumulative conditions in a subordinate *if* clause:

4) The Minister / shall grant a licence to an applicant / *if he has passed the test / and paid the fee.*

In the fifth example the fact-situation again precedes the statement of law; however, another notable change occurs. The element of the case is expressed in a relative clause embedded in a subordinate *where* clause containing the original condition:

5) *Where an applicant who has passed the test / pays the fee /* the Minister / shall grant him a licence.

Retaining the structure of the previous example, Driedger interchanges the elements of the fact-situation, expressing the original condition in a relative clause embedded in the subordinate *where* clause containing the case:

6) *Where an applicant who has paid the fee / has passed the test /* the Minister/ shall grant him a licence.

In the last three examples the fact-situation and the statement of law are inverted. First of all, the element of the case is expressed in a relative clause, the condition in an *if* clause:

7) The Minister / shall grant a licence to an applicant / *who has passed the test / if he pays the fee.*

The elements in the relative and conditional clauses of the fact-situation are then interchanged in the eighth example:

8) The Minister / shall grant a licence to an applicant / *who pays the fee / if he has passed the test.*

The final example marks a complete departure from Coode's model. Here the basic conditional sentence is replaced by a relative sentence in which both elements of the fact-situation are expressed consecutively in a relative clause:

9)   The Minister / shall grant a licence to an applicant / *who has passed the test / and paid the fee.*

According to Driedger, his experimental provision could be expressed in at least 54 additional ways. In regard to the examples cited above, he admits that some forms are more exact and some are better English. Despite the semantic shift, the substance remains the same in all examples (1976:xxvii).

Translators should note that the statement of law (*'The Minister shall grant a licence to an applicant'*) remains unchanged in all examples of Driedger's sample provision. Regardless of the length and complexity of a provision, the statement of law is always in the main clause (or clauses). While the legal action is expressed by the principal predicate, the legal subject (if one exists) is usually expressed by the principal subject. The fact that these elements remain unchanged in Driedger's sample provision serves as a warning to translators to refrain from rearranging elements of the statement of law, unless such changes are deemed necessary. On the other hand, flexibility is normally permitted in the formulation and arrangement of the elements constituting the fact-situation, provided the intended logical relations are clearly expressed. As seen in Driedger's examples, the elements of the fact-situation may be formulated as adverbial modifiers in a subordinate *if* or *where* clause, or even as adjective modifiers in a relative clause. Sometimes the modifiers are embedded in the statement of law. Although variety is permitted, translators must proceed with caution when formulating the fact-situation, taking care not to alter the propositional content or create an ambiguity that could endanger uniform interpretation and encourage litigation.

6.3. ARRANGEMENT OF ELEMENTS

According to Coode's general rule, the fact-situation describing the case and conditions under which a legal rule is operative must precede the statement of law specifying the legal subject and prescribing the action to be taken. Although some of Coode's rules have been criticized as being too rigid, his basic rule on word order is still widely recommended today (Cornu 1990:290; Thornton 1987:23). However, strict adherence to Coode's basic rule sometimes depends on the subject-matter of the piece of legislation. For example, as a major form of social control, criminal provisions must be absolutely clear and unambiguous. Therefore, the Swiss Guidelines of 1976 explicitly required drafters to place the fact-situation before the statement of law in criminal provisions as this best expresses the logical relations of the underlying thought process:

> Vom logischen Aufbau der Strafbestimmung in Tatbestand and Rechtsfolge soll nur aus zwingenden Gründen abgewichen werden (Richtlinien der Gesetzestechnik 1976:25).

Although the Guidelines are deemed mandatory for both drafters and translators, it sometimes occurs that the drafter of the German source text complied with the above rule, but one or both translators did not. This is the case, for instance, in

Article 221(2) of the Swiss Penal Code, where the fact-situation and the statement of law are reversed in the French and Italian texts:

Fact-situation
Bringt der Täter wissentlich Leib und Leben von Menschen in Gefahr,

Statement of law
so ist die Strafe Zuchthaus nicht unter drei Jahren.

Statement of law
La peine sera la réclusion pour trois ans au moins

Fact-situation
si le délinquant a sciemment mis en danger la vie ou l'intégrité corporelle des personnes.

Statement of law
La pena è della reclusione non inferiore a tre anni

Fact-situation
se il colpevole mette scientemente in pericolo la vita o l'integrità delle persone.

The basic rule on the arrangement of the fact-situation and statement of law in criminal provisions is repeated in the new Swiss *Gesetzgebungsleitfaden*, however; the wording ('folgende Grundsätze sind zu beachten') now implies that it is a recommendation rather than a requirement (1995:273). Moreover, exceptions are explicitly permitted in provisions in which the fact-situation contains several elements relating to the same statement of law. Despite these changes, Swiss drafters and translators are still expected to observe Coode's general rule when formulating criminal provisions. As provided by the Swiss Guidelines of 1976, this rule need not be observed in provisions prescribing administrative sanctions (Richtlinien der Gesetzestechnik 1976:25). Thus it is safe to conclude that reversing the order of the fact-situation and statement of law does not disrupt the thought process after all. When no specific guidelines apply, clarity and emphasis seem to be the main considerations. It is well known that, for the sake of emphasis, the most important part of a message is placed at the beginning of a sentence. This also applies to legal rules (Cornu 1990:327; Fleiner-Gerster 1985:39). Since one of the main goals of criminal provisions is to make the punishable conduct known to the public, this is another reason for placing the fact-situation at the beginning of such provisions.

Flexibility is generally permitted when arranging the elements of the fact-situation; however, translators must preserve causal relations at all times so as to express the desired cause and effect. As a general rule, each modifier should be placed 'as near as possible to the sentence element it modifies, thus making it appear "logically and naturally connected to that element"' (Thornton 1987:23). In some provisions, the case and condition constituting the fact-situation are separated, with one appearing before and the other after the statement of law. The fact-situation may also consist of a sequence of conditions with one or more conditions embedded in the statement of law. For example, Article 289a(2) of the Swiss Obligations Act contains two cumulative conditions. Instead of enumerating the conditions consecutively, the drafter separates them, emphasizing the latter by expressing it as an excluded condition (*see also* 6.5.3 below). While the French translation follows the arrangement of elements in the German text, the first condition in the Italian text is embedded in the statement of law. The elements of the fact-situation are in italics:

DE: *Hat der Verpächter zugestimmt,* / so kann er die Wiederherstellung des früheren Zustandes *nur* verlangen, / *wenn dies schriftlich vereinbart worden ist.*

FR: *Lorsque le bailleur a donné son consentement,* / il ne peut exiger la remise en état de la chose / *que s'il en a été convenu par écrit.*

IT: Il locatore, / *se ha consentito,* / può esigere il ripristino dello stato anteriore / *soltanto se pattuito per scritto.*

Canadian drafting and translation practices are considerably more flexible in regard to the arrangement of elements, especially in recent legislation. At the offset of the legislative reform, Meredith encouraged translators to rearrange the elements of legal rules if such changes would render the new text more clearly:

> A translator should not feel bound to follow the construction in the source text. If the meaning of an article can be rendered more clearly by reversing the word order, this should be done, but with care (1979:61).

At that time, such 'interventions' were regarded as acts of drafting previously reserved strictly for legislative drafters (Meredith 1979:61). Having finally won the right to formulate legislation in the genius of their own language, translators began making more extensive changes in syntax. Although this right is not a *carte blanche* to make unlimited changes, translators gradually became bolder in their creativity with language as they took on greater drafting responsibilities. Today they do not hesitate to use variations of the conditional sentence when formulating rules of law, even if this requires making 'interventions' in the statement of law. Such decisions, however, require both legal and language competence (*see* Chapter 4, 4.7.2).

6.4. VARIATIONS OF THE CONDITIONAL SENTENCE

As Driedger showed in his experiment above, it is possible to use a variety of constructions to express the same idea without altering the substance and affecting the thought process. Like drafters, translators are now widely permitted to select the formulation which expresses the propositional content of the fact-situation most clearly and effectively in their own language. Not surprisingly, translators most frequently use the variations of the basic conditional sentence shown in Driedger's exercise above. Although some translation theorists might regard Driedger's experiment as a mere exercise in transformational grammar, lawyers are concerned mainly about the logical forms underlying syntactic structure, not about grammar as an end in itself (*cf.* Bowers 1989:211). Logic plays a key role in legal reasoning and argumentation. Therefore, it is not by chance that one of the tests of adequacy is whether the surface structures used by translators are variations of the deep structure expressing the basic 'if/then' thought process.

6.4.1. Drafting practices and styles

Due to cultural and language differences, different drafting practices have developed in various jurisdictions, thus resulting in distinctive drafting styles, each with a preference for certain modes of expression. For instance, common law drafters tend to favor the use of the basic conditional sentence because it expresses commands and permissions more directly. For their part, civil law drafters often use variations of the conditional sentence which express the same substance in a less direct manner. This is particularly true in regard to criminal provisions, the majority of which are commands. Speaking for civil law lawyers, Bocquet comments: 'La particularité de ces ordres est celle de n'être jamais directement exprimés: ce sont des ordres implicites et paradoxaux' (1994:15). Furthermore, common law drafters attempt to limit judicial discretion by making statutes more detailed and complex than civil law legislation. Supposedly for the sake of precision, common law drafters repeat individual words and entire phrases, while their civil law colleagues avoid repetition whenever possible (Cornu 1990:332; Fleiner-Gerster 1985:39). Accordingly, civil law drafters frequently avoid using conditional sentences in which the same subject is repeated in both the fact-situation and statement of law as follows:

– If P does X, then P is liable to punishment Y.

Without altering the substance, the propositional content of the fact-situation can be formulated in a relative clause[2] modifying P, the subject of the statement of law:

– P who does X is liable to punishment Y.

Characterized by generality, legal rules do not apply to specific individuals (*see* Cornu 1990: 276). Particularly in areas of public law, such as criminal law, legal rules often apply to all persons.[3] In universal norms, as they are called, P equals all persons or everyone who performs a certain act:

– Everyone who does X is liable to punishment Y.

In some languages the same propositional content is formulated more naturally in a subject clause which is the grammatical subject of the statement of law:

---

2.   The function of a relative clause is to restrict or qualify the word it modifies (*see* Bowers 1989:289). Relative clauses are often used to qualify the principal subject of a provision, especially in civil law legislation. In a series of related provisions the subject can then be repeated without the qualifier, which is implied from the context.

3.   Public law norms such as criminal provisions usually prescribe rules of conduct which are binding on all persons; non-compliance is punishable by sanction. On the other hand, private law norms create obligations and rights for certain classes of persons (*see* Chapter 3, 3.1.2); parties realize their rights and claim damages for non-performance of obligations by taking court action. On differences between public law and private law norms and the consequences for structure, *see* Fleiner-Gerster 1985:34.

– Whoever does X is liable to punishment Y.

Such variations of the conditional clause are common in Swiss criminal provisions. While universal norms are expressed in the German text by a subject clause introduced by *wer*, the French and Italian texts use a relative clause embedded in the statement of law introduced by *celui qui* and *chiunque*, respectively. According to Bocquet, the use of *celui qui* is obligatory whenever *wer* is used as the subject of criminal provisions in the German text of Swiss law (1994:17). This can be seen in the expression of the universal norm in the three texts of Article 24(2) of the Swiss Penal Code:

DE: *Wer* jemanden zu einem Verbrechen zu bestimmen versucht, / wird wegen Versuchs dieses Verbrechens bestraft.
FR: *Celui qui* aura tenté de décider une personne à commettre un crime / encourra la peine prévue pour la tentative de cette infraction.
IT: *Chiunque* tenta di determinare altri a commettere un crimine / incorre nella pena prevista per il tentativo di questo crimine.

In legal rules in which the subject is a class of individuals or a thing, the subject is often repeated in common law provisions, whereas civil law drafters and translators tend to favor abbreviated forms. There are numerous examples of such structural variations in provisions of Canadian federal legislation. Despite structural differences in the English and French texts of subsection 3 of s. 729.9 of the *Canadian Act to amend the Criminal Code* [*SC* 1988], the substance remains the same:

Where the court does not make an order under subsection (1), the court shall...	*Le tribunal qui ne rend pas l'ordon-nance visée au paragraphe (1)* est tenu...

Following the drafting practices in the French Civil Code, the drafters of the new Civil Code of Quebec commonly formulate the propositional content of the fact-situation in a relative clause modifying the subject of the statement of law. In such cases, the anglophone translator sometimes reverts to a conditional sentence, formulating the fact-situation in a subordinate *where* or *if* clause. This is done in the following provision from Article 2158:

Le mandataire qui outrepasse ses pouvoirs est personnellement tenu...	*Where a mandatory exceeds his powers,* he is personally liable...

At other times the anglophone translator follows the structure of the French text by using the relative pronoun *who*. More commonly, however, the English text is abbreviated with a gerund as in Article 413 of the Civil Code of Quebec:

Le jugement qui attribue un droit d'usage ou de propriété équivaut à titre et en a tous les effets.	*A judgment awarding a right of* use or ownership is equivalent to title and has the effects thereof.

6.4.2. Provisions with a hidden fact-situation

Whereas the above examples are reminiscent of Driedger's exercise, the changes are more radical in other provisions. In the following example, the original English text does not follow the basic 'if/then' structure but contains a so-called hidden fact-situation embedded in the statement of law. In provisions having the same fact-situation, it has become common practice to use cross references, thus eliminating the necessity of repeating the entire fact-situation or parts thereof. This practice is especially popular in common law provisions, some of which contain several cross references. In such instances one or more cross references may be embedded in the statement of law, as in the English source text of subsection 9 of s. 727.6 of the *Canadian Act to amend the Criminal Code* [*SC* 1988]. Instead of following the English text, the francophone translator places the cross reference at the beginning of the provision in an abbreviated conditional clause, thus making the fact-situation easier to identify. The following example is of interest not only because of structural differences but also because of the rearrangement of elements in the French text. In addition to its clarity and readability, the French text is a technically effective provision that will promote uniform interpretation and application of the single instrument:

A court shall not	Dans le cas d'un ordonnance rendue en vertu des articles 725 ou 726,
extend	
the period within which payment of restitution is to be made	le tribunal ne peut,
	en vertu du paragraphe (7),
pursuant to subsection (7)	prolonger
to a date later than the expiration of the fourth year after the day on which the order of restitution was made	de plus de quatre ans à compter de la date de l'ordonnance
	la période pendant laquelle le dédommagement doit être versé.
under section 735 or 726, as the case may be.	

As in the above provision, francophone Canadians often formulate the fact-situation in a phrase introduced by the expression *dans le cas* or *en cas de*. Although francophone drafters are not fond of Coode's rigid rules (Didier 1990:293), their *dans le cas* phrases contain elements of the fact-situation which Coode referred to as case. As in French law (*see* Cornu 1990:285), such phrases are placed at the beginning of the provision, thus complying with Coode's rules on word order. In English provisions, elements of Coode's case are usually expressed in a subordinate *where* clause. Such clauses are often translated by *dans le cas* phrases in French when the verb in the English clause can be deleted without affecting the substance. It should be noted that francophone drafters and translators prefer to use nouns to convey the information expressed in verbal phrases in the English text, thus resulting in a more natural syntax in French (*cf.* Didier 1990:295). This has been done, for example, in the provision of section 31(1) of the *Marine Transportation Security Act* [*SC* 1994]:

Where a fine imposed on a person convicted of an offence is not paid when required, ...	En cas de défaut de paiement, à la date fixée, d'une amende pour une infraction prévue à la présente loi, ...

The same techniques are also used by the francophone drafters of the new Civil Code of Quebec. In this case, French provisions commencing with *en cas de* are often translated literally with *in the event of* (Art. 416). Other gerund clauses in French are rendered with an introductory *where* clause, as in the following provision of Article 276 of the Code:

Le tribunal saisi de la demande d'ouverture d'un régime de protection prend en considération...	Where the court examines an application to institute protective supervision, it takes into consideration...

As shown in the above examples, being creative with language requires legal competence and intuition. Like the draftsman, an accomplished translator should 'be able to express the same qualification in different ways so that he can select the one with precisely the correct shade of meaning, and can smoothly combine all his modifiers so as to produce not only a readable and grammatically correct sentence, but one that expresses a complete, exact and workable law' (Driedger 1976:4).

6.5. THE USE OF NEGATIONS

Drafting rules generally discourage the use of negative provisions in normative texts. This is because affirmative statements are more direct and straightforward and thus easier to understand (Thornton 1987:32). Nonetheless, there are numerous exceptions where negative provisions are either more effective or necessary to achieve the desired legal effects. In contrast to translators of ordinary language, legal translators are warned against translating negative phrases positively and vice versa. As a rule, if a provision is negative in the source text, it should be translated as a negative provision. In such cases, however, the translator may select the mode of negation most commonly used in the target language. For example, while negative subjects are commonly used in English provisions, francophone translators usually prefer to negate the verb instead.[4] This has been done in the French version of section 20(4) of the *Official Languages Act* of Canada [*SC* 1988]:

---

4.   German guidelines for the drafting of treaties explicitly recommend that the verb be negated, not the subject (Standardformulierungen 1992:83).

No decision ... is invalid...	Les décisions... *ne sont pas* invalides...

Conversely, anglophone translators commonly translate a negative verb in French by negating the subject, as in Article 401 of the *Civil Code* of Quebec:

Un époux ne peut,... aliéner, hypothéquer ni transporter hors de la résidence familiale les meubles qui servent à l'usage du ménage.	*Neither spouse may,... alienate, hypothecate or remove* from the family residence the movable property serving for the use of the household.

Negating the subject extends the scope of negation backwards, placing the emphasis on the subject. Therefore, it is common practice in universal prohibitions to negate the subject in all languages, thus stressing that the prohibition applies to all persons without exception.[5] The following example is from Article 43(3) of the Swiss *Federal Constitution*:

DE: *Niemand darf* in mehr als einem Kanton politische Rechte ausüben.
FR: *Nul ne peut* exercer des droits politiques dans plus d'un canton.
IT: *Nessuno può* esercitare diritti politici in più d'un Cantone.

6.5.1. Negations affecting the facts to be established

In legal translation, the translator's primary consideration is effect. Hence, translators should select a formulation that guarantees that the particular provision will produce the desired effects in practice. Effects relating to the law of evidence should also be taken into account. In particular, translators should refrain from translating negative provisions as positive and vice versa whenever such transformations could interfere with the burden of proof and the facts to be established as evidence. In the law of evidence it is generally accepted that the existence rather than the non-existence of certain facts must be established as proving the latter is much more difficult (Fasching 1990:463). For example, pursuant to the Swiss Federal Code on Private International Law, a foreign award can be recognized if none of the grounds for refusal exists. Unless proven otherwise, it is presumed that no such ground exists. Thus the burden of proof is on the respondent to establish facts that would prove the existence of any of the grounds for refusal. The general ground for refusal is expressed in the public policy clause of Article 27(1) which reads as follows:

DE: Eine im Ausland ergangene Entscheidung wird in der Schweiz nicht anerkannt, *wenn die Anerkennung mit dem schweizerischen Ordre public offensichtlich unvereinbar wäre.*
FR: La reconnaissance d'une décision étrangère doit être refusée en Suisse *si elle est manifestement incompatible avec l'ordre public suisse.*

---

5.   On the use of *Nul* and *Aucune* to commence provisions in French law, *see* Cornu 1990:277–278.

171

IT: Non è riconosciuta in Svizzera la decisione straniera *il cui riconoscimento sia manifestamente incompatibile con l'odrine pubblico svizzero.*

The principal verb in the German and Italian texts (*wird nicht anerkannt/non è riconosciuta*) is negative because the award shall *not* be recognized if the respondent provides evidence to prove incompatibility, i.e., that recognition would be manifestly incompatible with Swiss public policy. Instead of using a negative verb, the franco-phone translator changes the principal verb to *doit être refusée (shall be refused)*; the substance, however, remains unchanged (*see* 6.5.3 below). Further grounds for refusal of recognition follow in paragraph 2, which specifies that recognition shall be refused if one of the parties establishes that:

1) he/she was *not* properly served,
2) the judgment was rendered *in violation of* Swiss procedural law, or
3) litigation on the same matter has already been initiated in Switzerland.

Translators are warned against transforming negative conditions into positive ones and vice versa in such provisions as this would inversely affect the facts to be established. This is also true in provisions on the validity of legal instruments and the nullity of legal actions. On the other hand, transformations are generally acceptable if the substance remains unchanged in the context of the provision as a whole. In the following example from section 8(1) of the *Canada Mortgage and Housing Corporation [RSC* 1985], the English text has a negative subject in the statement of law and positive conditions (except b) in the fact-situation, while the statement of law is positive in the French text with negative conditions (except b) in the fact-situation. In this provision, the conditions of the fact-situation specify the facts to be established as requirements for candidacy:

No person shall be appointed as a President or Vice-President or as a director from outside the public service of Canada and no person shall continue to hold any such office, if that person
(a) is a director, officer or employee of a lending institution;
(b) is not a Canadian citizen or otherwise a British subject ordinarily resident in Canada; ...

Pour exercer la charge de président ou de vice-président, d'administrateur choisi à l'extérieur de l'administration publique fédérale, il faut remplir les conditions suivantes:
a) ne pas relever d'un établissement de crédit, à titre d'administrateur, de dirigeant ou d'employé;
b) être soit citoyen canadien, soit sujet britannique résident habituellement au Canada; ...

6.5.2. Expressions of time

Generally speaking, transforming negative provisions into positive ones and vice versa is not recommended; however, there are occasional exceptions where such transformations can be performed without affecting the substance. In some instances (as in the above provision), the transformation is optional, whereas in others it is mandatory. Particularly in procedural and other provisions expressing periods of time, it frequently occurs that a negative in one text is expressed more effectively or naturally by a positive in the other text. This, however, is a question of language, not of law. For example, in subsection (4) of s. 727.6 of the *Canadian Criminal Code*, the period of limitation is rendered in English by the expression *No proceedings... shall be initiated,* in French by the technical verb *se prescrire* (= *becomes time-barred*):

No proceedings under subsection (1) shall be initiated more than 6 years after the date of the alleged failure or refusal to comply or alleged default.	*Les procédures visées au paragraphe (1) se prescrivent* par six ans à compter du prétendu défaut ou refus de se conformer à l'ordonnance.

Just as the formation of negations varies from language to language, so does usage. If the use of a negation is awkward or illogical in the target language, the translator should usually not hesitate to use a positive formulation to express the information. While francophone drafters and translators avoid negating the subject whenever possible, they make frequent use of verbal negations, some of which are unknown in English. For example, prior to the revision of the English translation of the old *Civil Code of Lower Canada*, the English text of the provision on demurrage was translated literally as 'Demurrage does not begin until the laydays expire.' For the sake of clarity, Meredith proposed the following revision (1979:61):

Les surestaries ne commencent à courir qu'à partir du moment où le délai des staries est expiré.	Demurrage begins when the laydays expire.

While the transformation in the above example is mandatory for the sake of clarity, the use of *ne sont pas comptés* to express exclusion in the French text of section 29(8) of the *Canada Evidence Act [RSC* 1985] is purely stylistic and thus optional:

Holidays shall be excluded from the computation of time under this section.	Dans le calcul des délais prevus au présent article, les jours fériés ne sont pas comptés.

Optional transformations made solely for the sake of diversity are not always in the best interest of the single instrument. An example is the unorthodox transformation in the French text of section 38(2) of the *Canada Evidence Act [RSC 1985].*[6] As a rule, requirements specifying time periods for filing applications are expressed positively, stating when the application must be made. This is the case in the English text of the said provision, whereas the French text contains a negation stating when the application can no longer be made. Despite the different approaches, the results are the same:

---

6. *Cf.* section 172.1 of the *Canada Labour Code* [SC 1993] where the English phrase 'The employer shall comply with the result of the vote within thirty days after...' is rendered in the French text as 'l'employeur est tenu *dans les trente jours suivant la date...*' [emphasis added].

173

An application under subsection (1) *shall be made within ten days* after the objection is made...	Le délai dans lequel la demande visée au paragraphe (1) *ne peut être faite est de dix* jours suivant l'opposition...

6.5.3. Obligations, permissions, prohibitions

In general translation it is not uncommon for a term to be 'decomposed' into a negative and its contrary or contradictory term (Newmark 1982:162). Sometimes it occurs that a permission is translated negatively or even transformed into a prohibition. For example, 'Women only' could be negated and translated as 'No males' or even 'Males prohibited.' Despite the obvious semantic shift in both negations, the results are the same. Although such radical transformations are not acceptable in legal texts, there are instances where a negated permission is translated as a prohibition. Since prohibitions prescribe acts that persons are not permitted to perform (Chapter 5, 5.10), it follows that 'P is not permitted' is equivalent to 'P is prohibited.' Because there are no exceptions, the legal effect is always the same (Weinberger 1988:68). Following this reasoning, the francophone translator deviates from the German source text of Article 793(2) of the Swiss *Civil Code* by using *prohibé* to translate *nicht gestattet*. The Italian translation follows the German text, placing the negation at the beginning for emphasis:

DE: Die Bestellung anderer Arten des Grundpfandes ist *nicht gestattet.*
FR: Toute autre forme est *prohibée.*
IT: *Non è ammessa* la costituzione di pegno immobiliare sotto altra forma.

Similarly, prohibitions are negative obligations that can sometimes be expressed positively by changing the verb and subject. A pertinent example is in the statement of law of Article 27(1) of the Swiss Federal Code on Private International Law cited above (*see* 6.5.1). Here the German prohibition *wird nicht anerkannt* is translated in the French text by the negative obligation *doit être refusée*. Although this transformation requires completely rewriting the statement of law, the substance remains unchanged:

DE: Eine im Ausland ergangene Entscheidung *wird* in der Schweiz *nicht anerkannt.*
FR: La reconnaissance d'une décision étrangère *doit être refusée.*

Since a prohibition can sometimes be expressed as a negative permission, the question arises as to whether it is acceptable to express a permission by negating a prohibition. Permissions are acts that are not prohibited. They include acts that are cancellations of prohibitions, acts that are exceptions to prohibitions and other acts that are explicitly permitted (Weinberger 1988:62). While it is conceivable that the first two types of permissions could be formulated by stating that a particular act is no longer prohibited (cancellation) or is not prohibited (exception to a general prohibition), such formulation is highly unconventional. On the other hand, it is not uncommon for prohibitions with excluded negative conditions to be transformed into permissions with excluded positive conditions, and vice versa. Prohibitions with excluded negative conditions permit an otherwise prohibited act to be performed under the specified condition(s). They are formulated in English by negating the verb in the statement of law and placing the condition(s) constituting the fact-situation after the conjunction *unless* or *except*, as in example (A) and its abbreviated form in example (B):

(A) The identity of X and Y may not be revealed, / unless they grant their consent.
(B) The identity of X and Y may not be revealed / without their consent.

Such prohibitions can be transformed into permissions by making the statement of law positive as well as the excluded condition. In English *only if* or *only* is used to introduce the condition:

(A) The identity of X and Y may be revealed / only if they grant their consent.
(B) The identity of X and Y may be revealed / only with their consent.

Despite the semantic shift, the results are the same. Thus such transformations are acceptable in legal rules and are sometimes used in multilingual legal texts. In Article 85 of the Belgian Constitution both the Dutch and French texts are prohibitions with an excluded negative condition, whereas the recently authenticated German text is a permission with an excluded positive condition embedded in the statement of law. The abbreviated form is used in all three texts:

NL: De Koning *kan niet* tegelijk hoofd van een andere Staat *zijn / zonder in-stemming van beide Kamers.*

FR: Le Roi *ne peut être* en même temps chef d'un autre Etat, / *sans l'assentiment des deux Chambres.*

DE: Der König *darf / nur mit der Zustimmung der beiden Kammern /* gleichzeitig Oberhaupt eines anderen Staates *sein.*

6.6. USE OF THE IMPERSONAL

Characterized by the impersonal, legal texts are written in the third person singular (*see* Cornu 1990:281). As Bowers remarks, 'the third person form implies a neutral transmitter and it is the form in which to present a statement as authoritative' (1989:30). Since laws prescribe rules for the regulation of human affairs, they are directed to legal personalities. The persons whose rights and duties are affected by a particular law are legal subjects. In his analysis of the basic elements of legal rules, Coode defined the legal subject as 'the person on whom the obligation is imposed or on whom the right, privilege or power is conferred' (in Driedger 1976:2). According to Coode, the legal subject is the grammatical subject of the statement of law (*see* Chapter 5, 5.7). Coode's definition has been criticized by both common law and civil law drafters as being too rigid (*see* Didier 1990:293). Above all, both agree that the grammatical subject is not always a legal person and in numerous legal rules there is no legal subject at all (Driedger 1976:2). In particular, civil law drafters reject Coode's notion of the legal subject as an attempt to personalize the law (Didier 1990:293). For their part, francophone drafters use all the linguistic means at their disposal to ensure that legislative expression remains impersonal (Ray 1926:85; Sourioux and Lerat 1975:45–46; Cornu 1990:279).

Sometimes legal subjects are classes of things (courts, contracts, applications, etc.) or persons (husbands, judges, employers, etc.); however, in numerous instances provisions are applicable to everybody. Anglophone drafters commence universal provisions with *every person, all persons, each person* (*see* 6.4.1 above) or the negative *no person* (*see* 6.5). In contrast, francophone drafters prefer impersonal formulations which express universal commands, prohibitions, and permissions less directly (Bocquet 1994:15), such as *il est interdit* for *no person shall*[7] and *il peut* for *every person may*. In section 3 of the *Canada Evidence Act* [*RSC* 1985], the French text uses the universal negation *Nul n'est inhabile...* for *A person is not incompetent....* In criminal and other provisions prescribing sanctions, *every person* has usually been translated as *quiconque* (*cf.* the usage of *celui qui* by Swiss francophones, *see* 6.4.1 above). In recent criminal legislation, however, the English phrase *every person who... is guilty* is rendered in French by commencing with the statement of law and placing *est coupable* in the initial position, thus making the provision even more impersonal. The following example is from section 279(2) of the *Criminal Code* [*SC* 1994]:

Every one who, without lawful authority, confines, imprisons or forcibly seizes another person *is guilty* of an indictable offence and liable to imprisonment for a term not exceeding five years.	*Est coupable* d'un acte criminel et passible d'un emprisonnement maximal de cinq ans *quiconque*, sans autorisation légitime, séquestre, emprisonne ou saisit de force une autre personne.

The degree of impersonalization is even greater in the new Penal Code of France of 1994. As if not to be outdone, French drafters took the innovative step of removing the personal pronouns *celui qui* and *quiconque* from universal criminal provisions, replacing them with the neutral phrase *le fait de* (*see* Bocquet 1994:16). By saying that 'the fact of having committed X is punishable' instead of 'everyone who commits X is guilty and liable to punishment,' drafters place the emphasis entirely on the act and consequent punishment. This is done in the following provision from Article 221(1) of the new French Penal Code:

Le fait de donner volontairement la mort à autrui constitue un meurtre. *Il est puni* de trente ans de réclusion criminelle.

---

7. In 1843 Coode insisted that *it shall not be lawful* is expressed more clearly by *no person shall*. As a result, *No person shall* became the accepted form in Britain and the Commonwealth for expressing a universal prohibition (Driedger 1982b:5). While Driedger regards it as 'an eminently correct form' (*ibid.*), Dickerson points out that *no person shall* can be interpreted as a negation of a prohibition in the sense that nobody is required to act (1965:130; *see also* Bowers 1989:250).

A similar but less radical technique is used in the French text of the *Marine Transportation Security Act* [*SC* 1994]. Whenever possible, the francophone drafter/translator deletes *quiconque* in provisions prescribing sanctions and uses a neutral subject to express the same substance. Despite extensive structural variations, the basic thought process is retained, as illustrated in the French provision from section 21(3):

Every person who contravenes this section is guilty of an offence punishable on summary conviction and liable...	L'inobservation du présent article constitue une infraction passible, sur déclaration de culpabilité par procédure sommaire...

The French text above transforms the active English text into a passive provision without a personal subject. Using passive forms is one of the most common methods of emphasizing the impersonal in all languages. Nonetheless, drafters are generally advised to avoid the use of the passive voice in legal norms (*cf.* Kindermann 1979:32). Regarding the legal subject as a mandatory element of all legal norms, Coode explicitly opposed the use of the passive voice in rules of law (*see* Driedger 1976:3). Taking Coode's lead, Thornton claims that passive constructions are frequently imprecise and ambiguous because they do not identify the person on whom a power or duty is conferred or imposed (1987:52). On the other hand, Driedger maintains that the form of the verb is immaterial if the victims or beneficiaries of a provision can be satisfactorily identified by other means (1976:3). As a rule, the Swiss *Gesetzgebungsfaden* does not recommend passive forms; however, this is because such forms tend to be more complicated and thus more difficult to understand: 'Die Passivform is komplizierter als die Aktivform; darunter kann die Verständlichkeit eines Satzes leiden' (1995:303). At the same time, the *Gesetzgebungsleitfaden* cites three exceptions where the use of passive forms is not only permitted but also preferred. These include provisions where a duty is imposed on various different persons who are not identifiable, where the subject need not be mentioned because it cannot be precisely identified or its identification would be irrelevant, and where the meaning would be clearer by expressing the idea of the provision as the subject (1995:303–304). These exceptions can serve as useful guidelines for translators as well.

Legal translators were formerly advised not to transform active into passive provisions and vice versa, as this would be overstepping their authority. Generally speaking, such transformations are now deemed acceptable if the substance remains unchanged. Moreover, translators are sometimes encouraged to use such transformations as a means of improving clarity or shifting emphasis. This, however, varies from jurisdiction to jurisdiction. As mentioned above, civil law drafters prefer an impersonal, less direct style and are encouraged to use all the linguistic means available to create such provisions (Sourioux and Lerat 1975:46). Taking their cue from French drafting practices, francophone translators in Canada now use passive forms whenever the subject of an active provision can be deleted without altering the substance. In the provision cited above from section 21.3 of the *Marine Transportation Security Act* [*SC* 1994], the francophone translator is justified in deleting the subject *Everyone who*. As is the case in all universal provisions, the person of

177

such subjects is not precisely identified. Moreover, transforming the verbal object of the English text *contravenes this section* into the subject of the French text *L'inobservation du présent article* is effective because it places the main emphasis on the idea of the provision. Thus the translator's use of the passive form in this provision is in keeping with the exceptions set forth in the Swiss *Gesetzgebungsleitfaden*. As a word of caution, when transforming active into passive forms, translators should avoid deleting any elements essential to the meaning and operation of the provision.

Unlike their anglophone counterparts, francophone drafters and translators frequently commence provisions with natural impersonal verbs such as *il faut* (Cornu 1990:280). Similarly, they are fond of using the neutral pronoun *il* followed by a passive verb, regardless whether the subject in the English text is a person or thing. Not by chance, there is an abundance of such impersonal phrases in the French text of recent Canadian legislation where part of or an entire provision has been reformulated in the impersonal passive.[8] Though purely stylistic, the following transformations are acceptable as a French drafting technique that makes the text more impersonal and less direct without altering the substance, causing ambiguity, or adversely affecting the results:

S. 205(3), *Canada Labour Code*
The onus is on the employer to show...

Il incombe à l'employeur de prouver...

S. 239.1 (6), *Canada Labour Code*
...the employee is responsible for..

Il incombe à l'employé...

S. 38(3), *Canada Evidence Act*
An appeal lies...

Il y a appel...

S. 251.12, *Canada Labour Code*
No order shall be made...

Il n'est admis aucun recours...

S. 276 (4), *Criminal Code of Canada*
The notice given under subsection (2)... shall not be published in any newspaper or broadcast.

Il est interdit de diffuser dans un journal, à la radio ou à la télévision, l'avis donné conformément au paragraphe (2).

---

8. *See* note 7 above on Coode's comment on the former usage of the English phrase *it shall not be lawful*. While Sourioux and Lerat refer to the French use of *il* and passive verbs as *transformations impersonnelles* (1976:46), Cornu uses the term *la voix impersonnelle*. In this context he notes: 'La voix impersonnelle marque justement le caractère impersonnel de la règle. La règle est posée dans l'abstrait, sans référence à un sujet logique. La voix impersonnelle exprime une réalité objective, et donc une sorte de vérité générale' (1990:279).

6.7. PUNCTUATION

Punctuation is now regarded as a device of syntax that assists the reader 'comprehend more quickly the intended meaning by providing sign-posts to sentence structure' (Thornton 1987:33). This, however, was not always the role of punctuation. In fact, the oldest Hebrew and Greek writings were completely without punctuation. And when the Greeks did start punctuating, their system of dots was not intended to supplement meaning but rather to show the proper places for breathing and accent (Mellinkoff 1963:152). Highly inflected, Latin could be understood without mechanical aids in the form of punctuation. Similarly, it is said that old English statutes were unpunctuated and that dotting was first used as an aid to oral delivery. According to Mellinkoff, punctuation did not become a concern in England and elsewhere until the invention of the printing press and the commencement of printing in the fifteenth and sixteenth centuries. Nonetheless, it appears that the main concern of printers was not usage but how to print the various dots (Mellinkoff 1963:150, 159). As a result, there was no such thing as consistency and uniformity in punctuation. In regard to German, the written form of New High German and its rigid rules of syntax and punctuation were developed in the first half of the seventeenth century.

Drafters are advised to follow conventional rules of punctuation in legal texts (Thornton 1987:34). Like other rules of syntax, the rules of punctuation vary from language to language and are more rigid in some languages than others. Although English is a germanic language, English rules of punctuation are not rigid, thus permitting a measure of individuality as long as communication is not impeded. For a long time, courts in the United Kingdom did not regard punctuation 'as part of the text alterable only by amendment' (Thornton 1987:34). As a result, the traditional position in England was not to take punctuation into account when construing statutes. While confirmed in *IRC* v. *Hinchy* [1960], this view was challenged in *Slaney v Kean* [1970] and again in *Marshall* v *Cottingham* [1981]. More recently, the Law Commission took a favorable view towards punctuation that was subsequently adopted by the Renton Report on the Preparation of Legislation (*see* Thornton 1987:33). On the other hand, punctuation has long been considered part of the text in civil law jurisdictions. In regard to Quebec, Meredith comments that 'once a bill has become law, no one may change one comma in the text, except by an amending statute tabled in the Assembly' (1979:56). In the same token, it is common practice for the courts of civil law countries to take punctuation into account when construing statutes and other legislative texts. In legal translation and multilingual drafting, it is generally agreed that the rules of punctuation of one language should not be imposed on another. In view of the rigid rules of punctuation in German, the Guidelines issued by the Foreign Office of the Federal Republic of Germany explicitly require that the rules of German punctuation set forth in the most recent edition of *Duden* be observed in German legal instruments:

> Im deutschen Wortlaut einer Überkunft ist ungeachtet der Interpunktion in den fremdsprachigen Texten nach den deutschen Zeichensetzungsregeln zu verfahren, wie sie in der jeweils neuesten Auflage des *Duden*, Band 1, und in der *Sonderreihe zum Großen Duden*, Band 1, zusammengefaßt sind (Standardformulierungen 1992:7).

Back in the days of strict literal translation, the view that the syntax of the source text was sacrosanct included punctuation as well. As a result, the source text was faithfully reproduced word for word and comma for comma. When literal translation became the rule of the day, the translator was permitted to follow the rules of syntax of the target language. Nonetheless, legal translators continued to follow the syntax of the source text as closely as possible, allowing for exceptions only when deemed absolutely necessary. This often resulted in an unnatural word order that made the translation difficult to understand, especially when English was the target language. In such cases the use of commas became a mechanical means of making the target text more intelligible by showing which groups of words belong together. Moreover, the position of the commas was often identical in both the source and target texts. This is still the case in some of the provisions of the English text of the new *Civil Code* of Quebec [1993]. For example, the syntax in the English text of Article 368 follows that of the French text so closely that it would be almost unintelligible without the commas, which are placed in the same position as in the French text, the only exception being at the beginning:

On doit, avant de procéder à la célébration d'un mariage, faire une publication par voie d'affiche apposée, pendant vingt jours avant la date prévue pour la célébration, au lieu où doit être célébré le mariage.	Before the solemnization of a marriage, publication must be effected by means of a notice posted up, for twenty days before the date fixed for the marriage, at the place where the marriage is to be solemnized.

Whereas the English text of the above provision was taken word for word from Article 413 of the revised version of the 1980 Civil Code, the anglophone translator disregards the word order of the French source text in most new provisions of the 1993 Civil Code. Properly worded, the English text reads smoothly without an excess of commas. For example, the English text of Article 2087 suffices with two commas, while the original French text requires four:

L'employeur, outre qu'il est tenu de permettre l'exécution de la prestation de travail convenue et de payer la rémunération fixée, doit prendre les mesures appropriées à la nature du travail, en vue de protéger la santé, la sécurité et la dignité du salarié.	The employer is bound not only to allow the performance of the work agreed upon and to pay the remuneration fixed, but also to take any measures consistent with the nature of the work to protect the health, safety and dignity of the employee.

Finally, it should be mentioned that any punctuation which is an integral part of the standard format cannot be changed. This is the case, for example, in judgments following the French technique, especially cassation judgments (*see* Chapter 5, 5.3.1).

6.8. THE CANADIAN EXPERIMENT IN CO-DRAFTING

Translators previously took painstaking care to ensure that the target text is a mirror image of the source text, particularly when the parallel texts were printed side by side. For many lawyers this provided visual evidence that the authentic language versions constitute a single instrument. In fact, the reliability of the single instrument was frequently measured by the degree of the interlingual concordance between the parallel texts, i.e., the consistency of terminology and presentation between each and all authenticated texts of the same instrument (*see* Chapter 7, 7.4.1). As mentioned earlier, it is necessary to follow the standard format prescribed for a particular instrument, thus preserving the organizational plan, division into parts, etc. It is well known that plurilingual communication could not function without a method of guaranteeing uniform citation of the provisions of the parallel texts of a given instrument. If reference is made by citing page numbers, as is frequently the case in respect of judgments, care must be taken to unify pagination. In other words, the same text must appear on each page in all parallel texts. This method of citation is used even in long judgments such as those of the European Court of Justice, which are printed in parallel volumes of the *Reports of Cases before the Court*. In addition to citing page numbers, a system of marginal enumeration makes it possible to cite individual textual units of the Court's judgments. In legislative texts it goes without saying that the division of text into parts, sections, paragraphs, and subparagraphs (or other textual units) must correspond in order to guarantee uniform citation.

In view of such constraints, most institutions observe the general rule: one instrument, one format, one style. In regard to style, we are reminded of the difficulty experienced at the European Court of Justice when each of the language divisions was permitted to select its own style. As a result of an error and its subsequent correction in the authentic German judgment in case 57/65, over 200 000 appellate proceedings were initiated at German courts (*see* Chapter 5, 5.3.2). Despite the traditional belief that strict concordance promotes uniform interpretation and application, the view is generally held that there is room for stylistic diversity in parallel texts. There appears, however, to be no consensus as to how much diversity can be tolerated without posing a threat to the unity of the single instrument. After the introduction of bilingual drafting in the early eighties (Chapter 4, 4.4.1), this question took the form of an open debate in Canada. Today, a mere glance at the *Statutes of Canada / Lois du Canada* suffices to convince even non-lawyers that considerable stylistic diversity is tolerated in the English and French texts of Canadian federal legislation. Since the parallel texts are still printed side by side, notable differences immediately catch the eye.

The question of stylistic diversity in parallel texts is a matter not only of language but also of drafting and interpretation practices. In regard to stylistic diversity in common law and civil law legislation, Driedger maintains that many differences are merely 'cosmetic' and do not affect the substance:

> There are differences in style between statutes in different languages, or between statutes in different countries, arising largely out of differences in grammatical structure, differences in political and legal institutions and their histories, and out of customs,

habits and traditions. But many of these are cosmetic only, having little, if any bearing on substance (1982a:78).

During the legislative reform, Quebecers took Driedger by his word and began to insist on the right to formulate the French texts of federal legislation in a style more reminiscent of that of civil law jurisdictions. Although common law lawyers warned that two distinctive styles cannot be tolerated in one and the same jurisdiction, farreaching innovations were already visible in the French texts of *The Revised Statutes of Canada* of 1985 [RSC]. Apparently more interested in the theoretical aspects of co-drafting, lawyers have generally paid little attention to their application in practice.[9] In an attempt to illustrate the practical implications of the new co-drafting techniques, the examples cited in this section show how far francophone translators and drafters have gone in their campaign to incorporate characteristics of civil law drafting into the French texts of federal legislation.

6.8.1. Disregarding the one-sentence rule

One of the first steps taken by francophone translators and drafters was to cast aside the one-sentence rule that dominates common law style. While common law lawyers continue to uphold British tradition by formulating each section and subsection in one sentence (*see* Chapter 5, 5.4.2), civil law lawyers prefer to express each idea in a separate sentence (*cf.* the Swiss *Gesetzgebungsleitfaden* 1995:288; *cf.* Cornu 1990:293). As a result, civil law legislation frequently contains articles or paragraphs consisting of more than one sentence. This is common not only in monolingual legislation such as the *Code civil de Napoléon* and the German BGB, but also in plurilingual legislation in Switzerland, Belgium, and the European Union. When a provision of plurilingual legislation consists of more than one sentence, the division into sentences is consistent in all the parallel texts of the same instrument. Thus civil law lawyers and EU lawyers are able to cite the article, paragraph, and even sentence of a piece of legislation and be assured that they are referring to the same text in all language versions. On the other hand, sentences are not cited in references made to common law legislation. For this very reason, francophone translators and drafters of federal legislation in Canada were able to convince their counterparts that the division of a section or subsection into more than one sentence does not affect uniform citation. Having proven their point, they are no longer bound to honor the one-sentence rule. Thus it is now common for compound and compound-complex sentences in the English text to be formulated as two or more sentences in the French text. This is illustrated by the following example from section 7(2) of *The Official Languages Act* [SC 1988]:

---

9. A linguist, Gémar does not even mention the new methods of co-drafting in his recent work on legal translation (1995–II). Nor does he cite examples to illustrate the revolutionary techniques currently used by his countrymen in the French version of Canadian federal legislation. The examples reproduced in his Annex include only one excerpt from contemporary Canadian federal legislation (1995–II:204–206).

All instruments made in the exercise of a prerogative or other executive power that are of a public and general nature shall be made in both official languages and, if printed and published, shall be printed and published in both official languages.	Les actes qui procèdent de la prérogative ou de tout autre pouvoir exécutif et sont de nature publique et générale sont établis dans les deux langues officielles. Leur impression et leur publication éventuelles se font dans ces deux langues.

6.8.2. Deletions

At the beginning of the twentieth century the letter of the law was still regarded as inviolate and it was generally believed that, for the sake of promoting uniform interpretation by the courts, every word of the source text had to be faithfully reproduced in the target text.[10] Today the pendulum has swung in the opposite direction, and even lawyers widely acknowledge that it is the sense that counts, not the words (*cf.* Bocquet 1994:8). In order to convey the sense, Koutsivitis contends that the deletion of words is perfectly legitimate in translations of legislation:

> En effet, laisser tomber des mots en gardant le sens tout à fait intact n'est pas un défault, mais un processus traductif absolument légitime (1988:362).

Although it is generally agreed that deletions are permitted, there is no consensus on which words can be deleted and how extensive the deletions can be. When the legislative reform began in Canada in the early eighties, the view was held that expressions which are 'standard equipment' in the source text may be deleted in the target text, provided the substance is not affected (Meredith 1979:61). Among other things, the so-called 'standard equipment' of common law statutes includes archaic expressions and formal words (*see* Mellinkoff 1963:13, 19) that are often regarded as 'clutter' by civil law lawyers. Sometimes vague referential words such as *aforesaid, herein, hereafter,* and *hereinbefore* are retained in the French text in the form of cross references, as are *thereto, thereof,* and *therewith* as possessive pronouns; however, in most cases they are simply omitted. Another Old English tradition that is still preserved in common law drafting is the use of coupled synonyms. In keeping with the fashion of the fifteenth century, coupled synonyms found their way into legal English, some of which were bilingual such as *fit and proper* (old English + French) and *maintenance and upkeep* (French + English). Doubling thus became a habit, resulting in Old English paired with synonyms such as *each and every* and even coupled French synonyms (some of Latin origin) such as *null and void*. It goes without saying that coupled synonyms should be translated with one word in the target text. For example, the expression *full and equal access* is translated as *l'universalité d'accès* in the preamble of *The Official Languages Act*.

10. This is in keeping with Cesanna's third guideline for translators of legislative texts, which reads as follows: 'Die Vollständigkeit. Es bedeutet einen groben Verstoß gegen die Übersetzungstechnik, eigenmächtig Wörter und Wortverbindungen einfach wegzulassen, weil man sie für belanglos hält, oder deren Übertragung als unbequem erachtet' (1910/10:152).

The English affection for doubling is characteristic of the verbose style of common law legislation. From the point of view of civil law drafters, their common law counterparts frequently use more words than necessary to express an idea. Although anglophone drafters claim that this is done for the sake of emphasis or clarity, francophone drafters and translators are now generally permitted to delete any words deemed superfluous as long as the substance remains unchanged. The following excerpt from the Oath of Fidelity and Secrecy in the Schedule of the *Canada Mortgage and Housing Corporation Act* [RSC 1985] shows how extensive such deletions can be:

<table>
<tr><td>I, ... do solemnly swear that I will faithfully, truly and to the best of my judgment, skill and ability, execute and perform the duties required of me as a director (officer *or* employee *as the case may be*) of the Canada Mortgage and Housing Corporation and which properly relate to any office or position in the Corporation held by me.</td><td>Je, ..., jure de bien et fidèlement remplir les fonctions, attachées à l'emploi (*ou* au poste) que j'occupe à la Société canadienne d'hypothèques et de logement.</td></tr>
</table>

In the above text, the formal expression *solemnly* is deleted as superfluous, and the word *truly* as repetitive; the expression *to the best of my judgment, skill and ability* is expressed simply by *bien* in the French text; *execute and perform the duties* by *remplir les fonctions*. The phrase *as the case may be* is omitted, as is the entire phrase *which properly relate to...*, the sense of which is already expressed by the general phrase *attachées à l'emploi (ou au poste) que j'occupe....* In view of these radical deletions, it can be said that the translator has *de facto* formulated a new text. While this example is not a legal rule, extensive changes are now permitted in substantive provisions as well, thus showing to what extent translators have assumed new decision-making authority formerly reserved for drafters.

Anglophone drafters are not always happy with the deletions made by their francophone colleagues. As a general rule, no deletions should be made which could cause ambiguity or alter the substance. Not surprisingly, anglophone and francophone drafters do not always agree on this point. For example, the expression *on, from and after the said day* is rendered as *à compter de la date* in section 2 of the *Manitoba Act* and elsewhere. While the French expression eliminates the redundancy of *from and after*, anglophone drafters claim that it also omits the meaning of *on*. To avoid possible confusion, section 27(3) of *The Interpretation Act* explains that in such cases the time period is computed on the specified day as well.[11] Since judges cannot

---

11.   This is a case in hand where the English text has been improved as a result of increased co-operation with francophone drafters. The expression *on, from and after the said day* has been revised in more recent legislation to read *after the day on which*. The corresponding French text is formulated in several ways, including: *à compter de la date de* (s. 727.6 (9) of the Criminal Code of Canada, as amended in 1988) and *après l'expiration d'un délai de X jours suivant la date de* (s. 251.15 (1), Canada *Labour Code* [SC 1993].

always rely on rules of interpretation to clarify plurilingual texts, translators should exercise caution and refrain from making any deletions that could endanger uniform interpretation of the parallel texts.

At the same time, translators should be aware that superfluous words in the target text can sometimes impede interpretation and even lead to undesired results. Since the parallel texts of a single instrument are construed as independent texts in their own right, superfluous words that run counter to the spirit of the target language can become a 'source of contention.' Thornton's general warning applies to plurilingual legislation as well:

> In legislation, a word used without purpose or needlessly is not merely a tedious imposition upon the time and attention of the reader; it creates a danger because every word in a statute is construed so as to bear a meaning if possible. A superfluous word is therefore a potential source of contention (1987:50).

With this in mind, translators must decide which deletions are justified and how far-reaching they can be without endangering uniform interpretation. Whereas deletions were previously justified only as a means of avoiding unnecessary repetition or increasing clarity, they are now made for reasons of style as well. Having won the right to make stylistic changes, francophone drafters and translators take the liberty of making extensive deletions and reformulating entire provisions. This applies to the statement of law as well as to the fact-situation.

One of the main differences between civil law and common law legislation is the tendency for civil law drafters to rely more on context and inference, thus resulting in a looser texture that is not cluttered with detail. While civil law legislation is a broad statement of principles, common law legislation is an enumeration of instances (Driedger 1982b:12). Believing that each section and subsection of a statute should be self-contained (Driedger 1976:77), common law lawyers intentionally repeat words and entire phrases. As a result, words and phrases that are deemed superfluous by civil law drafters are considered necessary by common law drafters. As a gesture of compromise, francophone drafters and translators of Canadian federal legislation are now permitted to create a looser textured text.

6.8.3. Creating a looser texture

As an initial step in their campaign to create a distinctive style that is more reminiscent of the looser texture of civil law legislation, francophone drafter/translators began to use pronouns instead of repeating the same nouns several times in the same section or subsection. While common law drafters contend that the use of pronouns can result in ambiguity, their francophone counterparts restrict their use of pronouns to instances where the intended reference is clear from the context of the subsection or section as a whole. In the following provision from section 7(1) of the *Canada Mortgage and Housing Corporation Act* [RSC 1985], a pronoun is used in the French text instead of repeating *Governor in Council*. By making the French text active, the drafter/translator shifts the emphasis to the new subject (*gouverneur en conseil*), thus making the reference clear:

185

The President shall be appointed by the *Governor in Council* to hold office during pleasure for such term as the *Governor in Council* deems appropriate.	Le *gouverneur en conseil* nomme le président à titre amovible pour le mandat qu'*il* estime indiqué.

In the following provision of section 34 of the *Canada Mortgage and Housing Corporation Act*, the French text has been entirely reformulated to reduce repetition. By placing the phrase *sur demande de la Sociéte* at the beginning and using the pronoun *lui,* the term *Société* is repeated only twice. Repetition of *gouverneur en conseil* is avoided by using the pronoun *celui-ci*:

The minister of any department or the officer in charge of any other portion of the Government of Canada, or any agent of Her Majesty in right of Canada, may, on request of the *Corporation* and with the approval of the *Governor in Council*, agree to assist the *Corporation* on such conditions as may be approved by the *Governor in Council* by providing such services as the Executive Committee may deem advisable for carrying out the business of the *Corporation*.	Sur demande de la *Sociéte*, les ministres, les responsables de secteurs de l'administration publique fédérale et les mandataires de Sa Majesté du chef du Canada peuvent *lui* fournir, avec l'agrément du *gouverneur en conseil* et aux conditions qu'approuve *celui-ci*, les services que le comité de direction juge utiles aux activités de la *Société*.

As a rule, civil law provisions are formulated in general terms, while common law provisions are particular. Convinced that they can express the same idea in more general terms, francophone drafters and translators began to use a generic term in the French text to express a series of subordinate terms in the English text, a practice that is now widely accepted in Canadian federal legislation. An example can be found in section 9 of *The Official Languages Act* [*SC* 1988] where the English expression *all rules, orders and regulations governing the practice or procedure...* is rendered in French as *les textes régissant la procédure et la pratique....* In this case, the generic term *textes* is acceptable because it includes *rules, orders and regulations.* Such changes involve a high degree of risk as the translator must be absolutely certain that the generic term covers all the subordinate terms yet is not too broad so as to unintentionally widen the scope of application. To avoid possible ambiguity, francophone drafters and translators sometimes identify the items covered by the generic term in a hyphenated appositive and then use the generic term in a subsequent subsection. For example, the subject of subsection 1 of s. 11 of *The Official Languages Act, A notice, advertisement or other matter* is rendered as *Les textes – notamment les avis et annonces* in the French version. Instead of repeating the subject and part of the qualifier in a lengthy cross reference as in subsection 2 of the English text, the French translator simply uses the generic term:

> *Where a notice, advertisement or other matter is printed in one or more publications pursuant to section (1),* it shall be given equal prominence in each official language.

> Il est donné *dans ces textes* égale importance aux deux langues officielles.

No longer bound by the traditional rules of legal translation, francophone translators in Canada have become text producers or, more precisely, co-drafters[12] who formulate new texts in the genius of the target language with a distinctive style of their own. As a result, it is becoming more difficult to distinguish between a source and target text. Instead, both texts can be regarded as originals in the legal, as well as the linguistic sense. Attempts to create a loosely textured text have resulted in less repetition, thus enabling greater concision in the French version of federal legislation. The following provision from section 4(3) of the *Canada Evidence Act* [RSC 1985] shows to what extent diversity is tolerated in the French text for the sake of achieving concision. While many reject such changes as too radical, a closer look reveals that the results are the same. Whereas the English text consists of a compound sentence containing two co-ordinate clauses, the same effect is achieved in a simple sentence in the French text by using the generic term *conjoint* (spouse):

> No husband is compellable to disclose any communication made to him by his wife during their marriage, and no wife is compellable to disclose any communication made to her by her husband during their marriage.

> Nul ne peut être contraint de divulguer une communication que son conjoint lui a faite durant leur mariage.

6.8.4. The use of paragraphing

The use of paragraphing is a common law technique for 'presenting complicated sentences in a digestible state' (Thornton 1987:64). Dick refers to the device as 'sculpturing' or 'paragraph sculpture' (1985:117) which is an adequate description because it emphasizes the visual aspect. Paragraphing, i.e., indenting certain lines of a sentence provides 'a visual aid to comprehension by breaking up solid blocks of type' (Driedger 1982a:78), thus enabling the reader to distinguish between the main and dependent clauses. Set off in separate paragraphs, the dependent clauses usually enumerate a list of contingencies, alternatives, requirements, or conditions which are to be applied cumulatively or alternatively. Although common law drafting experts claim that paragraphing helps remove syntactic ambiguity and avoid repetition, the same subject is often repeated in every condition. Arguing that the device is not always used to its best advantage, francophone drafters and translators began reformulating the text set off by paragraphing. For example, in the English

---

12.   *Cf.* Didier's statement: 'Lorsqu'il s'agit d'un traducteur, celui-ci joue alors effectivement un rôle quasi-législatif' (1990:289).

text of section 16(1) of *The Official Languages Act*, the subject of paragraphs a, b, and c (*every judge or other officer who hears those proceedings*) is repeated three times. To avoid this repetition, the francophone translator places the general phrase *celui qui entend l'affaire* in the introductory part followed by a colon:

Every federal court, other than the Supreme Court of Canada, has the duty to ensure that
(a) if English is the language chosen by the parties for proceedings conducted before it in any particular case, *every judge or other officer who hears those proceedings* is able to understand English without the assistance of an interpreter;
(b) if French is the language chosen by the parties for proceedings conducted before it in any particular case, *every judge or other officer who hears those proceedings* is able to understand French without the assistance of an interpreter; and
(c) if both English and French are the languages chosen by the parties for proceedings conducted before it in any particular case, *every judge or other officer who hears those proceedings* is able to understand both languages without the assistance of an interpreter.

Il incombe aux tribunaux fédéraux autres que la Cour suprême du Canada de veiller à ce que *celui qui entend l'affaire*:
(a) comprenne l'anglais sans l'aide d'un interprète lorsque les parties ont opté pour que l'affaire ait lieu en anglais;
(b) comprenne le français sans l'aide d'un interprète lorsque les parties ont opté pour que l'affaire ait lieu en français;
(c) comprenne l'anglais et le français sans l'aide d'un interprète lorsque les parties ont opté pour que l'affaire ait lieu dans les deux langues.

In common law provisions of criminal law, elements of the fact-situation or statement of law are frequently enumerated in dependent clauses set off by paragraphing. For example, to express alternative punishments in the statement of law, the phrase *is guilty* is repeated at the beginning of each of the paragraphs in the statement of law. To avoid repetition, francophone drafters and translators place *Est coupable* at the very beginning of the provision. While the anglophone drafter uses the connector *or* to express that the punishments are to be applied alternatively, paragraphs a and b both commence with *soit* in the French text.[13] In the following provision from section 96(3) of the Canadian *Criminal Code* [RSC 1985], the fact-situation precedes the statement of law in the English text; the order is reversed in the French text:

Every one who imports any restricted weapon when he is not the holder of

Est coupable:
a) *soit* d'un acte criminel et pas-

---

13. Criminal provisions with alternative punishments are currently formulated according to the following formula in Canadian federal legislation:
   – Every one who ... (a) is guilty of X; or (b) is guilty of Y.
   – Est coupable: a) soit d'un X; b) soit d'un Y, quiconque....

a permit authorizing him to possess that weapon

> (a) *is guilty* of an indictable offence and liable to imprisonment for a term not exceeding five years; *or*
>
> (b) *is guilty* of an offence punishable on summary conviction.

sible d'un emprisonnement maximal de cinq ans;

> b) *soit* d'une infraction punissable sur déclaration de culpabilité par procédure sommaire,

quiconque importe une arme à autorisation restreinte sans être titulaire d'un permis l'autorisant à la posséder.

6.8.5. Restructuring the text

In the late seventies, the Law Reform Commission was established for the purpose of revising the French texts of federal legislation. Insisting that drafters and translators have the right to render the substance of each rule in terms and in a form appropriate to each language, the Commission made proposals to incorporate certain civil law drafting techniques. One of the steps taken by the Commission in its experimental translations was the widespread elimination of paragraphing. Defending its actions, the Commission wrote in its *Report on Evidence*:

> To facilitate this endeavour we have avoided the technique of breaking up sections into paragraphs, except in the case of long or complicated enumerations. Whatever advantage this technique may have is more than outweighed in a bilingual country by the fact that this tends to cast one of the versions in a mould created for the other language. The marginal increase in clarity that such paragraphing yields is easily offset by that resulting from a comparison with another version expressed in accordance with the specific characteristics of the other language (cited in Beaupré 1986:186).

Although numerous proposals submitted by the Law Reform Commission were rejected as too radical, a compromise was reached on paragraphing, allowing francophone drafters and translators to restructure entire sections and subsections without paragraphing. This new freedom resulted in radical changes which, for the first time, affect the actual composition of individual provisions. Each alteration, however, requires careful reflection by drafters and translators who must guarantee that the substance remains unaltered, that the new text is not ambiguous and that the results will be the same in practice. A comparison of the two texts of section 18 of *The Official Languages Act* [SC 1988] shows how far civil law drafters and translators have gone in their attempt to produce a text with a distinctive style of its own. In addition to eliminating paragraphing, the French translator uses the pronoun *elle* to avoid repeating the subject. The result is a concise, loosely textured provision consisting of two sentences:

Where Her Majesty in right of Canada or a federal institution is a party to civil proceedings before a federal court,

> (a) Her Majesty or the institution

Dans une affaire civil à laquelle elle est partie devant un tribunal fédéral, Sa Majesté du chef du Canada ou une institution fédérale utilise, pour les plaidoiries ou les actes de la

concerned shall use, in any oral or written pleadings in the proceedings, the official language chosen by the other parties unless it is established by Her Majesty or the institution that reasonable notice of the language chosen has not been given; and

(b) if the other parties fail to choose or agree on the official language to be used in those pleadings, Her Majesty or the institution concerned shall use such official language as is reasonable, having regard to the circumstances.

procédure, la langue officielle choisie par les autres parties à moins qu'elle n'établisse le caractère abusif du délai de l'avis l'informant de ce choix. Faute de choix ou d'accord entre les autres parties, elle utilise la langue officielle la plus justifiée dans les circonstances.

While the hand of the drafter is visible in the example above, the sequence of information in the French text more or less follows that in paragraphs a and b of the English text. This is not always the case in more recent statutes. For example, in the provision from section 10(3) of the *Marine Transportation Security Act* [SC 1994], the information content of paragraphs a and b of the English text is neither presented in the same sequence nor as two separate points in the French text. Such restructuring is possible in provisions where the information applies cumulatively, not alternatively, i.e., only in provisions where the English paragraphs are connected by *and*. The information content of paragraph b is italicized in the French text:

The Minister may, by notice in writing, request the operator of a vessel or marine facility

(a) to formulate rules respecting any matter specified in the notice relating to the security of the vessel or facility; *and*

(b) to submit the rules to the Minister within any period specified in the notice.

Le ministre peut, par avis écrit, demander à un exploitant *de lui soumettre dans le délai imparti* des règles concernant toute matière qu'il indique pour la sûreté du bâtiment ou de l'installation maritime.

Since each text is independent yet dependent on the other, francophone drafters and translators have been warned not to go too far in their endeavor to restructure the text. Above all, the order and enumeration of sections and subsections must be strictly preserved in order to assure uniform citation. Some flexibility, however, has been allowed in regard to definitions. Since Canadian federal legislation follows the common law practice, francophone drafters and translators have no choice but to place all the definitions in a special section in the preliminary provisions, as in the English text. As a token of conciliation, however, they have been granted limited freedom to develop their own method of presentation. Among other things, this includes the right to change the order of the definitions within the section so that the French terms appear in proper alphabetical order. As a result, the corresponding definitions are no longer printed side by side. To facilitate those wishing to compare definitions, both the French and English terms are listed in the marginal notes of the English as well as the French text. As for the text itself, francophone drafters and translators no longer use the introductory formula *In this Act* and do not follow the English model of formulating definitions: X means Y, or X includes Y and Z. Moreover, the one-sentence rule has been abandoned and a period is placed after each definition in the French text. Paragraphing is also eliminated, thus resulting in a text that not only reads but also looks significantly different than the English text (*see* examples in Chapter 5, 5.13).

6.9. DIVERSITY: HOW MUCH IS TOO MUCH?

At the offset of the legislative reform, the Law Reform Commission of Canada and the Conseil de la langue française of Québec were invited to produce a *Study Paper* containing experimental translations and proposals for creating a distinctive French drafting style that would be more reminiscent of civil law legislation. Made public in 1980, many of the proposals in the *Study Paper*[14] were considered too radical, and the Commission and Conseil were reprimanded for having gone too far. This raises the question: How much diversity can be tolerated without posing a threat to the single instrument?

Although the goal of the Commission and Conseil was to create a new drafting style that could eventually be adopted as a pan-Canadian French drafting style, the proposed revisions were so extensive that the English original had to be subsequently revised to correspond to the new French text. Such actions were criticized by experts who rejected the translations as totally unacceptable. One of the experts, Justice Pigeon, agreed in principle that the French text could have its own distinctive style; however, he accused his fellow francophones of 'putting the shoe on the other foot' by undermining the English version and savaging the common law for the sake of creating a new text in the spirit of the French language and civil law drafting practices. According to Pigeon, his francophone colleagues had overstepped their authority by creating a new text according to civil law standards. Moreover, their proposals modified the substance of the law in numerous provisions of both texts (1982b:185–186). A pertinent example is section 3(1) of the *National Dairy Products Commission Act*. To correspond to the new French text,[15] the English text was to be modified as follows:

14. Among others, the Law Reform Commission made the following proposals: Use a short title and include a purpose clause in the preliminary provisions. Omit the definition section and incorporate as few definitions as possible in the principal provisions. Reorganize the arrangement of provisions in accordance with the principles of deductive reasoning so as to allow the reader to progress from the essential to the subordinate. Use the present indicative of verbs, etc. *See* the summary of suggestions in the *Study Paper* 1981:281–283.

15. The proposed French text of the provision reads as follows: 'Une Commission nationale des produits laitiers est créée.'

191

Present text	*Proposed text*
There shall be a corporation to be known as the Canadian Dairy Commission.	A National Dairy Products Commission is established.

Anglophone drafters raised two objections to the proposed text. First of all, the English expression *there shall be* is not a mandatory form but indicates a creative provision. As Driedger points out, the present tense is not suitable because this kind of provision does not have continuing operation. On the other hand, if the present tense is used, the acceptable formulation would be: *There is hereby established* (Driedger 1976:13). The major objection involves a substantive issue: the deletion of the term *corporation.* Such deletion is totally unacceptable as it changes the status of the Commission from an incorporated to an unincorporated body, thus eliminating the rights and duties accorded to it as a legal entity. As specified in section 21(1) of the *Interpretation Act,* a corporation has 'the power to sue and be sued, to contract and be contracted with by its corporate name, to have a common seal and to alter or change it at pleasure, to have perpetual succession, to acquire and hold personal property for the purposes for which the corporation is established and to alienate that property at pleasure.' Although the authors of the proposed text readily acknowledged that corporate personalty 'is essential to the life of Canadian institutions,' they nevertheless omitted the term *corporation.* The fact that they were unable to agree on a suitable French equivalent is no justification for such an irresponsible decision (Pigeon 1983:693).

Emphasizing the need to reach a compromise, Pigeon advised francophone drafters and translators to strike a balance with the English text and the common law in federal statutes (1982b:185–186). One of the results of that compromise can be seen in section 3 of the *Canada Mortgage and Housing Corporation Act [RSC 1985].* Today, in provisions establishing a corporation, francophone drafters and translators use the term *Société* for *corporation.* In addition, the phrase *avec personnalité morale* is included in the French text to indicate that the particular *société* is a corporate body.[16] As part of the compromise, the act of creating is expressed in the present tense in both texts:

There is hereby established a *corporation* to be called the 'Canada Mortgage and Housing Corporation' consisting of...	Est constituée la *Société* canadienne d'hypothèque et de logement, *dotée de la personnalité morale* et composée du...

Reaching a compromise on the limits of stylistic diversity in federal legislation is absolutely essential. Generally speaking, the limited use of civil law drafting practices is acceptable as long as it does not pose a threat to uniform interpretation. As a rule, any stylistic diversity is deemed unacceptable if it changes the substance and/or interferes with the rules of interpretation used by federal judges and the justices of the Supreme Court of Canada. Since successful communication pre-

---

16. For an excellent comparative law analysis of the terms *société, association, compagnie,* and *corporation, see* Vanderlinden 1995:87–117.

supposes that the rules of interpretation are coordinated with the drafting style and vice versa, any significant change in drafting style is likely to require a corresponding change in the accepted rules of interpretation (Dale 1977:292). Therefore, common law lawyers have made it clear that the French version of federal statutes cannot be written in a style that is incompatible with the common law rules of interpretation:

> The Supreme Court of Canada interprets legislation by common law methods, and statutes must therefore be written to fit those methods (Driedger 1982a:72).

Bound to the text when ascertaining the legislative intent, common law judges must ascertain the intent by giving meaning to the words in the text. As Driedger put it: 'The law is what the legislature has said, no more and no less' (1982a:80). For this reason, common law texts tend to be an enumeration of circumstances and exceptions rather than broad principles. On the other hand, civil law judges are not bound to the text but are permitted to resort to inference when ascertaining the intent. Having considerable more discretion, they are usually permitted to supplement statutory and customary law by filling in gaps (*see* Chapter 3, 3.2.1).

While francophone drafters and translators must refrain from creating an overly loose text that would be incompatible with the common law rules of interpretation, they still have ample freedom to be creative. Taking advantage of their new freedom, they combine the elements of stylistic diversity mentioned above to create a new French text that is not bound to the English text. The goal is to produce two independent texts, both of which express the same legislative intent and lead to the same results in practice. The following example from section 10 of the *Marine Transportation Security Act* [SC 1994] illustrates to what extent diversity is tolerated in the French text. Whereas each subsection of the English text is self-contained, the French text relies on context and inference, thus resulting in a loosely textured, natural French text with a distinctive style of its own:

(6) Within one hundred and twenty days after the rules have been submitted, the Minister shall decide whether to approve them and shall notify the operator of the decision in writing and, if the Minister approves the rules,
    (a) the Minister may make the approval subject to any conditions the Minister considers appropriate:
    (b) the operator shall notify the persons who were consulted that the rules have been approved; and
    (c) the operator shall carry out the rules and any conditions of their approval until the approval is revoked.

(7) If the Minister decides not to

(6) Le ministre fait connaître sa décision par écrit dans les cent vingt jours. En cas d'approbation, il peut assortir les règles de sûreté des conditions qu'il juge utiles et l'exploitant est tenu, d'une part, d'aviser les personnes consultées de leur approbation et, d'autre part, de mettre en oeuvre les règles de sûreté et leurs conditions jusqu'à révocation de l'approbation.

(7) En cas de rejet, le ministre fait

193

approve the rules, the Minister shall give the operator reasons for the decision and the Minister may request the operator to revise and resubmit the rules within any period that the Minister may specify.	connaître à l'exploitant les motifs de sa décision et peut lui impartir un délai pour soumission de règles révisées.
(8) Amendments to security rules may be submitted and approved in the same way as are the security rules they amend and, when approved, have the same effect.	(8) La procédure de soumission et d'approbation des règles de sûreté est la même pour leur modification et leur confère le même effet.
(9) The Minister may revoke the approval of security rules, either at the request of the operator or otherwise.	(9) L'approbation est révocable.

The upper limits of diversity are undoubtedly reached in the French text of subsection 9 above. Here the same idea is conveyed in an abbreviated passive sentence that repeats neither the subject *the Minister* nor the object *security rules*. Moreover, the entire phrase describing the situations in which approval may be revoked (*either at the request of the operator or otherwise*) is deleted. It can be argued that such deletion is justified because the word *otherwise* broadens the fact-situation to include all situations, thus making an enumeration of situations unnecessary. Similar proposals were made by the Law Reform Commission (*see Study Paper* 1981:245–247).

Francophone drafters agree that a compromise must be reached in order to guarantee the harmonious co-existence of the two texts. Nonetheless, the debate on style is still not closed. In regard to the future, Driedger outrules the possibility that the English text will be written in common law style and the French text in civil law style. Instead, he foresees the creation of a common style, a Canadian style. To achieve this end, anglophone drafters must also be willing to make concessions by giving up some of their common law drafting practices:

> I hope and believe that eventually, although not in my time, we will have one style for English and French statutes in Canada that will not be designated as being in either common law style or civil law style, but simply Canadian style (1982a:81).

Perhaps this is the ultimate compromise that the late Justice Pigeon had in mind when he wrote: 'Il faudrait, à mon avis, que... les deux textes reflètant également le compromis entre les deux communautés culturelles, leurs juristes et leurs rédacteurs...' (1982b:185–86). To guarantee uniform interpretation and application of the single instrument, any significant changes in drafting style will also require that an agreement be reached on adequate rules of interpretation. Such a compromise is likely to be more difficult to achieve.

7 The Translation of Multilateral Instruments

7.1. ADDITIONAL CONSTRAINTS ON TRANSLATORS

International lawyers were winding up their first project in simultaneous multilingual drafting when the Canadians launched their co-drafting experiment. The results, however, are strikingly different. Confronted by additional constraints which restrict their creativity, drafters and translators of multilateral instruments must exercise extreme caution in their decision-making process. Thus their main concern is not how much diversity can be tolerated but rather how to ensure the concordance of the parallel texts of instruments of international and supranational law. This Chapter deals primarily with the translation of treaties and conventions produced under the auspices of the United Nations and other international institutions, as well as instruments of the European Union.

Treaties are international agreements concluded between sovereign states (the heads or Governments of States or Government Departments). Treaties concluded between two states are bilateral, between more than two states, multilateral. *Treaty* is a generic term denoting all types of international agreements; at the same time it is also a hyponym of itself denoting 'more solemn agreements such as treaties of peace, alliance, neutrality, arbitration' (McNair 1986:22). Whereas such treaties are more like contracts, rival forms of treaties have developed that are similar to legislation: conventions, declarations, protocols, acts, final acts, and general acts. Attempts at establishing uniform laws at the international level have resulted in numerous conventions regulating areas of private law such as commercial law, transport, arbitration, banking, and conflicts of laws, as well as public domains such as maritime law, treaty law, human rights, and others. One of the primary sources of international law, conventions are drawn up and adopted at diplomatic conferences convened for that purpose.

While conventions and other uniform laws produced under the auspices of the International Institute for the Unification of Private Law in Rome (UNIDROIT) and The Hague Conference on Private International Law are bilingual (French and English), UN-sponsored instruments are currently produced in six parallel texts. Since the latest expansion of the European Union in January of 1995, instruments of primary European law are produced in 12 parallel texts (Chapter 1, note 11). In regard to the production of multilingual instruments, Tabory once remarked that the difficulties grow with every addition to the number of authentic texts (1980:146). While Tabory is referring mainly to linguistic problems resulting from the increased number of language versions, one must not forget that the situation of reception, i.e., the interpretation process is also affected by the increased number of participants and legal systems involved in the communication process. As shown in this Chapter, the decision-making process of translators is significantly influenced by both the multilingual and multilateral aspects of the communication process involving treaties and conventions.

7.2. THE EMERGENCE OF MULTILINGUALISM

The history of international law shows that the original practice was to have one recognized language of diplomacy. In particular, Sumerian, Akkadian, Assyrian, Persian, Armaic, Chinese, Greek, and Arabic each served at some time as the *lingua franca* of diplomacy among the early centers of civilization in Africa, Asia, and Asia Minor (Tabory 1980:4). After 753 B.C. Latin was the language of Rome and Roman diplomacy; from 31 B.C. it became the language of the Roman Empire and the Catholic Church, of Roman law and canon law. Apparently the only written medium at the time,[1] Latin continued to dominate treatymaking practice in central and western Europe, remaining the principal diplomatic language during and even after the Middle Ages. Toward the end of the fifteenth century, Latin supremacy was briefly challenged by Castilian Spanish, which had become the diplomatic idiom in numerous courts (Tabory 1980:4). The final challenge, however, came from France. As a result of the success of the armies of Louis VIX and the growing importance of French literature, the French language gained such prestige and widespread recognition that it replaced Latin as the accepted language of diplomacy at the beginning of the eighteenth century. When Latin demonstrated its impracticability at peace congresses, French also became the exclusive medium of multilateral and most bilateral treaties (Verzilj 1973:187). This was confirmed by its use even in international agreements marking the defeat of France, such as the Acts of the Congress of Vienna of 1815 and the Frankfurt Peace Treaty of 1871 (Hilf 1973:6). Despite objections on the part of the British, French dominated the language of diplomacy for nearly two centuries. Its continued acceptance was regarded as a diplomatic usage, not as a precedent in international law (Satow 1957:59).

After World War I, English was granted the status of an official language together with French at the 1919 Paris Peace Conference, thus ending the dominance of one language in diplomatic affairs. The new practice of declaring international agreements equally authentic in more than one language version was also initiated with the Treaty of Versailles, which was declared equally authentic in both French and English. An integral part of the Treaty of Versailles, the Covenant of the League of Nations also granted French and English equal status as the working languages of the organization. After World War II, the position of French weakened, causing it to struggle to retain parity with English in the initial years of the United Nations. Although French and English were recognized as the working languages of the UN, they had to share their status as official languages with Chinese, Russian, and

---

1. Sir Satow writes: 'Formerly the language in universal use was Latin, which may be said to have been at first the only language in which men knew how to write, at least in central and western Europe' (1957:57).

196

Spanish (Art. 11 of the UN Charter). According to the rules of procedure of the General Assembly, the verbatim records, documents, and the Official Journal were made available in the working languages. On the other hand, only the resolutions, important documents and summary records were translated into the other official languages. As a result of the growing importance attributed to the principle of the equality of states, the distinction between working and official languages gradually disappeared in the various UN bodies. As the largest language group within the UN, Spanish was granted the status of a working language of the General Assembly and its committees and subcommittees in 1948; Russian followed in 1968, and Chinese in 1973. Upon the request of the Arab countries, Arabic was recognized as both an official and a working language of the General Assembly and its main committees in 1973 (*see* Tabory 1980:7–9; *also Yearbook of the ILC* 1966:II-106).

The parallel texts of multilateral instruments are drawn up on the basis of a basic text which is usually prepared in advance. In regard to conventions concluded within the General Assembly, the basic text may be drawn up by the substantive services of the Secretariat, by a special commission attached to the General Assembly, or by the delegates themselves. For example, the basic text of the Convention on the Prevention and Punishment of the Crime of Genocide (1948) was drawn up by the substantive Secretariat in French; the translation service of the Secretariat translated the draft into English; and a drafting committee approved and coordinated the two drafts. The remaining authentic texts were translated by the Secretariat in accordance with the procedure described in its memorandum on the 'Preparation of Multilingual Treaties' (A/CN.4/187 in *Yearbook of the ILC* 1966 II:104–111). Unfortunately, the memorandum describes procedural formalities without mentioning translation techniques. As regards the International Convention on the Elimination of All Forms of Racial Discrimination (1965), the basic text was prepared by the Commission on Human Rights in cooperation with the Sub-Commission on Prevention of Discrimination and Protection of Minorities. The draft articles in English were then translated by the Secretariat into French. Since there was no coordination committee, suggestions for harmonizing and coordinating the parallel texts were made by the General Assembly's Third Committee. The Secretariat was also responsible for preparing the Russian, Spanish, and Chinese translations (Tabory 1980:95–96).

When multilateral conventions are adopted by conferences convened by the General Assembly, the draft articles are usually prepared by a drafting committee of the International Law Commission (ILC). At the offset, the ILC resumed responsibility only for the drafting of the English and French texts; Spanish was added in 1964, sixteen years after becoming a working language of the General Assembly. Despite the fact that Russian, Chinese, and Arabic have also been elevated to the status of working languages, the work of the ILC has remained basically trilingual (Tabory 1980:97). Often prepared by one or more special reporters, the basic texts of the draft articles are commonly written in the language(s) of the reporter(s). For example, at the first Conference on the Law of the Sea in 1958, the basic texts of the draft articles were written in French, then translated into English. A Conference drafting committee was appointed at an early stage to review all the articles and coordinate the English, French, and Spanish texts. At the Conference on Diplomatic Intercourse and Immunities in 1963, the basic texts were drawn up in both English and French. At the Conference on the Law of Treaties (1969), the

197

basic texts were in English only; however, the negotiations and the actual drafting were trilingual. In all instances, the final Acts and the Russian and Chinese translations were prepared by the Secretariat with the assistance of interested delegations and representatives (Tabory 1980:96–99).

7.3. INTERPRETATION AND THE PRINCIPLE OF EQUAL AUTHENTICITY

Earlier it was common practice to insert a language clause in the final provisions specifying which text was to prevail in the event of a divergence in the meaning of the authentic texts of a treaty or convention. In the absence of such a clause, it was left to the courts to determine the prevailing text. In most cases, priority was given to the original text, which was generally held to be the most reliable (*see* Chapter 3, 3.4.1). General recognition of the principle of equal authenticity made the task of interpreting treaties more complicated by obliging judges to compare the various language versions and reconcile any discrepancies in meaning that might occur. Theoretically, if each text is open to several interpretations, the judge should give effect to all the authentic texts by determining the meaning common to all texts (*see* Chapter 3, 3.4.1). Accordingly, if one or more meanings is broader than the other(s), the meaning signifying the lowest common denominator of all the texts should prevail. This appears to have been the reasoning behind the Permanent Court of Justice's decision in its ruling in the *Mayrommatis Palestine Concessions*, a dispute emanating from the Palestine Mandate embodied in a resolution of the League of Nations. Here the Court opted for the restrictive meaning of the English expression *public control* over the broader meaning purported by the French term *contrôle public*. Apparently the decision was motivated by the reasoning that, if one or more meanings is broader than the other(s), the meaning signifying the lowest common denominator of all the texts should prevail. In its reasons, however, the Court also acknowledged that it favored the English expression because the instrument set forth obligations for Great Britain in her capacity as Mandatory for Palestine and because 'the original draft of the instrument was probably made in English.' In an attempt to prove that the English text was the original, Judge Moore maintained in his dissenting opinion that the fact that *public control* is a technical expression, while *contrôle public* is vague, suggests that the latter is a literal translation of the former (Hardy 1962:77, 79 note 4).

Since arguments favoring the original text still carried weight in courts, attorneys attempted to win cases or set aside unfavorable decisions by discrediting translations. For example, in *Naomi Russel (United States)* v. *Mexico*, the United States tried to set aside the decision on the ground that the Claims Commission appointed to adjudicate claims relating to loss or damage caused to US citizens favored the Spanish text 'which was a mere translation prepared without leave from the authors of the treaty.' One of the disputed questions turned on the following phrase in Article III of the Convention of September 10, 1923:

(2) By revolutionary forces as a result of the triumph of whose cause governments *de facto* or *de jure* have

(2) Por fuerzas revolucionarias que hayan establecido al triunfo de su causa gobiernos *de jure* o *de facto*, o

been established, or by revolutionary forces opposed to *them*. [emphasis added]

por fuerzas revolucionarias contrarias a *aquéllas*. [emphasis added]

Whereas the Spanish word *aquéllas* clearly refers to *fuerzas*, the US Commissioner argued that the pronoun *them* referred to *governments* and thus the phrase also covered insurgents who had not succeeded in forming a government. Following this reasoning, he claimed that Mexico was bound to make reparation for damages caused by supporters of Orozco, an insurgent General who had failed to seize power. Remarking that both texts were equally authentic, the Presiding Commissioner ruled on the basis of the clear Spanish text, which was more favorable to Mexico. This is apparently because Mexico had assumed its obligation *ex gratia* (*see* Hardy 1962:85–87).

The above ruling favoring the translation as the clear text is an exception. Although one text should not prevail over the other(s), international jurisprudence shows that the principle of equal authenticity has not been strictly upheld from the very beginning. In numerous cases judges have felt 'entitled to establish an order of precedence among [the texts], at least on a specific point, and to recognize the superiority of the original version' (Hardy 1962:98). In view of the tendency for courts to favor the original text on the pretense of 'translation defects,' it is not surprising that lawyers came to mistrust translations, relegating them an inferior status. It soon became evident that, in order for the principle of equal authenticity to be respected, judges needed clearer guidelines for interpreting the parallel texts of multilateral instruments.

An initial step in this direction was taken in Article 33 of the Vienna Convention on the Law of Treaties of 1969, which directly addresses the problem of interpreting plurilingual treaties. Paragraph 1 of Article 33 codifies the equal authenticity principle by declaring that the text of a treaty authenticated in two or more languages is equally authoritative in each language, unless the treaty or parties provide that a particular text shall prevail. The new importance attached to the principle of equal authenticity was intended to confer undisputable authority on each of the authentic texts, *de facto* eliminating the inferior status of authoritative translations. As specified in paragraph 3, equal authenticity rests on the presumption that the terms of a treaty have the same meaning in each authentic text. Despite the lofty intentions behind the presumption of equal meaning, lawyers were the first to acknowledge that 'some degree of divergence between the language texts of a multilingual treaty is inevitable' (Kuner 1991:958; *see* Chapter 3, 3.3.2), thus making it necessary to establish special rules of interpretation. Encouraging judges to establish a common meaning by reconciliation, paragraph 4 provides that, in cases of divergence, obscurity or ambiguity, every reasonable effort should be made to reconcile the texts, having regard to the object and purpose of the treaty. This approach is compatible with the idea that the authentic texts of a single instrument derive their meaning from one another.

While lawyers have generally praised the codification of rules of interpretation in the 1969 Vienna Convention as an achievement, Article 33(4) has also been criticized for its failure to specify concrete methods to be used to reconcile the meaning of divergent texts (Tabory 1980:215). For this reason, international tribunals have generally refrained from reading too much into Article 33(4) (Rosenne 1983:783). Despite the absence of firm guidelines designating specific techniques for ascertaining the common meaning and/or resolving ambiguities and other textual discrepancies, one tendency is clear: The practice of giving priority to the original text has been declared incompatible with the principle of equal authenticity. The new practice is enshrined in the award rendered in the *Young Loan* case (*Belgium, France, Switzerland, the United Kingdom and the United States of America v. Federal Republic of Germany*),[2] in which the Arbitral Tribunal explicitly refused to give the English text of the German External Debts Agreement 'special interpretative weight' merely because the disputed clause was originally drafted in that language:

> The Tribunal takes the view that the habit occasionally found in earlier international practice of referring to the basic or original text as an aid to interpretation is now, as a general rule, incompatible with the principle, incorporated in Article 33(1) of the [Vienna Convention on the Law of Treaties], of the equal status of all authentic texts in plurilingual treaties. The interpretational maxim of the special importance of precedence... of the original text would relegate the other authentic texts again to the status of subordinated translations (cited in Rosenne 1983:767).

While supporting the principle of equal authenticity, Rosenne is also one of its main critics. Acknowledging that 'the interpretation of multilingual texts cannot be divorced from the manner of their preparation,' Rosenne challenges the unconditional acceptance of equal authenticity, warning that it can be counterproductive and even threaten the unity of the single instrument (1987b:694). In particular, Rosenne questions the interpretative value of translations authenticated in irregular proceedings. Fearing that such translations could reduce the principle of equal authenticity to a mere fiction, he encourages judges to determine the reliability of the parallel texts of multilateral instruments by examining their drafting history (1983:782).

7.4. TRANSLATION AND THE SPECIAL NATURE OF TREATIES

One of the few international lawyers to have tried his hand at translation, Rosenne is among the best qualified to question the practice of unconditionally assigning the same interpretative value to all authentic texts. By no means does Rosenne underestimate the skills of translators. On the contrary, he is fully aware of the potential pitfalls that can befall translators and, particularly, of the grave consequences that can be triggered by differences between the language versions of treaties and diplomatic texts. As shown by past diplomatic incidents, even slight discrepancies in the parallel texts of highly sensitive political agreements can endanger the peace and stability of the international order. A well-known example is the first Italian-

---

2. *Young Loan* Arbitration, award of May 16, 1980; *see International Law Reports* vol. 59 at 529–530.

Ethiopian war which was allegedly caused by a discrepancy between the equally authentic Italian and Amharic texts of the Treaty of Friendship and Commerce, signed at Uccialli in 1889. The dispute turned on Article 17 of the Treaty, which in the Amharic text permitted the Ethiopian Emperor Menelik to use the Italian Government's services to conduct foreign relations. In the Italian text the same provision was expressed as a command, not a permission. The conflict developed because Italy is said to have proclaimed a protectorate over Ethiopia on the grounds of the mandatory form of Article 17. Rejecting such interpretation, the Ethiopian Emperor denounced the Friendship Treaty, an act that ironically led to war (*see* Tabory 1980:5; *also* Verzilj 1973:199).

It is presumed that all the authentic texts of treaties and diplomatic texts reflect the intent of the States parties (*cf.* Chapter 4, 4.2). Misrepresenting the intent is a grave error that has evoked fatal consequences in international affairs. For instance, the decision to drop the first atomic bombs on Nagasaki and Hiroshima is allegedly due to a translation error in the English text of the communique sent by the Japanese Prime Minister in response to the Allies' ultimatum at the end of July 1945. The Japanese text apparently contained the polysemous expression *mokusatsu,* which can mean 'to consider' but also 'to disregard or ignore.' With the intention of winning time, the Premier had used *moskusatsu* in the sense of 'consider.' Unfortunately, the translator of the official Japan Foreign Information Center misinterpreted the intent and translated the term in the second sense, thus giving the Allied Powers reason to believe that Japan had rejected the ultimatum (cited in Reiß 1995:59).

By now it should be clear that decisions of translators of treaties and diplomatic texts may have farreaching and irreversible effects. The fact that sophisticated telecommunications systems now link the countries of the world does not diminish the awesome responsibility of translators of instruments of international law. Regardless of the sensitivity of the subject matter, incongruencies in the parallel texts of international agreements can result in international disputes and unnecessary litigation or legal uncertainty (*cf.* Verzilj 1973:199). Numerous disputes, such as the Soviet charges against the United States regarding nuclear testing in 1987,[3] could have been avoided if the treatymakers would have taken greater pains to ensure the concordance of the parallel texts. The demand for flawless decision-making automatically places additional pressure on translators, forcing them to carefully weigh each and every word and give special consideration to all possible interpretations and misinterpretations when formulating the text. While the above examples are from bilingual documents, the difficulties of drafting and translation 'grow with every addition to the number of authentic versions,' as a result of which 'the probability of confusion, errors and discrepancies is multiplied in direct proportion to the number of authentic texts' (Tabory 1980:146). Translators of multilingual instruments must take account not only of the basic text(s) but of all the parallel texts of that instrument. Although they are now widely permitted to formulate the text in the spirit

---

3. The then USSR based its charges on the Russian text of the 1963 Threshold Test Ban Treaty. The US defended its actions by reference to the English text of the same treaty, which differed from the Russian text on that point (*see* Kuner 1991:953).

of the target language, their main priority is to preserve the unity of the single instrument by ensuring concordance of the parallel texts.

7.4.1. Reliability and interlingual concordance

International lawyers commonly distinguish between concordance and harmonization. While harmonization is the process of ensuring internal consistency of terminology and presentation within a given text, concordance is the process of ensuring consistency of terminology and presentation between each and all the authentic texts (Rosenne 1983:775–776). Since the two processes overlap in numerous aspects, they are sometimes regarded as one translation operation. This, however, is not the case in international law. Due to the sensitivity of the subject-matter, as well as the increased number of texts involved in the communication process, translators of instruments of international law are under constant pressure to achieve interlingual concordance (sometimes called intertextual symmetry or correspondence). While translators of Canadian federal legislation are encouraged to experiment with stylistic diversity (*see* Chapter 6, 6.8), it is usually too risky for translators of multilateral instruments to be creative with language. Regardless of the communicative situation, their main concern is to promote uniform interpretation and application by preserving the unity of the single instrument.

For many lawyers the yardstick for measuring the reliability of the parallel texts of multilateral instruments is the degree of their interlingual concordance, more specifically, how closely the terminology and syntax of the parallel texts of the same instrument are coordinated. As Sager points out, parallel texts with structural diversities are often regarded with mistrust. Although he calls such attitude 'naive,' he admits that it is effective:

> Paralleltexte, vor allem in verwandten Sprachen, werden oft im Verlgeich miteinander gelesen und kritisiert, wenn sie keine deutlich erkennbare strukturelle Ähnlichkeiten aufweisen. So naiv eine derartige Kritik auch ist, kann sie dennoch Ausdruck eines erschutterten Vertrauens in den Text sein, und dadurch wird dessen Wirkung geschwächt (1986:344).

Believing that linguistic conformity promotes uniform interpretation and application, international lawyers require strict concordance between the parallel texts of multilateral instruments. For a long time, the preference for strict interlingual concordance was interpreted as implying that translations of instruments of international law should be literal. Later, however, lawyers began to criticize translations of treaties inhibited with the 'word-for-word mentality' (Hardy 1962:89), advising translators to respect the genius of each language to the extent possible. Eventually lawyers came to the conclusion that absolute concordance is neither possible, nor desirable:

> Language possesses its own genius which influences the choice of words and the arrangement of the sentence. It is therefore rarely possible to maintain, either in form or in meaning, a perfect concordance between the different texts of a plurilingual treaty (Hardy 1962:82).

Other lawyers were more emphatic and encouraged translators of treaties to render the contents 'clearly and idiomatically,' even if this requires grasping 'syntax by the neck and vigorously [shaking] it, changing the order of paragraphs and words, substituting many words for one when necessary and vice versa...' (cited in Rosenne 1971:366). Although this liberal view is clearly an exception, today it is agreed that translators of treaties should strive to produce an idiomatic text that reads like an original, yet preserves sufficient interlingual concordance so as to prevent ambiguity and possible misinterpretations. In view of the increased pressure on translators of treaties 'to get the message right,' the difficulty of this task should not be underestimated. According to Hardy, translation defects are due mostly to the inability of translators to render the intended ideas while respecting the genius of each language (1962:99). Therefore, even highly skilled translators are cautious about being overly creative with language, usually preferring to give interlingual concordance priority over linguistic purity, particularly as the number of authentic texts increases.

As a rule, drafters of treaties and conventions make a conscious effort to express the intent of the parties in general terms, using a simple and straightforward style with uncomplicated syntax that can be easily understood and translated into other languages. This is the case, for example, in Article 30 of the UN Convention on Contracts for the International Sale of Goods (1980), which is cited below in English, French, Spanish, and Russian. Each of the four language versions is clear and unambiguous, and all texts are adequately coordinated so as to preserve the unity of single instrument. While the Spanish and Russian texts follow the English word order, the slight deviations in the French text do not affect the substance. It is clear that all obligations are mandatory and must be performed as required by the contract and the Convention:

The seller must deliver the goods, hand over any documents relating to them and transfer the property in the goods, as required by the contract and this Convention.

Le vendeur s'oblige, dans les conditions prévues au contrat et par la présente Convention, à livrer les marchandises, à en transférer la propriété et, s'il y a lieu, à remettre les documents s'y rapportant.

El vendedor deberá entregar las mercaderías, transmitir su propiedad y entregar cualesquiera documentos relacionados con ellas en las condiciones establecidas en el contrato y en la presente Convención.

Продавец обязан поставить товар, передать относящиеся к нему документы и передать право собственности на товар в соответствии с требованиями договора и настоящей Конвенции.

Despite the good intention of drafters to use clear and simple language, this is not always possible in international agreements, especially treaties. This is because they are negotiated texts.

7.4.2. Treaties are negotiated texts

Treaties are agreements prepared by negotiators authorized to represent the interests of the participating States parties.[4] There are no particular requirements as to the manner of negotiation, or reaching agreement, or the form of a treaty. Negotiations normally result in the adoption of an agreed text setting out the mutual undertakings of the parties. In numerous instances, however, the negotiating parties are unable to reach agreement on certain points of contention, as a result of which the 'agreed text' is little more than a 'disagreement reduced to writing' (cited in Tabory 1980:227). Failing consensus, they frequently resort to a compromise that glosses over their differences with vague, obscure, or ambiguous wording. Sacrificing clarity for the sake of obtaining consensus occurs not only in treaties of a political nature but also increasingly in international legislation, especially in the form of conventions. As confirmed by Ramberg, it is becoming more and more difficult to reach consensus on legal solutions in international legislation. Attributing this tendency to increased differences of opinion among the contracting States, Ramberg notes that 'in most cases, compromises are necessary in order to reach any result at all.' Furthermore, he acknowledges that such compromises 'might entail intentional obscurity so that it is difficult to distinguish winners and losers in the clash of opinion' (1992:107). As a result, treaties and conventions which are negotiated texts leave very little, if any *Spielraum* for translators to be creative. The warning is clear: Translators should avoid attempts to clarify vague points, obscurities, and ambiguities. Those who do, run the risk of upsetting the delicately achieved balance and misrepresenting the intent of the parties.

Since it is presumed that each of the authenticated texts is an agreed text that expresses the true intent of the parties, one of the greatest fears of international lawyers is that translators will scuttle the intent of the parties by attempting to clarify clauses that are intentionally vague, obscure, or even ambiguous (Rosenne 1983:783). Since this fear is not unfounded, Rosenne maintains that authentic texts which are not 'the fruit of negotiation' pose a threat to the unity of the single instrument, making it even more difficult for judges to ascertain the true intent. In particular, he disapproves of authenticated translations that are 'the product of a technical service supplied by an international secretariat operating virtually independently of the contracting parties' (1954:384). With each additional authenticated translation, the chances increase that the common meaning of all the texts will no longer reflect the true intent of the negotiated instrument. Aware of the potential danger of this possibility, Rosenne challenges the principle of equal authenticity by encouraging judges to distinguish between 'negotiated language versions' and those 'produced mechanically by some translation service, however competent' (1971:361).

---

4. Exceptions are so-called unequal treaties in which the bargaining power of one of the parties is significantly reduced or one of the parties has no bargaining power at all. An example of the latter is a peace treaty whose terms have been dictated by the victorious state(s), *see International Law Reports* 1951:419.

As a means of monitoring the reliability or interpretative value of authenticated translations, Rosenne urges judges to examine how the texts were actually prepared (when, where, by whom) and which steps were taken to ensure interlingual concordance (1983:782–783). Coordinating the parallel texts of international instruments is a delicate and responsible process involving both linguistic and legal decisions. In essence, those comparing and coordinating the terminology and syntax of parallel texts are responsible for deciding in which instances linguistic diversity does not alter the substance and is therefore justified and, vice versa, when linguistic diversity should be avoided to ensure greater conformity as a means of protecting the interests of the parties. In order to preserve the true intent, it is imperative that the decision-makers have first-hand knowledge of the intent of the negotiating parties. Even then, however, it can occur that an apparently harmless linguistic diversity later leads to major differences in interpretation.

A classic example is the disputed clause in UN Security Council Resolution 242 (1967) which reads as follows in the English text:

> Withdrawal of Israeli armed forces *from territories* occupied in the recent conflict...
> [emphasis added].

The phrase *from territories* appears in the other authentic texts as *des territoires*, *s territorii*, and *de los territorios*, all of which are correct grammatical renditions of the English text. However, the use of the definite article in the French and Spanish texts, as opposed to no article in the English and Russian texts later raised the question as to whether the intention of the negotiators was to oblige Israel to withdraw its forces from *all* or just *some* of the occupied territories. While Israel bases its arguments on the English text, Arab supporters cite the French text. Submitted by the United Kingdom, the draft resolution was in English and the original text was also English, the language of the negotiations between the members of the Security Council and other interested parties. Prepared by the language services of the UN Secretariat, the other texts (translations) were reviewed by the substantive Secretariat officials in the Department of Political and Security Council Affairs of the Secretariat assigned to the Security Council and subsequently by members of the Security Council in informal meetings. It is noteworthy that the Spanish text had previously read *de territorios* in the draft resolution and was later revised by the Spanish-speaking members of the Security Council. This revision is significant because it aligned the Spanish with the French text, thus resulting in two texts with and two without definite articles. In regard to the French text, legal experts have found it to be 'an accurate and idiomatic rendering of the original English text, and possibly even the only acceptable rendering into French' (Rosenne 1971:363, 360–364).[5]

---

5. From Gémar's point of view, the French text is defective: 'On notera la traduction française "from territories" par "des territoires", ce qui, grammaticalement parlant, n'est pas une équivalence et constitue même une faute (de traduction)' (1995–II:141).

7.4.3. Authentication and the time element

Rosenne's criticism of authenticated translations drew attention to irregularities in the authentication procedure which challenge the presumption that each of the parallel texts expresses the true intent of the negotiating parties. As shown in Chapter 4 (4.2.3), the time element is an essential factor in the authentication procedure. From the legal point of view, in order for a text to be authentic, the first condition is that 'it should have been adopted by the treaty-adopting body itself.' If that was not the case, then Rosenne concludes that despite 'all its political and psychological importance, the designation of a text as "authentic" carries in itself little if any weight' (1983:782). In practice, however, technical difficulties and time pressures often make it impossible to complete one or more translations in time for adoption. Nonetheless, it has become common to adopt all the texts cited in the language clause and declare them equally authentic, regardless of whether they have been reviewed and approved by the delegates. Not surprisingly, the Chinese text has caused the most problems. For example, in the case of the Convention on the Elimination of Racial Discrimination, the English, French, Russian, and Spanish texts were distributed prior to the adoption of the draft convention by the General Assembly on December 21, 1965. Although the Chinese text was not available until February 7, 1966, it was officially approved at the time of adoption (Tabory 1980:96).

In an attempt to rectify such shortcomings, treatymakers now insist that formal authentication is not the act of adoption but rather that of signature or other procedure agreed upon by the parties. A provision to this effect has been incorporated into Article 10 of the Vienna Convention on the Law of Treaties. Unfortunately, this step only confirms Rosenne's fears that the principle of equal authenticity is being reduced to a fiction (*see* Rosenne 1983:782). The most flagrant example (Verzijl 1973:198) is the Chicago Convention on Civil Aviation, which was adopted on December 7, 1944. At that time it was hoped that the missing translations in French and Spanish would be supplied by the date of signature. In this sense, the final clause stated that 'a text drawn up in the English, French and Spanish languages, each of which shall be of equal authenticity, shall be opened for signature...' Not only were the translations not ready by the date of signature, they had not yet been completed when the Convention entered into force. In fact, unofficial translations were used for a period of 24 years. The protocol on the authentic trilingual text of the Convention was officially approved and signed by the contracting States at the OCAO Conference held in Buenos Aires on September 24, 1968 (*see* details in Hilf 1973:41). Apparently the situation did not improve significantly after the signing of the 1969 Convention on the Law of Treaties. According to UN Official Documents, when a delegate inquired about the production of the authentic Chinese text of the Single Convention on Narcotic Drugs of 1972, the legal adviser to the Conference replied that 'arrangements had been made to produce the Chinese text at a later stage, after the original of the Protocol had been transmitted to United Nations Headquarters for deposit.' As he explained, this procedure had been adopted for financial reasons. Since the People's Republic of China had not been represented at the Conference, it would have been too expensive to bring 'a staff of Chinese translators and calligraphers to Geneva to prepare the Chinese text' (UN Official Records 1972 II: 64 (14th plenary meeting)).

The main issue raised by Rosenne is not a procedural formality, i.e., whether all the parallel texts are physically present for initialling at the signature ceremony, but whether the signatories have duly reviewed and approved each of the texts prior to signature. As regards this point, Hardy once said that 'a considered and nuancee translation' can be very useful to judges for the purpose of interpretation 'if the parties, after due consideration, have placed thereon the seal of authenticity' (1962:89). Reminding his colleagues that the signatories are equally bound by each authentic text, Rosenne was more emphatic, insisting that 'each Government is nominally responsible in law' to review and approve each text before becoming a party to the instrument (1954:382). To make this possible, the Secretariat should produce all translations within the framework of the particular conference or at least submit them to the conference prior to adoption, allowing sufficient time to have them duly reviewed and coordinated by competent persons. Although the practice varies according to the procedural rules adopted at each conference, a drafting committee is usually appointed to harmonize each text and coordinate all the texts adopted by committees or the plenary. The fact that some translations are not duly reviewed and coordinated prior to approval by the negotiating parties raises doubts as to whether such texts should be regarded as equally authentic. At stake is the interpretative value of translations authenticated in irregular proceedings. As a means of evaluating the reliability of authenticated translations, Rosenne advises judges to reserve the right to determine whether the negotiating parties have actually reviewed the translations and which steps were taken to ensure concordance. According to Rosenne's criteria, judges would be justified in assigning a lower interpretative value to authenticated translations prepared exclusively by a secretariat without being reviewed and coordinated by persons participating in the negotiations. Inversely, the interpretative value would increase in proportion to the degree to which the negotiating parties participated in the comparison and coordination of the texts (*cf.* Hardy 1962:105).[6]

Another question which arises in this context is whether subsequently produced authentic texts should be regarded as equally authentic for the purpose of interpretation. According to Tabory, subsequently produced authentic texts should be of 'lesser interpretative value' than those produced earlier, at least in cases of divergence in meaning (1980:84). In regard to the disputed trilingual Civil Aviation Convention, some delegations to the Buenos Aires Conference felt that there should

---

6.   Authenticated translations which are proved to be defective may be shortlived. A pertinent example is the authenticChinese text of the Genocide Convention prepared by the Secretariat. In this case, Chinese had not been used in the debates, nor was a Chinese text available when the General Assembly adopted the Convention on December 9, 1948; nor had Chinese delegates assisted the Secretariat in the preparation of the text. Having found numerous errors in the authenticated translation that entered into force on January 12, 1951, the Chinese Government (Nationalist China) submitted a new Chinese text that corrected these errors. In addition, the new text was intended 'to bring the official Chinese text into greater harmony with the other four official texts and to make the wording of the Chinese text closer to the terminology used by the executive and judicial organs of China and more intelligible to the Chinese people' (Yuen-Li Liang 1953:269). Since the revisions were found to be language corrections which did not affect the substance, the General Assembly voted to approve the 'corrected' text and to recommend that it be accepted by the States signatories as the authentic Chinese text (*ibid.*:271).

be no discrimination between the 1944 English text and the French and Spanish texts added in 1968. Others, however, criticized this view as well as the practice of recognizing subsequently produced language versions as authentic. Remarking that some of the linguistic choices made by the French translators pose a threat to its uniform interpretation, Mankiewiez concluded: 'Seule la conférence qui élabore la Convention semble qualifiée pour approuver les différentes versions linguistiques' (1968:488, 490).

Despite criticism such as Mankiewiez's, the delegates to the Vienna Conference on the Law of Treaties adopted a provision recognizing texts produced in a language other than one of those in which the treaty was authenticated. As a restriction, Article 33(2) stipulates that such texts shall be considered authentic only if the treaty so provides or the parties so agree. This makes it possible for a conference to change the authentic texts of an existing treaty, as was the case in regard to the 1944 Convention on Civil Aviation, or to permit the accession of new members, as occurs, for example, when new Member States are admitted to the European Union. In view of the EU's unique position between international and municipal law, Tabory agrees that subsequent authentication of the Rome Treaties (now amended by the Single European Act and the Treaty on European Union, *see* 7.9 below) in the languages of the new members is 'legally justifiable,' however, only in regard to their application in the municipal law of those states. In this sense, she suggests that any additional language versions of the Treaties ought to be attributed an inferior status for the purpose of interpretation at the multilateral level (1980:194).

7.5. EXPERIMENT IN MULTILINGUAL DRAFTING

As a means of improving the quality and reliability of parallel texts of instruments of municipal law, conscious efforts were made to coordinate the situational factors of text production (*see* Chapter 4, 4.3). While these efforts succeeded in bringing about widespread drafting reforms, there was no such intention when preparations began for the third UN Conference on the Law of the Sea (UNCLOS III) in December 1970. The unique experiment in multilingual drafting undertaken at UNCLOS III can be attributed to the unusual circumstances of the Conference. First of all, the task of drawing up the draft articles of the basic text had not been assigned to the ILC but to the UN Sea-Bed Committee which, however, was unable to agree on a set of draft articles. In view of the widely conflicting interests of the 150 states participating in the Conference, it was decided that political compromises had to be worked out before a draft text could be drawn up. Thereafter, the General Assembly confirmed the convening of the Conference without a draft text, and the first session was held in December 1973. At that time, the General Assembly expanded the scope of the Conference to include all matters relating to the law of the sea (Koh and Jayakumar 1985:47–51).[7]

---

7. The Law of the Sea Convention (1982) is one of the most comprehensive and complex multilateral treaties ever concluded. Dealing with almost every aspect of the law of the sea, the Convention governs the limits of national jurisdiction over ocean space, access to the seas, navigation,

Though appointed in 1973, the Drafting Committee did not commence its actual work until 1975 when it received the Single Negotiating Text prepared in English by three committees and revised in 1976. In June 1977, the Conference requested its President and the three Chairpersons to prepare an 'informal composite negotiating text' (ICNT) in treaty language to be used as the basis for further negotiations. Two parts of the ICNT were submitted in English, the other in Spanish. Translations were made by the UN Secretariat into all languages of the Conference and submitted to the Drafting Committee for harmonization and coordination. The resulting Concordance Text, in which the six language versions appear side by side on opposite pages of three columns each, was distributed to all delegations for discussion. Above all, it was the flexible timetable of the Conference that made this remarkable feat possible. One of the longest conferences in the history of international law, UNCLOS III lasted almost ten years. At the close of the tenth session in 1981, the Conference decided to revise the ICNT, officially producing a Draft Convention. Although the Draft Convention and four Resolutions were formally adopted on April 30, 1982, the Convention did not enter into force until November 16, 1994. Due to opposition by major maritime powers (including the US and Great Britain) to Part XI on the Deep Sea-Bed, the Treaty did not receive the 60 signatures necessary for ratification until the controversial provisions were revised in 1994.

It is primarily the innovative work of the Drafting Committee that had such a decisive impact on the drafting process. The fact that the Drafting Committee worked as an integral part of the machinery of the Conference shaped the Committee's procedure, ensuring that all the authentic texts reflect the intent of the negotiating States. The Committee itself consisted of 23 members selected primarily on the basis of equitable geographical distribution. Since no State could be represented on more than one main organ of the Conference, there were some significant omissions. To provide the Committee with a more adequate representation, six special language groups were established, one for each authentic text: Arabic, Chinese, English, French, Russian, and Spanish. Moreover, all interested delegations were encouraged to participate in the work of the language groups, thus ensuring nearly universal representation. The six language groups selected coordinators who met regularly among themselves, as well as with the chairman of the Drafting Committee. As interest grew in the drafting process, the meetings were opened to all members of the language groups and the Drafting Committee. The bulk of the hands-on work was done by the language groups, each of which discussed drafting proposals submitted by its own members, by the other groups, and occasionally by the Secretariat. Suggestions for specific drafting changes were then discussed at joint meetings of the coordinators and, if approved, passed on to the Drafting Committee for deliberation and finally submitted to the Conference in the form of recommendations (Nelson 1987:172).

The competence of the Drafting Committee was set forth in Rule 53 of the Rules of Procedure of the Conference. In accordance with the usual formula, Rule 53

protection and preservation of the marine environment, exploitation of living resources and conservation, scientific research, sea-bed mining and other exploitation of non-living resources, as well as the settlement of disputes (*see* details in Platzöder and Grunenberg 1990:295–489).

specified that the Drafting Committee shall 'formulate drafts and give advice on drafting as requested by the Conference or by a Main Committee, co-ordinate and refine the drafting of all texts referred to it, ... without altering their substance, and report to the Conference or to the Main Committee as appropriate.' The restrictive clause 'without altering their substance' was inserted to ensure that the Drafting Committee would not be a forum for negotiations. Moreover, additional restrictive clauses prevented the Drafting Committee from 'reopening substantive discussions on any matter' and emphasized that it 'shall have no power of or responsibility for initiating texts.' Like the Conference itself, the Drafting Committee operated on the basis of consensus at all levels, thus making it even more difficult to approve changes that would have improved the texts (Nelson 1987:173). Despite these restrictions, the work of the Drafting Committee sometimes resembled that of the Drafting Committee of the ILC, which often acts in the capacity of an informal negotiating body when generating draft articles of the basic texts of UN treaties (Rosenne 1983:778).

7.5.1. The harmonization process

The main tasks of the Drafting Committee consisted in harmonizing the individual texts and ensuring concordance between all six language versions. The bulk of the work was done by the six language groups and their coordinators, while the final decision-making was the responsibility of the Drafting Committee, the Chairpersons of the Main Committees, and the Conference. In accordance with the principle of terminological consistency (*see* Chapters IV, 4.8.1 and VIII, 8.10), each language group had the task of harmonizing the recurring words and phrases within its own text. The importance of this task should not be underestimated; due to its broad scope and length (320 Articles with 9 Annexes), various parts of the Convention had been drafted by different committees and were based on different sources. In particular, the choice of terminology was influenced by previous conventions and other instruments, the language of which was not always consistent.[8] Although the actual wording of the source articles was frequently retained, in some instances it had to be modified, a task that the Secretariat would not have been authorized to perform (*see* Nelson 1987:83). The work of the Arabic language group was further complicated by the fact that there were no authentic texts of the source instruments in Arabic, thus requiring the group to do the pioneer work of selecting appropriate terminology (Rosenne 1983:777, note 54). Apparently the results were not always satisfactory. This follows from Egypt's remarks at signature, criticizing the 'imprecision of expression' in certain provisions of the Arabic text relating to the legal regime of

---

8. Above all, the terminology of the Convention on the Law of the Sea (LOS 1982) was influenced by the Geneva Conventions on the Law of the Sea (1958), the International Convention relating to Intervention on the High Seas in Cases of Oil Pollution Casualties (1969), the Convention on the Prevention of Marine Pollution by Dumping of Wastes and Other Matter (1972), the Declaration of Principles Governing the Sea-Bed and the Ocean Floor, and the Subsoil thereof, beyond the Limits of National Jurisdiction (1970).

oceans (*Traités multilatéraux déposés auprès du Secrétaire Général,* État au 31 décembre 1994:892).[9]

The harmonization process (including grammar, syntax, and spelling) was coordinated in all six language groups in an attempt to ensure consistent usage of terminology and phraseology throughout each text. In addition to examining their own text and proposing changes in that text, the language groups reviewed proposals for changes in the other texts as well. The interaction between the six language groups was one of the key factors contributing to the success of the multilingual drafting experiment. To facilitate communication, each proposal was translated into all other languages before being submitted to the coordinators. This proved to be a tedious task as it required that proposals for stylistic and grammatical changes in only one language be translated as well. Although such translations were technically difficult and time consuming, the documentation was needed to prove that a proposal submitted for a stylistic or grammatical change was in fact what it purported to be. The result was a voluminous mass of complex documentation dealing with almost every Article of the Convention. It is estimated that up to 1981, the Drafting Committee and its subsidiary organs together produced something like a quarter of a million pages of documentation (in Rosenne 1983:776, note 52).

The decision whether a particular recommendation for harmonization should be incorporated into a text was left mainly to the discretion of the Chairpersons of the Main Committees. For example, the Chairpersons decided to replace the expression *States with special geographical characteristics* in Articles 69 and 70 of the English text by the phrase *geographically disadvantaged States*, which also appears in later provisions. In the final texts, the terms *geographically disadvantaged States* (EN), *les Etats géographiquement désavantagés* (FR), *Estados en situación geográfica desventajosa* (ES), государства в географически неблагоприятном положении (RU), 地理不利国 (*dili buli guo*) (CH), الدول المتضررة جغرافيا (*al-duwal al-mutaḍarrirah ǧuġrāfiyyan*) (AR) are used consistently throughout the respective texts. While the consistent use of the same terms implies that they have the same meaning in all parts of the Convention, this is perhaps not the intention after all. Doubts in this regard have been raised as a result of a subsequent change made in the texts of Article 70 where the term is defined in Part V. The fact that the phrase *for the purposes of this Convention* was replaced by *for the purposes of this Part* seems to imply that the same definition does not apply to other Parts of the Convention where the expression *geographically disadvantaged States* and its equivalents appear (*see* Nelson 1987:177), thus leaving it to the courts to determine how the term should be interpreted in other Parts of the Convention.

As a rule, the same term should always be used to refer to the same referent (*see* Chapters IV, 4.8.1 and VIII, 8.10).[10] In some instances, however, the Drafting

---

9. Egypt's concern goes so far that it takes the unusual step of declaring its readiness to adopt 'l'interprétation qui est la mieux corroborée par les divers textes officiels de la Convention' (*Traités multilatéraux déposés auprès du Secrétaire Général,* État au 31 décembre 1994:892).

10. *Cf.* the following statement made by the Franco-Italian Conciliation Commission in its response to the *Pertusola Claim* in 1951: 'If it is good drafting to employ, in the same treaty, the same expression every time the same thing is referred to, it sometimes happens, even in international

Committee was unable to agree on a single term. A relevant example is the use of the words *ship* and *vessel* in the English text. With few exceptions the word *ship* is used in the provisions prepared by the Second Committee of the Conference (Parts II, III, IV, V, and VII), whereas the word *vessel* is used in the provisions drafted by the Third Committee (with the exception of Article 233). For its part, the Third Committee objected to replacing the term *vessel* by *ship* in provisions relating to the protection and preservation of the marine environment. As it pointed out, 'the broader term *vessel* is more appropriate, for it would cover not only ships but also other floating structures whose use or operation might cause pollution of the marine environment' (cited in Nelson 1987:178). As confirmed by the Drafting Committee, the two terms are not intended to mean different things. This is also strongly suggested by the fact that this difference is not present in other texts where the following terms are used consistently: *buque* (ES), *navire* (FR), *судно* (RU), and سفينة (*safīnah*) (AR). An exception is the use of the terms 船只 (*chuánzhi*) and 船舶 (*chuánbo*) in the Chinese text. In addition, 军舰 (*junjian*) is used in the Chinese and *военный корабль* in the Russian text for *warship* (Articles 29–32). On the other hand, in the French text the phrase *des bateaux de pêche* was changed to *les navires de pêche* in the third revision of the ICNT. To make it clear that the terms *ship* and *vessel* have the same meaning, the Drafting Committee recommended inserting a provision to that effect in Article 1 of the English text. The recommendation, however, was defeated in the interest of preserving the interlingual concordance of all texts (*cf.* Nelson 1987:177, *also* note 49).

7.5.2. Ensuring the concordance of six language versions

The second stage of the work of the language groups involved the actual article-by-article comparison of all texts to ensure concordance. As a result of the early interaction between the language groups, this stage overlapped to some extent with the harmonization process. This was fortunate because in 1981 the Conference set the first and only deadline requiring that the final texts of the Convention be completed for adoption and signature by the end of 1982. The article-by-article comparison commenced at an intersessional meeting of the Drafting Committee from January 12 to February 27, 1981, and continued up to the final intersessional meeting of the Drafting Committee from July 12 to August 20, 1982. In 1981 the language groups together held some 700 meetings, the Coordinators 75, and the Drafting Committee 30. Approximately 1500 recommendations were submitted by the Drafting Committee in that year alone. All recommendations were considered at informal plenary meetings of the Conference and not in the main Committee, as a result of which they are not considered part of the formal records constituting the *travaux préparatoires* used for interpretation (Nelson 1987:180).

instruments which are drafted with care, that that principle is no more followed than the other, equally excellent, rule that one should use different expressions to indicate different things' (*International Law Reports*, Year 1951:418).

In numerous instances there was either difficulty in reaching consensus on recommendations or no consensus was obtained. At this late date, some delegations feared making any changes that might affect the substance. Even in cases involving ambiguities, they were sometimes reluctant to clarify the text. For example, when the Chinese language group noticed an ambiguity in the English text of Article 216(1), it was decided not only to retain the ambiguity but to preserve and strengthen it by making the French and Spanish texts ambiguous as well. The disputed text reads as follows in English, French, and Spanish:

> *Laws and regulations adopted in accordance with this Convention and applicable international rules and standards* established through competent international organizations or diplomatic conference for the prevention, reduction and control of pollution of the marine environment by dumping shall be enforced:...

> *Les lois et règlements adoptés conformément à la Convention et aux règles et normes internationales applicables* établies par l'intermédiaire des organisations internationales compétentes ou d'une conférence diplomatique en vue de prévenir, réduire et maîtriser la pollution du milieu marin par immersion de déchets sont mis en application:...

> *Las leyes y reglamentos dictados de conformidad con esta Convención y con las reglas y normas internacionales applicables* establecida por conducto de las organizaciones internacionales competentes o en una conferencia diplomática para prevenir, reducir y controlar la contaminación del medio marino causado por vertimientos serán ejecutados:...

In the English text the question arises as to whether the phrases *Laws and regulations* and *international rules and standards* are intended to be parallel subjects or whether *Laws and regulations* is the only subject. Although it is clear from the French and Spanish texts that the latter interpretation is correct, the Drafting Committee voted against changing the English text. Instead, the prepositions *aux* and *con* were deleted from the French and Spanish texts, making those texts ambiguous as well (Nelson 1987:187).

This decision raises a question about general principles of multilingual drafting. Should one text have priority when making decisions relating to concordance? More specifically, should the 'other' texts be aligned on the language version in which the draft articles were drawn up? In regard to the Convention on the Law of the Sea (LOS 1982), the suggestion that the English text should enjoy special status was rejected, also for the purpose of ensuring concordance. It appears that decisions regarding concordance were made on a case-by-case basis. This is in keeping with Rosenne's warning that, in order for the drafting process to be truly multilingual, drafters should not attempt to align a text on only one of the other language versions, regardless whether it is the basic or original text (1983:783). As Sir Humphrey Waldock remarked during the Vienna Convention on the Law of Treaties in 1966, the basic text may also be a source of language defects (*Yearbook of the ILC* 1966: I pt. 2, 874th meeting). Therefore, in each case of textual divergence, drafters/ negotiators should determine which text expresses the common intent and align the other text(s) on that one (*Yearbook of the ILC* 1966 II:109).

Nonetheless, the Chinese language group confirmed that it resolved a number of problems relating to Chinese terminology and phrases by using the English text as

213

its principal reference (*see* Nelson 1987:173, note 28). Reliance on the English text also caused some problems. In particular, several language groups raised questions about the intended meaning of abstract English words which could be translated by two or more terms in another language. For example, the Chinese language group pointed out that the English word *mechanism* in Article 140(2) could be conveyed by two sets of Chinese characters: one concrete in the sense of *institutional machinery* and the other abstract in the sense of *method*. After consultation the Chinese group opted for the concrete term; however, its recommendation that a more specific word be used in the English text was turned down (Rosenne 1987:429).

The article-by-article comparison of the six parallel texts was a complicated process in which every article was given three or four readings in each language. The differences detected raised linguistic, technical, and legal issues which were resolved in a series of consultations.[11] Some of the Drafting Committee's proposals pertained to one language, others to several; frequently a revision in one version required subsequent changes in others as well. While some of the proposals concerned the use of definite or indefinite articles, prepositions, and Latin phrases, others aimed at unifying language expressing the normative content of the statement of law. For example, in Article 280 the English phrase *Nothing in this Part shall impair the right* was replaced by *Nothing in this Part impairs the right,* the French phrase *Aucune disposition de la présente partie ne porte atteinte au droit* by *Aucune disposition de la présente partie n'affecte le droit,* the Russian phrase *Ничто в настоящей Части не ущемляет права* by *Ничто в настоящей Части не затрагивает права.* In short, all the other texts (Chinese and Arabic included) were revised to make them correspond with the Spanish text *Ninguna de las disposiciones de esta Parte menoscabará el derecho,* which was deemed to express the intended meaning (UN Document A/CONF.62/L.75/Add.4).

As in municipal law, drafting guidelines for treaties recommend the use of positive over negative provisions (*cf.* Chapter 6, 6.5). While some negations are acceptable, such as the one in Article 280 above, others are not. In any case, drafters of instruments of international law prefer to use language which expresses a uniform thought process in all texts. With this in mind, the Drafting Committee recommended transforming the negative provision in Article 295 of the French text into a positive one. Although the results are the same, preference was given to the positive formulation which is used in the other language versions, with the exception of the Arabic text.[12] The two French versions read as follows:

Old text	*Revised text*
Aucun différend entre Etats Parties relatif à l'interprétation ou à l'ap-	Un différend entre Etats Parties relatif à l'interprétation ou à l'ap-

11. Recommendations for improving concordance are contained in the following UN documents: A/CONF.62/L.67/Rev. A/Add. 1–16; A/CONF.62/L.75/Add.1–13; A/CONF.62/L.85/Add.1–9; A/CONF.62/L.142/Rev.1/Add.1; and A/CONF.62/L.152/Add.1–17.

12. The English text of Article 295 reads as follows: 'Any dispute between States Parties concerning the interpretation or application of this Convention may be submitted to the procedures provided for in this section only after local remedies have been exhausted where this is required by international law.'

plication de la Convention *ne peut* être soumis aux procédures prévues à la présente section *avant seulement épuisement des recours internes* selon ce que requiert le droit international.

plication de la Convention *peut* être soumis aux procédures prévues à la présente section *après que les recours internes ont été épuisés* selon ce que requiert le droit international.

7.5.3. Fidelity to the single instrument

Total interlingual concordance of all language versions is neither possible nor desirable. Thus the Chairman of the Drafting Committee, J. Alan Beesley of Canada, emphasized that the main goal of the article-by-article comparison was to improve the linguistic concordance of the six authentic texts 'to the extent possible, and to achieve juridical concordance in all cases' (UNCLOS Official Records, vol. XV (A/Con.62/L.67/Rev. 1, para. 6). Beesley's comment is reminiscent of Beaupré's advice that legal equivalence must always prevail in translations of Canadian federal legislation (*see* Chapter 2, 2.8.4). The comparison, however, seems to end here. About the same time Beaupré was encouraging translators of Canadian federal legislation to strive for 'linguistic purity' and not 'verbal and grammatical parallelism' (1986:179), Beesley was advising drafters to eliminate linguistic diversity and coordinate the authentic texts of the Convention on the Law of the Sea (1982) as closely as possible. Reviewed and coordinated simultaneously by delegates participating in the negotiations, the French, Spanish, Russian, Chinese, and Arabic texts of the Convention are not 'mere translations' (Nelson 1987:198). Nonetheless, the principle of fidelity to the single instrument retains priority.

In keeping with the principle of fidelity, drafters and translators of parallel texts of multilateral instruments are advised to strive for interlingual concordance. The degree to which interlingual concordance is achieved in the parallel texts of the Convention on the Law of the Sea can be seen in paragraph 1 of the English and French texts of Article 45 below. Above all, the presentation is uniform. The entire paragraph is formulated in one sentence and expresses one idea. There is no restructuring (as in the French texts of Canadian federal legislation). Hence, the paragraphing is consistent and sub-paragraphs a and b contain the same information content in both texts. Since deletions are not common, the length of the provision is nearly the same in each language version. Syntactic and stylistic diversity is kept to a minimum:

1. The régime of innocent passage, in accordance with Part II, section 3, shall apply in straits used for international navigation:
(a) excluded from the application of the régime of transit passage under article 38, paragraph 1; or
(b) between a part of the high seas or an exclusive economic zone and the territorial sea of a foreign State.

1. Le régime du passage inoffensif prévu à la section 3 de la partie II s'applique aux détroits servant à la navigation internationale qui:
a) sont exclus du champ d'application du régime du passage en transit en vertu de l'article 38, paragraphe 1; ou
b) relient la mer territoriale d'un Etat à une partie de la haute mer ou à la zone économique exclusive d'un autre Etat.

Despite attempts to discourage syntactic diversity, some basic transformations are permitted, provided the substance remains unchanged. Although drafters and translators are advised to formulate provisions in the active voice (*see* Chapter 6, 6.6), active and passive transformations are generally tolerated. A typical example can be found in the following provision from Article 27(1)[13] where the English text is formulated in the passive, the French text in the active voice:

The criminal jurisdiction of the coastal State should not be exercised on board a foreign ship passing through the territorial sea...	L'Etat côtier ne devrait pas exercer sa jurisdiction pénale à bord d'un navire étranger passant dans la mer territoriale...

While the above transformation is more or less standard, the same cannot be said of the active and passive formulations in the English and French texts of paragraph 2 of Article 45 below. In this provision, the active English text is a prohibition, the passive French text a negative permission. The diversity is tolerated only because the end result is the same (*see* Chapter 6, 6.5.3). A comparison of the other texts shows that the Spanish, Chinese, and Russian texts are formulated as prohibitions, the Arabic text as a negative permission:

2. *There shall be no suspension* of innocent passage through such straits.	2. *L'exercice du droit* de passage inoffensif dans ces détroits *ne peut être suspendu.*

7.6. HOW RECEPTION AFFECTS TRANSLATION STRATEGY

Despite numerous similarities between the multilingual drafting experiment at UNCLOS III and the bilingual drafting reform in Canada, the results are very different. Whereas the Canadian experiment introduced revolutionary translation techniques and encouraged creativity in the translation of instruments of municipal law, the UNCLOS III experiment brought about no such liberalization. This, however, does not imply that translators of instruments of international law have less decision-making power. As shown above, the sensitivity of the subject-matter often makes it too risky for translators of treaties and conventions to be creative, as does the fact that such instruments are largely negotiated texts.[14] Above all, however, it is the changed circumstances of the communication process that prevent translators

---

13. As for the other language versions of Article 27(1), the Arabic and Chinese texts are active, the Spanish and Russian texts passive.
14. *Cf.* the following statement from the official German guidelines for translators of treaties and diplomatic texts: 'Allerdings ist [bei völkerrechtlichen Übereinkünften] die Forderung nach einem durchsichtigen und möglichst knappen Satzbau viel schwerer zu erfüllen, da zumeist die fremdsprachigen Vertragstexte mit den anderen Vertragsparteien ausgehandelt werden und der Übersetzer an den ausgehandelten fremdsprachigen Wortlaut gebunden ist. Vom dem Übersetzer wird daher die Bereitschaft gefordert, sich um den stilistisch besten und sprachlich eindeutigen Ausdruck bei möglichst genauer Entsprechung von deutschem und fremdsprachigem Text zu bemühen' (*Standardformulierungen* 1992:30).

from being overly creative with language in multilingual, multilateral instruments. In regard to the multilingual aspect of the communication process, it is inevitable that the increased number of parallel texts complicates production, requiring translators to take account of all language versions. As for the multilateral aspect, each increase in the number of States parties participating in the negotiations makes it more difficult to agree on the wording of each of the parallel texts, thus leaving little to no room for translators to experiment with diversity. But what about reception? How do the multilingual and multilateral aspects of communication in international law affect the interpretation and application of parallel texts? It follows that each increase in the number of authentic texts complicates the interpretation process, placing additional burden not only on translators but also on judges, who are expected to consult all the language versions and determine the common meaning. More important, however, is the multilateral aspect of the communication process, i.e., how the large number of signatory States participating in the communication process affects the interpretation process, making it extremely difficult and sometimes impossible to achieve uniform interpretation and application of the parallel texts of a given instrument. This, in turn, automatically places greater pressure on translators, requiring them to take precautionary measures to preserve the unity of the single instrument. In numerous cases, however, linguistic measures alone are insufficient, thus making legal intervention necessary in the form of judicial controls.

7.6.1. The interpretation and application of multilingual, multilateral instruments

The drafting experiment at UNCLOS III proved that it is possible to coordinate the production of the parallel texts of multilingual, multilateral instruments. However, it is not enough to control the conditions of text production; one must also attempt to control the interpretation and application of treaties and conventions. Past experience has shown that the latter task is considerably more difficult as it requires establishing judicial controls. As a result of the large number of States parties, each of which is determined to safeguard its own interests, reaching agreement on such sensitive issues has proved almost impossible in international law. Other factors come into play as well. For instance, since the relationship between domestic and international law is regulated by the constitutional law of each state, the methods of implementing international instruments vary from country to country. In some states, the treaty (or convention) must first be incorporated into municipal law in the usual parliamentary process before becoming binding. This may be done by incorporating the actual text of the treaty into domestic law, in which case the treaty is the law, or by enacting a special statute which then becomes the law, rather than the treaty itself. In Canada and Great Britain, for instance, treaties must be implemented by statute in order to become internally binding (Tetley 1990:432). As a result, some judges may not even be aware that they are interpreting an instrument of international law (on decisions of German courts *see* Drobnig 1986:615).

Treaty law is binding and must be upheld by the courts; however, the question arises by which courts? From the very beginning the League of Nations attempted to introduce judicial control by establishing the Permanent Court of International

Justice in 1921. The United Nations followed suit in 1946 by establishing the International Court of Justice as its major judicial organ.[15] Despite the intention to create an effective judicial mechanism, the Court's jurisdiction is limited and, as a rule, non-compulsory. For example, it can adjudicate civil cases brought by and against sovereign states only with the consent of the parties. Its jurisdiction also confers cases which the parties refer to it by special *ad hoc* agreement and cases covered by special clauses in treaties, by treaties of pacific settlement or by the optional clause of the Statute (*see* Walker 1980:632). On the other hand, claims of individuals and legal entities are settled by an *ad hoc* tribunal or by the national courts of a contracting State connected with the case. This results in almost inevitable diversity.

7.6.2. Diversity in decisions of national courts

Without a doubt, the greatest threat to the uniform interpretation of multilingual, multilateral instruments is the diversity of decisions by national courts. Whereas most plurilingual countries have incorporated a system of checks and balances into their municipal judicial systems, the growing number of states and consequently national courts participating in the interpretation process makes this practically impossible in international law. In view of the conflicting interests at stake, it is highly unrealistic to expect that judges of national courts will interpret and apply treaties, conventions, model laws, and other multilateral instruments uniformly. The tendency for judges of national courts to use their own domestic rules of interpretation is especially detrimental. This occurs particularly in jurisdictions where treaties are incorporated into domestic statutes, such as in Canada and Great Britain. As Kuner points out, 'whatever the merits of the English courts' literal method of interpreting domestic statutes, it is out of place when interpreting modern multilingual treaties' (1991:961). Generally speaking, international lawyers agree that preserving the unity of multilingual instruments requires that a common meaning be found for all language versions by comparing the parallel texts of the particular instrument (*cf.* Tabory 1980:195). This, however, requires sophisticated methods of plurilingual interpretation. Although one of the goals of the Vienna Convention on the Law of Treaties (1969) was to provide uniform rules for the interpretation of plurilingual treaties, the Convention has been criticized for its failure to provide concrete methods (*see* 7.3.1 above). Furthermore, judges of national courts are not always qualified to compare multilingual texts on a routine basis.

---

15. Although judges are encouraged to determine the common meaning of multilingual multilateral instruments by consulting all the language versions on a regular basis, this practice is rarely followed. Composed of 15 judges from different countries, the International Court of Justice has only two working languages: French and English. As a result, even when interpreting the United Nations Charter, the Court has almost always consulted only the English and French versions, although the Chinese, Russian and Spanish versions are equally authentic (Kuner 1991:957). Apart from this unsatisfactory practice, it appears that the Court has not been seriously troubled by problems of plurilingual interpretation (Rosenne 1987:425).

Since judges of national courts are seldom experts of international law, they tend to consult authentic texts exclusively in their respective national languages, unless there is a contention of a difference in meaning among the texts. The prevailing view under English law goes so far as to preclude reference to non-English versions of a treaty incorporated into a domestic statute, unless it is contended that the texts are in conflict or that the English text is ambiguous. In disapproval, Kuner reminds his English colleagues that the rights of the citizens of England 'are controlled not only by the English text but by the common meaning of all the texts' (Kuner 1991:960–961). The threat to uniformity becomes even greater in countries where national judges rely completely on non-authentic translations in their own language (*see* Hilf 1973:200).

The fact that treaties tend to be less technical than national legislation should facilitate their interpretation and application. Unfortunately, this is not always the case. Although drafters are encouraged to avoid the use of technical terms from a particular legal system, treaties frequently contain elements of a foreign law. Instead of attempting to qualify such elements according to the foreign legal system of origin, national judges frequently take the easy way out by interpreting them according to their own legal system. This occurs particularly when technical terms of one legal system are translated with the closest equivalent technical term of another system (*see* Chapter 8, 8.8.4). Moreover, regardless of the degree of their technicality, treaties often contain elements that are common to all or most legal systems but are conceptually incongruent, thus making diversity in interpretation practically unavoidable. For example, though the English term *debts* and the French term *dettes* are etymological equivalents, they are conceptually incongruent (*see* Chapter 8, 8.3). While *debt* denotes an obligation to pay a fixed sum stipulated for damages, *dettes* is much broader and includes any kind of obligation, whether liquidated or not. Accordingly, when interpreting the Varsailles Treaty, English judges limited the term to claims for a certain sum, whereas French and Belgian judges treated unliquidated claims as *dettes* (Schlesinger 1980:815).

While diversity in the decisions of national courts sometimes occurs without the knowledge of the judge, in numerous cases judges knowingly take conflicting stands on substantive issues because of differences in their municipal laws. In particular, van den Berg encourages judges of national courts to compare existing decisions of foreign courts and to make efforts to align their opinions on such decisions. Unfortunately, case law shows that judges of national courts rarely use the method of comparative judicial interpretation, as van den Berg calls it. A notable exception occurred in the initial phase of the implementation of the New York Convention on the Recognition and Enforcement of Arbitral Awards (1958). At the beginning, Italian and American judges held considerably different views on what constitutes a written arbitration agreement. Nonetheless, in the interest of promoting uniform interpretation, they were able to agree on a common approach. Thus it follows that the success or failure of a convention may depend on the good will of the courts of the signatory States to agree not to disagree (van den Berg 1996:26).

Good will was obviously failing on the part of the national courts of the signatory States when it came to interpreting the disputed fact-situation of Article 25(1) of the Convention for the Unification of certain rules relating to international carriage by air (Warsaw Convention). In the said article, which determined whether the carrier's

219

liability could be limited or excluded, the term *dol* in the French original is translated by *wilful misconduct* in the English version. This unfortunate translation was approved despite warning by the English delegate that *wilful misconduct* includes acts performed with intention as well as acts performed carelessly without regard for the consequences. Instead of searching for a common meaning or agreeing on the intended meaning, judges of continental courts tended to rule in favor of limited liability in similar cases where American courts declared the carrier to have unlimited liability. Such conflicting decisions occurred particularly in cases involving deaths and bodily injuries resulting from acts not caused with intention (*see* cases in Mankiewicz 1962:467). Since this key provision served as an exclusion clause enabling plaintiffs/claimants to evade the thresholds of limited liability provided by the Convention, the conflicting decisions not only frustrated the object of the treaty but also directly encouraged plaintiffs/claimants to evade the treaty and shop for a more favorable forum, thus resulting in the failure of the Convention (*see* text of Art. 25(1) in Chapter 5, 5.12.1).

7.7. ATTEMPTS TO ESTABLISH JUDICIAL CONTROLS

In view of the diversity in decisions of national courts in disputes arising under multilingual, multilateral instruments, it is not surprising that drafters and translators seek to avoid possible sources of contention by coordinating parallel texts as closely as possible. Obviously there can be no liberalization of translation methods in international law without effective measures to control the interpretation process. Even then, however, it is questionable whether liberalization would be desirable. Attempts to establish judicial controls to promote the uniform interpretation and application of multilateral instruments began long ago when it became evident that the future of multilingualism was at stake. In particular, the failure of the Warsaw Convention made lawyers realize that real uniformity cannot be achieved by merely agreeing on a uniform text in various languages (Mankiewicz 1962:457). Fearing that the objective of unification could be defeated by conflicting and even contradictory court decisions, lawyers emphasized the need to introduce judicial controls similar to those in the municipal law of some plurilingual countries. Their concern is reflected in the following remarks in the *1959 Annuaire* of UNIDROIT:

> The danger of conflicting judicial decisions is inherent in the judicial function, but it is reduced and controlled at the national level by such devices as the establishment of a Supreme Court or the doctrine of *stare decisis*. No such device has yet been adopted at the international level, but something similar is required because contradictory judicial decisions are likely to endanger the attainment of the very aim of a Convention for the unification of law by destroying eventually the internationally agreed rules (1960:319).

International lawyers were quick to recognize that the most effective way to promote the uniform interpretation and application of parallel texts is to establish an international court whose decisions have the force of binding precedents on the national courts of the signatory States (*Annuaire* 1960:321). Going a step further, it was proposed to limit or, if possible, exclude the jurisdiction of national courts by establishing a specialized court with exclusive jurisdiction for the settlement of disputes arising under a particular treaty or convention. From the legal point of view, establishing a specialized court has several advantages. First of all, the judges have ample opportunity to establish the common meaning of the single instrument by routinely comparing all the authentic texts of that and related instruments. Moreover, they are able to develop and consistently use methods of interpretation that take account of the object and purpose of the instruments in question. Finally, the creation of a specialized court facilitates interaction between judges and treatymakers, thus increasing the chances that judges will define the common meaning of the single instrument as intended by the treatymakers. The role of a specialized court can be compared to that of the highest court in the judicial system of municipal law, especially if its decisions have the authority of precedents.

Although specialized courts seem to be the most effective way of promoting the uniform interpretation of parallel texts of multilateral instruments, they are still rare in international law. Despite repeated requests by both the International Civil Aviation Organization and the International Law Association, the attempt to salvage the Warsaw Aviation Convention by establishing an international court for the settlement of international claims against carriers proved unsuccessful. In this case, however, the damage had already been done and it was considered too late to create such a court. One of the best examples of a successful specialized court is the European Court of Human Rights in Strassbourg, which has been conclusive in taking a stand on conceptual differences in disputes involving discrepancies between the authentic texts of the European Convention on Human Rights (*see* cases in Rosenne 1983:772; Tabory 1980: 166, note 318).

In an attempt to provide effective judicial control, the delegates to UNCLOS III agreed on the establishment of a new and autonomous specialized tribunal in Annex VI to the Convention on the Law of the Sea (1982): the International Tribunal for the Law of the Sea. In Part IV on the Settlement of Disputes, the Convention obliges parties to settle their disputes peacefully and designates a selection of methods for doing so. In the event they are otherwise unable to reach agreement, states may make a prior determination of the fora they would be amenable to. For this purpose, Article 287 allows a choice among the International Court of Justice, *ad hoc* arbitration, or the International Tribunal for the Law of the Sea. Although the International Tribunal is to have shared jurisdiction over all matters relating to the law of the sea, its specialized chamber, the Sea-Bed Disputes Chamber, is to have exclusive jurisdiction over all disputes involving the international sea-bed area (*see* Platzöder and Grunenberg 1990:628–655). From the legal point of view, the creation of the International Tribunal marks an advance in the evolution of the law of international institutions of its kind not only because of the structural autonomy of the Sea-Bed Disputes Chamber and the fact that the Chamber has exclusive jurisdiction over sea-bed matters, but also because private and legal persons will have direct access to the Chamber on an equal footing with states.

As far as the communication process is concerned, the establishment of a specialized court marks a significant achievement by enabling the disputes arising from a particular instrument to be resolved at the same place, by the same judges and under the same conditions, regardless of the language of the case. In defiance

221

of traditional translation theory, which presupposes that source and target texts are received at a different time and place (*see* Chapter 3, 3.5), this eliminates the distinction between source and target text receivers, thus resulting in a unique communicative situation of reception.

Figure 8: *Coordinating the Situational Factors of Reception*

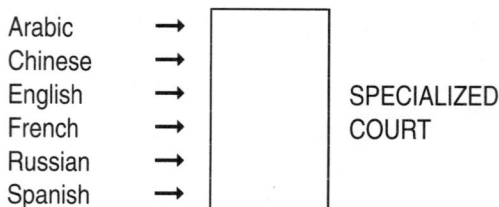

Arabic	→	
Chinese	→	
English	→	SPECIALIZED
French	→	COURT
Russian	→	
Spanish	→	

7.8. JUDICIAL CONTROLS IN THE EUROPEAN UNION

Due to their multilateral character, the original founding instruments of the EC are designated as treaties: Treaties establishing the European Coal and Steel Community, the European Economic Community, and the European Atomic Energy Community. Constituting the primary source of law of the EC, the so-called Rome Treaties are *de facto* legislative texts, as are the Single European Act of 1986 (the amending instrument establishing the institutions for creating the European Union) and the Maastricht Treaty on European Union of 1992. Both primary and secondary legislation of the EU is usually drafted in French and then translated into the other official languages.[16] After four expansions, the EU has retained its unique linguistic policy of language equality (Brackeniers 1991:2). As its membership grew from six to nine, ten, twelve, and currently to fifteen Member States, the number of official languages gradually increased to twelve (counting Irish). All language versions of EU legislation, regulations and directives are equally authentic and have the force of law in all Member States. Although this puts tremendous pressure on EU translators, it does not seem to intimidate them. On the contrary, Koutsivitis speaks of creativity in translations of EU instruments (1988:345), thus suggesting that EU translators enjoy more freedom than their UN counterparts. How is this possible?

Having learned from the mistakes of international lawyers, European lawyers took it upon themselves to create a judicial mechanism that would not only limit the jurisdiction of national courts but also make them accountable to a specialized court with special powers to ensure the uniform interpretation and application of European law. In 1958 the European Court of Justice was established in Luxembourg for the purpose of securing observance of the Treaties establishing the EC and protecting the rights of Member States, companies, and individuals. To safeguard uniform

16.   According to Madero, about 60 percent of all EU instruments are drafted in French, 25 percent in English, and 10 percent in German (1992:345).

interpretation of the Treaties, the Court of Justice has exclusive jurisdiction over disputes between Member States concerning application of the terms of the treaties, as well as disputes relating to the object and purpose of the Communities in general. In its relations to national legal systems, the European Court resembles the chief federal court in a federal state (Walker 1980:437). In particular, the Court has exclusive jurisdiction in direct actions initiated by states, companies, and individuals in matters concerning Community law. Since the Court cannot decide all disputes involving questions of Community and national law, the national courts of the Member States must also interpret and apply Community law in numerous instances. As a means of controlling the decisions of national courts, the European Court is empowered to interpret and rule on the validity of Community law by issuing preliminary rulings. Whenever questions concerning the interpretation or validity of Community law arise in cases being heard by national courts, the particular national court is required to refer the case to the European Court for a preliminary ruling, on the basis of which it then resolves the case. Preliminary rulings have the authority of binding precedents on the national courts of all Member States (Klinke 1989:12–21).

As of January 1995, the European Court of Justice consists of fifteen judges, one from each of the Member States and nine advocates-general. It hears cases in any of the twelve official languages (including Irish), depending on the choice of the parties. Above all, it is the well-defined limitation of jurisdiction that has enabled it to act in the capacity of a specialized court. This, in turn, has made it possible for the Court to develop special rules of interpretation for multilingual, multilateral instruments that set it apart from both international and national courts of law. Particularly important in this regard is the fact that EU treaties are essentially legislative texts, not highly sensitive political texts. As a result, the European Court presumes that the 'occasional differences in the different versions of the Treat[ies] are not normally the result of different meanings put on the Treaty by the negotiators for different countries, but rather accidents due to the haste in which the various translations were prepared' (Morgan 1982:110). This basic presumption has enabled the Court to take a considerably different approach when dealing with linguistic and conceptual diversity. Regardless of the large number of language versions, the European Court compares all the texts of a given instrument on a routine basis; however, instead of attempting to ascertain the common meaning which best reconciles all the texts, the Court prefers to ascertain the intended meaning of the single instrument, using the purposes of the instrument as its primary criterion (Morgan 1982:111). Accordingly, teleologic and systematic interpretation rank highest in the hierarchy of its rules of interpretation, literal and historic interpretation lowest (Volman 1988:42). Although its methods vary from case to case, the Court tends to favor resolving disputes by taking account of the object and purpose of the particular instrument within the framework of the whole of European law. If the Court has to make a choice between solutions, one of which favors European law and the other national law, the result is almost always in favor of European law (Case No. 80/76 *North Kerry Milk Products v. Minister for Agriculture and Fisheries* [1977] E.C.R. p. 425; *see also* Volman 1988:62). The Court does not commit itself to resolving discrepancies on the basis of the principle of the majority and in several cases has even favored a single text that differed from the others. Conceptual incongruency is often but not always resolved on the basis of the principle of the highest common denominator (*see* cases in Volman 1988:60–73; Morgan 1982:111). From this brief description, it follows that the Court enjoys a great deal of discretion. In several instances, the Commission has even corrected individual language versions to bring them in line with the Court's decisions (Case No. 29/69 *Erich Stauder v. City of Ulm, Sozialamt* [1969] E.C.R. p. 419).

7.9. CREATIVITY IN TRANSLATIONS OF EU INSTRUMENTS

The fact that the European Court is more concerned with broad purposes than narrow wording has also had a notable impact on translation by permitting translators a limited amount of creativity. In his analysis of the translation of EU legislation, Koutsivitis (translator at the Commission) differentiates between restricted and non-restricted or 'free' parts of EU instruments. While the restricted parts are dominated by standard formulae and technical terms, the non-restricted parts consist mainly of ordinary discourse containing 'pure' idiomatic phrases or idiomatic phrases mixed with technical terms and formulae (*see* Chapter 4, 4.8.1). It follows that creativity is permitted only in non-restricted parts where the translator is essentially free to write in the spirit of the target language as long as the sense of the original is conveyed correctly:

> Dans la traduction du texte libre, le traducteur est libre des obligations lexicales imposées par les termes techniques et des contraintes morphosyntaxiques imposées par les formules standardisées. Sa seule règle de conduite est le transfert du sens, toujours dans ses dimensions cognitives et stylistiques. Le traducteur est libre de choisir les mots, les expressions, les tournures; il doit transmettre le sens (Koutsivitis 1988:344).

The essence of the above statement is repeated in a later article where Koutsivitis proposes two main principles for the translation of non-restricted parts of EU instruments:

> Transférer le sens de l'original à la traduction et respecter le génie de la langue-cible sont les deux soucis principaux du traducteur quand il opère avec le texte libre (1990:146).

Although Koutsivitis' principles are too general to be of much use for translators, they reveal a considerably more liberal approach to translation than in international treaty law. Thanks to the special rules of multilingual interpretation developed by the European Court, EU translators are under less pressure to ensure strict concordance, despite the increased number of parallel texts.

As an example of the creativity permitted in non-restricted parts of legislation, Koutsivitis refers to the diversity in the title of the Annex to R 1887/84 in the then nine official languages. Although the French version serves as the source text, this does not mean that all the other language versions must be aligned on that text (*cf.* Rosenne's remark in 7.5.2 above). Translators are generally encouraged to compare as many language versions as possible. In the following example, the Danish,

German, Greek, Italian, and Dutch versions follow the French original, while the Spanish and Portuguese versions follow the English translation in which the French adjective *négative* is rendered with the explanatory phrase *which the Fund may not assist*. As Koutsivitis admits, the English version expresses the sense more clearly (1990:148; *also* 1988:346):

FR: Liste négative des catégories d'infrastructures
DA: Negativliste over kategorier af infrastrukturprojekter
DE: Negativliste der Infrastrukturkategorien
EN: List of categories of infrastructures which the Fund may not assist
ES: Lista de las categorias de infraestructuras que le FEDER no podrà financiar
GR: Αρνητικός κατάλογος κατηγοριών έργων υποδομής
IT: Elenco negativo delle categorie di infrastrutture
NL: Negatieve lijst van infrastructuurcategorieën
PT: Lista das categorias de infra-estruturas que não podem beneficiar da contribuição do Fundo.

Although strict concordance is not a requirement in EU instruments, syntactic and stylistic diversity appear to be the exception rather than the rule in substantive provisions, a distinction that Koutsivitis does not make. Nonetheless, the fact that diversity is permitted is definitely leaving its mark on the parallel texts of EU instruments. This is illustrated by the example below from subparagraph 7 of Article J3 of the Treaty on European Union. A comparison of the English, French, German, and Spanish texts reveals differences in all texts. While the English and German texts favor the conditional clause, the French and Spanish texts use the abbreviated *en cas de* form frequently used by francophone Canadians (*cf.* Chapter 6, 6.4.2). The word order is natural in each text; it is uniform only in the second sentence. Because of its rigid syntax, the German text places the information in the main clause of the statement of law before the fact-situation (*Ein Mitgliedstaat befaßt den Rat*). The remaining information, which is expressed in a relative clause in the other texts, is formulated in a main clause following the fact-situation (*der Rat berät...*). While the French text is the only one to join the subparagraphs of Article J3 by semicolons (thus *en cas de* is not capitalized), the division of subparagraph 7 into two sentences is also observed, thus ensuring concordance in all texts. Other minor stylistic diversities include the use of nouns in the German and Spanish texts to express the verbal phrase *implementing a joint action* and the use of pronouns in the French and German texts instead of repeating *solutions*:

Should there be any major difficulties in implementing a joint action, a Member State shall refer them to the Council which shall discuss them and seek appropriate solutions. Such solutions shall not run counter to the objectives of the joint action or impair its effectiveness.

en cas de difficultés majeures pour appliquer une action commune, un État membre saisit le Conseil, qui en délibère et recherche les solutions appropriées. Celles-ci ne peuvent aller à l'encontre les objectifs de l'action ni nuire à son efficacité.

225

Ein Mitgliedstaat befaßt den Rat, wenn sich bei der Durchführung einer gemeinsamen Aktion größere Schwierigkeiten ergeben; der Rat berät darüber und sucht nach angemessenen Lösungen. Diese dürfen nicht im Widerspruch zu den Zielen der gemeinsamen Aktion stehen oder ihrer Wirksamkeit schaden.

En caso de que un Estado miembro tenga dificultades importantes para aplicar una acción común, solicitará al Consejo que delibere al respecto y busque las soluciones adecuadas. Estas soluciones no podrán ser contrarias a los objetivos de la acción ni mermar su eficacia.

As in the translation of international treaties and conventions, the main objective of EU translators is to create a text that will promote uniform interpretation and application of the parallel texts. Nonetheless, as shown in the above provision, EU translators are permitted to strive for linguistic purity, provided the substance remains the same. The fact that linguistic diversity is not only tolerated but also welcomed in the parallel texts of EU instruments would not be possible without the effective judicial controls mentioned above. Despite these controls, translators are urged to proceed with caution. Since they are dealing with multilingual and multilateral instruments, EU translators are subject to considerably more restrictions than their Canadian colleagues. Hence, the real challenge is deciding when one can be creative without altering the substance and when one should exercise constraint in the interest of preserving the single instrument. Like judges, EU translators are expected to consult several texts, not only the original. Moreover, all existing parallel texts should be consulted when making subsequent translations occasioned by the admission of new Member States (*cf.* Chapter 4, 4.2.2).

7.10. OUTLOOK FOR THE TRANSLATION OF MULTILINGUAL, MULTI-LATERAL INSTRUMENTS

The changed circumstances of the communication process and special nature of multilingual, multilateral instruments place additional constraints on translators, making it doubtful whether UN and other translators of treaties and conventions will experience any liberalization in the near future. While the multilingual drafting experiment at UNCLOS III made considerable progress in coordinating the production of the parallel texts of the Convention on the Law of the Sea (1982), this did not have any visible effect on translation and drafting methods. Instead, additional steps were taken to preserve interlingual concordance in all parallel texts. As in the European Union, the ultimate goal of international lawyers is to control not only the production but also the interpretation of parallel texts of multilateral instruments to the greatest extent possible (*see* Chapter 4, 4.5). Again, attempts to achieve this goal have been most successful at UNCLOS III where the delegates agreed to establish the International Tribunal for the Law of the Sea. While the International Tribunal has only shared jurisdiction over matters relating to the law of the sea, all disputes concerning the international sea-bed area are to be resolved by the Sea-Bed Disputes Chamber, which is empowered to act in the capacity of a specialized court (*see* 7.7 above). Now that the Convention on the Law of the Sea has finally entered into force, final preparations are being made for the International Tribunal to begin its work.

Despite shortcomings, the completion of this process marks a special achievement in multilingual communication. Ideally it can be said that the situative factors of production and interpretation of all parallel texts of the Convention will be coordinated in one basic act of communication. Controlling the communication process by coordinating the situational factors of production and reception of parallel texts of multilateral instruments should promote uniform interpretation and application despite inevitable divergences in the six language versions. Even under such conditions, it is doubtful whether drafters and translators of future treaties and conventions will relinquish the principle of fidelity to the single instrument.

Because of the large number of states participating in negotiations at international conferences, it has become common practice to insert so-called opting out clauses into multilateral conventions which enable a state to declare that it will not be bound by certain provisions. In particular, the Convention on the Law of the Sea has been called a 'package deal that is very much the result of a bargain between states with different priorities' (Dixon 1993:168). As a result, it is questionable how effective the provisions will be in section 2 of Part XV, which provides for compulsory procedures for the resolution of disputes and designates all decisions rendered by such courts or tribunals as final and binding. In section 3, however, Article 297 contains a list of limitations and exceptions to the applicability of section 2, and Article 298 makes it possible for states to exempt themselves from one or more of the procedures provided for in section 2. Taking advantage of this opting out clause, the then Soviet Union declared at signature that it accepts no obligatory procedures resulting in obligatory decisions concerning disputes relating to sea boundary delimitations and military activities, as well as disputes in respect of which the UN Security Council exercises the functions assigned to it by the UN Charter. As regards the choice of procedures under Article 287, it selected the arbitral tribunal designated in Annex VII as the principal means of resolving disputes concerning the interpretation or application of the Convention. Moreover, it explicitly limited the jurisdiction of the International Tribunal for the Law of the Sea to disputes concerning the prompt release of vessels and crews (*see Traités multilatéraux déposés auprès du Secrétaire Général*, État au 31 décembre 1994, Nationes Unies, 892–893).[17] If this Declaration is an indication of the readiness of states to accept the jurisdiction of a specialized court, it does not speak well for the future of judicial controls in international law. On the other hand, if states accept the exclusive jurisdiction of the Sea-Bed Disputes Chamber and recognize its decisions as final and binding, then progress will be made. Generally speaking, there appears to be a common desire for a greater degree of predictability and legal certainty in international law.

By the time the Convention on the Law of the Sea entered into force in November 1994, many of its rules had already been recognized as customary law (Dixon 1993:169) and were being applied by *ad hoc* arbitral tribunals appointed to resolve disputes relating to the law of the sea. An example of such a case is *La Bretagne*,

---

17. Russia has endorsed the Declaration made by the Soviet Union in 1982. As in the original declaration, it authorizes the arbitral tribunal specified in Annex VIII to resolve disputes concerning fishing, protection and preservation of the marine environment, marine scientific research, and navigation (including pollution).

a dispute between Canada and France concerning filleting within the Gulf of St. Lawrence. Invoking Article 6 of the 1972 Agreement governing France and Canada's mutual fishing relations, Canadian authorities refused to grant a license for fishing and the use of fish filleting equipment in the Gulf of St. Lawrence to the French vessel *La Bretagne*. In order to determine whether Canada's regulatory authority covered filleting equipment, the Tribunal referred to Article 62, subparagraph 4(a) of LOS 1982. In an effort to determine the common meaning of all the parallel texts, the arbiters voluntarily consulted and compared all six language versions of the said provision. Maintaining that filleting equipment cannot be assimilated to *fishing equipment* in the ordinary meaning of the terms used in the six authentic texts,[18] the Tribunal concluded that the regulation of filleting at sea cannot *a priori* be justified by coastal State powers under the new law of the sea rules (*International Law Reports* 1990:630). Unfortunately, it appears that most *ad hoc* tribunals are not as thorough in their comparisons of parallel texts. Lacking the authority of precedents, decisions of *ad hoc* tribunals will not be binding on the International Tribunal for the Law of the Sea when it commences its work in Hamburg.

Numerous disputes arising under multilateral instruments turn on terminological issues due to the conceptual incongruency of corresponding terms and institutions of different legal systems. Distinguishing between interlingual and conceptual incongruency, Rosenne does not hesitate to advise translators and drafters of treaties and conventions to strive for 'conceptual concordance in all cases, if necessary at the expense of formal linguistic concordance' (1987:784). As acknowledged by Nadelmann and von Mehren, the difficulty of achieving conceptual congruency increases not only with the number of parallel texts, but also with the number of signatory States participating in the communication process. In their words: 'The equivalence problem causes difficulty in bilateral conventions written in two languages,' and can 'become unmanageable for multilingual, multilateral conventions' (1966:196). The problem of conceptual incongruency is dealt with in the next Chapter.

---

18. Consulting the six language versions of Article 62(4)(a) of LOS 1982, the Arbitral Tribunal found *fishing vessels and equipment* in the English text, рыболовных судов и оборудования in the Russian text, *navires et engins de pêche* in the French text, *buques y equipo de pesca* in the Spanish text, *yu chuan* (fishing vessels) and *pu lao she bei* (fishing equipment) in the Chinese text, and *lisoufon al sayed oua mouadatiha* (fishing vessels and their equipment) in the Arabic text (*International Law Reports* 1990:630, note 16).

8 Terminological Problems of Legal Translation

8.1. LEGAL TRANSLATION IS NOT TRANSCODING

Long convinced that all legal translation had to be literal, lawyers frequently focus their attention on terminological issues. In fact, most existing studies on legal translation deal primarily if not exclusively with terminology (*cf.* Bocquet 1994:ii). Unfortunately many of these studies are mere exercises in contrastive linguistics, thus giving the false impression that legal translation is a mechanical process of transcoding, i.e., substituting words and phrases of the source legal system by corresponding expressions of the target legal system. LSP scholars have also had a hand in spreading this misconception by overly emphasizing the role of technical terms in specialized languages (Fluck 1985:137). Despite the continued emphasis on preserving the letter of the law in legal translation, the basic unit of translation is not the word but the text. Since a text derives its meaning from one or more legal systems, legal translation is essentially a process of translating legal systems (*see* Chapter 1, 1.4). Accordingly, it follows that, if legal translation is to be effective, the so-called search for equivalents cannot be reduced to a process of matching up 'equivalents.'

Regardless of the type of text involved, all legal translators must deal with the problem of terminological incongruency. As Rosenne warned, terminological incongruency presents the greatest single threat to the uniform interpretation and application of parallel legal texts (1987:784). Addressing the problem of terminological incongruency, this Chapter attempts to assist translators in their decision-making process by analyzing the options available to them when selecting equivalents and by proposing ways of compensating for terminological incongruency. When determining whether a potential equivalent is acceptable in a given context, the translator should take account of the specific communication process, in particular the communicative situation of reception by the courts. Since the translator's task is to select terminology that will achieve the desired results, the success or failure of a legal translation may depend on his/her ability to predict how the courts will interpret and apply the terms of the particular text. For the purpose of legal translation, the acceptability of a potential equivalent is determined primarily by the results in practice, i.e., the legal effects.

8.2. A SYSTEM OF REFERENCE

Each legal system has its own language(s) and its own system of reference. Although reference has been defined in different ways by different authors who do not even use the same terms, it is generally agreed that reference 'has to do with the relationship which holds between an expression and what that expression stands for on particular occasions of its utterance' (Lyons 1977:174). In an attempt to improve communication, linguists have long investigated the relationship between words and things. Among others, Odgen and Richards supported the theory that the relationship between a word and the object it identifies is indirect, being mediated by a concept. In their triangle of signification (1923), Odgen and Richards employed the term *referent* for any object or state of affairs in the external world that is identified by means of a word or expression, and *reference* for the concept that mediates between the word or expression and the referent (*see* Lerat 1995:37). In the following illustration of the triangle of signification, A, B, and C represent the word, reference, and referent respectively, or in the currently accepted terminology, the sign, concept, and object.

Figure 9: *Triangle of Signification*

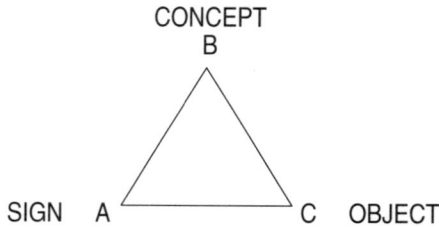

```
            CONCEPT
               B
              /\
             /  \
            /    \
           /      \
          /        \
SIGN   A ‾‾‾‾‾‾‾‾‾‾ C   OBJECT
```

While AC represents the indirect relationship between the sign and its object, AB and BC represent the two basic relationships of signification: the sign signifying the concept and the concept signifying the object. It should be noted that, for Odgen and Richards, the relation of reference is between B and C, and not between A and C, as is usually the case, in philosophy as well (Lyons 1977:97, 175).

Though maintaining the view that the meaning of a word is what it signifies, some linguists have attempted to eliminate either B or C. Arguing that C is of no direct concern in semantics, Ullmann maintained that the properties of things relevant to determining the meaning of words are abstracted from things and represented in B. Following Saussure's 1916 analysis (*see* Lerat 1995:37), he regarded A and B as a composite entity and meaning as a reciprocal relation between A and B, which 'enables them to call up one another' in the mind (cited in Lyons 1977:99). Rejecting the idea that meaning is a mental entity, other scholars preferred to eliminate B, the concept mediating between a word and its object. In their opinion, a word refers directly to a particular object and thus the meaning of a word is simply the object or class of objects that it stands for (Lyons 1977:99). Since terminologists focus their attention primarily on signs and concepts, for them the relation of reference is between A and B, both of which are aspects of reference. Terminologists generally agree that terms are symbols (signs) which refer to concepts; however, there is still no agreement on a definition of concept. It appears, however, that most definitions make explicit reference to mental activities and to objects, thus showing that terminologists do not eliminate the third component of the triangle entirely.[1] Since the advent of the information age, terminologists have attempted to establish multidimensional models of knowledge in which individual concepts occupy sets of points along orthogonal axes in hyperspace (*see* Sager, Dungworth and McDonald 1980:71). This, however, has not significantly changed the traditional principles of terminology, including the triadic notion of reference.

While it may appear that lawyers are concerned primarily with terms and concepts, they cannot disregard the objects they stand for. In fact, law is very much dependent on the triadic notion of reference. From Kelsen's point of view, the meaning of a linguistic sign is the object it refers to. As he points out, signs refer not only to material objects but also to relationships, acts, procedures, etc. Accordingly, an object can be real, i.e., it actually exists in reality, or it can be something that exists only in our imagination (Kelsen 1979:26; *see also* Mincke 1991:452). Belonging to the group of languages for special purposes (LSP), the language of the law consists of technical or legal terms, as well as non-technical terms from ordinary language (*see* Gémar 1995–II:96; *also* Cornu 1990:61–65). Confusion arises when a term is assigned a legal meaning that has little or nothing to do with the object referred to by the term in ordinary language (*see* 8.10.4 below). Numerous terms used in legal discourse derive their general meaning from ordinary language (e.g., *thing, property, theft, rent*) but are assigned a special legal meaning by each legal system. Other legal terms are used exclusively in legal discourse (e.g., *negligence, legal capacity, joint stock company*) (*cf.* Lampe 1970:28). Whereas terms of the exact sciences are monosemous, i.e., each term refers to only one object, legal terms are characterized by polysemy (*see* Cornu 1990:89–117; Gémar 1995–II:130). Normally this does not create a serious problem for translators as they should be able to determine the intended meaning from the context. On the other hand, the fact that most legal terms derive their meaning from a particular legal system makes legal terminology inherently congruent.

8.3. TERMINOLOGICAL INCONGRUENCY

In international standardization, the terminology of a special subject area can be standardized in different languages only after the objects and consequently the concepts they signify have been standardized (*see* Sager 1990:114–128). This process is considerably easier in the natural sciences because in the majority of

---

1. For example, the British Standard Recommendation for the selection, formation and definition of technical terms (BS.3669:1963) defines concepts as 'mental constructs, abstractions which may be used in classifying the individual objects of the inner and outer world.' Similarly, the UK proposal for the revision of ISO document R 704 reads: 'The objects of all fields of knowledge and human activity, such as things, their properties, qualities, phenomena, etc., are represented by concepts' (cited in Sager 1990:23).

instances the same objects exist in each society. This is no longer the case in the field of law where legal terms or 'terms of art,' as they are called in English law, usually refer to objects, relationships, acts, and procedures that are peculiar to a particular national legal system. The product of different institutions, history, culture, and sometimes socio-economic principles, each legal system has its own legal realia and thus its own conceptual system and even knowledge structure (Vanderlinden 1995:328–337). Consequently, the legal terminology of different legal systems is, for the most part, conceptually incongruent (Šarčević 1989:278; *also* Arntz 1993:6).

As in Hjelmsley's analysis of terminological incongruency in ordinary languages, it can be shown that the boundaries between the meanings of concepts of different legal systems are incongruent. For example, the concept of *décision* in French law corresponds with two, more specific concepts in German law *Entscheidung, Beschluß* and three in Dutch law *Beschikking, Besluit, Beslissing* (Bauer-Bernet 1982:192). Although etymological equivalents such as *contract* and *contrat* even signify the same object, they are not identical at the conceptual level. The English concept of *contract* is considerably broader than its French equivalent *contrat*, which is restricted to transactions involving mutuality of agreement and obligation (*see* Tallon 1990:284–290; *see also* Chapter 5, note 9).

Moreover, it occurs that, within the same language, the same term designates different concepts in different legal systems. For instance, *domicile* has one meaning in English law and quite different meanings in American jurisdictions (*see* Nadelmann and von Mehren 1966:195; Vanderlinden 1985:321). Even such a basic term as *Sache* has different meanings in German and Austrian law (*see* Pasternak 1996:46). Conversely, the same concept is sometimes designated by different terms in different jurisdictions having the same official language. For example, a preventive measure consisting of a *retención de bienes* is designated in various Spanish-speaking jurisdictions as *embargo, secuestro, retención, depósito, occupación, anotación preventiva* and *comiso* (cited in de Torres Carballal 1988:449).[2] Even terms whose concepts have been directly transplanted into another legal system take on different meanings once the concepts have been assimilated into the foreign legal system and culture (on legal transplants *see* Watson 1974:21). As a result, the civil law terminology in Turkey is not interpreted strictly in the sense of the Swiss ZGB although the latter was adopted almost word for word in the Turkish Civil Code of 1926. Rich in transplants from French law (Code Napoléon), German law (BGB) and after 1945 the common law, the law of Japan and its legal terminology strongly reflect the 'style of translation.' According to Kitamura, the strict legal sense of the foreign concepts has been successfully assimilated into Japanese law; however, the historical, philosophical, and sociological connotations were lost in translation (1987:787; on the concept of domicile in Japan *see* Vanderlinden 1995:410).[3] Even general terms change their effective meaning when adopted by other legal systems. This was the case, for example, when terms such as *family, land, person, wife, child,*

---

2. Variations in the basic terminology of criminal procedure used in 13 Spanish-speaking countries are listed in the United Nations glossary *Derechos Humanos* (1985:vii).
3. According to Kitamura, the German influence on Japanese law was so strong from 1890 to 1945 that all lawyers had to know German (1987:755).

provocation, and *reasonable* were transposed from England to the developing legal systems of Africa (*see* Allott 1974:134).

In addition, all legal systems contain a number of terms with no comparable counterparts in other legal systems or families. This is because the actual object, relationship, action, or procedure does not exist in other legal systems. System-bound terms, as I refer to them in earlier works (Šarčević 1988b:455), designate concepts and institutions peculiar to the legal reality of a specific system or related systems. System-bound terms are frequently regarded as untranslatable. This includes technical terms such as *equity* and *trust*, as well as terms signifying cultural-specific realia such as the Soga (Uganda) term *nkoko*, which literally means hen. Originally a hen was the symbolic payment made by a person acquiring land to the headman controlling that land; the term is still used for the payment, though it is now a substantial premium charged for the allocation of land (Allott 1974:132).

On the other hand, there are numerous indefinite or vague terms, such as *the best interests of the child*, *due care and attention*, and *good faith*, which are easily translated and already exist in most legal systems, but are interpreted differently by courts of different jurisdictions. Other terms such as *human rights* and *democracy* have a high ideological content and thus have different connotations in countries with different socio-political and/or religious principles such as the United States, Iran, and China. For instance, the Chinese term for democracy 民主 (*minzhu*) literally means 'people's rule,' not however in the western sense of 'rule by the people' but rather 'the ruling people.' In the PR of China the term 民 (*min*) (people) has a narrower sense as it includes only citizens who support the Communist Party of China (*see* von Senger 1994:204). Translators should be aware of the effects of ideological connotations on interpretation although there is little they can do to prevent them.

8.4. NATURAL VS. LINGUISTIC EQUIVALENTS

As a result of the tremendous burden placed on translators by the incongruency of legal terminology, some lawyers have openly doubted whether texts can be translated from one legal system into another (*see* Beaupré 1987:736). Belonging to these pessimists, the comparativist René David complained about the lack of adequate equivalents in French and English law:

> Les concepts du droit anglais sont différents de ceux du droit français, et il n'existe, et ne peut exister, aucun vocabulaire satisfaisant, traduisant en français les mots de la langue juridique anglaise ou traduisant inversement en anglais les termes usités par les juristes français (cited in Pigeon 1982:277).

Despite David's pessimism, legal texts have been translated for centuries. As shown in the historical review in Chapter 2, literal translation dominated legal translation until relatively late in the twentieth century. Literal translation is characterized by the use of linguistic equivalents such as literal equivalents, borrowings, and naturalizations (*see* 8.10.2 and 8.10.3 below). While the majority of linguistic equivalents are terms created to designate concepts foreign to the target legal system, natural equivalents are terms that actually exist in the target legal system.[4] The debate on the use of natural as opposed to linguistic equivalents dates back to Professor Rossel's revolutionary translation of the Swiss Civil Code in the early 1900s. At that time Cesana attacked Rossel's use of natural French equivalents as heresy, insisting that the new progressive concepts in the German text could be rendered accurately only by literal or word-for-word translation of the German terms. Invoking the principle of language equality, Rossel defended his practice of using natural French terms to express Swiss German concepts (*see* Chapter 2, 2.7).

More than half a century later, Quebecers also invoked their right to language equality, thus setting the stage for the Canadian debate that led to the legislative reform of the eighties. One of the most respected reformers, the late Justice Pigeon rejected the use of literal equivalents which correspond only in appearance:

> Mais, encore une fois, ce qui me paraît être carrément à rejeter, c'est la traduction 'littérale' par un mot qui ne correspond qu'en apparence à celui qu'il s'agit de traduire (1982:280).

J.C. Clarence Smith also supports the use of natural equivalents whenever possible or, as he put it, the use of equivalents in 'universal French' for common law terms. In contrast to David's pessimistic view, Smith claims that 'equivalents in universal French... are applicable in ninety-five percent of cases in common law' (1983:595). Later it will be shown that the acceptability of natural equivalents must be determined on a case-by-case basis.

Before continuing, a few words should be said about the term *equivalent* and its usage in translation theory. In mathematics and logic, if X and Y qualify as equivalents, this means that they are in a one-to-one correspondence. Similarly, if X and Y are translation equivalents, this is often interpreted as meaning that they are 'of equal value' or are 'the same thing.' On the other hand, in ordinary English, if X is said to be an equivalent of Y, this implies that they are 'virtually the same' (*cf.* Snell-Hornby 1986:14; 1991:80). According to Snell-Hornby, the same difference exists in regard to *équivalent* in technical and ordinary French, however not in regard to *Äquivalent* in technical and ordinary German (1986:15; 1988:16–17). When translation theorists finally acknowledged that absolute equivalence cannot be achieved at the level of the text in translation, the term *equivalence* was temporarily purged from translation theory (*see* Reiß and Vermeer 1984:131) until its revival in the early nineties (*see* Chapter 2, 2.8.4). As far as terminological studies are concerned, equivalence has always remained a relevant factor (Snell-Hornby 1988:106; Felber 1993:38; Arntz 1993:5–19) although, as Reiß points out, absolute one-to-one correspondence exists only in cases where the technical terms of a given discipline have been assigned the same definition in two or more languages (Reiß 1995:54). Today the term *equivalent* continues to be used in translation theory, however, not in its technical sense. Accordingly, if X and Y are said to be equivalents, this simply means that X can be used to translate Y and vice versa, without

---

4. It may occur that a natural equivalent is also a linguistic equivalent. This, however, is an exception, as in the case of *cour d'appel* and *court of appeal*. *See* 8.10.3.

implying that they are identical at the conceptual level. This was Heck's definition of the German term *Äquivalent* long before modern translation theory began (1931:9).

Because of the inherent incongruency of the terminology of different legal systems, legal translators cannot be expected to use natural equivalents of the target legal system that are identical with their source terms at the conceptual level. Nonetheless, it is perfectly legitimate to require them to use the 'closest natural equivalent' of the target legal system, i.e., the equivalent that most accurately conveys the legal sense of the source term and leads to the desired results.[5] This, however, may prove to be a formidable task at times.

8.5. THE SEARCH FOR EQUIVALENTS

Govert van Ginsbergen compares the translator's search for equivalents with the legal process of qualification. In cases with a foreign element, the judge must determine which law is to be applied in respect of certain terms, parts of an instrument, or the entire instrument. In the first step of the process, the judge must determine the nature of the substantive problem. For instance, is it a matter of tort or of contract? Thereafter he/she consults the choice-of-law rules. If the relevant choice-of-law rule points to foreign law, the next step is to investigate how the substantive issues in question are resolved in the foreign legal system (van Ginsbergen 1970:7). This is a process requiring considerable comparative law skills. Unlike branches of law such as criminal law or contract law, comparative law does not consist of a body of rules but of methods for comparing concepts and institutions of different legal systems and even entire legal systems. One of the methods of comparison that has found widespread support is the functional approach. Since most legal systems provide solutions for basically the same problems, comparative lawyers maintain that concepts and institutions of different legal systems can be meaningfully compared only if they are capable of performing the same task, i.e., if they have the same function. As Zweigert put it:

> Unvergleichbares kann man nicht sinnvoll vergleichen, und vergleichbar ist im Recht nur, was dieselbe Aufgabe, dieselbe Funktion erfüllt (Zweigert and Kötz 1984:34).

In order to identify the concept in the foreign legal system that has the same function as a particular concept in his/her own legal system, the judge departs from the problem at hand and investigates how that problem is resolved in the foreign legal system.

Similarly, when searching for equivalents in the target legal system, translators should approach the matter as if they were solving a legal problem (*cf.* Mincke 1991:464). Like the judge, they should identify the nature of the issue at hand and determine how that issue is dealt with in the target legal system. This should lead

---

5. In general translation theory it was Nida who recommended that translators use the 'closest natural equivalent' in the target language. *See* Nida and Taber 1974:13.

the translator to the concept or institution in the target legal system that has the same function as the concept concerned in the source legal system. For instance, if the translator is searching for the common law equivalent for the French concept of *hypothèque*, he/she should investigate how security is pledged for the payment of a debt on land in the target legal system. This will bring him/her to the concept of *mortgage*. *Hypothèque* and *mortgage* are functional equivalents.

The term *functional equivalence* is used not only in general translation theory (Wilss 1977:56; Reiß and Vermeer 1984:129; Reiß 1995:113) but also in comparative law (Bartels 1982:66). To my knowledge, Canadian lawyers were the first to use the term *functional equivalent* as a *terminus technicus* in legal translation. In 1979 Jean Kerby mentioned two types of equivalents in legal translation, one of which was the *équivalent fonctionnel*.[6] Without defining the term, he merely identified it as an equivalent used in the absence of an exact equivalent (1979:18). The late Justice Pigeon also spoke about functional equivalents in legal translation but offered no definition. While their notion of *functional equivalence* is legal, some linguists such as Gémar (1995–II:165; *also* Gémar 1987:495) use the term in the sense attributed to it in general translation theory. In an attempt to define the term as a technical term of legal translation, I defined *functional equivalent* in an earlier article as a term designating a concept or institution of the target legal system having the same function as a particular concept of the source legal system (Šarčević 1989:278–279; 1988:964). Thereafter, Groffier and Reed mention the use of functional equivalents in this context (1990:81) as do Weston (1991:21–23) and de Groot (1991:287–289). Weston goes so far as to say that 'the technique of using a functional equivalent may be regarded as the *ideal* method of translation' (1991:23).

Identifying the functional equivalent is only the first step in a complex decision-making process. The fact that a functional equivalent has the same function as the source concept does not necessarily mean that it is acceptable for the purpose of translation. According to Justice Pigeon, the essence of functional equivalence lies in the principle of analogy:

> Le principe même de l'équivalence fonctionnelle signifie que l'on traduit en utilisant un mot qui ne correspond pas rigoureusement au même concept juridique mais à un concept analogue (1982:280).

Although Justice Pigeon strongly advocated the use of functional equivalents, his statement serves as a warning to translators, reminding them that some functional equivalents may not be sufficiently accurate. In fact, some functional equivalents can be misleading to the point that they encourage litigation. Therefore, a functional equivalent should not be used until its acceptability has been proven. In order to determine the acceptability of a functional equivalent, translators must compare the target and source concepts to establish their degree of equivalence. This process is

---

6. Kerby also speaks of semantic equivalents, however, the examples he cites – *offer* and *offre* – imply that he is referring to etymological equivalents. Translators should examine etymological equivalents carefully since many of them are *faux amis*. Kerby also mentions untranslatable terms for which there are no equivalents, such as *Common law* and *equity*.

so important that Bocquet makes it the second step in his three-step process of translation (Bocquet 1994:7; *cf.* Forti and Vesco 1991:274).[7]

8.6. MEASURING THE DEGREE OF EQUIVALENCE

Translators of authentic texts must have a well-stocked library of reference and legal materials at their disposal; however, they rarely have time to do the research necessary to make reliable decisions about the degree of equivalence of functional equivalents. For this and other reasons, they should be assisted by a group or department of terminologists, preferably lawyer linguists who are able to conduct comparative law studies. To date, some of the most successful comparative studies on legal terminology have been performed by lawyers at the Internationales Institut für Rechts- und Verwaltungssprache in Berlin (hereinafter: Berlin Institute). Published in a series of bilingual legal dictionaries (*Europaglossar der Rechts- und Verwaltungssprache*), the studies focus on specialized areas of the law of selected source and target legal systems (*see* Lane 1982:231). Regretfully, the dictionaries cover only a small number of terms and legal systems, as a result of which their practical value is limited for translators. On the other hand, the methods of conceptual analysis used therein can serve as a model for others.

The purpose of conceptual analysis is to establish the constituent features or characteristics of particular concepts. As in other disciplines of the social sciences, it has been proposed that the characteristics of legal concepts be divided into two groups: *essentialia* (vital, necessary) and *accidentalia* (additional, possible, but not inevitable) (Dahlberg 1981:19; *cf.* Felber's comment, 1993:41). Such classification permits flexibility, thus allowing a characteristic to change categories depending on the use of the term in context. For example, the concept of *lawful wedded wife* has certain essential characteristics in family law that are accidental in inheritance law, although the concept remains the same (Picht and Draskau 1985:48).

The above system has been used by the Berlin Institute to classify the characteristics of functional equivalents of different legal systems. According to Alexander Lane, the first step in the comparative process is to determine the conceptual characteristics of the source term and qualify them as essential or accidental. Thereafter, the same process is repeated for the functional equivalent in the target legal system. The final evaluation is essentially a process of matching up the characteristics of the two terms. If all the essential characteristics of the source term match up with those of the functional equivalent and only a few of the accidental ones do not, the concepts are considered to be 'identical,' which is indicated by the

---

7. Bocquet's three-step process of legal translation is modelled on translation theories of the sixties and seventies when translation was regarded as a transcoding process consisting of two steps: decoding the message in the source language and encoding it into the target language. Following the decoding phase he inserts a new step: comparing legal institutions of the source and target legal systems. The translations Bocquet refers to are apparently non-authentic texts. This follows from his recommendation that the translator adapt the content of the message in the encoding phase so as to make it intelligible to the target readers (1994:7).

mathematical symbol '='. On the other hand, if most of the essential and only some of the accidental characteristics are the same, the concepts are regarded only as 'similar' and the symbol '±' is used. Finally, if only a few or none of the essential characteristics coincide, the two concepts are considered non-equivalent. In such cases, the functional equivalent is discarded and the symbol '≠' indicates the lack of an acceptable functional equivalent (Lane 1982:224–225; on the dispute regarding the acceptability of functional equivalents in Canada *see* Šarčević: 1988c:311).

By providing three general categories of equivalence, the Berlin Institute presents valuable guidelines for evaluating the acceptability of functional equivalents. However, as a note of caution, it should be pointed out that using the term *identity* and the symbol '=' is misleading since not all characteristics of the two concepts coincide. Moreover, it is helpful to go a step further and distinguish between intersection and inclusion. Although making such a distinction is extremely difficult when dealing with legal concepts, it is useful for translators. Generally speaking, intersection occurs when concepts A and B contain common characteristics but also additional ones not shared by the other concept; inclusion occurs when concept A contains all of the characteristics of concept B, plus one or more additional features.

Based on these remarks, I propose the following categories of equivalence for translators in the field of law: near equivalence, partial equivalence, and non-equivalence, each of which includes both intersection and inclusion. The optimum degree of equivalence is referred to as near equivalence which is indicated by the symbol '~'. Near equivalence occurs when concepts A and B share all of their essential and most of their accidental characteristics (intersection) or when concept A contains all of the characteristics of concept B, and concept B all of the essential and most of the accidental characteristics of concept A (inclusion):

Figure 10: *Near Equivalence*

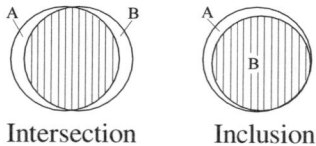

Intersection   Inclusion

In the majority of cases functional equivalents are only partially equivalent (±). Partial equivalence occurs when concepts A and B share most of their essential and some of their accidental characteristics (intersection) or when concept A contains all of the characteristics of concept B but concept B only most of the essential and some of the accidental characteristics of concept A (inclusion):

Figure 11: *Partial Equivalence*

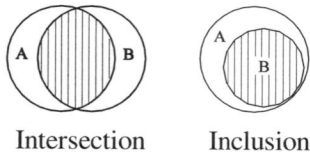

Intersection   Inclusion

If only a few or none of the essential features of concepts A and B coincide (inter-section) or if concept A contains all of the characteristics of concept B but concept B only a few or none of the essential features of concept A (inclusion), then the functional equivalent can no longer be considered acceptable. In such cases, one speaks of non-equivalence. Furthermore, non-equivalence also occurs in cases where there is no functional equivalent in the target legal system for a particular source concept. In such cases one speaks of exclusion. Non-equivalence is designated by the symbol '≠':

Figure 12: *Non-Equivalence*

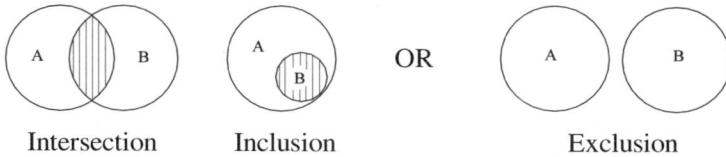

A	B	A B		A B
Intersection		Inclusion	OR	Exclusion

8.7. ESTABLISHING THE CHARACTERISTICS OF LEGAL CONCEPTS

From the general description above one could get the false impression that conceptual analysis in the field of law is not so difficult after all. Not mentioned above, the main problem is to establish the constituent characteristics of the concepts being analyzed. In most subject areas this is done by examining the definition of the terms in question. Definitions provide the link between concepts and terms 'by means of an equation in which the definiendum is the term' (Sager 1990:39). For the most part, a definition lists the essential characteristics of a concept that 'distinguish or differentiate it from its immediate hyperonym and co-hyponyms' (Sager 1990:44). Whereas terminologists in the exact sciences rely primarily on the definitions of monolingual dictionaries to establish the constituent characteristics of concepts (*cf.* Arnzt and Picht 1982:140; Arntz 1993:11), monolingual law dictionaries are frequently insufficient for this purpose. For one thing, the definitions of such dictionaries usually list the characteristics constituting the intension of terms while disregarding their extension.

When analyzing the properties of legal concepts, one must take account of both intension and extension (*cf.* Sourioux and Lerat 1975:59). According to Lyons, the intension of a term includes 'the set of essential properties which determines the applicability of the term' (1977:159). For example, the term *bankruptcy* in English law is defined as 'the name given to a variety of judicial or quasi-judicial proceedings, having for their main object the distribution of the property of an insolvent person among his creditors' (*Jowitt's Dictionary of English Law* 1977:183). On the other hand, the extension of a term is 'the class of the things to which it is correctly applied' (Lyons 1977:158). In legal methodology, the extension also includes types or classes of transactions, cases, situations, or proceedings (*cf.* Wank 1985:35). For example, the extensional definition of *bankruptcy* in English

239

law includes the various types of insolvency proceedings such as compulsory winding-up, creditor voluntary winding-up, bankruptcy (in the narrow sense), administration, corporate voluntary arrangements, and individual voluntary arrangements.

Since the number of characteristics constituting the intension of general terms is relatively small, it is not uncommon for the general terms of different legal systems to have the same intension but different extensions. For example, the German term *Konkurs* has the same intension as the English term *bankruptcy* (*cf. Creifelds Rechtswörterbuch* 1996:707); however, in German law there are only two types of insolvency proceedings: *Konkurs* (in the narrow sense) and *Vergleichsverfahren*. Thus it can be said that, although both *bankruptcy* and *Konkurs* happen to be hyponyms of themselves, these hyponyms are not congruent. In other words, the congruency is limited to intension. Conversely, it may occur that, as in Frege's example of the morning star and the evening star, the extension is the same but the intension differs. Especially in criminal law, it is possible that the same case or cases can be subsumed under different offenses in different legal systems.

Since such information is rarely included in monolingual law dictionaries, users sometimes prematurely conclude that they are dealing with congruent terms. Generally speaking, users of monolingual law dictionaries should proceed with caution as deficiencies occur not only in extensional but also in intensional definitions. For this reason, L.-J. Constantinesco's advice still holds true that the best way to establish the constituent characteristics of concepts is to examine all the original sources of the law of the particular legal systems: legislation, doctrine, case law, and customary law (1974:135). Even then, however, there is no guarantee that one will find ready definitions. By their very nature, legal terms seem to defy being defined (*see* Groffier and Reed 1990:52). While it is not surprising that indefinite or vague concepts are inaccurately defined or not defined at all, the fact that there are often no ready definitions of definite concepts is rather disquieting for terminologists. Although legislation is the primary source of such definitions, the number of statutory definitions is relatively small. Nonetheless, terminologists must be on the alert because the same term may be defined differently in different statutes or even in the same statute (de Groot 1991:285). Moreover, statutory definitions are subject to change (*see* 8.11 below).

At present, the number of empirical studies on comparative legal terminology is still very limited,[8] thus forcing terminologists to research practically each and every functional equivalent. If all sources of the law have been examined and no reliable definitions can be found, terminologists should determine the essential and accidental characteristics of concepts by legal analysis, posing a series of practical questions as if solving a legal problem. Lacking the know-how to pose the proper questions, terminologists without training in law tend to be at a loss. Similarly, once the characteristics of corresponding concepts have been established, they frequently have

---

8. Exceptions are Vanderlinden's excellent comparative analysis of the concept of *domicile* in various legal systems worldwide (1986) and, more recently, the analytical comparison of *association, compagnie, corporation* and *sociéte* in his book *Comparer les droits* (1995:87–109).

difficulty determining whether a functional equivalent is acceptable. According to the three categories of equivalence established above, partial equivalence is required for minimum acceptability. In other words, most of the essential features of the source concept and the functional equivalent must coincide; otherwise, the functional equivalent should be rejected as non-equivalent. Having determined the degree of equivalence, it is up to the translator to decide whether partial equivalence suffices for acceptability or whether near equivalence is required.

8.8. ESTABLISHING CRITERIA TO DETERMINE ACCEPTABILITY

Determining the acceptability of functional equivalents is surely one of the most important decisions made by legal translators. Since terminological issues are one of the main sources of litigation, the success or failure of a text may depend on the choice of equivalents, as in the case of the Warsaw Convention (*see* 8.9.2 below). In regard to contracts, de Vries warns that a careful translator and/or draftsman 'must take into account that a translation satisfactory for merely informational purposes may be inadequate and even harmful in an adversary proceeding conducted with the animus of skilled advocacy' (1962:20). Despite his warning, de Vries offers no criteria for evaluating the acceptability of translation equivalents. More to the point, Martin Weston (translator at the European Court of Human Rights) regrets that no criteria have been established 'by which the translator may decide whether a term peculiar to the TL culture is or is not an admissible translation.' Furthermore, he comments: 'This omission is the more curious – and serious – as the problem confronts translators quite regularly' (1991:23). Unfortunately, Weston's suggestion that acceptability be tested by the distinction between generic and specific greatly simplifies the matter (1991:23). While the test apparently works with national institutional terms such as *Master of the Rolls*, *House of Lords,* and *Minister of Foreign Affairs*, such terms constitute only a small percentage of the legal terms used in authoritative instruments of law, thus making it necessary to fill the gap by proposing more specific criteria for evaluating acceptability.

While some functional equivalents are always acceptable (near equivalence) or never acceptable (non-equivalence), most functional equivalents fall into the category of partial equivalence. Accordingly, the question of acceptability arises primarily when a functional equivalent and its source term are only partially equivalent. In such cases, the acceptability of a functional equivalent usually depends on context, thus requiring the translator to analyze each textual situation before deciding whether a functional equivalent is acceptable in that particular context (*cf.* Arntz 1993:17). Translators should be aware that acceptability is not always reciprocal. Thus it sometimes occurs that A can be used to translate B, but B cannot be used to translate A.

For the most part, lawyers are content to say that a translation equivalent is acceptable if it would not be misleading. Obviously this statement offers little help to translators who need to know in which circumstances a functional equivalent could be misleading. In any test of acceptability, function serves only as a starting point. Accordingly, the fact that *mortgage* and *hypothèque* are both forms of security pledged for the payment of a debt is not sufficient to make a decision on their

241

acceptability as translation equivalents. When determining the acceptability of a functional equivalent, the translator should take account of the structure/ classification, scope of application, and legal effects of both the functional equivalent and its source term. If a functional equivalent does not correspond with its source term in these three aspects, it may lead to results other than those intended by the legislature, contracting parties, or other. Finally, since the translator's goal is to create a text that will promote uniform interpretation and application of the single instrument, he/she must always take account of the situational factors of reception of the particular communication process, i.e., how the courts are likely to interpret the equivalent and how this will affect the application of the provision and the text as a whole. In the end, this may be the overriding consideration in the translator's decision-making process.

8.8.1. Structure/classification

Despite Schlesinger's postulation of the 'existence and vast extent of a common core of legal systems' (1980:36), different legal techniques are sometimes used to solve the same problem. Thus it may occur that, although a functional equivalent is capable of solving the same problem(s) as its source term, the legal techniques used to solve the problem are considerably different, even though the results are more or less identical. This is due to structural differences between legal systems. All lawyers think in terms of structure by automatically classifying a problem as a matter of contract law, property law, procedural law etc. This process is not purely a formal one because classification automatically implies that certain legal techniques will be applicable while others are excluded. Thus it follows that, if a functional equivalent and its source term are not structurally equivalent, the legal techniques used to solve the particular problem tend to be different. Accordingly, translating source terms by functional equivalents that do not belong to the same branch of law should be avoided if possible (*cf.* de Groot 1991:289). For example, translating *délit* and *unerlaubte Handlung* as *tort* (civil wrong independent of contract) would put common law lawyers on the wrong track. Furthermore, translating *délit* as *unerlaubte Handlung* and vice versa could cause some confusion for both German and French lawyers. Since the term *unerlaubte Handlung* is not used in criminal law, this means that it could eventually be used to translate *délit* when the context relates to civil law. In addition, however, German law makes no distinction between what the French call *délit* and *quasi-délit*, as a result of which *unerlaubte Handlung* covers both *délit* and *quasi-délit*. Moreover, the underlying concept of *faute* includes elements of both *Rechtswidrigkeit* and *Verschulden* (Schroth 1986:58, note 24).

Although structural differences also exist between legal systems belonging to the same legal family, they tend to be more pronounced in legal systems of different legal families. In regard to English and French law, René David commented: 'English legal structure is not the same as that of French law and it poses the greatest difficulty for a continental jurist since it is, in fact, totally different to anything with which he is familiar' (David and Brierley 1985:334). This applies particularly to property law which has been heavily influenced by the hand of history. Contrary to a *hypothèque*, which is considered a contract and is thus regarded primarily as a term of contract law, *mortgage* is used primarily as a term of property law. Historically, this applied to mortgages on personal property (chattel mortgage) as well as to those on real property. More recently, however, chattel mortgages tend to be subsumed under a contract theory, as *créances mobilières* are in French law.

Classification serves as a catalyst to put the lawyer's mind on the right track, calling up the related concepts and institutions involved in solving the particular problem. Thus terminologists should not deal with isolated concepts but need to compare the conceptual structures of the functional equivalent and its source term by analyzing the conceptual hierarchies to which each belongs. For example, the diagrams of the conceptual hierarchies of *mortgage* and *hypothèque* below show that their conceptual structures more or less coincide as far as realty is concerned (with the exception of the historical characterization of leaseholds as personal property). As for personalty (personal property), its conceptual structure is similar to that of *bien meubles* (with the exception of the category of chattels real):

Figure 13: *Conceptual Hierarchies of 'mortgage' and 'hypothèque'*

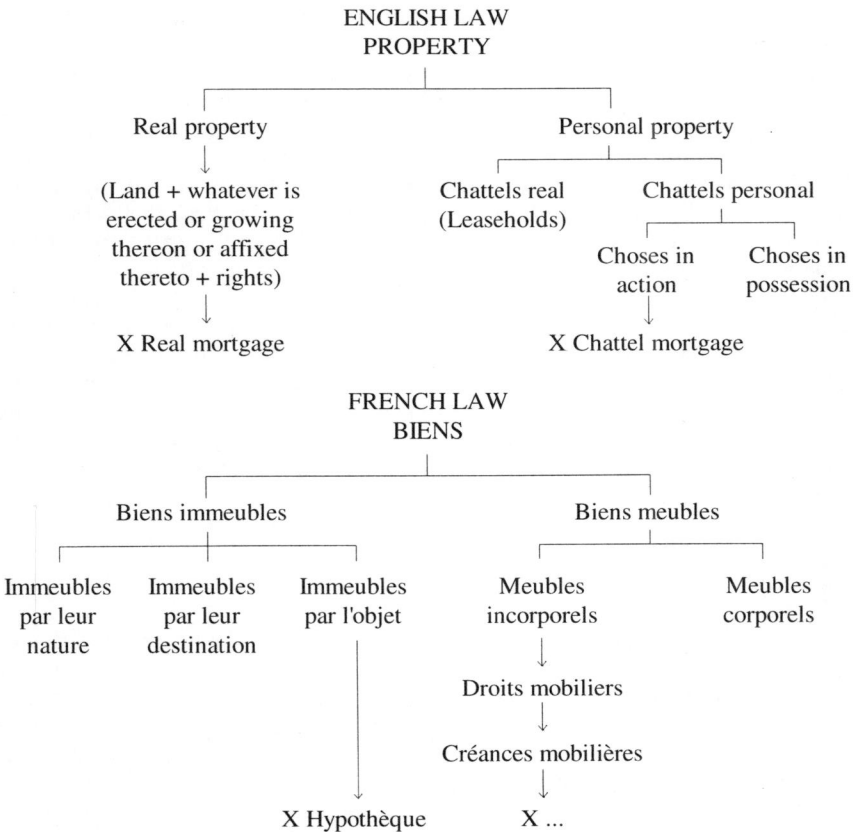

ENGLISH LAW
PROPERTY

Real property

Personal property

(Land + whatever is
erected or growing
thereon or affixed
thereto + rights)

Chattels real
(Leaseholds)

Chattels personal

Choses in
action

Choses in
possession

X Real mortgage

X Chattel mortgage

FRENCH LAW
BIENS

Biens immeubles

Biens meubles

Immeubles
par leur
nature

Immeubles
par leur
destination

Immeubles
par l'objet

Meubles
incorporels

Meubles
corporels

Droits mobiliers

Créances mobilières

X Hypothèque

X ...

Comparing the position of concepts within their respective conceptual hierarchies is important for another reason as well. From the linguistic point of view, analyzing the structure of a concept involves determining its relationship to other concepts within the same hierarchy. Since the level of abstraction of legal concepts of different legal systems varies, terminologists should establish the generic-specific relationship of a functional equivalent and its source term. Based on logical relationships, one distinguishes between superordinate, coordinate, and subordinate concepts. Ideally, a functional equivalent and its source term should be coordinate concepts, i.e., concepts having the same level of abstraction and falling under the same superordinate concept (Felber, Galinski and Nedobity 1987:13; Felber 1993:36–37).

The above diagrams confirm that *real mortgage* and *hypothèque* are coordinate concepts. The starting points coincide (*property* and *biens*) as does the level of abstraction of their direct superordinate terms *real property* and *biens immeubles*. On the other hand, when it comes to *chattel mortgage*, we see that there is no coordinate *terminus technicus* in French law. Nevertheless, the superordinate terms *personal property* and *biens meubles* more or less coincide as do the direct superordinate terms *choses in action* and *meubles incorporels*. The division of personal property into *chattels real* and *chattels personal* is unknown in the civil law systems.

Although it is best when a functional equivalent and its source term are coordinate concepts, this is not always possible. Take the example of the Anglo-American concept of *consideration*, a generic term of contract law meaning 'that which is given, done or forborne in return for the promise or act of another party' (Walker 1980:274). The attempt by Canadian translators to naturalize the term into French by using the anglization *considération* failed, probably because the term already existed in ordinary French but with another meaning. Lacking a coordinate concept in Quebec law, Quebec translators finally proposed translating *consideration* by naming the specific thing used in each particular context to evidence the contract or ensure that it was not undertaken lightly. As Walker points out, consideration 'may be a promise to do or forbear from doing something'; normally, however, it is 'a payment, transfer of goods, doing of services or surrender of another legal claim' (1980:274). In light of this, Schwab recommends the following French equivalents depending on context: *à titre onéreux, contrepartie, cause* (bonne et valable), *dédommagement, paiement, prix, provision* (d'une lettre de change), *rémunération, rétribution*, or *valeur* (1984:122).

8.8.2. Scope of application

The scope of application of a concept is important because it determines whether the concept can be applied in a concrete fact situation. As such it is one of the main factors determining the extension of a concept. Although a functional equivalent solves the same problem as its source term, their scope of application may differ. For example, concept A may also solve other problems which concept B is incapable of solving and vice versa (intersection), or concept A may solve the same problem(s) as concept B and additional problems as well (inclusion). A functional equivalent whose scope of application is significantly broader or narrower than that of its source term poses a threat to the uniform application of the single instrument and should be avoided if possible.

For example, in *Gulf Oil Can. Ltd.* v. *Canadien Pacifique Ltée* ([1979] C.S. 72), an action for damages for breach of contract, Canadian Pacific invoked the provisions of an order made under the *National Transportation Act* and the *Transport Act.* Whereas the English text of the disputed provision stated that a carrier is not liable for loss caused by an *act of God,* the French version used the phrase by *cas fortuit ou de force majeure.* This led to a problem because fact situations which qualify as *cas fortuit* under Quebec law do not always qualify as an act of God at common law. Despite this discrepancy in the scope of application of the two terms, the Superior Court of Quebec upheld Quebec law and ruled according to the French version. Maintaining that the act of the third party – in this case, a truck that hit a locomotive – was a *cas fortuit,* the Court exonerated the defendant railway company from liability, although the same fact situation would not qualify as an act of God in a common law province (*see* Beaupré 1986:133–134).

In regard to the disputed word pair *hypothèque* and *mortgage,* it is important to note that the scope of application of *mortgage* is broader than that of *hypothèque.* Whereas a *mortgage* can be pledged for both real and personal property, a *hypothèque* applies only to immovables (realty). Technically speaking, this means that the narrower term *hypothèque* can be translated as *mortgage* in all contexts, the broader term *mortgage,* however, as *hypothèque* only in contexts pertaining to realty. Despite these technical differences, the term *hypothèque* is often used as an equivalent for *mortgage* regardless of context. For example, section 15 of the *Bill of Sale Act* of New Brunswick [1973] deals specifically with chattels (i.e., personal property). Nonetheless, the francophone translator consistently uses *hypothèque* for *mortgage, créancier hypothécaire* for *mortgagee,* and other related forms. The discrepancy is particularly noticeable in the phrase 'by reason of the fact that the grantee has subsequently taken possession of the chattels sold or mortgaged...' which is translated as 'en raison du fait que l'acquéreur a par la suite pris possession des biens personnels vendus ou hypothéqués....' While this mistranslation is apparently harmless, this is not always the case.

As a rule, conceptual differences are much greater between common law and civil law systems; however, there are also notable differences between the corresponding concepts of individual civil law systems. In fact, these differences are so great that many comparative lawyers regard the 'romanistic' systems modelled on the French Code civil and the 'germanic' systems which follow the German BGB as distinct legal families (Zweigert and Kötz 1984 I:80). As illustrated by the following example, conceptual differences in the scope of application of a functional equivalent and its source term can sometimes be decisive in determining the admissibility of specific types of claims. The question whether an insurer's claim was admissible in a dispute initiated in 1925 before the Oberlandesgericht Breslau hinged on the conceptual differences between *bien meubles* and *bewegliche Sachen* (personal property) in French and German law. The claimant, an Insurance Agency in the part of Oberschlesien ceded to Poland under the Treaty of Versailles (1919), invoked the German Revaluation Law of 1924, requesting the revaluation of an insurance claim destroyed by inflation, namely its personal rights secured by a land mortgage that had been discharged at face value and consequently significantly deflated due to hyperinflation. As required under Article 312 of the Versailles Treaty, Germany had agreed to pay Poland a fixed compensation for insurance agencies operating in Oberschlesien and, moreover, to transfer to Poland 'das Eigentum an allen beweglichen Sachen, die ein Träger der genannten Versicherungen in Polnisch-Oberschlesien besaß.' Pursuant to §§ 90, 854, 903 and 929 of the German BGB, the concept of *bewegliche Sachen* is limited to physical objects and thus excludes personal rights. While this appeared to be sufficient grounds to reject the Insurance Agency's claim, claimant's counsel argued that the German text was merely a translation of the authentic French text of the agreement. The French text used the term *biens meubles*, which pursuant to Articles 516, 527, 528, 529, and 535 of the French Code civil includes 'les corps qui peuvent se transporter d'un lieu à un autre' as well as 'les obligations et actions qui ont pour objet des sommes exigibles.' Although it seemed clear that the intent had not been to apply French law, the agreement was based on the Treaty of Versailles which mentions 'biens, droits et intérêts privés en pays ennemi' in Articles 297 and 298. Thus the claim was declared admissible on the basis of the French text (Entscheidungen des Reichsgerichts in Zivilsachen 1931:251–260).

8.8.3. Legal effect

Lawyers agree that the meaning of parallel legal texts cannot be identical; however, they are expected to lead to the same legal effects in practice (Pigeon 1982:281). Thus the main task of the translator is to formulate the text in appropriate language so as to achieve the desired effect. Due to their inherent normative function, legal concepts automatically imply certain legal effects within a given system (*see* Lampe 1970:25). This led to the so-called theory of relativity of legal concepts, according to which the meaning of a legal term can be grasped only as a process of interaction between fact and legal effect within the total mechanism of the particular legal system (*see* Wank 1985:75–76). Thus it follows that the translator must also investigate the legal effect(s) of the functional equivalent in the target legal system. Since the same concept may have different legal effects in different situations, they are often disregarded. In numerous instances, however, the legal effect(s) of a concept are vital to its intension and thus are decisive in determining the acceptability of a functional equivalent.

In regard to the term *mortgage* and the German term *Hypothek*, Collins and Teichman comment that 'the idea that land can be charged would seem to be almost universal. However, when *mortgage* is used as the translation of the (seemingly) equivalent German concept confusion may result.' Firstly, there are various types of land charges in Germany, all of which could be called *mortgages*. In their opinion, there would be little sense in choosing different English terms to express the various types of German land charges because the English terms would not 'have exactly the same legal meaning as the German terms.' More significant, however, is the difference in legal effect if the mortgagor fails to meet his obligations, regardless of the type of land charge:

Specifically, an English lawyer talking about a mortgage may have it in the back of his mind that, under English law, the mortgagee may be granted the right to dispose of the mortgaged property by private sale if the mortgagor fails to meet his obligations. A German colleague who tells him that his clients may obtain a mortgage in Germany may not realize this and may have difficulty to explain later why such a private sale is not possible in Germany (German law in fact prescribes a special court procedure in the course of which the mortgaged property is sold by court auction) (Collins and Teichman 1986:51).

These differences are not just procedural but result from the fact that, in its strict sense, a mortgage effects the actual conveyance of legal title to the creditor, thus creating all the incidents of legal ownership, including the right to possession. On the contrary, the civil law concepts of *Hypothek* and *hypothèque* merely create a charge upon the property of the debtor, not a title to the property (Baumann 1984:198). In normal circumstances this essential difference would suffice to disqualify the use of *mortgage* and *Hypothek* or *hypothèque* as translation equivalents.

The problems of interpretation which may arise when *mortgage* and *hypothèque* and/or related terms such as *nantir* and *nantissement* are used as equivalents in parallel texts are illustrated in *Laliberté* v. *Larue, Trudel and Picher et al.*, a case that reached the Supreme Court of Canada ([1931] S.C.R. 7). The defendant bondholders based their argument on the English version of the Civil Code of Lower Canada, claiming that the use of the terms *mortgage* and *mortgaging* as equivalents for *nantir* and *nantissement* implied conveyance of title to the real estate in question. Since the property was located in Quebec, the Court rejected their argument, summarizing the problem as follows:

> The translation of the words *nantir* and *nantissement* by *mortgage* and *mortgaging* in the English version of the statute is not appropriate and may be misleading: there is no connection between the *nantissement* of the civil law and the *mortgaging* of the English common law... (cited in Beaupré 1986:121).

Insisting that the intention had not been to introduce a new legal institution into the Quebec law of property, the Court ruled that the 'statute should not be interpreted according to the rules governing *mortgage* of the English common law.' This ruling later became statute law in section 8(2)(c) of the *Official Languages Act* of 1969, which *de facto* provides that common law terms used as equivalents for technical terms in civil law statutes shall be interpreted according to the original civil law concepts (and vice versa) (*see* Chapter 3, 3.4.4).

8.8.4. The role of the judiciary

In normal circumstances translators would not even consider using a functional equivalent which fails to meet the conditions of minimum acceptability. The above example, however, illustrates to what extent some translators rely on the courts to correct terminological incongruency. In fact, the translator's final decision on whether to use a particular functional equivalent may well depend on the number of legal systems participating in the communication process and the interpretation practices of the competent courts in jurisdiction(s) where the instrument is applicable. In particular, the question arises as to whether the competent courts have well-developed techniques of interpreting bilingual and/or multilingual instruments and whether they can be relied on to promote uniform interpretation and application of the single instrument. In other words, is there a reliable system of checks and balances built into the judicial system to protect against excesses by limiting judicial discretion, thus making it 'safe' to allow the courts to ascertain the intended meaning of functional equivalents?

In regard to Canada, Beaupré remarks: 'Interpretative methodologies have been devised by the courts over time to compensate for the linguistic limitations to achieving exact equivalence' (1987:740). The Canadian situation appears to be unique in this regard. By providing a built-in mechanism to mechanically limit discretion and promote uniform application despite terminological incongruency, the provision of paragraph c of section 8(2) gave a green light to translators and drafters, encouraging them to use functional equivalents of technical terms, without being overly concerned about their acceptability. According to Didier, widespread use of functional equivalents is evident in the Revised Statutes of Canada of 1985 (1990:234). Didier also notes that, for some unexplained reason, section 8 of the *Official Languages Act* of 1969 was omitted in its entirety in the Revised Statutes of 1985, thereby reducing paragraph c of section 8(2) to an ordinary rule of interpretation, i.e., it is no longer statute law (1990:248; on shortcomings of section 8 *see* Beaupré 1986:162). The fact that it was also omitted in the revised *Official Languages Act* of 1988 does not mean that the former practice has been discontinued. Judges are still faced with the problem of ensuring that private law institutions set forth in provincial statutes are applied without importing 'foreign' elements from other provinces on the grounds of authoritative translations. As suggested in the ruling in *Laliberté* v. *Larue, Trudel, Ficher et al.*, the purpose of translations of provincial statutes is not to import civil law concepts into the common law provinces and vice versa but to provide French-speaking citizens of common law provinces and English-speaking citizens of Quebec access to provincial legislation and the courts in their mother tongue (*cf.* Didier 1990:210). Regardless of the equivalents used for system-bound technical terms in translations of provincial statutes, the courts will interpret them in the sense of the source legal system. Thus the rule of former paragraph c of section 8(2) remains in tact. To ensure that common law concepts are not read into the civil law of Quebec, Quebec's *Interpretation Act* provides that, in the event of a discrepancy between the two language versions of any enactment, the French version prevails (Brierley 1987:17).

The real test of bilingual interpretation in Canada begins at the federal level. The broad discretion enjoyed by the federal courts in resolving terminological disputes was expressed in former paragraph d of section 8(2) of the *Official Languages Act*, which allowed them to give preference to the version that, 'according to the true spirit, intent and meaning of the enactment, best ensures the attainment of its objects.' Although the rule is no longer statute law, lawyers have not challenged the court's use of broad discretionary power to ascertain the intent when terminology is unclear or ambiguous in one version or the two versions have a conflicting meaning. As a result of the constant contact of the two legal systems, the federal courts in Canada have developed a respectable practice in interpreting bilingual, bilegal texts. Furthermore, the courts are subject to the control of the Supreme Court, which is in the unique position of having the final say in all disputes and handing down precedents in cases concerning bilingual interpretation (*see* Chapter 3, 3.5.3). According to Beaupré, the Canadian Supreme Court has approached 'equal authenticity with a good deal of flexibility,' as a result of which the judiciary can be expected 'to continue to perform their interpretative function with their usual pragmatism, that is, with the overall content continuing to be their primary guide' (1986:156). Thus many Canadian lawyers prefer to leave it up to the courts to correct the 'imperfections' of translation through codified and uncodified rules of interpretation (Pigeon 1982:280–281); Didier 1990:248).[9]

Despite the highly praised pragmatism of the federal courts in Canada, others have come to regard their broad discretion as a potential threat to uniform interpretation and application. Recognizing the necessity of cultivating interaction between text producers and receivers, they have called on drafters and translators to strive for greater precision as a means of limiting judicial discretion. This also applies to the selection of equivalents. By selecting a certain type of equivalent, the translator effectively sends a signal to the courts as to how that term should be interpreted, i.e., according to which legal system it should be qualified. Confusion arises when the signal is unclear or imprecise, thus forcing judges to use their discretion to ascertain the intended meaning. For instance, in the ruling in *Gulf Oil Can. Ltd.* v. *Canadien Pacifique Ltée* (*see* 8.8.2 above), the judge explained that, if the translator had used the literal equivalent *acte de Dieu*, they would have qualified it as a common law term and interpreted it according to the common law concept of *act of God*; however, since the translator used the French technical term *cas fortuit ou de force majeure*, they interpreted it according to Quebec law (Beaupré 1986:133–134). For this reason, the National Program recommends widespread use of literal equivalents in federal statutes (*see* 8.10.3).

Since most jurisdictions do not have built-in interpretation mechanisms to compensate for terminological incongruency, translators should always strive to express the intent of the single instrument in language that is clear and precise, particularly when there is less judicial control and courts from several jurisdictions are involved in the interpretation process. Among other things, this means that translators need to be more critical in their evaluation of functional equivalents, especially those that are partially equivalent. Moreover, translators are encouraged to achieve greater precision by compensating for terminological incongruency in the text itself. As a last resort translators should attempt to compensate for terminological incongruency before disqualifying a functional equivalent.

9. According to von Overbeck, the Swiss Federal Court enjoys large discretionary power when interpreting trilingual texts of national legislation (1984:986); in regard to multilingual, multilateral treaties and conventions *see* Dölle 1961:14, 38. Herbots is of the opinion that the large discretionary power of judges has disadvantages as well as advantages. He advises legal translators to make their translations as accurate as possible (1987:844).

8.9. COMPENSATING FOR TERMINOLOGICAL INCONGRUENCY

A functional equivalent is inadequate when one or more of its essential characteristics differ from those of the source term in all or some contexts. In such cases, translators can sometimes compensate for the incongruency by using methods of lexical expansion to delimit or expand the sense of the functional equivalent.

8.9.1. Lexical expansion

In particular, Canadian translators seem willing to use lexical expansion as a means of compensating for terminological incongruency. For example, in *Mart Steel Corp. v. R.,* a case before the Federal Court in Montreal ([1974] 1 F.C. 45 (T.D.)), the Crown was said to be liable in respect of a tort committed by its servants. Basing its argument on the meaning of *tort* the Crown argued that, 'by using the word *tort* the *Crown Liability Act* was intended to have no application in the province of Quebec, where the concept of *tort* is foreign.' The argument was easily dismissed by reference to the French version which uses the term *délit civil*, a lexical expansion that delimits the sense of the functional equivalent *délit* to civil wrongs. To make it clear that *délit civil* is to be interpreted according to Quebec law, it is defined as meaning *délit* or *quasi délit* in respect of any matter arising in Quebec. Furthermore, in the English text it is explicitly stated that the common law concept of *tort* is deemed to be equivalent to the civil law concept of *délit* in respect of any matter arising in Quebec (Beaupré 1986:133).

Cooperation between drafters and translators of parallel texts of the same instrument can be very helpful in attempts to compensate for terminological incongruency. The following example shows that lexical expansion sometimes entails adding a single word and, furthermore, that lexical expansion can also be used to delimit the meaning of the source term, thus making it correspond with a narrower functional equivalent. In fact, the dispute in *Azdo* v. *Min. of Employment & Immigration* ([1980] 2 F.C. 645 (C.A.)] could have been avoided if the legislator's intent had been clarified by delimiting the meaning of the broader source term. In the said case, the Canadian Federal Court of Appeal had to decide whether the ambiguous concept of *guardian* in section 29 of the *Immigration Act*, 1976, included counsel who was not the minor's legal guardian. Applying the principle of the highest common meaning, the judge concluded that the term *guardian* should be interpreted in its narrow sense because this was the meaning it shared with the French equivalent *tuteur.* Accordingly, the court ruled that the minor had to be represented by his legal guardian (Beaupré 1986:61). The dispute could have been avoided if the drafter had delimited the meaning of the English term by using the expression *legal guardian.*

Although translation theory favors delimiting broader terms, functional equivalents whose sense is narrower than that of the source term may also be extended by lexical expansion, however, only as a last resort. As mentioned above, the term *hypothèque* applies only to immovables (realty), as a result of which there is no adequate equivalent for the common law term *chattel mortgage.* This gap can be filled by expanding the sense of *hypothèque* to include movables as well. This can be done by adding the lexeme *mobilier* or one of the phrases *sur biens meubles / sur biens mobiliers,* thus creating *hypothèque mobilière* (*Vocabulaire de la 'common law'* 1980:36), *hypothèque sur biens meubles* (Herbst 1979:659), and more recently *hypothèque sur biens mobiliers* (Lindbergh 1993:90). These solutions, however, only partially correct the incongruency between the two concepts.

As we recall, the concepts of *mortgage* and *hypothèque* also differ in respect of their legal effect. In fact, from the legal point of view, this aspect should be given priority. This might be disputed in this particular case on the ground that a modern concept of *mortgage* has developed, according to which a mortgage is regarded as a mere lien and not as creating a title. In contrast, the classical concept of *mortgage* automatically effects conveyance of title. Although the modern concept has been adopted in some of the US states, the Western provinces of Canada and Ontario, this is not a valid reason to overlook such a significant aspect of incongruency. On the contrary, it makes it all the more important to emphasize that the source term in question is the historical common law term by choosing an equivalent which expresses conveyance. Otherwise, this could be a potential point of contention. Obviously it is much more difficult to expand the sense of *hypothèque* to include the conveyance of title; however, J.A. Clarence Smith has come up with an acceptable proposal: *hypothèque translative* (1984b:759). As a means of compensating for both incongruencies (legal effect and scope of application), Smith proposes expanding the sense of *hypothèque* by using two qualifiers *translatif* and *mobilier,* thus creating the expression *hypothèque (translative) mobilière.* In so doing, he has succeeded in converting a non-equivalent functional equivalent into a near equivalent one.

When searching for an adequate equivalent for *hypothèque,* the easy way out would be to use the lexical expansion *mortgage without conveyance* which nicely compensates for the incongruency in legal effect. In this case, however, there is an existing term which expresses nearly the same thing, i.e, a charge. In English law *charge* is defined as 'a form of security for the payment of a debt or performance of an obligation, consisting of the right of a creditor to receive payment out of some specific fund or out of the proceeds of the realization of specific property' (*Osborn's Concise Law Dictionary* 1993:66). The use of the English term *charge* as an equivalent for *hypothèque* leads, however, to problems in Canada where it is commonly used as an equivalent for the French term *charge* although the latter is a much wider concept in French law (*see Droit des biens, Supplément* 1993:F-17).

It should be noted that lexical expansions are not true natural equivalents because, technically speaking, the concepts they denote do not exist in the target legal system. By expanding or delimiting the sense of functional equivalents, the lexical expansions cited above modify concepts of the target legal system, making them artificially correspond to the source concepts or vice versa. While some lexical expansions are acceptable, translators are warned against going too far merely for the sake of retaining the functional equivalent. If the above methods of lexical expansion are not possible or would be too artificial, translators can sometimes compensate for the incongruency by using descriptive paraphrases and definitions.

8.9.2. Descriptive paraphrases and definitions

From the legal point of view, probably the most effective method of compensating for terminological incongruency is to spell out the intended meaning in neutral language that can be understood by lawyers worldwide. This method is particularly effective in the parallel texts of multilateral instruments of international law elaborated by a large number of States parties. Since such instruments are subject to less judicial control (*see* Chapter 7, 7.6), drafters and translators are advised to refrain from using technical terms of national legal systems which have no adequate equivalents. If this is not possible, steps should be taken to compensate for the incongruency. As shown in Chapter 5, the failure of the Warsaw Aviation Convention could possibly have been averted if the French term *dol* had not been translated by *wilful misconduct* in the English text of Article 25, a key provision specifying the situations in which the Convention does not apply. In the Hague Protocol of 1955 amending the Convention, the incongruency of the disputed terms is corrected by discarding both terms and incorporating a definition of *dol* into the fact-situation of both texts enumerating in which circumstances acts or omissions qualify as *dol*. Adding the qualifier *recklessly and with the knowledge that damage would probably result* to the fact-situation prevents common law judges from applying the provision in respect of acts that would qualify as *wilful misconduct* but not as *dol*.[10] The amended provision provides that the limits of liability specified in the Convention shall not apply if the damage resulted from an act or omission 'done with intent to cause damage or recklessly and with the knowledge that damage would probably result' or 'soit avec l'intention de provoquer un dommage, soit témérairement et avec conscience qu'un dommage en résultera probablement' (*see* details in Chapter 5, at 5.12.1). Interlingual congruency of the French and English texts is achieved by omitting the technical term and explaining the meaning of *dol* in the French text as well. Although substantive equality is achieved in the amended texts, it was considered too late to rectify the damage already done.

After the failure of the Warsaw Convention, drafters and translators of multilateral instruments made conscious efforts to compensate for terminological incongruency, also in provisions containing commonly used terms such as *ordre public* and *public policy*. This can be seen, for example, in Article 5 of the Hague Convention on the Recognition and Enforcement of Foreign Judgments in Civil and Commercial Matters. Probably comprising all the elements of due process of law, *ordre public* is much broader than *public policy* as used in Anglo-American recognition practice (Nadelmann and von Mehren 1966:200). To compensate for the difference, the Conference retained the term *public policy* in point 1 of the English text of Article 5 and added the other situations covered by *ordre public*. As regards the French text, the Conference decided to retain the term *ordre public,* thus achieving conceptual congruency at the expense of interlingual concordance:

---

10. *Dol* is narrower as *wilful misconduct* which includes not only acts performed with intention but also acts performed carelessly *without* regard for the consequences; *see* Chapter 5, 5.12.1.

La reconnaissance ou l'exécution de la décision peut néanmoins être refusée dans l'un des cas suivants: 1. la reconnaissance ou l'exécution de la décision est manifestement incompatible avec l'ordre public de l'Etat requis;	Recognition or enforcement of a decision may nevertheless be refused in any of the following cases – (1) if recognition or enforcement of the decision is manifestly incompatible with the public policy of the State addressed *or if the decision resulted from proceedings incompatible with the requirements of due process of law or if, in the circumstances, either party had no adequate opportunity fairly to present his case;* [emphasis added]

As Nadelmann and von Mehren put it, this technique 'courageously abandons at the textual level a misleading symmetry between the two authentic versions in order to obtain symmetry at the level of substance' (1966:201). Praised as a 'significant advance,' this technique is particularly effective in multilateral instruments in two languages. Nonetheless, it is rarely used, probably because it distorts interlingual congruency and is thus regarded with suspicion by conservative lawyers who still expect a translation to follow the wording of the source text as closely as possible. While compensating for terminological incongruency is 'more manageable' in bilingual instruments of international law, it threatens to become 'unmanageable' in multilingual, multilateral instruments (Nadelmann and von Mehren 1966:196). Since a different formulation would be required in practically each language version, such interlingual diversity could create confusion, thus doing more harm than good.

Thanks to the authoritative role of the European Court of Justice, EU drafters and translators sometimes dare to be more creative in this respect as well (*see* Chapter 7, 7.8). Since the European Court has developed special rules of multilingual interpretation, EU drafters and translators usually rely on the Court to correct any incongruency resulting from the use of technical terms of national law in the parallel texts of EU instruments. In some cases, however, they have also attempted to compensate for the resulting incongruency by resorting to descriptive paraphrases and lexical expansion in some or all of the parallel texts of a particular instrument. This has been done, for example, in Article 5(3) of the Brussels Convention on Jurisdiction and the Enforcement of Judgments in Civil and Commercial Matters which deals with *matière délictuelle ou quasi délictuelle* (French text), *matters relating to tort* (English text), and *unerlaubte Handlung* (German text). To compensate for the incongruency in the German text, the fact-situation is extended by adding *oder eine Handlung, die einer unerlaubten Handlung gleichgestellt ist, oder wenn Ansprüche aus einer solchen Handlung den Gegenstand des Verfahrens bilden.* In the English text, the terms *delict* and *quasi-delict* are used in addition to the technical term *tort*. The Danish, Dutch, Greek, and Portuguese texts also use technical terms with additional qualifiers where necessary:

FR: en matière délictuelle ou quasi délictuelle
DA: i sager om erstatning uden for kontrakt

253

DE: wenn eine unerlaubte Handlung oder eine Handlung, die einer unerlaubten Handlung gleichgestellt ist, oder wenn Ansprüche aus einer solchen Handlung den Gegenstand des Verfahrens bilden
EN: in matters relating to tort, delict or quasi-delict
ES: en materia delictual o cuasidelictual
GR: ως προς ενοχές εζ αδικοπραζίας ή οιονεί αδικοπραζίας
IT: in materia di delitti o quasi-delitti
NL: ten aanzien van verbintenissen uit onrechtmatige daad
PT: em materia extracontractual

As a note of caution, only skilled translators with legal training should attempt to use descriptive paraphrases to compensate for terminological incongruency. By using such methods, the translator is essentially taking on tasks traditionally reserved for drafters. Accordingly, the translator must have first-hand knowledge of the intent of the treatymakers or contracting parties. In addition, there must be close cooperation between the drafters and translators of all parallel texts of the same instrument. Probably the most common and efficient method of compensating for conceptual incongruency in multilingual, multilateral instruments is to incorporate definitions of the disputed terms into all the parallel texts of the same instrument, explaining how the term is to be interpreted in that particular instrument or part thereof. Such definitions are used for both technical and vague terms and can be placed either in the principal provisions or the definition section. This, however, is purely a matter of drafting, as only treatymakers or lawmakers are authorized to assign a meaning to a particular term.

8.10. ALTERNATIVE EQUIVALENTS

If the translator rejects a functional equivalent because it could be misinterpreted or lead to different results, and if it is impossible to compensate for the incongruency by using the above methods, the translator will be forced to select an alternative equivalent. Moreover, in cases of non-equivalence where no functional equivalent exists in the target legal system for system-bound source terms, the translator must automatically select an alternative equivalent. Once the alternative equivalent has been selected, the translator must uphold the principle of language consistency by using the same equivalent whenever reference is made to that concept. Otherwise the user could think that reference is being made to a different concept (Weston 1991:32–33; Morgan 1982:114). English courts, for instance, presume that a difference of terminology implies a difference of meaning (Akehurst 1972:28). For this reason, the use of synonyms is discouraged in parallel legal texts (*cf.* Gesetzgebungsleitfaden 1995:307).

The choice of an alternative equivalent is important because it serves as a signal for judges, indicating the legal system according to which the term is to be defined. Accordingly, when selecting an alternative equivalent, the translator should take into account whether the intent is to have the term interpreted according to a specific legal system or whether its meaning is intended to be system neutral, i.e., independent of a particular legal system. In this sense it can be said that the selection of alternative equivalents also involves the process of qualification.

8.10.1. Neutral terms

According to Akehurst, one of the translators of the final English text of the E.E.C. Treaty, the best solution when there is no adequate functional equivalent is to use neutral terms, i.e., non-technical terms (1972:260). This is because neutral terms are usually broader in meaning than technical terms (*see* Šarčević 1988b:456; *also* Sacco 1991:13). The use of neutral terms is especially recommended when the intent is for the source term and its equivalent(s) to have a meaning independent of a particular legal system. For these reasons, neutral terms are frequently used in multilingual, multilateral instruments. For example, the French title of the UN Convention on Contracts for the International Sale of Goods (1980) is Convention des Nationes Unies sur les contrats de vente internationale de *marchandises*. While the term *goods* appears in the English text of all previous conventions, the technical legal term *objet mobilier corporel* is used in the French text of the Sales Conventions of 1955, 1958, and the two Hague Conventions of 1964. The term *marchandise* appears for the first time in the Convention on the Limitation Period in the International Sale of Goods of 1974. *Marchandise* is a term derived from commercial practice which covers any movable object that may be traded or marketed.[11] From the legal point of view, the term *objet mobilier corporel* is more correct because it distinguishes such objects from immaterial movables and also from immovable objects. Nonetheless, in this case the delegates decided not to use a technical term of the civil law which could falsely imply that the Convention is to be interpreted according to the civil law systems, especially French law. Moreover, concern was raised that the technical term *objet mobilier corporel* cannot be adequately translated into English because the common law does not have the same system of classification (*see Actes et documents de la Session extraordinaire* 1987:51).

If the meaning of the neutral term is not sufficiently clear, a definition can be included, specifying how the term is to be interpreted and applied in that and related instruments. A classic example is the disputed technical term *domicile* which is frequently translated by the terms *Domizil* (German), *domicilio* (Spanish), *domicile* (French), *domicilio* (Italian). Although these terms have the same etymological origin, they are actually *faux amis* because their underlying concepts differ from legal system to legal system. In his excellent comparative study, Jacques Vanderlinden shows that the national concepts of domicile generally consist of one or both of the following elements: residence as a matter of fact and/or the intention of the individual. However, the criteria for determining one's residence and intent, as well as the combination of criteria vary, regardless of the legal family to which a legal system belongs (1985:305). Because of its decisive role in resolving questions of

---

11. To avoid possible confusion as to the scope of the Convention, the delegates emphasized that the use of the term *marchandise* does not restrict application of the Convention to commercial sales only (*Actes et documents de la Session extraordinaire* 1987:51, 55).

255

jurisdiction and determining the applicable law,[12] attempts were made at Hague Conferences to adopt a uniform definition for *domicile*. For example, in the Convention of June 15, 1955 Designed to Regulate Conflicts between the National Law and the Law of Domicile, *domicile* is defined as 'the place where a person resides habitually.' Because of different legal connotations associated with *domicile*, the technical term was later dropped and replaced by the neutral terms *habitual residence* and *résidence habituelle*. This, however, did not resolve the problem. 'Believing that the contours of [these terms] might not be sufficiently clear,' some delegations requested at a later Hague Conference that States be granted the option of using the term *domicile*. As a result, the Convention on the Recognition and Enforcement of Foreign Judgments in Civil and Commercial Matters permits the contracting countries to add the term *domicile* to the list of bases for assumption of jurisdiction where *habitual residence* is cited in paragraph 1 of Article 10. Furthermore, since two countries have to conclude a supplementary agreement in order to put the Convention into operation between them, it was suggested that they also agree on criteria for defining *domicile* if their national definitions differ (*see* Nadlemann and von Mehren 1966:197).

8.10.2. Borrowings

In cases where a technical term of a given legal system is to be applied in all the parallel texts of a single instrument, the translator(s) may decide to use the foreign term as a borrowing in the other text(s). Borrowings are usually set off by inverted commas or printed in italics. Sometimes the functional equivalent is retained but is followed by the borrowing in parenthesis, thus making it clear that the term derives its meaning from the foreign legal system. This method is used in Canada and in instruments of international law in provisions where it is customary to apply the concept of a particular legal system as, for example, in the *ordre public* clause mentioned above. Instead of continuing to expand the meaning of *public order* by adding the additional situations covered by *ordre public* (*see* 8.9.2 above), it later became common practice in Hague conventions to retain the functional equivalent *public policy* and place the borrowing *ordre public* in parenthesis. This is done in Article 18 of the Convention on the Law Applicable to Succession to the Estates of Deceased Persons, which reads as follows:

L'application d'une des lois désignées par la Convention ne peut être écartée que si cette application est manifestement incompatible avec l'ordre public.	The application of any of the laws determined by the Convention may be refused only where such application would be manifestly incompatible with public policy (*ordre public*).

---

12. In municipal law the domicile of a person often controls the jurisdiction of the taxing authorities and determines the place where a person may exercise the privilege of voting and other legal rights and privileges.

In most cases, however, the functional equivalent is discarded and the borrowing is used either alone or with supplementary information in parenthesis. For example, the UN *Derechos Humanos* glossary cites the term *amparo* as a borrowing and instructs translators to '[l]eave in Spanish, underline and add in parenthesis "enforcement of constitutional rights" [...]' (1985:vii). Most frequently, however, the borrowing itself suffices to signalize the intended meaning.

Whereas linguists often believe that borrowings should be used only as a last resort (Weston 1991:26), lawyers strongly favor their use (Sacco 1991:19; Mincke 1991:459). Above all, they are effective in the parallel texts of international instruments adopted for the purpose of establishing uniform laws. Since national courts usually prefer to apply their own national law, the use of a borrowing eliminates their discretion, forcing them to apply the foreign concept. As a means of promoting uniform interpretation and application, the working group of UNIDROIT[13] decided to use the terms *force majeure* and *hardship* as borrowings in the parallel texts of all instruments drafted under the auspices of the Rome Institute (Tallon 1995:343, note 13).

Another system-bound term without an adequate functional equivalent is *trust*, a common law institution that developed as a result of the historical separation of law and equity. Although the concept signifies a fiduciary relationship with respect to property, it has long been held that using functional equivalents such as *fiducia* and *Treuhand* is unsatisfactory and misleading (Gutteridge 1946:46). In the Hague Convention on the Law Applicable to Trusts and on their Recognition, the terms *trust* and *trustee* are designated as *le trust* and *le trustee* throughout the French text. The use of borrowings in this Convention is of interest because of legal considerations raised in the debate on the Convention's scope of application. While some lawyers argued that the use of borrowings in the French text strongly implies that the Convention's scope of application is limited to trusts established in common law jurisdictions, others insist that a statement in the Preamble suggests that such interpretation would be too restrictive. Moreover, if the wording of the Preamble is to be interpreted literally, this could be taken to mean that the Convention's scope of application should be broadened to include 'other jurisdictions' where the common law concept of trust has been 'adapted with some modifications.' According to Kötz, this would also include the *fideicomiso* of several Latin American countries, the *fiducie* of Quebec and functional counterparts in Israel and South Africa (1986:566). Going a step further, Kötz comments that, from the German point of view, if the terms *Treuhand* and *Treuhändler* were used and the technical meaning of the German terms disregarded, the descriptive definition of *trust* in Article 2 would also apply to the German concepts, although they have nothing to do with the concept of *trust* in the technical sense of the common law (1986:565). This reasoning prompted other lawyers to suggest that the Convention's scope of application should be extended to include even functional counterparts of trust which possess the characteristics cited in the general definition in Article 2. This view was opposed

---

13. The International Institute for the Unification of Private Law was established in Rome in 1926 under the aegis of the League of Nations. As its name indicates, it was established for the purpose of unifying private law.

by lawyers who insisted that the Convention should apply only to legal institutions which are 'structurally similar' to the Anglo-American trust (*see* Kötz 1986:566, note 12).

This example shows that the choice of an alternative equivalent can sometimes have a significant effect on the interpretation and application of the entire instrument. Thus it follows that translators must take account of all possible legal implications when selecting an alternative equivalent. To facilitate the decision-making process, interaction is needed between translators and drafters, on the one hand, and the courts, on the other. The interaction should be in both directions, thus ensuring that the equivalent selected by the translator conveys the meaning intended by the treatymakers or lawmakers and, furthermore, that the courts interpret the translator's signals as intended. Not only do the translator's signals need to be clear, they should also be systematic, leaving no doubt as to the intent and whether a particular equivalent is to be attributed a restrictive or broad interpretation. This is particularly important in international law where the large number of courts involved in the interpretation process makes it particularly difficult to establish interaction between producers and receivers.

Although borrowings can be very useful in parallel texts, drafters and translators should guard against their overuse. This also applies to naturalizations, i.e., borrowings that have been modified phonologically or graphologically, thus making them more similar to the native words of the target language. Prior to the Silent Revolution in Quebec, the French language of the law was characterized by a large number of borrowings and naturalizations of English terms (*see* examples in Schwab 1984:112–154). For example, it is said that there were more than 400 anglicisms in the area of commercial law alone. The inflation of anglicisms can be explained by the fact that the majority of Quebec's laws were originally drafted in English and then translated into French, a practice that finally ended in the 1920s (Didier 1990:216). The purification of the French language in Quebec began in the 1970s, at which time the most obtrusive anglicisms were eliminated. Today the situation in Quebec is reversed; both the laws and codes are drafted in French and translated into English. The *Code Civil du Bas-Canada* (1866) was always bilingual, thus providing one of the few versions of a civil code in English. Despite conscious attempts to reduce the number of borrowings and naturalizations in both texts of the new *Code civil du Québec* (1993), many have been retained, especially those which have been used for years in legal parlance. For example, even anglophone lawyers of Quebec admit that the naturalization *creance* renders the concept of the French term *créance* more fully than the existing English terms *claim*, *indebtedness*, and even *credit*, the term used in Louisiana (Brierley 1987:18, note 25).

Borrowings and naturalizations are common in French translations of Canadian federal legislation, as well as statutes of the bilingual common law provinces. While the naturalization *chatel* is acceptable for *chattel* (*Droit des biens II*:1987:25), borrowings and naturalizations should be avoided whenever an acceptable equivalent already exists in the target legal system. In accordance with this general rule, J.A. Clarence Smith argues against the use of *aviseur légal* for *legal advisor* because, in his opinion, the functional equivalent *conseiller juridique* is acceptable and should be used instead (1983:598). Moreover, a term should not be naturalized if the same expression already exists but has a different meaning in the target legal system.

Accordingly, Smith rejects the term *entreplaiderie* as a naturalization for *interpleader* because the term already exists in French law (1983:602; *also* Smith 1984a:743).

8.10.3. Literal equivalents

If translators reject the use of a borrowing and cannot find adequate neutral terms to express the intended meaning, they will be forced to create neologisms. In institutions like the UN and EU, neologisms are usually created by lawyer linguists or terminologists from the Terminology Division. There are basically three possibilities for creating a new legal lexicon in a bilingual or multilingual jurisdiction: existing terms of ordinary language or another area of specialization can be assigned a legal meaning, existing terms of a third legal system can be used, or new terms can be created (on the Belgian experience, *see* Chapter 2, 2.9.3). All of the above can be regarded as neologisms (*Encyclopedia of Language and Linguistics* 1994–III:1568).[14] The process of creating new legal terms does not differ significantly from ordinary methods of designation. Thus it follows that legal neologisms should be grammatically acceptable and semantically motivated or transparent (*cf.* Newmark 1982:81, 75) so as to enable the target users to grasp the general meaning of the source term. As in other areas of LSP, literal equivalents are the most popular type of neologism in the field of law.

Literal equivalents should be used only when there is no acceptable functional equivalent; in some instances, however, the functional equivalent may be a literal equivalent. In regard to the literal equivalent *court of appeal,* Weston remarks that it is 'the only possible translation' for the French *cour d'appel* (1991:25). On the other hand, Crabb, the American translator of the French Civil Code into English, points out that 'such translation is accurate only in the general sense of resort from the level of first instance to a higher court.' While the *cour d'appel* reconsiders issues of fact as well as questions of law and may receive additional evidence on them, this is unknown in Anglo-American procedure. Its judicial *appeal* is similar, though not identical, to what is know in French law as *cassation*, which involves only issues of law. Thus, as Crabb suggests, it would be more accurate to translate *cour d'appel* with a neutral expression such as *court of review*; however, most translators yield to what Crabb calls 'the irresistible impulse' to use the literal equivalent *court of appeal* (1977:16–17).

Proper names of institutions are frequently translated literally to facilitate their identification, for example, *National Assembly* for *Assemblée nationale* and *International Labour Organization* for *Organisation internationale du Travail* (*see also* Newmark 1988:70 and 1982:74). Official translations of international institutional terms are usually provided by the terminology division of the particular organization. Similarly, individual countries often appoint special commissions or

---

14. According to some linguists, borrowings are also neologisms; *see* Groffier and Reed 1990:86, note 40. On the other hand, German linguists generally regard only *Neubildungen* as neologisms, *see* Fleischer 1975:14, note 19.

259

government offices to recommend official translations of national institutional terms.[15] As a rule, official translation equivalents should be used even though translators believe they can produce a better one (Newmark 1988:89 and 1993:93).

In Canada, the National Program for the Integration of the Two Official Languages in the Administration of Justice was established in 1981 for the purpose of promoting terminological consistency in the French translations of federal legislation and statutes of the common law provinces (Manitoba, New Brunswick, and Ontario) and the Northwest Territories (*see* Patry 1987:3). Saskatchewan later joined the group, which also includes the Yukon since the beginning of 1994 (Pardons 1995:279). Under the auspices of the Ministry of Justice and the Secretary of State Department, the National Program has produced the *CLEF* (Common Law en Français) series of bilingual vocabularies: *Droit de la preuve* (1984), *Droit successoral* (1984), *Droit des biens I* (1986), *Droit des biens II* (1987), *Droit des biens III* (1989), *Droit des biens IV* (1990), *Droit des biens V* (1993), *Droit des biens, Supplément* (1993).

Among other things, all the vocabularies contain French equivalents for the source common law terms and definitions of the source terms in English. To avoid confusion as to the meaning of the French terms, it is stated in the Introduction to *Droit de la preuve* that 'the French equivalent is intended to play the same role as the English term to which it is matched and to cover the same concepts' (1984:xii). Like borrowings, the French equivalents simply refer the user back to the source concepts from which they derive their meaning. To ensure that the users can easily identify the source terms, the National Program has taken the liberty of creating a large number of literal equivalents, such as *bail à vie* for *lease for life*, *action personnelle* for *personal action*, *bien corporel* for *corporeal property*, etc. While these examples are sufficiently transparent to awaken associations in readers, others have been criticized for sounding unnatural and even absurd. A member of the Standardization Committee (*see* 8.12 below), L.-P. Pigeon strongly criticized the decision to approve the literal equivalents *bien réel* and *bien personnel* for *real property* and *personal property*. According to Pigeon, the terms *réel* and *personnel* make good sense in French; however, when combined with the term *bien*, the expressions are a complete nonsense (Pigeon 1982:280; *cf.* Smith 1984:755–756). On the other hand, those who favor the use of such equivalents point to the fact that the terms in the *CLEF* series are intended strictly for domestic use, thus emphasizing that the criteria for selecting equivalents depend on the communicative situation in each individual case. Accordingly, an equivalent that is acceptable in one jurisdiction may not be in another. For example, for the sake of accuracy, Canadian lawyers insist on using *common law* as a borrowing in French, while some French sources in France are content to use the literal equivalent *droit commun* (*see* Šarčević 1988a:972; *cf.* de Groot 1991:291).

While the new French lexicon created by the Canadian National Program is clearly a language of translation, the terminology departments of the European Union have made painstaking efforts to create a more natural lexicon for the ever growing

---

15. In Germany, for example, this is the responsibility of the Ministry for Education and Science and the German Foreign Office; *see* examples of official translations for names of German courts in Arntz 1993:17.

multilingual jurisdiction. In this case, however, a completely new nomenclature is being established: new concepts are being defined and adequate designations selected in all the official languages. Despite the large number of languages, there is essentially one system of reference because all equivalents derive their meaning from the same conceptual system. From the very beginning, conscious attempts were made to avoid using existing national legal terms to designate new Community concepts. For the sake of promoting uniform interpretation, care has been taken to create terms which are reasonably transparent and can be easily translated. Since the terms must be easily recognizable in all languages, literal equivalents have clearly had priority in the formation of Community terminology (*cf.* Bauer-Bernet 1982:192; Koutsivitis 1988:332). For example, the expression *taxe sur la valeur ajoutée* denotes a tax based on the net value added to a taxable product by each person concerned with a distinct stage of manufacture or service rendered. Following their respective rules of word formation, terminologists came up with the following literal equivalents: *mervaerdiafgiften* (DA), *Mehrwertsteuer* (DE), *value added tax* (EN), *impuesto al valor agregado* (ES), Φόρος προστιθέμενης αξίας (GR), *imposta sul valore aggiunto* (IT), *belasting op de toegevoegde waarde* (NL), and *imposto sobre o valor acrescentado* (PT). Note that the Spanish, Italian, Portuguese, and even the Dutch equivalents render the French expression word for word. Similar methods were used to create equivalents for the French expression *taxe sur le chiffre d'affaires,* which designates a tax imposed on the sale of a commodity every time it changes hands or is 'turned over,' hence the English expression *turnover tax.* The following equivalents are used consistently in EU instruments: *omsaetningsafgift* (DA), *Umsatzsteuer* (DE), *turnover tax* (EN), *impuesto sobre el volumen de negocios* (ES), Φόρος κύκλου εργασιών (GR), *imposta sulla cifra di affari* (IT), *omzet-belasting* (NL), and *imposto sobre o volume de vendas* (PT). Although literal equivalents are used in some of the languages to designate a particular concept, this does not mean that all language divisions must follow that policy. For example, the term *acquis communautaire* was created to denote all Community acts adopted under the Rome Treaties and all decisions taken since establishment of the Communities. The equivalents in the other language versions include borrowings, naturalizations, one hybrid term, and literal equivalents. Literally *acquis communautaire* means 'that which has been acquired by the Community.' While the literal equivalents *gemeinschaftlicher Besitzstand* and *gaeldende faellesskabsret* have been retained in German and Danish, the earlier English equivalent *community patrimony* (*see* Šarčević 1988a:975) has been rejected in favor of the borrowing. The following equivalents appear in Article C of the *Treaty on European Union* (1992):

FR: acquis communautaire
DA: gaeldende faellesskabsret
DE: gemeinschaftlicher Besitzstand
EN: acquis communautaire
ES: acervo comunitario
GR: κοινοτικό κεκτημένο
IT: 'acquis' comunitario
NL: acquis communautaire
PT: acervo comunitário

8.10.4. Other neologisms

Instead of assigning existing legal terms new meanings, new legal terms are often created by assigning a legal meaning to terms from ordinary language or even other special languages. The legal criteria for such terms, i.e., how they are to be interpreted and applied in respect of that instrument, are usually set forth in a definition. This procedure is particularly common in international law where new concepts frequently emerge in customary law and are later codified in conventions. For example, the term *continental shelf* was originally a geographic term; however, when various states began to claim the natural resources of the subsoil and sea-bed of the continental shelf, it became necessary for lawyers to take regulatory action. When establishing the legal criteria of the term in the Convention on the Continental Shelf (1958), the delegates completely disregarded the physical features of the actual shelf, thus resulting in a number of disputes (*see* cases in Dixon 1993:179). Since then attempts have been made to achieve a greater correlation between the 'physical' and 'legal' shelf. Significant progress in this respect has been made in the 1982 UN Convention on the Law of the Sea although, as Dixon points out, the match is still not perfect (1993:178). The current legal criteria of *continental shelf* (EN) and its equivalents *plateau continental* (FR), *platforma continental* (ES), *континентальный шельф* (RU), 大陆架 (*dalujia*) (CH), الجرف القاري (*al-ǧuruf al-qārrī*) (AR) are set forth in Article 76 of the Convention on the Law of the Sea (1982) (*see* Chapter 5, 5.13.3). Since the physical continental shelf is a universally known object, the existing geographic terms are used as equivalents in the various language versions. Note the use of the naturalized term *шельф* in Russian.

The problem of using existing terms to serve as neologisms becomes more acute when the object, relationship, act, or procedure does not exist in the target society. In some instances, however, it or something similar may have existed at some point in history. Following the recommendation of some French linguists (Mounin 1974:229–230; *see also* Wijnands 1985:13–36), Canadian lawyers also resort to archaisms as a method of creating neologisms. For instance, the French term *préclusion*, which was widely used in the fifteenth and sixteenth centuries, has been proposed as an equivalent to replace the borrowing *estoppel* (*see* Groffier and Reed 1990:87). Although the word *préclusion* can no longer be found in contemporary French dictionaries, it is apparently used in international law today. Nevertheless, the decision to adopt the expression as an equivalent for *estoppel*, a common law term that is strictly a concept of private law, is based primarily on the archaic meaning of the word as an act of stopping or deferring (Bastarache and Reed 1982:213–215). While *préclusion* is an archaism revived from ordinary French, legal archaisms are also used by Canadian lawyers, in particular, Norman French terms that were part of the 'law French' used in England following the Norman Conquest (*see* Mellinkoff 1963:103). An example is the archaic Norman French term *le mort-gage*, which was used as an equivalent for *mortgage* in French translations of New Brunswick statutes (Didier 1990:282). It appears, however, that the archaism has been replaced by the functional equivalent *hypothèque*, thus complying with the popular usage that has dominated French legal parlance of the common law provinces for more than 75 years (*see* Bastarache and Reed 1982:211; Pardons 1995:287).

According to Didier, the resurrection of archaisms has not always been successful (1990:272).

Instead of using archaisms, Quebec lawyers prefer to create neologisms by borrowing legal terms from a third legal system. For instance, to translate civil law terms, equivalents are occasionally borrowed from mixed legal systems where English is spoken, above all the law of the US state of Louisiana and Scottish law, both of which have elements of common law and civil law. Probably the best-known example is the Scottish term *hypothec* which is consistently used as an equivalent for *hypothèque* in English translations of civil law legislation (*see* e.g. Book Six of the Quebec Civil Code). In the bilingual edition of the *Dictionnaire de droit privé*, published after many years of preparation by the Quebec Research Centre of Private and Comparative law of McGill University, the term *hypothec* is cited as an equivalent for *hypothèque* and related terms, thus confirming a usage dating back to the original translation of 1866 (*Dictionnaire de droit privé* 1991:287; *cf.* Meredith 1979:55).

8.10.5. Latin equivalents: friend or foe?

Since Latin was once the universal language of the law in western civilization, it has often been suggested that Latin equivalents be used to translate common law and civil law terms. Unfortunately, such a remedy would not improve matters to any substantial extent. Unlike the civil law systems of continental Europe and related systems based on Roman law, English law did not experience a 'renewal' through Roman law, nor was it transformed by means of codification. Although law Latin dominated English law in the eleventh and twelfth centuries and remained the written language of the law even longer (Mellinkoff 1963:71–82), Latin expressions borrowed from the *Institutes* of Justinian, the *Digest*, or the canon law are generally used in a sense that is peculiar to English law. As Gutteridge once said: 'It is almost impossible to convey to continental lawyers the exact sense in which an English lawyer uses the terms *in rem* and *in personam*' (1946:123). For example, the distinction in English law between *rights in personam* and *rights in rem* is based, though not accurately, on the Roman distinction between *actio in rem* and *actio in personam* (*see* details in Walker 1980:1071). Nonetheless, the term *right in rem* is used as an equivalent for the continental European concepts of *droit réel, derecho real, diritto reale, dingliches Recht, zakelijk recht* etc. in Article 16 of the Brussels Convention on Jurisdiction and the Enforcement of Judgments in Civil and Commercial Matters.

On the other hand, the delegates to UNCLOS III consciously omitted the vague term *bona fides* from Article 281 of the Convention on the Law of the Sea (1982) (*see* Chapter 7, 7.6). Although *bona fides* is a term of international law, it is also widely used in municipal law. As a result, the expression means one thing in English law and another in the law of the Continent. Moreover, it appears that French and German lawyers take different views of the precise meaning of *bona fides*, a fact that became evident at the Geneva Conference on the Law on Bills of Exchange in 1930 (Gutteridge 1946:123).

263

Not only was Roman law received differently in France and Germany, but as Pascale Berteloot points out, Latin phrases take on 'national coloring' wherever they are used. As a result of the national influence on Latin phrases, there are numerous *faux amis*, such as the English *prima facie case* and the German *prima facie Beweis* (Berteloot 1988:19). Therefore, instead of serving as a reliable source for alternative equivalents, the use of Latin phrases by lawyers generally makes the translator's task more difficult. This is particularly true in the European Union where translators are constantly confronted with Latin phrases in different languages. In regard to translations of EU legislation, Koutsivitis remarks that Latin phrases sometimes appear in all language versions of a provision; at other times they are used only in several language versions. Moreover, there are provisions in which Latin terms are used to translate non-Latin terms. The examples cited by Koutsivitis are not technical legal terms (1988:358).[16]

8.10.6. A glance eastward

In addition to their historical ties to Roman law, most Indo-European languages have common roots in Latin and Greek, thus making it considerably easier to create new terms which correspond in sound and meaning. This is not the case when one must create neologisms in Japanese or Chinese. On the one hand, the Japanese have developed a method of naturalizing western legal terms by imitating them phonetically and recording them in special characters called *katakana*. Most frequently, however, they create new terms by using Chinese characters, the method of writing adopted by the Japanese around the fifth century (*see* Kitamura 1987:767). As for the Chinese, they rarely use the Japanese method of naturalizing western terms (Pasternak 1996:36). As a rule, new words are created by using Chinese characters, i.e., ideograms. Contrary to popular opinion, ideograms are now generally perceived neither as pictures of objects nor as inherently meaningful symbols. Dating back almost 3000 years, Chinese ideograms have developed into conventional signs representing old but also completely new ideas. Like alphabets they must also be learned (*see* Hansen 1993:387). Otherwise, the system of reference operates the same way as in other languages: The signs refer to objects, the meaning of which is mediated by a concept (*see* 8.2 above).

The Chinese had their first introduction to western legal concepts via the Japanese, who not only translated but also transplanted elements of the Code Napoléon and the German BGB and ZPO into Japanese law in the late nineteenth and early twentieth century (Kitamura 1987:775). Since most of the terms were recorded in Chinese characters, the Chinese simply adopted Japanese designations for western terms; however, they also began creating their own neologisms. Translating terms of western (and other) legal systems is essentially a process of sinization: Chinese

---

16. Citing the French, Greek, and English texts of provisions from Lomé III, Koutsivitis notes that *ad hoc* is used in all texts, *instuitu personae* in the French and Greek texts but *on a personal basis* in the English text; the French term *notamment* is translated as ιδίω ς in the Greek text and *inter alia* in the English text.

characters are used to signify some property or other essential characteristic of the foreign concept, thus conveying at least a general idea of the intended meaning by way of association. Needless to say, there is a significant loss of information which translators should attempt to restore by supplying explanations, usually in the form of footnotes. New terms can be formed in Chinese by combining two, three, or four ideograms, similar to the process of making composita in German. Sometimes the new terms consist of words from ordinary language or a combination of legal terms and ordinary words. For example, 民 (*min*, people) + 法 (*fa*, law) = 民法 (*minfa*, civil law), literally 'people's law' or 'law concerning people' in the sense of private law relations. Frequently the Chinese combine characters in a way which translates the source term literally. For example, in treaties and conventions the term *habitual residence* is translated by the Chinese expression 惯常居住地 *guanchang juzhu di*, literally 'habitual residing place' or 'place where one habitually resides' (*guanchang*, usual, habitual + *juzhu*, resides, residence + *di*, place). The term, however, has quite different connotations when used in Chinese laws (*see* von Senger 1994:192). While some Chinese neologisms can pass for literal equivalents of western terms, others combine characters which attempt to 'describe' the meaning by signifying the particular function or other essential characteristic of the original concept. For instance, the term for *communism* is 共产主义 (*gong chan zhuyi*) which literally means 'common property -ism.' In some instances, adequate equivalents already exist in Chinese and can be used as functional equivalents. In regard to the English term *contract* and the Chinese term 合同 (*hetong*), even their etymology is stikingly similar. On the one hand, the English term *contract* is derived from the Latin term *contractus* meaning transaction, hence agreement. Going a step further, this breaks down into the following: *con* + *trac* [ptp.s. of *trahere* = draw] + *tus* = state of drawing together (*Webster's Encyclopedic Unabridged Dictionary* 1989:317). The Chinese expression *hetong* is derived from 合 (*he,* come together) and 同 (*tong,* agree), hence agreement. In this case, however, the Chinese term signifies the 'coming together' of pieces of wood. According to a custom dating back to the seventh to nineth century, parties 'formed a contract' by breaking a document into two pieces. The party seeking performance of the obligations had to present his/her piece of the document to prove that the pieces fit together (*Hanyu Da Cidian*, vol. III, 1994:147). As a word of warning, the fact that the two terms are used as equivalents and are etymologically similar does not mean that the Chinese term has the same meaning as western concepts of contract (on contracts in Chinese law, *see* von Senger 1994:190).[17]

17.   My special thanks go to Dr. Dr. Harro von Senger for his advice and assistance in preparing this general survey on Chinese terminology. Von Senger is professor of sinology at the Albert Ludwig University in Freiburg (Germany) and expert for Chinese law at the Swiss Institute of Comparative Law in Lausanne.

8.11. EVOLUTION OF LEGAL TERMINOLOGY

As a reflection of social reality, the lexicon of a language is in constant flux. New words are created to express new objects and relations, and the meanings of old words change and/or take on additional meanings. As Hardy commented: 'Words have no intrinsic significance; their meaning is that which is given to them in a given milieu at a given time' (1962:82). Accordingly, translators must take care to use terms which aptly express the intended meaning of the source text at the time it was produced. As illustrated by the following example, serious consequences can sometimes arise if a translator neglects to take account of the evolution of legal terminology. In New York a translation was made of an Austrian judgment authorizing the applicant's *Scheidung* from his wife. The judgment was rendered prior to 1938, at which time the term *Scheidung* in Austrian law did not mean divorce as it does today, but rather separation. The translator, however, used the term *divorce*, which was correct according to German, but not Austrian law. As a result of the translation error, the man was permitted to remarry in New York although he was only legally separated from his first wife (Herbots 1987:840).

Translators cannot disregard the fact that legal terms are porous, i.e., subject to change. While the change in the statutory definition of *Scheidung* came about as a result of legislative reform (*see* Schlesinger 1980:816), statutory definitions can also be redefined by national courts, especially in common law systems where it is primarily judges who exercise their power of discretion to shape, define, and redefine terms by broadening or restricting their scope. Not only are most national courts empowered to redefine concepts or extend a definition to another case by analogy, but in the continental European systems, the opinions of legal scholars (doctrine) are also influential and may indirectly affect existing definitions or lead to new definitions if accepted by the court (Wank 1985:63–72). In exceptional cases, decisions of international courts can also compel national legislatures to revise rules and definitions, bringing them in line with regional or international treaties and conventions to which the States are parties. A pertinent example is the decision of the European Court of Human Rights of July 13, 1979, in the *Marckx* case, in which the Court ruled that the provisions of the Belgian Civil Code on affiliation violated Article 8 of the European Convention for the Protection of Human Rights and Fundamental Freedoms by discriminating against 'illegitimate' children. As a result, Belgium was forced to revise its legislation to guarantee equal rights for all children (*see* Pintens 1988:20–24). The legislative reform that swept through Europe as a result of this and other conventions on children's rights[18] affected the legal lexicon as well. In addition to the discriminatory terms *legitimate* and *illegitimate child*, less offensive expressions such as *l'enfant naturel* and *uneheliches Kind* were also eliminated and replaced by the expression *child born out of wedlock (l'enfant né hors mariage)* and especially by the generic neutral phrase *all children*. This development was by no means limited to Europe. The terms *concubin, concubinage,*

---

18.   In particular, the 1975 European Convention on the Legal Status of Children born out of wedlock / Convention européenne sur le statut juridique des enfants nés hors mariage.

enfant adultérin and *enfant incestueux* were subsequently removed from the Civil Code of Quebec (Groffier and Reed 1990:24).

Since the late 1980's lawyers and terminologists have been exceptionally busy in the new democracies of eastern and central Europe where the sudden fall of communism brought about a terminological revolution as well. As the legislative mechanisms went into high gear churning out new legislation effecting the transition to free market economies, lawyers and terminologists were suddenly confronted with the task of completely renewing the legal and economic lexicons in the affected countries. In Croatia, which at that time was still part of former Yugoslavia, the economic reform of 1989 sent drafters and translators scrambling to create a new lexicon in Croatian to express the new market economy concepts. In numerous instances, Croatian terms from the presocialist era were simply revived, occasionally the old meanings as well. Whereas the socialist regime had attempted to establish a new vocabulary that set it apart from both east and west, the new approach is to transplant western concepts into Croatian law. Because of structural similarities, German law frequently serves as a model for new legislation, including company law. Whenever possible, new terms are created by translating the foreign terms literally into Croatian, for example, *dioničko društvo* for *Aktiengesellschaft, društvo s ograničenom odgovornošću* for *Gesellschaft mit beschränkter Haftung, komanditno društvo* for *Kommanditgesellschaft*, etc. The characteristics of the Croatian companies are similar to but not identical with those of their German counterparts (*see* Šarčević 1993:337–343). In January 1995 a new Croatian company law entered into force which follows German law very closely.

8.12. STANDARDIZATION OF LEGAL TERMINOLOGY

'Overburdened' by their own legal background, language, and culture, lawyers tend to resist any interference or change. Thus the process of unifying and standardizing the national laws of EU Member States has met with considerable resistance. As part of the unification process, the Member States need to adopt a common nomenclature by harmonizing divergent definitions and systems of concepts. Since this requires a considerable amount of tampering with established definitions, it is easier to create new legal regimes with a new conceptual system. Once agreement has been reached on definitions, the selection of appropriate designations (terms) is a naming process (*see* Forti and Vesco 1991:273). The multilingual lexicon of European law has essentially been created in this way. Consistency in the use of terms is promoted by Community glossaries which are intended to facilitate translation, not to standardize terminology. The search for equivalents is also facilitated by the terminological database of the European Commission, EURODICAUTOM, which contains more than 2.5 million terms in areas of Commission activity, including administration, trade, economics, environment, finance, law, etc. The database is updated monthly and grows at an annual rate of 20,000 to 30,000 terms. The entries also contain a reliability code with values from 0 to 5, where 5 represents standardized terminology (Directory of Public Databases, Office for Official Publications of the EU, 1993:49). In 1989 the Terminology Section of the Swiss Federal Office

267

began building its own database TERMDAT by incorporating Swiss legal and administrative terms into EURODICAUTOM (*see* Gesetzgebungsleitfaden 1995:324).

As a means of facilitating the harmonization of national laws, the Council of Europe attempts to standardize basic legal concepts of national and international law. Again, this is a slow and tedious process as it entails unifying concepts that are interpreted and applied differently in different jurisdictions. Despite attempts by the Hague Conference to unify the concept of *domicile* for the purpose of international law (*see* 8.10.1 above), the Council of Europe decided to proceed with a 'progressive standardization' of the concepts of *domicile* and *residence*. Aware that states are unwilling to relinquish their national concepts, the Council of Europe passed a resolution in 1972 recommending that the governments of Member States harmonize the concepts of *domicile* and *residence* by applying uniform rules for determining domicile and residence in certain relations in international as well as municipal law. In addition, the Resolution permits Member States to assign special meanings to *domicile* and *residence* for particular purposes (*see* Resolution (72) I, Documents of the Council of Europe). In essence, the Resolution shows that a certain degree of standardization of concepts can be achieved if states are willing to apply identical or at least very similar rules in concrete cases. On the other hand, to provide certainty in international relations, it is sometimes necessary to adopt special choice-of-law rules that designate which national law shall apply when qualifying a particular concept in given situations. In this sense, the choice-of-law rules in Article 52 of the Brussels Convention on the Recognition and Enforcement of Judgments in Civil and Commercial Matters specify the applicable law for determining the domicile of parties in cases falling under the Convention.[19]

The process is considerably less complicated if the goal is to standardize terms, not concepts. From the offset the Canadian National Program made it clear that its *CLEF* vocabularies were intended to standardize terminology for usage in French translations of common law statutes in the provinces and at the federal level. The fact that the new terms in the *CLEF* series are deemed to derive their meaning from the source legal concepts made it unnecessary to tamper with concepts (*see* 8.10.3 above). As a result, the task of creating French equivalents for common law terms has been largely reduced to a naming process. The same is essentially true in respect of the terminology project in Quebec that resulted in the publication of the *Dictionnaire de droit privé*, a bilingual vocabulary with English equivalents for civil law terms. Here, however, the equivalents have been selected on the basis of their ability to reflect the legal culture of the civil law system (Brierley 1987:18). In both cases, the task of selecting and creating adequate terms should not be underestimated. Unlike the *CLEF* vocabularies, the bilingual edition of the *Dictionnaire de droit privé* does not claim to have standardization ambitions. Nonetheless, the equivalents therein are attributed considerable authority.

---

19. To avoid possible confusion, Article Vc(^{1}) of the Protocol to the Brussels Convention provides that provisions relating to *residence* in provisions of the English text of the Convention for the European Patent for the Common Market (1975) shall operate as if *residence* were the same as *domicile* in Articles 52 and 53 of the Brussels Convention.

As to the question whether the *CLEF* vocabularies will be authoritative, the Chairman of the National Program admits that decisions on standardization cannot be binding on users; however, he points out that 'the members of the Standardization Committee, all of whom have decision-making roles in the drafting or translation of legislation [...], are committed to using the standardized terms in the future.' Thus he is optimistic 'that [the terms] will also be used by judges, practising lawyers, notaries, law professors, jurists in general and translators' (cited in Šarčević 1988a:977). After completion of seven volumes of vocabularies, the Standardization Committee is still faced with the dilemma of how it can 'enforce' its decisions. According to Reed, the main problem is that most federal and New Brunswick statutes had already been translated into French some ten years before the National Program commenced the project. As a result, the terminology used in those statutes remains the 'law' until the particular statute is repealed or amended (1993:83). To facilitate access to the vocabularies and promote its standardization project, the Canadian National Program cooperates closely with the TERMIUM data bank, which has been operated by the Canadian Government Translation Bureau since 1975. In addition to its data collection of bilingual terminology used within the federal govern-ment, TERMIUM also has data collections of proper names, translation problems, and multilingual terminology. Also available on CD-ROM, TERMIUM currently contains over one million records.

9 The Future of Legal Translation

9.1. MULTILINGUALISM AND THE RELIABILITY OF AUTHENTICATED TRANSLATIONS

In our age of telecommunications and the Internet, multilingual communication is an accepted fact of everyday life. Despite extraordinary progress in technology, modern man is still dependent on legal translation. In fact, the international community is more dependent on legal translation than ever before. The globalization of trade, financial markets, and even peacekeeping keeps legal translators in high demand. The greatest volume of translation is done in the European Union, the entity currently with the largest number of official languages. At the national level, new plurilingual jurisdictions are being born, among other things, to insure language equality in the administration of justice. Thus, as we move towards the twenty-first century, it is safe to say that multilingualism has a bright future in national, supranational, and international law.

On the other hand, the future of multilingualism in the law depends on the ability of translators to produce reliable texts. In view of the significant and sometimes irreversible effects of legal translation, this is not a matter to be taken lightly. Furthermore, the fact that the parallel texts of legal instruments are usually equally authentic makes it essential for translators to guarantee the reliability of authenticated translations. Since reliability can be ensured only if there is greater professionalism in the field of legal translation, lawyers and linguists have responded by organizing special courses and graduate programs which provide interdisciplinary training in law and translation. Such programs are now available, among other places, in Canada (*see* Chapter 4, 4.7.2), Uruguay (Torres Carballal 1988:450), the Netherlands (Rayar 1990:644), and more recently in Hong Kong.[1] While each of the programs emphasizes terminological aspects of translation, mastering the technical terminology of the source and target legal systems is insufficient to make a translator competent.

To develop translation competence, translators also need instruction in translation theory. In this case, however, a special theory of legal translation is needed which takes account of legal criteria. As this study has attempted to show, a theory of legal translation must be practice oriented in order to be effective. Thus legal translation is regarded in this study as an act of communication in the mechanism of the law.

---

1. At the initiative of the linguist K.K. Sin, terminology oriented courses in legal translation from English into Chinese are now offered at the City University in Hong Kong as part of a new M.A. program in Translation and Interpretation (*see* Pasternak 1996:36).

Analyzing the communication process and the role of the translator in this process, the first part of the study shows how legal texts are produced and how they are interpreted and applied by the courts. Like general translation theory, a theory of legal translation can also be regarded as a theory in action if it helps translators become responsible decision-makers. To this end, this study attempts to provide concrete criteria to assist legal translators evaluate the pragmatic aspects of various communicative situations.

No longer isolated from the drafting process, the modern legal translator has assumed a dynamic role in the communication process, enabling him/her to interact with the other text producers and even receivers who interpret and apply the texts. Since it is the results that count in legal communication, perfect communication can be said to occur when the parallel texts of a single instrument are interpreted and applied uniformly as intended by the legislator, States parties, or contracting parties, as the case may be. Perfect communication is extremely difficult and sometimes impossible to achieve.

Despite traditional constraints, legal translators are now encouraged to achieve linguistic purity, however, not at the expense of substantive equality. To be effective in their new role as text producers, they must know when, where, and how they can be creative and still honor the restrictions of the profession. In particular, the new techniques of co-drafting developed in Canada permit legal translators to use all the linguistic means at their disposal to achieve the desired results. Such freedom, however, requires considerable legal competence as well. The Canadian experiment and the resulting stylistic diversity now characteristic of the parallel texts of Canadian federal legislation raise the question as to how much diversity is tolerable in parallel legal texts. As shown in the practical part of this study, the answer to this question depends on the specific communicative situation, in particular on the legal characteristics of the communicative situation of reception, i.e., how the texts are interpreted and applied by the courts having jurisdiction over disputes arising under the instrument in question. This brings us to the question whether the new methods of co-drafting developed in Canada can serve as a model for translators in other jurisdictions.

9.2. FOLLOWING THE CANADIAN MODEL?

The Canadian experiment in co-drafting has succeeded in revolutionizing legal translation and thus serves as a 'source of inspiration' for legal translators worldwide, as suggested by Levert (1995:266). On the other hand, it is questionable whether the Canadian methods of co-drafting can be applied successfully in other jurisdictions and whether the results would be similar. In regard to the situation in Switzerland, francophone Canadians from the Legislative Section of the Ministry of Justice in Ottawa have been in contact with their Swiss counterparts in the Language Section of the Swiss Federal Office in Berne for over ten years. Nonetheless, the Swiss have developed their own methods of co-drafting with the intent of improving quality without encouraging stylistic diversity (*see* Chapter 4, 4.4.1). While Belgian lawyers praise the new Canadian techniques, they quietly concede that it is too early to experiment with such methods in Belgium (Verrycken

1995:368). Searching for solutions for translating common law terms into other languages and civil law terms into English, British lawyers have also expressed interest in the Canadian model (Levert 1995:265–266).

Before adopting any of the Canadian equivalents and translation methods, translators should take account of the unique communication process in Canada and Quebec. This is precisely what occasioned lawyers and translators from Hong Kong to study the Canadian model. In search of a model to assist them in their transition to a bilingual common law system, they found numerous similarities between the communicative situation in the bilingual common law provinces of Canada and their new bilingual system in which the common law of Hong Kong must be interpreted and applied in Chinese as well (K.K. Sin 1989:513).

After Hong Kong officially became bilingual in 1986, translators were faced with the formidable task of translating existing legislation and even case law into Chinese, as well as enacting all new principal ordinances in equally authentic English and Chinese texts (as of April 1989). In view of the specific communicative situation in Hong Kong, the difficulties encountered in translating common law legislation into Chinese and producing equally authentic legislation in both languages seemed insurmountable. Above all, the conceptual, structural, historical, and ideological differences between the common law of capitalist Hong Kong and the socialist system of communist China based on civil law make it extremely difficult and often impossible to find adequate legal equivalents. Furthermore, translators must resolve problems arising from the linguistic and cultural differences between English and Chinese. The situation is complicated even more by the fact that the written and spoken Chinese of Hong Kong differs from that of the P.R. of China, not to mention Taiwan and Macao (*see* Pasternak 1996:45). Taken these differences, it is legitimate to ask how translators and drafters can be expected to produce two authentic texts which are presumed to be equal in meaning, effect, and intent. Hong Kong lawyers and translators found a solution in the Canadian model.

9.3. MANIPULATING THE SYSTEM OF REFERENCE

The success of an authenticated translation often depends on the ability of the translator to interact with the judiciary. Above all, the translator should produce a text consisting of clear and unambiguous signs, leaving no doubt in the judge's mind as to how the text, parts thereof, and individual terms are to be interpreted and applied. Due to inherent incongruencies between legal systems, this is not always possible. Although Canadian drafters and translators are generally skilled in compensating for conceptual incongruencies, linguistic means are sometimes insufficient for this purpose. As a result, Canadian drafters and translators have been forced to seek legal intervention as a last resort.

At an early date, Canadian lawyers attempted to promote the uniform interpretation and application of parallel texts by building checks and balances into the judicial system. At the top of the hierarchy of courts in Canada and Quebec, the Supreme Court of Canada has developed a respectable system of bilingual interpretation enabling the justices to resolve problems with a high degree of professional pragmatism (Beaupré 1986:44–64; 156). In cases of divergences between the authentic

273

texts or an ambiguity in either text, the Supreme Court reserves the right to ascertain the intended meaning of the single instrument after comparing the two language versions. Decisions of the Supreme Court are vested with the authority of precedents and its recommendations are binding.

Suddenly fearing that judges and justices had too much discretion, lawmakers attempted to limit judicial discretion by enacting legislative guidelines for bilingual interpretation. In addition to adopting special rules on specific linguistic questions in the *Interpretation Act*, they also enacted general rules of bilingual interpretation in the *Official Languages Act* of 1969. For instance, the main objective of section 8 was to provide a means of assuring that the two equally authentic texts of federal legislation would have the same effect in all parts of Canada, i.e., in both common law and civil law jurisdictions (*see* Chapter 3, 3.4.2 – 3.4.4). Although section 8 has since been repealed, the principles therein still constitute the most commonly observed guidelines for construing bilingual legislation in Canada (*see* Beaupré 1986:162). This includes paragraph 2c of section 8, which contains an escape mechanism for resolving terminological conflicts involving technical terms of the common law and civil law. In essence, this provision authorizes the courts to determine which legal system Parliament intended to apply in each concrete case and to construe the technical term in question according to that legal system. In other words, paragraph 2c manipulates the system of reference by authorizing the courts to construe a concept, matter or thing that is incompatible with the legal system where the enactment is intended to apply 'as a reference to the concept, matter or thing in that version of the enactment that is compatible therewith' (*see* cases in Chapter 3, 3.4.4). The same method is also used by the Canadian National Program in the *CLEF* series of bilingual vocabularies. Instead of deriving their meaning from the conceptual system of the civil law of Quebec, the French equivalents are to be construed as a reference to the concept of the common law source term. For this reason, the authors acknowledge that the French equivalents of common law terms appearing in the *CLEF* series are intended strictly for domestic use.

Hong Kong lawyers were attracted above all to the idea that legal means can be used to compensate for conceptual incongruency. Following the Canadian model, they enacted legislative controls as a last resort to ensure that the new equivalents in the Chinese texts of common law ordinances will not be construed as a reference to Chinese law. Pursuant to the *Interpretation and General Clauses Ordinance* [Laws of Hong Kong 1989], the English and Chinese texts of Hong Kong Ordinances are equally authentic and the provisions therein are presumed to have the same meaning in each authentic text. While paragraph 3 of section 10B specifies that judges should strive to reconcile any conceptual differences between the two authentic texts, lawmakers went a step further and enacted their own escape mechanism to prevent judges from reading concepts of Chinese law into the common law of Hong Kong. Paragraph 1 of section 10C reads as follows:

> Where an expression of the common law is used in the English language text of an Ordinance and an analogous expression is used in the Chinese language text thereof, the Ordinance shall be construed in accordance with the common law meaning of that expression.

As Pasternak comments, it remains to be seen whether Chinese judges will always comply with the special rule in paragraph 1 (1996:44). On the other hand, Section 10C eased some of the pressure on translators and terminologists, enabling them to go about their task of building a common law vocabulary in Chinese. As emphasized by Sin, a linguist at the City University of Hong Kong, 'a Chinese Common Law vocabulary is not to be found – it is to be created' (1990:55). Since the new terms are assigned a common law meaning, the meaning of the Chinese text will be derived from the English source text 'until legal Chinese has fully developed into an autonomous language of the Common Law' (Sin 1990:56). During this 'feeding and checking period' (ibid.) it is important that judges refrain from using the common law rule of literal interpretation (Pasternak 1996:44; see examples of proposed Chinese equivalents for common law terms of Hong Kong in Pasternak 1996:49–87). As for the question of stylistic diversity, translators are advised against following the Canadian model in this respect, at least for the time being, thus giving judges time to develop a reliable system of bilingual interpretation.

Figure 14: *The System of Reference in Hong Kong's Bilingual Legislation*

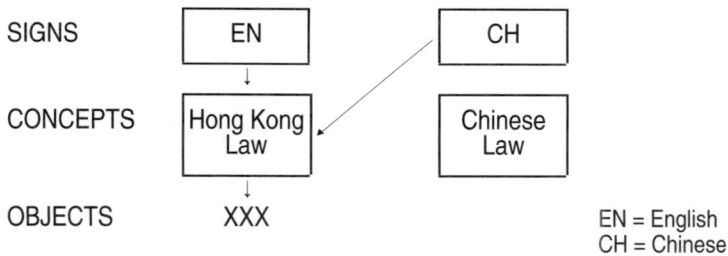

9.4. MULTILINGUALISM IN INTERNATIONAL LAW

In view of the large number of states participating in the communication process, it is extremely difficult to impose judicial and legislative controls at the international level. Lacking the means to adopt rules of interpretation similar to those mentioned above, international lawyers at best provide instructions on interpretation by spelling out how terms are to be interpreted and applied in the definition section of the authentic texts of the particular instrument. Undoubtedly the best method of controlling the interpretation and application of multilingual, multilateral instruments is to establish specialized courts to resolve disputes arising under that and related instruments governing the particular subject-matter. The main problem is that such courts usually do not have exclusive jurisdiction over all matters governed by the particular instrument. For instance, LOS 1982 provides for the establishment of a special Tribunal for the Law of the Sea. While the International Tribunal has shared jurisdiction over all matters relating to the law of the sea, its specialized chamber, the Sea-Bed Disputes Chamber, is to have exclusive jurisdiction over all disputes concerning the international sea-bed area (*see* Chapter 7, 7.7).

To promote uniform interpretation and application, the ultimate goal in international law is to coordinate the situational factors not only of reception but also of production. Ideally, the production and reception of all the parallel texts of a single instrument should be coordinated to the point that they can be regarded as constituting one and the same act of communication. This is truly a unique communication process that defies present models of communication in translation theory. Realizing that the reliability of equally authentic texts cannot be divorced from the manner of their preparation, international lawyers made conscious efforts to coordinate the production of all the parallel texts of the draft Convention on the Law of the Sea. Although the actual success of the multilingual drafting experiment at UNCLOS III will be measured by the results, interested parties immediately raised the question whether the new practice of simultaneous multilingual drafting will be used at future conferences. The Sixth Committee of the General Assembly considered the question serious enough to take the matter up in an agenda item entitled 'Review of the Multilateral Treaty-Making Process.' During the debates, which concluded with the adoption of Resolution 39/90 on December 13, 1984, some representatives favored establishing an international language drafting bureau, however, 'many representatives preferred either to increase the role of the Sixth Committee (for treaties drawn up within the General Assembly) or to create a drafting committee within each plenipotentiary conference' (*United Nations Legislative Series* 1984–I, Part III, section VII, p. 129). While positive support was shown for simultaneous multilingual drafting, practical problems remain which must be resolved on a case-by-case basis. First and foremost is the question of the time element. As Rosenne points out, transferring the practice at UNCLOS III 'to a conference lasting but a few weeks, working on a "basic text" in which concordance problems have already had some treatment, would be almost impossible' (1983:783).

Unlike the drafting reform in Canada, the multilingual drafting experiment at UNCLOS III did not 'liberate' drafters and translators by encouraging them to be more creative with language. Due primarily to the changed circumstances of the communication process in international law, greater emphasis is placed on achieving interlingual and conceptual concordance in the equally authentic texts of treaties and conventions. Although limited linguistic diversity is tolerated, the principle of fidelity to the single instrument still prevails as the best method of promoting the uniform interpretation and application of multilingual, multilateral instruments. Without tighter legislative and judicial controls, linguistic and stylistic diversity will certainly be kept to a minimum in the parallel texts of treaties and conventions.

9.5. THE TRANSLATION OF 'OTHER' LANGUAGE VERSIONS

Although this study deals exclusively with authenticated translations of legal instruments having the force of law, it is appropriate in closing to mention the translation of other language versions as well, i.e., non-authentic translations.[2] Non-authentic translations of sources of law are usually made for information purposes. For instance, it is common for governments, law institutes, and even private individuals to translate the constitution and other important laws of a country into foreign languages, frequently in connection with comparative law studies. This is especially true when the authentic text(s) of a country's laws are written in so-called lesser known languages (on the translation of laws from lesser known languages, *see* Šarčević 1990:156–166; 1988b:455–461). Since the communicative function of the target text differs from that of the source text in non-authentic translations, it is appropriate to ask whether the shift in function justifies a change in translation strategy, as suggested by the *skopos* theory. For instance, it could be argued that, in light of the fact that non-authentic legal translations do not have the force of law, translators should have unlimited freedom to make an idiomatic translation in the genius of the target language. Most frequently, however, the opposite view is taken, i.e., that non-authentic translations of sources of law should be literal. In this regard, Newmark once said: 'In translating the laws of a source-language country, [the translator] cannot "bend" the text towards the second reader' (1982:11).

The truth of the matter is that neither generalization is correct. While the shift in function is significant, the communicative function is not the only factor determining translation strategy in legal texts. Legal considerations also come into play in such translations, requiring the translator to analyze the specific communication process. Generally speaking, it can be said that linguistic purity in the target language is necessary for the sake of comprehension. At the same time, translators should guard against using functional equivalents of the target legal system which could mislead target receivers into believing that such concepts or institutions exist in the source legal system. In the absence of adequate functional equivalents, translators should use alternative equivalents which convey the general sense of the source term. Neutral terms that are target language oriented usually have priority. In all instances, translators are encouraged to compensate for information lost in translation by providing comments and comparisons in footnotes or an explanatory foreword (*see* Šarčević 1990:157–163; 1988b:456–460). Stylistic diversity is usually not encouraged unless it enhances clarity and effect. Like authenticated translations, non-authentic translations of sources of law should also lead to the desired results, i.e., the effects intended by the legislator. This fact is often overlooked by translators who believe their task is simply to convey the information content of the source text. But why is it so important for translators of non-authentic translations to convey the true intent of the legislator?

Although non-authentic translations are not legally binding, they still have legal implications and can lead to legal consequences. As a rule, courts of law are permitted to use only authentic sources of law for the purpose of interpretation; however, in exceptional cases judges can be forced to rely on non-authentic translations as a source of foreign law. As a result of the greater movement of goods,

---

2.   The expression *other language versions* conforms with the current practice in international law where the term *version* is used instead of *text* to refer to all non-authentic translations of a legal instrument (*see* Chapter 1, 1.6.1).

capital, and persons, judges of national courts are increasingly being called upon to apply foreign laws in disputes with foreign elements. Since they cannot be expected to read the authentic texts of all foreign laws, they often consult non-authentic translations. According to Ulrich Drobnig, German courts take recourse to foreign law in private law disputes most frequently in family law matters (1986:613). To obtain information on substantive and procedural questions of foreign law,[3] they usually turn to German literature on comparative law, such as Bergmann and Ferid's *Internationales Ehe- und Kindschaftsrecht,* which contains translations of foreign laws relating to birth, marriage, adoption, death, and divorce.

Although it is presumed that the translations are accurate and complete, the possibility of error is ever present. Since such laws are written strictly for domestic use, drafters are not concerned about foreign receivers and translators who may be misguided by their choice of terms, especially in the case of system-bound concepts and institutions. An example showing what can happen when the translator fails to convey the intent of the legislator is illustrated by the German translation of Article 38 of the Indonesian Law of Marriage of 1974 published in Bergmann and Ferid's *Internationales Ehe- und Kindschaftsrecht.* The translator's use of the literal equivalent *Scheidung* instead of *Verstoßung* or *Scheidung durch Verstoßung* in Article 38 implies that a marriage can be dissolved or divorced only by means of a court decision, thus leading readers to the false conclusion that the new Indonesian law no longer recognizes the Islamic custom of *talaq,*[4] which is usually translated as *Verstoßung* in German. While it is true that the legislator did not use the term *talaq* in the Indonesian text of Article 38, it was used in the official commentary which the translator should have consulted. Obviously the translator did not read the official commentary and thus was unaware of the intended meaning. This shortcoming on the part of the translator occasioned further translation errors in Articles 14 through 17 of the Indonesian Ordinance No. 9/1975 concerning the Implementation of the Marriage Law. Whereas the said provisions regulate proceedings for the confirmation of a *talaq* divorce by the courts, they are translated as if they regulate ordinary divorce proceedings before the court.[5]

---

3. To facilitate the courts in their search for information on foreign law, the Member States of the Council of Europe adopted the European Convention on Information on Foreign Law (1968), which permits the judicial authorities of a Contracting State to request information from another Contracting State on its substantive and procedural law in certain areas. The requested State is required to supply excerpts from its laws and regulations, judicial decisions, and relevant information from commentaries and other scholarly works in the original language, unless provided otherwise. In the end, however, this means that the materials will have to be translated if the judge is unable to read the originals. Accordingly, the decision will again be based on a non-authentic translation.

4. According to the Islamic custom of *talaq,* a Moslem man can divorce his wife by repeating the phrase *anti talaq* three times.

5. My thanks go to Dr. Mathilde Sumampouw (T.M.C. Asser Institute, The Hague) for pointing out these errors. Written in 1976, the Chapter on Indonesian has still not been corrected in Bergmann and Ferid's *Internationales Ehe- und Kindschaftsrecht.* One of the consequences of the mistranslation is an article published by Christian Kohler ('Das indonesische Ehegesetz vom 2. Januar 1974' in *Das Standesamt* 11/1976:327–338) in which the author reports that the dissolution of marriage by *talaq* is no longer recognized by the new Indonesian Law on Marriage.

This example is noteworthy for several reasons. First of all, since these provisions are decisive in determining whether a divorce is valid, such a misrepresentation of the legislative intent could have serious consequences if used by a foreign judge. Furthermore, it shows that the use of literal translation can be dangerous in non-authentic texts as well. Above all, it illustrates how important it is for translators of non-authentic legal texts to understand the source text as intended by the legislator and to convey this intent in the translation. To this end, they cannot rely on the source text alone but need to do a significant amount of research and information gathering, preferably from experts who participated in the lawmaking or negotiating process.

Since non-authenticated language versions are not reviewed and approved by the authorized lawmaking body, the translators must take extra care when performing the final scrutinization and revision. Unlike authorized court translators, they need not attest to the accuracy of the translation; nonetheless, they are indirectly responsible for the information therein. As a precaution, some translators and publishers make a point of warning users that their translations are non-authentic and that the authentic source text should prevail in the event of a discrepancy between the source and target texts (*see* Publisher's note to *China's Foreign Economic Legislation* 1982:i). Others go so far as to exclude themselves from liability for any damages arising in cases where a party has relied on information in the translation.[6] This, however, is rare. Aware that their translations can lead to legal effects, translators of non-authentic sources of law must also strive to produce reliable translations. In the end, the translator's decision-making process should not differ significantly from that presented in this study.

6.   The following statement appears in the foreword to *China Laws for Foreign Business* published in 1988 by C.C.H. Australia Limited and China Prospect Publishing House: 'This publication (bilingual) is sold on the understanding that (1) the authors, editors and consultants are not responsible for the results of any actions taken on the basis of information in this work, nor for any errors or omissions....'

Bibliography

1. LEGAL TRANSLATION, TERMINOLOGY, LEXICOGRAPHY

Akehurst, Michael (1972) 'Preparing the Authentic English Text of the E.E.C. Treaty' in B.A. Wortley (ed.), *An Introduction to the Law of the European Economic Community*, Manchester: Manchester University Press, 20–31

Alvarez Calleja, Antonia (1994) *Traducción Jurídica (Inglés Español)*, Madrid: Universidad Nacional de Educación a Distancia

Balkema, J.P. and G.R. de Groot (eds.) (1987) *Recht en vertalen*, Deventer: Kluwer

Bastarache, Michel and David Reed (1982) 'La nécessité d'un vocabulaire français pour la Common law' sous la direction de J.-Cl. Gémar, *Langage du droit et traduction*, Montréal: Linguatech/Conseil de la langue française, 207–215

Beaupré, Michael (1987) Introduction to 'La traduction juridique' in *Les Cahiers de Droit* 28, 4:735–745

Bergmans, Bernhard (1987a) 'L'enseignement d'une terminologie juridique étrangère comme mode d'approche du droit comparé: L'exemple de l'allemand' dans *Revue internationale de droit comparé*, 1:89–110

Berteloot, Pascale (1988) 'Babylone à Luxembourg, Jurilinguistique à la Cour de Justice,' Vorträge, Reden und Berichte aus dem Europa-Institut/Nr. 136, Saarbrücken: Europa-Institut, 1–32

Bocquet, Claude (1994) *Pour une méthode de traduction juridique*, Prilly: CB Service

Cesana, G. (1910) 'Die drei Texte des schweizerischen Zivilgesetzbuches' in *Schweizerische Juristen-Zeitung* 10:149–156; 12:181–190

Cesana, G. (1918) 'Zum Problem der dreisprachigen Textierung der Bundesgesetze' in *Zeitschrift des Bernischen Juristenvereins und Monatsblatt für bernische Rechtsprechung* 54, 3:97–114

Collins, Anthony E. and Teichman, Christoph von (1986) 'Language and Phraseology' in *Drafting and Enforcing Contracts in Civil and Common Law Jurisdictions*, Deventer: Kluwer, 43–54

Comité de Terminologie Française, Ordre des Comptables Agréés du Québec (1984) 'Société – Association – Compagnie – Corporation' dans *Meta* 29, 3:297–306

Covacs, Alexandre (1980) 'Preparation of the French Language Version of Canadian Federal Legislation,' Ottawa: Department of Justice, 1–46

Covacs, Alexandre (1982) 'La réalisation de la version française des lois fédérales du Canada' sous la direction de J.-Cl. Gémar, *Langage du droit et traduction*, Montréal: Linguatech et Conseil de la langue français, 83–100

Crabb, John H. (1977), Introduction to English Translation of the French Civil Code (translated by Crabb), South Hackensack, N.J.: Rothman, 1–18

Crépeau, Paul-André (1995), 'La Transposition Linguistique' sous la direction de G. Snow et J. Vanderlinden, *Français Juridique et Science du Droit*, Bruxelles: Bruylant, 51–61

Didier, Emmanuel (1990) *Langues et langages du droit*, Montréal: Wilson & Lafleur

Didier, Emmanuel (1991) 'La Common law en français. Étude juridique et linguistique de la Common law en français au Canada' dans *Revue internationale de droit comparé*, 43, 1:7–56

Dievoet, G. Van (1980–81) 'De Commissie belast met de voorbereiding van de Nederlandse tekst van de Grondwet, de wetboeken en de voornaamste wetten en besluiten (1954–1981)' in *Rechtskundig Weekblad*, 44:2361–2368

Dievoet, G. Van (1987) 'Vertalen binnen een tweetalig rechtssysteem (Belgie). Wetgeving in het Nederlands en in het Frans' in J.P. Balkema and G.R. de Groot (eds.) *Recht en vertalen*, Deventer: Kluwer, 91–101

Dodova, L. (1989) 'A Translator Looks at English Law' in *Statute Law Review* 10:69–78

Forti, Gabrio e Enrico Vesco (1991) 'La traduzione dei termini normativi e il metodo della comparazione giuridica' in *Terminologie et Traduction* 3: 269–277

Frame, Ian (1985) 'Legal Translators and Legal Translation: A Personal View,' unpublished manuscript, European Court of Justice, 1–20

Gémar, Jean-Claude (1982) 'Fonctions de la traduction juridique en milieu bilingue et langage de droit au Canada' sous la direction de J.-Cl. Gémar, *Langage du droit et traduction*, Montréal: Linguatech et Conseil de la langue français, 121–137

Gémar, Jean-Claude (1987) 'La traduction juridique: art ou technique d'interprétation?' dans *Revue générale de droit* 18:495–514

Gémar, Jean-Claude (1995) *Traduire ou l'art d'interpréter, Langue, droit et société: éléments de jurilinguistique*, tome 2: *Application – Traduire le texte juridique*, Saint-Nicolas (Québec): Presses de l'Université du Québec

Groffier, Ethel and David Reed (1990) *La lexicographie juridique*, Cowansville (Québec): Yvon Blais

Groot, Gérard-René de (1987) 'Problems of Legal Translation from the point of View of a Comparative Lawyer' in *Netherlands Reports to the Twelfth International Congress of Comparative Law*, The Hague: T.M.C. Asser Institute, 1–19

Groot, Gérard-René de (1990) 'Die relative Äquivalenz juristischer Begriffe und deren Folge für mehrsprachige juristische Wörterbücher' in M. Thelen and B. Lewandowska-Tomaszczyk (eds.) *Translation and Meaning, Part I*, Maastricht: Euroterm, 122–128

Groot, Gérard-René de (1991) 'Recht, Rechtsprache und Rechtssystem' dans *Terminologie et Traduction* 3:279–316

Guide Canadien de rédaction législative française (mise en oeuvre 1984) Ministère de la Justice Canada

Hadi, Maher Abdel (1992) 'Géographie politique et traduction juridique' dans *Terminologie et traduction*, 2–3:43–55

Heck, Philipp (1931) *Übersetzungsprobleme im frühen Mittelalter*, Tübingen: Mohr

Herbots, Jacques H. (1987) 'La traduction juridique en Belgique' dans *Les Cahiers de Droit*, 28:813–844

Ivrakis, Solon Cleanthe (1954) 'Official Translations of International Instruments; Practice of the ILO, the LN and the UN' in *Revue Hellénique de droit international*, 213–226

Jessnitzer, Kurt (1982) *Ein Handbuch für die Praxis der Dolmetscher, Übersetzer und ihrer Auftraggeber im Gerichts-, Beurkundungs- und Verwaltungsverfahren*, Köln/Berlin/Bonn/München: Carl Heymanns Verlag

Kerby, Jean (1979) 'Problèmes particuliers à la traduction juridique au Canada' dans *La Revue de l'Université de Moncton*, 12, 2–3: 14–18

Kielar, Barbara (1977) *Langauge of the Law in the Aspect of Translation* (dissertation), Warszawa: Wydawnictwa Uniwersytetu Warszawskiego

Kitamura, Ichiro (1987) 'La traduction juridique: Un point de vue japonais' in *Les Cahiers de droit* 28:747–792

Koutsivitis, Vassilios (1988) *La traduction juridique, étude d'un cas: la traduction des textes législatifs des Communautés européennes, et en particulier à partir du français vers le grec* (these de doctorat), Université de la Sorbonne nouvelle Paris III

Koutsivitis, Vassilis (1990) 'La traduction juridique: liberté et contraintes,' sous la direction de Lederer, M. and Israel, F., *La liberté en traduction. Actes du colloque international tenu à l'E.S.I.T. les 7, 8 et 9 juin 1990*, Paris: Didier-Erudition, 139–149

Lane, Alexander (1982) 'Legal and Administrative Terminology and Translation Problems' sous la direction de J.-Cl. Gémar, *Langage du droit et traduction*, Montréal: Linguatech/Conseil de la langue française, 219–231

Lehto, Leena (1985) 'Methodological Aspects of Legal Translation' in *Papers from the Conference of Departments of English in Finland*, Turku: University of Turku, 147–176

Meredith, R. Clive (1979) 'Some Notes on English Legal Translation' in *Meta* 24, 1:54–67

Minck, Wolfgang (1991) 'Die Problematik von Recht und Sprache in der Übersetzung von Rechtstexten' in *Archiv für Rechts- und Sozialphilosophie* 77:446–465

Moreau, Michel (1995) 'L'avenir de la traduction juridique' sous la direction de G. Snow et J. Vanderlinden, *Français juridique et Science du droit*, Bruxelles: Bruylant, 267–277

Pasternak, Volker (1996) *Chinesisch als Rechtssprache in Hongkong*, Frankfurt am Main: Peter Lang

Rayar, Louise (1990) 'Law and Language – Postgraduate Training of Legal Translators' in *Translation, a creative profession. XIIth World Congess of FIT*, Belgrade: Prevodilac, 643–646

Reed, David G. (1993) 'Some Terminological Problems of Translating Common Law Concepts from English to French' in H. Sonneveld and K. Loening (eds.) *Terminology, Applications in Interdisciplinary Communication*, Amsterdam/Philadelphia: Benjamins, 79–86

Roberts, Roda P. (1987) 'Legal translator and legal interpreter training in Canada' in *L'Actualité Terminologique / Terminology Update* 20, 6:8–10

Rossel, Virgile (1911) 'Toujours les textes du Code civil suisse' dans *Schweizerische Juristen-Zeitung* 7, 13:201–203

Rossini Favretti, Rema (1994) 'Interpretazione e traduzione dei testi di legge' a cura di M. Lorgnet, *Atti della Fiera Internazionale della Traduzione II*, Bologna: Cooperativa Libraria Universitaria Editrice Bologna, 335–346

Saleilles, R. (1909) 'Le partage et la transmission intégrale dans le Code civil Suisse' dans *Revue trimestrielle de droit civil* 8:537–610

Šarčević, Susan (1988a) 'Bilingual and Multilingual Legal Dictionaries: New Standards for the Future' in *Revue générale de droit* 19, 4:961–978; also published in *Meta* (1991) 36, 4:615–626

Šarčević, Susan (1988b) 'Translation of legislation – with special emphasis on languages of limited diffusion' in P. Nekeman (ed.) *Translation, our future, XIth World Congress of FIT*, Maastricht: Euroterm, 455–462.

Šarčević, Susan (1988c) 'The Challenge of Legal Lexicography: Implications for Bilingual and Multilingual Dictionaries' in M. Snell-Hornby (ed.) *ZüriLEX '86 Proceedings*, Tübingen: Francke, 307–314

Šarčević, Susan (1989) 'Conceptual Dictionaries for Translation in the Field of Law' in *International Journal of Lexicography* 2, 4:277:293

Šarčević, Susan (1990) 'Strategiebedingtes Übersetzen aus den kleineren Sprachen im Fachbereich Jura' in *Babel*, 36, 3:155–166

Šarčević, Susan (1993) 'Zadatak leksikografa u privrednoj reformi' (Economic Reform: The Lexicographer's Task) u *Rječnik i Društvo*, Zagreb, Hrvatska akademija znanosti i umjetnosti, 337–344

Šarčević, Susan (1994) 'Translation and the Law: An Interdisciplinary Approach' in M. Snell-Hornby, F. Pöchhacker, K. Kaindl (eds.) *Translation Studies, An Interdiscipline*, Amsterdam/Philadelphia: Benjamins, 301–307

Schroth, Peter W. (1986) 'Legal Translation' in *American Journal of Comparative Law* 47–65

Sin, King-kui (1989) 'Meaning, Translation and Bilingual Legislation: The Case of Hong Kong' sous la direction de P. Pupier et L. Woehrling, *Langage et droit*, Actes du Premier Congrès de l'Institut international de droit linguistique comparé de droit linguistique comparé, Montréal: Wilson & Lafleur, 509–515

Sin, King-kui (1990) 'The Translatability of Law' in *Working Papers in Languages and Linguistics, No. 2*, Hong Kong: City Polytechnic of Hong Kong, 44–59

Smith, J.A. Clarence (1983) 'La Common Law en français' dans *The Canadian Bar Review* 61:595–608

Smith, J.A. Clarence (1984a) 'Revues de *Vocabulaire de la Common Law: Droit des biens – Procédure civile* (1980), *Droit des fiducies* (1982) et *Procédure civile – Preuve* (1983), par le Centre de traduction et de terminologie juridiques de l'Université de Moncton, dans *The Canadian Bar Review* 62:741–746

Smith, J.A. Clarence (1984b) 'Droit comparé et terminologie comparée' dans *Revue de la recherche juridique droit prospectif* 3: 755–761

Spevec, F.J. (1899) predgovor, *Opći austrijanski gradjanski zakonik,* Zagreb: Lav. Hartman (Kugli i Deutsch), iii-ix (2, privatno izdanje zakonika, prvo 1885, prijevodilac: Adolfo Rušnov)

Standardformulierungen für deutsche Vertragstexte (1992), Foreign Office of the Federal Republic of Germany, Berlin: de Gruyter

Torres Carballal, Pablo de (1988) 'Trends in legal translation: The focusing of legal translation through comparative law' in P. Nekeman (ed.) *Translation, our future, XIth World Congress of FIT*, Maastricht: Euroterm, 447–450

Trosborg, Anna (1994) '"Acts" in contracts: Some guidelines for translation' in M. Snell-Hornby, F. Pöchhacker, K. Kaindl (eds.) *Translation Studies, An Interdiscipline*, Amsterdam/Philadelphia: Benjamins, 309–318

Weisflog, W.E. (1987) 'Problems of Legal Translation' in *Swiss Reports presented at the XIIth International Congress of Comparative Law*, Zürich: Schulthess, 179–218

Weston, Martin (1987) *The Problems of Translating Legal French into Legal English*, thesis, Exeter

Weston, Martin (1991) *An English Reader's Guide to the French Legal System*, New York/Oxford: Berg

2. LINGUISTICS OF THE LAW, LANGUAGES OF THE LAW

Allott, Antony (1974) 'Law and Language in Africa' in *Zeitschrift für vergleichende Rechtswissenschaft* 74:124–136

Bauer, Roland (1994) 'Deutsch als Amtssprache in Südtirol' in *Terminologie et Traduction* 1:63–84

Bauer-Bernet, Hélène (1982) 'Le multilinguisme du droit de la Communauté européenne' sous la direction de J.-Cl. Gémar, *Langage du droit et traduction*, Montreal: Linguatech/Conseil de la langue française, 189–205

Bergmans, Bernhard (1986) *Die rechtliche Stellung der deutschen Sprache in Belgien*, Louvain-la-Neuve: Cabay

Bergmans, Bernhard (1987b) 'Die gesetzliche Lage' in *Die Entwicklung einer deutschen Rechtsterminologie für Belgien*, Brüssel: Belgisch-Deutsche Juristenvereinigung, 7–18

Blom, Bjarne and Anna Trosborg (1992) 'An analysis of Regulative Speech Acts in English Contracts – Qualitative and Quantitative Methods' in *Hermes, Journal of Linguistics* 9:83–111

Bowers, Frederick (1989) *Linguistic Aspects of Legislative Expression*, Vancouver: University of British Columbia Press

Brühlmeier, Daniel (1989) 'Mehrsprachigkeit und nationale Gesetzgebung am Beispiel der Schweizerischen Eidegenossenschaft' in *Zeitschrift für Gesetzgebung* 4, 2: 116–137

Brackeniers, Eduard (1991) 'Europäische Integration und Probleme der Sprachkommunikation' in *TEXTconTEXT*, 6:1–8

Brackeniers, Eduard (1992) 'Le multilinguisme dans la Communauté européenne' dans *Terminologie et Traduction*, 1:337–337–342

Brierley, John E.C. (1987) 'The English Language Tradition in Quebec Civil Law' in *L'actualité terminologique*, 20, 6:16–18

Caussignac, Gérard (1995) 'Corédaction, rédaction parallèle et rédaction bilingue des actes législatifs' sous la direction de G. Snow et J. Vanderlinden, *Français juridique et Science du droit*, Bruxelles: Bruylant, 71–92

Caussignac, Gerard et Daniel Kettiger (1991) 'Rédaction parallèlle au Canton de Berne / Koredaktion im Kanton Bern' in *Gesetzgebung heute / Législation d'aujourd'hui*, 3:77–87

Cornu, Gérard (1990) *Linguistique juridique*, Paris: Montchrestien

Dölle, Hans (1949) *Vom Stil der Rechtssprache*, Tübingen: J.C.B. Mohr

Dölle, Hans (1961) 'Zur Problematik mehrsprachiger Gesetzes- und Vertragstexte' in *Rabels Zeitschrift* 26, 1:4–39

Drafting Laws in French – Study Paper (1981), English version by M. Lajoie, W. Schwab, M. Sparer, Ottawa: Law Reform Commission of Canada

Everling, Ulrich (1967) 'Sprachliche Mißverständnisse beim Urteil des Gerichtshofes der Europäischen Gemeinschaften zur Umsatzausgleichsteuer' in *Außenwirtschaftsdienst des Betriebs-Beraters*, 5:182–184

Gémar, Jean-Claude (1990) 'Les fondements du langage du droit comme langue de spécialité. Du sense et de la forme du texte juridique' dans *Revue générale de droit* 21:717–738

Gerber, Philippe (1992) 'Rédaction bilingue d'une Constitution cantonale. L'exemple du projet de Constitution bernoise' dans *Gesetzgebung heute / Législation d'aujourd'hui*, 3:75–82

Gräf, Erwin (1974) 'Recht und Sprache im Islam' in *Vergleichende Rechtswissenschaft* 74:66–123

Haegen, Van der (1982) 'Das Sprachenproblem in den Europäischen Gemeinschaften' in *Lebende Sprachen* 27,1:13–14

Hauck, Werner (1990) 'Aktuelle Probleme der Mehrsprachigkeit in der schweizerischen Bundesverwaltung' in *Mehrsprachigkeit im Rechtsleben*, Bozen: Südtiroler Juristische Gesellschaft, 93–97

Hauck, Werner, Rolf Moos, Martin Keller und Rainer Schweizer (1982) 'Die Gesetzesredaktion in der Schweizerischen Bundesverwaltung' in H. Kindermann (Hg.) *Studien zu einer Theorie der Gesetzgebung 1982*, Berlin/Heidelberg/New York: Springer, 93–103.

Iturralde Sesara, Victoria (1989) *Lenguaje Legal y Sistema Jurídico*, Madrid: Editorial Tecnos

Ivainer, Théodore (1983) 'Introduction à un discours sur le langage du droit' dans *La Semaine Juridique* 57:4, no. 3097

Künssberg, Eberhard Frh. von (1930) *Der Wortschatz des österreichischen Allgemeinen Bürgerlichen Gesetzbuches*, Heidelberg: Carl Winter

Kremer, Edie (1994) 'Deutsch als dritte Landesprache in Belgien' in *Terminologie et Traduction* 1:85–103

Kurzon, Dennis (1986) *It is Hereby Performed... Explorations in Legal Speech Acts*, Amsterdam/Philadelphia: Benjamins

Kusterer, Hermann (1981) 'Das Sprachenproblem in den Europäischen Gemeinschaften' in *Lebende Sprachen* 26, 2:49–52

Lampe, Ernst-Joachim (1970) *Juristische Semantik*, Bad Homburg v.d.H./Berlin/Zürich: Gehlen

Legault, Georges A. (1977) 'Fonctions et structure du langage juridique' in *Meta* 24:1, 18–25.

Low, D.M. (1989) 'Les droits linguistiques en matière judiciaire devant les tribunaux fédéraux du Canada' sous la direction de P.Pupier and L.Woehrling, *Langue et droit, Actes du Premier Congrès de l'Institut international de droit linguistique comparé*, Montréal: Wilson & Lafleur, 195–201

Madero, Antonio Alonso (1992) 'Problèmes et perspectives de la communication écrite dans les Communautés européennes' dans *Terminologie et traduction*, 1:343–348

Mamić, Mile (1992) *Temelji Hrvatskoga pravnog nazivlja* [*Fundamentals of Croatian Legal Terminology*], Zagreb: Hrvatska Sveučilišna Naklada

Mathews, J. (1989) 'The Language of the Law: The Hong Kong Experience' in *New Zealand Law Journal*, 387–390

Mellinkoff, David (1963) *The Language of the Law*, Boston: Little, Brown and Company

Möhlig, Wilhelm J.G. (1973) 'Die Erforschung der traditionellen Rechtssysteme in Afrika als Aufgabe einer speziellen Semantik' in *Zeitschrift für vergleichende Rechtswissenschaft*, 229–244

Morgan, J.F. (1982) 'Multilingual legal drafting in the EEC and the work of Jurist/Linguists' in *Multilingua* 1, 2:109–117

Mounin, Georges (1979) 'La linguistique comme science auxiliaire dans les disciplines juridiques' dans *Meta* 24, 1:9–17

Patry, Réjean (1987) 'Le Programme national de l'administration de la justice dans les deux langues officielles: sa naissance, son évolution et son avenir' dans *L'actualité terminologique* 20, 6:2–4

Pescatore, Pierre (1985) *Vade-Mecum (Recueil de formules et de conseils pratiques à l'usage des rédacteurs d'arrêts)*, Luxembourg: Cour de Justice des Communautés Européennes

Le quadrilinguisme en Suisse – présent et futur. Analyse, propositions et recommandations d'un groupe de travail du Département fédéral de l'intérieur (1989) Berne

Ray, J. (1926) *Essai sur la structure logique du code civil français*, Paris: Librairie Félix Alcan

Richstone, Jeffry (1989) 'La protection juridique des langues autochtones au Canada' sous la direction de P. Pupier et J. Woehrling, *Langue et droit / Language and Law*, Montréal: Wilson & Lafleur, 259–278

Roebuck, D. (1989) 'The English Language and the Common Law' in *New Zealand Law Journal*, 391–396

Schneider, Christian (1992) 'Koredaktion von Gesetzestexten des Bundes' in *Gesetzbegung heute / Législation d'aujourd'hui*, 3:83–90

Schwab, Wallace (1984) *Les anglicismes dans le droit positif québécois*, Montréal: Conseil de la langue française

Seibert, Thomas-Michael (1977) *Zur Fachsprache in der Juristenausbildung*, Berlin: Duncker & Humblot

Seibert, Thomas-Michael (1981) *Aktenanalysen. Zur Schriften juristischer Deutungen*, Tübingen: Gunter Narr

Sourioux, Jean-Louis et Pierre Lerat (1975) *Le langage du droit*, Paris: Presses Universitaires de France

Trosborg, Anna (1991) 'An Analysis of Legal Speech Acts in English Contract Law' in *Hermes, Journal of Linguistics* 6:65–90

Verrycken, Mariette (1995) 'Le Français juridique en Belgique' sous la direction de G. Snow et J. Vanderlinden, *Français Juridique et Science du droit*, Bruxelles: Bruylant, 363–375

Weibel, Ernest (1992) 'La politique linguistique en Suisse' dans *Terminologie et traduction*, 2–3:25–42

Werk, Walther (1933) *Werdegang und Wandlungen der deutschen Rechtssprache*, Marburg: N.G. Elwert

Wydick, Richard (1985) *Plain English for Lawyers*, Durham, North Carolina: Carolina Academic Press.

3. GENERAL TRANSLATION THEORY, TERMINOLOGY, LANGUAGES FOR SPECIAL PURPOSES, LINGUISTICS

Albir, Amparo Hurtado (1990) *La notion de fidélité en traduction*, Paris: Érudition

Albrecht, Jörn (1990) 'Invarianz, Äquivalenz, Adäquatheit' in R.Arntz und G.Thome (Hg.) *Übersetzungswissenschaft, Ergebnisse und Perspektiven*, Tübingen: Gunter Narr

Arntz, Reiner (1986) 'Terminologievergleich und internationale Terminologie-angleichung' in M. Snell-Hornby (Hg.) *Übersetzungswissenschaft – eine Neuorientierung*, Tübingen: Francke

Arntz, Reiner (1988) 'Einleitung: Zum Verhältnis von Textlinguistik und Fachsprache' in R. Arntz (Hg.) *Studien zu Sprache und Technik*, Hildesheim: Olms, 3–5

Arntz, Reiner (1993) 'Terminological Equivalence and Translation' in H. Sonneveld and K. Loening (eds.) *Terminology. Applications in Interdisciplinary Communication*, Amsterdam/Philadelphia: Benjamins, 5–19

Arntz, Reiner und Erhard Eydam (1990) 'Was ist eine "fachlich schwierige Übersetzung"? – Versuch einer Präzisierung' in W. Wilss (Hg.) *Der Deutschunterricht*, 1. Themenheft: *Übersetzungswissenschaft*, 70–80

Austin, J.L. (1962) *How to Do Things with Words*, Oxford: Clarendon

Bastin, Georges L. (1990) 'L'Adaptation, Conditions et Concept' sous la direction de M. Lederer, *Études traductologiques en hommage à Danica Seleskovitch*, Paris: Lettres modernes Minard, 215–229

Beaugrande, Robert-Alain de and Wolfgang Dressler (1981) *Introduction to Text Linguistics*, New York: Longman

Bühler, Hildegund (1988) 'Übersetzungstyp und Übersetzungsprozeduren bei sogenannten Fachtexten' in R. Arntz (Hg.) *Studien zu Sprache und Technik*, Hildesheim: Olms, 281–297

Casagrande, J.B. (1954) 'The Ends of Translation' in *International Journal of American Linguistics* 20, 4:335–340

Catford, John C. (1965) *A Linguistic Theory of Translation*, London: Oxford University Press

Chau, Simon S.C. (1984) 'Hermeneutics and the Translators: The Ontological Dimension of Translating' in *Multilingual* 3, 2:71–77

Collas, John P. (1953) Introduction to *Year Books of Edward II* in *Selden Society* 70:xii–lxiv

Dahlberg, Ingetraut (1981) 'Conceptual Definitions for INTERCONCEPT' in *International Classification* 8, 1:12–22

Dancette, Jeanne (1995) *Parcours de traduction. Étude expérimentale du processus de compréhension*, Lille: Presses Universitaires de Lille

Durieux, Christine (1991) 'La créativité en traduction technique' dans *TEXTconTEXT*, 6:9–19

Durieux, Christine avec la collab. de Florence Durieux (1995) *Apprendre à traduire: prérequis et tests*, Paris: Maison du Dictionnaire

The Encyclopedia of Language and Linguistics (1994), R.E. Asher (editor-in-chief), Oxford/New York/Seoul/Tokyo: Pergamon

Fedorov, Andrei (1953) *Vvednie v teoriju perevoda*, Moskva

Felber, Helmut (1993) *Allgemeine Terminologie und Wissenstechnik – theoretische Grundlagen*, Wien: Term Net

Felber, Helmut; Galinski, C. and Nedobity, Wolfgang (1987) *A Method for Controlled Concept Dynamics,* Vienna: INFOTERM

Fleischer, Wolfgang (1975) *Wortbildung der deutschen Gegenwartssprache*, Tübingen: Niemeyer

Fluck, Hans-Rüdiger (3.Aufl. 1985) *Fachsprachen*, Tübigen: Francke

Fluck, Hans-Rüdiger (1992) *Didaktik der Fachsprachen*, Tübingen: Gunter Narr

Gémar, Jean-Claude (1995) *Traduire ou l'art d'interpréter, Fonctions, statut et esthétique de la traduction*, tome 1: *Principles*, Saint-Nicolas (Québec): Presses de l'Université du Québec

Gouin, Jacques (1977) 'La traduction au Canada de 1791 à 1867' dans *Meta* 22, 1:26–32

Habermas, Jürgen (1970) 'On Systematically Distorted Communication' in *Inquiry*, 13.3:205–218

Habermas, Jürgen (1981) *Theorie des kommunikativen Handelns*, Frankfurt am Main: Suhrkamp

Hansen, Chad (1993) 'Chinese Ideographs and Western Ideas' in *The Journal of Asian Studies*, 52, 2:373–399

Harwood Cline, Ruth and Joseph Mazza (1992) 'Beyond the Bilingual Dictionary: Research Tools in Translation' in *The Jerome Quarterly*, 7, 4;3–7

Hewson, Lance and Jacky Martin (1991) *Redefining Translation. The Variational Approach*, London/New York: Routledge

Hönig, Hans G. and Paul Kussmaul (1982) *Strategie der Übersetzung, Ein Lehr- und Arbeitsbuch*, Tübingen: Narr

Hoffmann, Lothar (2.Aufl. 1985) *Kommunikationsmittel Fachsprache, Eine Einführung*, Tübingen: Narr

Holz-Mänttäri, Justa (1984) *Translatorisches Handeln, Theorie und Methode*, Helsinki: Sumomalainen Tiedeakatemia.

Holz-Mänttäri, Justa (1986) 'Translatorisches Handeln – theoretisch fundierte Berufsprofile' in M. Snell-Hornby (Hg.) *Übersetungswissenschaft – eine Neuorientierung*, Tübingen: Francke, 348–374

Holz-Mänttäri, Justa (1988) 'Was übersetzt der Übersetzer? Zu Steuerfaktoren der Translatorhandlung und ihrer theoretischen Erfassung' in R. Arntz (Hg.) *Studien zu Sprache und Technik*, Hildesheim: Olms, 375–392

Holz-Mänttäri, Justa (1990) 'Das Transfer-Prinzip' in Arntz, Reiner und Gisela Thome (Hg.) *Übersetzungswissenschaft. Ergebnisse und Perspektiven. Festschrift für Wolfram Wilss zum 65. Geburtstag*, Tübingen: Gunter Narr, 59–70

Horguelin, Paul (1977) 'Les premiers traducteurs (1770–1791)' in *Meta* 22, 1:15–25

House, Juliane (1981) *A Model for Translation Quality Assessment*, Tübingen: Narr

Jumpelt, R.W. (1961) *Die Übersetzung naturwissenschaftlicher und technischer Literatur*, Berlin-Schöneberg: Langenscheidt

Kade, Otto (1968) 'Zufall und Gesetzmäßigkeit in der Übersetzung' in *Beihefte zur Zeitschrift Fremdsprachen* I. Leipzig.

Kade, Otto (Hg.) (1981) *Probleme des übersetzungswissenschaftlichen Textvergleichs*, Leipzig: Enzyklopädie

Kiraly, Donald (1995) *Pathways to Translation, Pedagogy and Process*, Kent, Ohio: The Kent State University Press

Kloepfer, Rolf (1967) *Die Theorie der literarischen Übersetzung*, München: Fink

Koller, Werner (1979 und 1992, 4.völlig neu bearb. Aufl.) *Einführung in die Übersetzungswissenschaft*, Heidelberg: Quelle & Meyer

Koutsivitis, Vassilis (1994) 'Organisation et gestion d'une équipe de traduction' dans *Terminologie et Traduction*, 2:343–353

Kussmaul, Paul (1995) *Training the Translator*, Amsterdam/Philadelphia: Benjamins

Lambert, José (1994) 'The cultural component reconsidered' in M. Snell-Hornby, F. Pöchhacker and K. Kaindl (eds.), *Translation Studies. An Interdiscipline*, Amsterdam/Philadelphia: Benjamins, 17–26

Larson, Mildred L. (1984) *Meaning-Based Translation*, Landham (Maryland): University Press of America

Lerat, Pierre (1995) *Les langues spécialisées*, Paris: Presses Universitaires de France

Lyons, John (1977) *Semantics*, vol. 1 and 2, Cambridge: Cambridge University Press

Mounin, Georges (1974) *Dictionnaire de la linguistique*, Paris: PUF

Möhn, Dieter und Roland Pelka (1984) *Fachsprachen, Eine Einführung*, Tübingen: Niemeyer

Needham, Joseph (1958) 'The translation of old Chinese scientific and technical texts' in *Aspects of Translation, Studies in Communication 2*, London: Secker and Warburg, 65–87.

Neubert, Albrecht (1973) 'Invarianz und Pragmatik' in Neubert und Kade (Hg.) *Neue Beiträge zu Grundfragen der Übersetzungswissenschaft*, Leipzig: Athenäum, 13–25

Neubert, Albrecht and Gregory M. Shreve (1992) *Translation as Text*, Kent, Ohio: The Kent State University Press

Newmark, Peter (1982) *Approaches to Translation*, Oxford: Pergamon

Newmark, Peter (1988) *A Textbook of Translation*, London: Prentice Hall

Newmark, Peter (1991) *About Translation*, Clevedon/Philadelphia/Adelaide: Multilingual Matters

Newmark, Peter (1993) *Paragraphs on Translation*, Clevedon/Philadelphia/Adelaide: Multilingual Matters

Nida, Eugene and Charles Taber (1974) *The Theory and Practice of Translation*, Leiden: E.J. Brill

290

Nord, Christiane (1988) *Textanalyse und Übersetzen*, Heidelberg: Gross

Nord, Christiane (1993) *Einführung in das funktionale Übersetzen*, Tübingen/Basel: Francke

Orth, Ernst Wolfgang (1984) *Dilthey und der Wandel des Philosophiebegriffs seit dem 19.Jahrhundert* (= Bd. 16 Phänomenologische Forschungen), Freiburg/München: Karl Alber

Paepcke, Fritz (1986) *Im Übersetzen Leben, Übersetzen und Textvergleich*, hrsg. von K. Berger und H.-M. Speier, Tübingen: Narr

Picht, Heribert and Jennifer Draskau (1985) *Terminology: An Introduction*, Surrey: University of Surrey

Poulsen, Sven Olaf (1990) 'Zur Problematik des textsortenbezogenen Übersetzens' in W. Wilss (Hg.) *Der Deutschunterricht 1. Themenheft Übersetzungswissenschaft*, 29–35

Reiß Katharina (1971) *Möglichkeiten und Grenzen der Übersetzungskritik*, München: Hueber

Reiß, Katharina (1976) *Texttyp und Übersetzungsmethode, Der operative Text*, Kronberg/Ts: Scriptor

Reiß, Katharina (1988) '"Der" Text und der Übersetzer' in R. Arntz (Hg.) *Studien zu Sprache und Technik*, Hildesheim: Georg Olms, 67–75

Reiß, Katharina (1990) 'Der Ausgangstext – das sine qua non der Übersetzung' in *TEXTconTEXT* 5:31–39

Reiß, Katharina (1995) *Grundfragen der Übersetzungswissenschaft, Wiener Vorlesungen*, M. Snell-Hornby und M. Kadric (Hg.), Wien: WUV-Universitätsverlag

Reiß Katharina and Hans J. Vermeer (1984) *Grundlegung einer allgemeinen Translationstheorie*, Tübingen: Niemeyer

Rothkegel, Annely (1984) 'Frames und Textstruktur' in *Text – Textsorten – Semantik*, A. Rothkegel und B. Sandig (Hg.), Hamburg: Helmut Buske, 238–261

Sager, Juan (1986) 'Die Übersetzung im Kommunikationsprozeß: der Übersetzer in der Industrie' in M. Snell-Hornby (Hg.) *Übersetzungswissenschaft – eine Neuorientierung*, Tübingen: Francke, 331–347.

Sager, Juan (1990) *A Practical Course in Terminology Processing*, Amsterdam: Benjamins

Sager, Juan (1993) *Language Engineering and Translation*, Amsterdam/Philadelphia: Benjamins

Sager, Juan, David Dungworth, and Peter McDonald (1980) *English Special Languages*, Wiesbaden: Oscar Brandstetter

Sandig, Barbara (1972) 'Zur Differenzierung gebrauchssprachlicher Textsorten im Deutschen' in E. Gülich und W. Raible (Hg.) *Textsorten, Differzierungskriterien aus linguistischer Sicht*, Frankfurt am Main: Athenaion, 113–134

Schmidt, Siegfried (1976) *Texttheorie*, München: Wilhelm Fink

Schmitt, Peter A. (1986) 'Die Eindeutigkeit von Fachtexten: Bemerkungen zu einer Fiktion' in M. Snell-Hornby (Hg). *Übersetzungswissenschaft – eine Neuorientierung*, Tübingen: Francke, 252–282.

Schröder, Hartmut (1993) 'Thematische Einleitung. Von der Fachtextlinguistik zur Fachtextpragmatik' in H. Schröder (Hg.) *Fachtextpragmatik*, Tübingen: Gunter Narr

Searle, John (1969) *Speech Acts*, Cambridge: University Press

Snell-Hornby, Mary (Hg.) (1986, 1994) 'Übersetzen, Sprache, Kultur' (Einleitung) *Übersetzungswissenschaft – eine Neuorientierung*, Tübingen: Francke, 9–29

Snell-Hornby, Mary (1988) *Translation Studies, An Integrated Approach*, Amsterdam: Benjamins

Snell-Hornby, Mary (1990a) 'Linguistic Transcoding or Cultural Transfer? A Critique of Translation Theory in Germany' in S. Bassnett and A. Lefevere (eds.) *Translation, History and Culture*, London/New York: Pinter, 79–86

Snell-Hornby, Mary (1990b) '"Slippery when wet": Paralleltexte als Übersetzungshilfe' in W. Wilss (Hg.) *Der Deutschunterricht*, 1. Themenheft: *Übersetzungswissenschaft*, 10–16

Steiner, George (1977) *After Babel*, Oxford: Oxford University Press

Störing, Hans Joachim (Hg.) (1963) *Das Problem des Übersetzens*, Stuttgart: Goverts

Stolze, Radegundis (2. Aufl. 1985) *Grundlagen der Textübersetzung*, Heidelberg: Groos

Stolze, Radegundis (1992) *Hermeneutisches Übersetzen*, Tübingen: Gunter Narr

Vermeer, Hans J. (1982) 'Translation als "Informationsangebot"' in *Lebende Sprachen* 27, 3: 97–100

Vermeer, Hans J. (1986) 'Übersetzen als kultureller Transfer' in M. Snell-Hornby (Hg.) *Übersetzungswissenschaft – eine Neuorientierung*, Tübingen: Francke, 30–53

Vermeer, Hans J. (1992a, 3.Aufl.) *Skopos und Translationsauftrag – Aufsätze*, Frankfurt/M.: Verlag für Interkulturelle Kommunikation

Vermeer, Hans J. (1992b) *Skizzen zu einer Geschichte der Translation*, Bd. 6.2, Frankfurt: Verlag für Interkulturelle Kommunikation

Vinay, J.-P. et Darbelnet, J. (1968, 4.ed.) *Stylistique comparée du français et de l'anglais. Méthode de traduction*, Paris: Didier

Weber, Harmut (1982) 'Language for Specific Purposes, Text Typology, and Text Analysis: Aspects of a Pragmatic-Functional Approach' in Høedt, Lundquist, Picht, and Qvistgaard (eds.) *Proceedings of the 3rd European Symposium on LSP, Pragmatics and LSP*, Copenhagen, 219–234

Wijnands, Paul (1985) 'Pour une redéfinition du néologisme lexicographique' in *La Banque des mots*, 3: 13–34

Wilss, Wolfram (1977) *Übersetzungswissenscahft. Probleme und Methoden*, Stuttgart: Ernst Klett

Wilss, Wolfram (1988a) *Kognition und Übersetzen*, Tübingen: Max Niemeyer

Wilss, Wolfram (1988b) 'Übersetzen als Entscheidungsprozeß' in R. Arntz (Hg.) *Studien zu Sprache und Technik*, Hildesheim: Olms, 7–20

Wilss, Wolfram (1992) *Übersetzungsfertigkeit. Annäherungen an einen komplexen übersetzungspraktischen Begriff*, Tübingen: Gunter Narr

Wölfflin, Eduard (Hg.) (1894) *Archiv für lateinische Lexikographie und Grammatik* Bd. 9, Leipzig: Teubner

292

4. LAW

Actes et documents de la Session extraordinaire d'octobre 1985, Conférence diplomatique sur la loi applicable aux contrats de vente, édités par le Bureau Permanent de la Conférence, La Haye: Imprimerie Nationale des Pays-Bas

Alen, André (1992) *Treatise on Belgian Constitutional Law*, Deventer: Kluwer

Annuaire 1959 (1960) 'Note on the Question of Divergencies in the Interpretation of Norms of Uniform Law,' Rome: UNIDROIT, 315–327

Baden, Eberhard (1977) *Gesetzgebung und Gesetzesanwendung im Kommunikationsprozeß*, Baden-Baden: Nomos

Bartels, Hans-Joachim (1982) *Methode und Gegenstand intersystemarer Rechtsvergleichung*, Tübingen: J.C.B. Mohr

Baumann, Jürgen (7.Aufl. 1984), *Einführung in die Rechtswissenschaft*, München: C.H. Beck

Baumann, Max (1991) *Recht/Gerechtigkeit in Sprache und Zeit*, Zürich: Schulthess.

Beaupré, Michael (1986) *Interpreting Bilingual Legislation*, Toronto: Carswell

Beaty, Stuart (1989) 'A New Official Languages Act for Canada – Its Scope and Implications' in P. Paupier and J. Woehrling (eds.) *Langue et droit / Language and Law*, Montréal: Wilson & Lafleur Ltée, 185–193

Berg, Albert Jan van den (1996) 'The New York Convention: Its Intended Effects, Its Interpretation, Salient Problem Areas'; also 'Court Decisions on the New York Convention,' both in *The New York Convention of 1958*, Zurich: Swiss Arbitration Association, 25–45; 46–99

Coing, Helmut (3.Aufl. 1976) *Epochen der Rechtsgeschichte in Deutschland*, München: Beck

Constantinesco, Léotin-Jean (1974) *Traité de Droit Comparé*, Paris: Librairie générale

Dale, William (1977) *Legislative Drafting: A New Approach*, London: Butterworths

David, René and John Brierley (3rd ed. 1985) *Major Legal Systems in the World Today*, London: Stevens

Dessemontet, François (1984) *Le droit des langues en Suisse*, Montréal: Conseil de la langue française

Dicey & Morris on The Conflict of Laws, vol. 2 (10th ed. 1980.) London: Stevens & Sons

Dick, Robert C. (1985) *Legal Drafting*, Toronto/Calgary/Vancouver: Carswell

Dickerson, R. (1954) *Legislative Drafting*, Boston: Little Brown

Dixon, Martin (2nd ed. 1993) *Textbook on International Law*, London: Blackstone Press

Driedger, Elmer A. (2nd ed. 1983) *Construction of Statutes*, Toronto: Butterworths

Driedger, Elmer A. (1982a) 'Legislative Drafting Style: Civil Law vs Common Law' in J.-Cl. Gémar (ed.), *Langage du droit et traduction*, Montréal: Linguatech et Conseil de la langue français, 61–81

Driedger, Elmer A. (1982b) *A Manuel of Instruction for Legislative and Legal Writing*, Ottawa: Department of Justice.

Driedger, Elmer A. (1976) *The Composition of Legislation*, Ottawa: Department of Justice.

Drobnig, Ulrich (1986) 'Rechtsvergleichung in der deutschen Rechtsprechung' in *Rabels Zeitschrift*, 50, 3–4:610–630

The Federal Legislative Process in Canada (1987), Ottawa: Department of Justice.

Fasching, Hans W. (2.Aufl. 1990) *Lehrbuch des österreichischen Zivilprozeßrechts*, Wien: Manz

Fleiner-Gerster, Thomas (1985) *Wie soll man Gesetze schreiben?*, Bern: Paul Haupt

Forsthoff, Ernst (1940) *Recht und Sprache*, Halle: Niemeyer.

Gadamer, Hans-Georg (4.Aufl. 1975) *Wahrheit und Methode*, Tübingen: J.C.B. Mohr.

Ginsbergen, Govert van (1970) 'Qualifikationsproblem, Rechtsvergleichung und mehrsprachige Staatsverträge' in *Zeitschrift für Rechtsvergleichung*, 11:1–15

Golding, Martin P. (1984) *Legal Reasoning*, New York: Alfred A. Knopf

Gutteridge, H.C. (1946) *Comparative Law*, Cambridge: University Press

Hardy, Jean (1962) 'The Interpretation of Plurilingual Treaties by International Courts and Tribunals' in *The British Year Book of International Law 1961*, London: Oxford University Press, 37:72–155

Hart, H.L.A. (1962) *The Concept of Law*, Oxford: Clarendon Press

Hattenhauer, Hans (1987) *Zur Geschichte der deutschen Rechts- und Gesetzessprache*, Hamburg: Joachim Jungius-Gesellschaft der Wissenschaften

Hauck, Werner (1985) 'Verständliche Gesetzessprache' in T. Öhlinger (Hg.) *Recht und Sprache, Fritz Schönherr – Gedächtnissymposium 1985*, Wien: Manz, 193–204.

Hegenbarth, Rainer (1982) *Juristische Hermeneutik und linguistische Pragmatik*, Königstein/Ts.: Athenäum

Hilf, Meinhard (1973) *Die Auslegung mehrsprachiger Verträge*, Heidelberg: Springer

Kaufmann, Ekkehard (1984) *Deutsches Recht, Die Grundlagen*, Berlin West: Erich Schmidt Verlag

Keating, Judith (1995) 'La corédaction et l'expérience Néo-Brunswickoise' sous la direction de G. Snow et J. Vanderlinden, *Français juridique et Science du droit*, Bruxelles: Bruylant, 203–217

Kelsen, Hans (1979) *Allgemeine Theorie der Normen*, K. Ringhofer und R. Walter (Hg.), Wien: Manz

Kelsen, Hans (1991) *General Theory of Norms* (translation), Oxford: Clarendon

Kindermann, Harald (1979) *Ministerielle Richtlinien der Gesetzestechnik*, Berlin/Heidelberg: Springer

Klinke, Ulrich (1989) *Der Gerichtshof der Europaischen Gemeinschaften – Aufbau und Arbeitsweise*, Baden-Baden: Nomos

Koch, Hans-Joachim und Helmut Rüßmann (1982) *Juristische Begründungslehre*, München: Beck

Kötz, Hein (1986) 'Die 15. Hager Konferenz und das Kollisionsrecht des trust' in *Rabels Zeitschrift* 50, 3–4:562–585

Koh, Tommy and Shanmugam Jayakumar (1985) 'The Negotiating Process of the Third United Nations Conference on the Law of the Sea' in M.H. Nordquist (ed.) *United Nations Convention on the Law of the Sea 1982, A Commentary*, Dordrecht: Nijhoff, 29–134

Koschaker, Paul (1947) *Europa und das römische Recht*, München/Berlin: Biederstein

Krüger, Paul (1912) *Geschichte der Quellen und Literatur des Römischen Rechts*, München/Leipzig: Duncker & Humblot

Krüger, Uwe (1969) *Der Adressat des Rechtsgesetzes*, Berlin: Duncker & Humblot

Kuner, Christopher (1991) 'The Interpretation of Multilingual Treaties: Comparison of Texts versus the Presumption of Similar Meaning' in *Comparative Law Quarterly* 40:4, 953–964

Larenz, Karl (5.Aufl. 1983) *Methodenlehre der Rechtswissenschaft*, Berlin/Heidelberg: Springer

Lashöfer, Jutta (1992) *Zum Stilwandel in richterlichen Entscheidungen*, Münster/New York: Waxmann

Leitfaden für die Ausarbeitung von Erlassen des Bundes (Gesetzgebungsleitfaden) (1995), Bern: Bundesamt für Justiz

Levert, Lionel (1995) 'Bijuridisme et bilinguisme législatifs: Un enjeu et un pari' sous la direction de G. Snow et J. Vanderlinden, *Français juridique et Science du droit*, Bruxelles: Bruylant, 255–266

Lewison Kim (1987) *The Interpretation of Contracts*, London: Sweet & Maxwell

Liang, Yuen-Li (1953) 'The Question of Revision of a Multilingual Treaty Text' in *American Journal of International Law*, 47:263–272.

Liebs, Detlef (1975) *Römisches Recht*, Göttingen: Vandenhoeck & Ruprecht

Mankiewiez, René H. (1962) 'Die Anwendung des Warschauer Abkommens' in *Rabels Zeitschrift*, 27:456–477

Mankiewiez, René H. (1968) 'Organisation de l'Aviation civile internationale' dans *Annuaire français de droit international*, 14:483–529

Mayer-Maly, Theo (1969) 'Auslegen und Verstehen' in *Juristische Blätter* 91:15/16, 413–417.

McNair, Lord (1986) *The Law of Treaties,* Oxford: Clarendon

Mehren, Arthur Taylor von and James Russel Gordley (2nd. ed. 1977) *The Civil Law System*, Boston/Toronto: Little, Brown & Co.

Mimin, Pierre (1978) *Le style des jugements*, Paris: Librairies techniques

Nadelmann, Kurt and Arthur von Mehren (1966) 'Equivalences in Treaties in the Conflicts Field' in *American Journal of Comparative Law*, 15:195–203

Nelson, L.D.M. (1987) 'The Drafting Committee of the Third United Nations Conference on the Law of the Sea: The Implications of Multilingual Texts' in *British Yearbook of International Law*, 57:169–199

Noll, Peter (1973) *Gesetzgebungslehre*, Reinbek bei Hamburg: Rowohlt

Overbeck, Alfred von (1984) 'L'interprétation des textes plurilingues en Suisse' in *Les Cahiers de Droit*, 24:973–988

Oxman, Bernard H. (1982) 'The Third United Nations Conference on the Law of the Sea: The Tenth Session (1981)' in *The American Journal of International Law*, 76, 1:1–23

Pardons, Claude (1995) 'Elaboration d'une terminologie française de common law' sous la direction de G. Snow et J. Vanderlinden, *Français juridique et Science du droit,* Bruxelles: Bruylant, 279–294

Pigeon, Louis-Philippe (1978) *Rédaction et interprétation des lois*, Québec: Éditeur officiel

295

Pigeon, Louis-Philippe (1982b) 'La rédaction bilingue des lois fédérales' dans *Revue générale de droit*, 13:177–186

Pigeon, Louis-Philippe (1983) Review of '*Drafting Laws in French – Study Paper*' by Marie Lajoie, Wallace Schwab and Michel Sparer, Ottawa Law Reform Commission of Canada 1982, in *Canadian Bar Review*, 61:691–697

Pintens, Walter (1988) 'Neues Abstammungs- und Adoptionsrecht' in *Standesamts Zeitung (StAZ)*, 1:20–24

Platzöder, Renate und Horst Grunenberg (1990) *Internationales Seerecht*, München: C.H. Beck

Ramberg, Jan (1992) 'Contractual Aspects of Privatization' in P. Šarčević (ed.) *Privatization in Central and Eastern Europe*, London, Graham & Trotman: 97–108

Rehbinder, Manfred (1972) 'Rechtskenntnis, Rechtsbewußtsein und Rechtsethos als Probleme der Rechtspolitik' in *Jahrbuch für Rechtssoziologie und Rechtstheorie*, Bd. III: 25–46

Rosenne, Shabtai (1954–II) *United Nations Treaty Practice*, in *ADI Recueil*, 86:281–444

Rosenne, Shabtai (1971) 'On Multi-lingual Interpretation' in *Israel Law Review*, 6:360–366

Rosenne, Shabtai (1983) 'The Meaning of "Authentic Text" in Modern Treaty Law' in R. Bernhardt, W.K. Geck, G. Jaenicke, H. Steinberger (eds.) *Festschrift für Hermann Mosler*, Berlin/Heidelberg/New York: Springer, 759–784

Rosenne, Shabtai (1987) 'Conceptualism as a Guide to Treaty Interpretation' in *International Law at the Time of its Codification. Essays in Honour of Roberto Ago*, vol: I, Milan: Giufré, 417–431

Rosenne, Shabtai (1987b) 'Publications of the International Court of Justice' in *American Journal of International Law*, 81:681–696

Sacco, Rudolfo (1991) 'Legal Formants: A Dynamic Approach to Comparative Law' in *American Journal of Comparative Law* 39:1–34 and 343–401

Satow, Sir Ernest (1957, 4th ed.) *A Guide to Diplomatic Practice*, ed. by Sir N. Bland, London: Longmans, Green & Co.

Schlesinger, Rudolf (1980) *Comparative Law, Cases-Text-Materials*, Mineola N.Y.: Foundation Press

Schönherr, Fritz (1985) *Sprache und Recht, Aufsätze und Vorträge*, hrsg. v. W. Barfuß, Wien: Manz.

Senger, Harro von (1985) 'Recent Developments in the Relations between State and Party Norms in the People's Republic of China' in S.R. Schram (ed.) *The Scope of State Power in China*, London: School of Oriental and African Studies, 171–185

Senger, Harro von (1994) *Einführung in das chinesische Recht*, München: Beck

Soetaert, R. (1980) 'Un arrêt de cassation est-il lisible ?' in *Journal des tribunaux*, 31 mai, 365–370

Sourioux, Jean-Louis (1990) *Introduction au Droit*, Paris: Presses Universitaires de France

Sumner, Colin (1979) *Reading Ideologies*, London/New York/San Francisco: Academic Press

Tabory, Mala (1980) *Multilingualism in International Law and Institutions*, Alphen aan den Rijn: Sijthoff & Noordhoff

Tallon, Dennis (1990) 'The Notion of Contract: A French Jurist's Naive Look at Common Law Contract' in D. Clark (ed.) *Comparative and Private International Law*, Berlin: Duncker & Humblot, 283–290

Tallon, Dennis (1995) 'Français juridique et science du droit: quelques observations' sous la direction de G. Snow et J. Vanderlinden, *Français juridique et Science du droit*, Bruxelles: Bruylant, 339–349

Tetley, William (1990) 'Interpretation and Construction of Maritime Conventions in Canada' in *Contemporary Law / Droit contemporain. Canadian Reports to the 1990 Congress of Comparative Law, Montréal*, Cowansville, Québec: Yvon Blais, 424–441

Thornton, G.C. (1987) *Legislative Drafting*, London: Butterworths

Vanderlinden, Jacques (1985) 'Ubi Domicilium, Ibi Ius Universale?' dans *Revue internationale de droit comparé*, 303–329

Vanderlinden, Jacques (1995) *Comparer les droits*, Bruxelles: Story-Scientia

Verzijl, J.H.W. (1973) *International Law in Historical Perspective*, Part VI: *Juridical Facts as Sources of International Rights and Obligations*, Leiden: A.W. Sijthoff

Villay, Michel (1974) 'Indicatif et impératif juridiques, Dialogue à trois voix' dans *Le Langage du droit, Archives de philosophie du droit* 19:4–61

Volman, Yvo, W.T. Eijsbouts et M. van Montfrans (1988) *La cour et les langues*, Amsterdam: Universiteit van Amsterdam

Voyame, J. (1989) 'le statut des langues en Suisse' sous la direction de P.Pupier & L.Woehrling, *Langue et droit, Actes du Premier Congrès de l'Institut international de droit linguistique comparé de droit linguistique comparé*, Montréal: Wilson & Lafleur, 343–350

Vries, Henry P. de (1962) 'Choice of Language in International Contracts' in W. Reese (ed.) *International Contracts: Choice of Law and Language*, Dobbs Ferry, N.Y.: Oceana, 14–22

Walker, David M. (1980) *The Oxford Companion to Law*, Oxford: Clarendon

Wank, Rolf (1985) *Die juristische Begriffsbildung*, München: Beck

Watson, Alan (1974) *Legal Transplants*, Edinburgh: Scottish Academic Press

Weinberger, Ota (1988) *Norm und Institution. Eine Einführung in die Theorie des Rechts*, Wien: Manz

Wetter, J. Gillis (1960) *The Styles of Appellate Judicial Opinions*, Leyden: Sythoff

Wieacker, Franz (1952) *Privatgeschichte der Neuzeit*, Göttingen: Vandenhoeck & Ruprecht

Woehrling, Jean-Marie (1989) 'La promotion des langues régionales et minoritaires dans le Projet de Charte du Conseil de l'Europe' sous la direction de P. Paupier and J. Woehrling, *Langue et droit*, Montréal: Wilson & Lafleur, 133–182

Wright, George (1987) 'On a General Theory of Interpretation: The Betti-Gadamer Dispute in Legal Hermeneutics' in *The American Journal of Jurisprudence* 32:191–243.

Wróblewsky, Jerzy (1987) 'Legal culture and axiology of law-making' in H. Schäffer (Hg.) *Gesetzgebung und Rechtskultur*, Wien: Manz, 11–23

Zweigert, Konrad und Hein Kötz (2.Aufl. 1984) *Einführung in die Rechtsvergleichung* Bd. I, II, Tübingen: Mohr

5. DICTIONARIES

La CLEF (Common Law en Français), Programme d'administration de la justice dans les deux langues officielles, Ottawa: *Droit de la preuve* (1984), *Droit successoral* (1984), *Droit des biens I* (1986), *Droit des biens II* (1987), *Droit des biens III* (1989), *Droit des biens IV* (1990), *Droit des biens V* (1993), *Droit des biens, Supplément* (1993)

Creifelds Rechtswörterbuch (13. Aufl. 1996), hrsg. v. H.C. Kaufmann, München: Beck

Dahl, Henry and Horacio Marull (1992) *Dahl's Law Dictionary / Diccionario jurídico*, Buffalo, New York: Hein & Co.

Derechos humanos/Human Rights/Droits de l'homme (1985), Language Service of the United Nations at Geneva

Dictionnaire de droit privé et Lexiques bilingues (2° éd. 1991), *Private Law Dictionary and Bilingual Lexicons* (2nd ed. 1991), Centre de recherche en droit privé et comparé du Québec, Cowansville: Yvon Blais

Hanyu Da Cidian [Great Dictionary of the Chinese Language] (1994) Shanghai

Herbst, R. (1979) *Dictionary – Commerce, Finance, Law* (English-German-French), Zug: Translegal Ltd.

Jowitt, E. and Walsh, C. (2nd ed. 1977) *Jowitt's Dictionary of English Law*, ed. by J. Burke, London: Sweet & Maxwell

Modern Dictionary of International Legal Terms / English, French, German (1993), Ernest Lindbergh, Boston: Little, Brown & Co.

Osborn's Concise Law Dictionary (8th ed. 1993) ed. by L. Rutherford and S. Bone, London: Sweet & Maxwell

Vocabulaire de la 'common law' (1980) Moncton: Centre de traduction et de terminologie juridiques de l'Université de Moncton

Webster's Encyclopedic Unabridged Dictionary of the English Language (1989) New York/Avenel, New Jersey: Gramercy Books

Index

African law, 70, 233
Austrian ABGB, 34-36, 130
Authentic texts, 20, 40, 64, 71, 76, 118, 195, 276
Authenticated (authoritative) translations, 19-21, 35, 40, 56, 64, 71, 93, 112, 116, 118, 271
    authentication, 20, 50, 56, 93-95, 206-208
    equal authenticity, 20, 35, 40, 56, 64, 71, 93-94, 112, 196–200, 204, 206, 249, 271, 276
    interpretative value of, 93-95, 198-200, 205-208
    theory of original texts, 20, 64

Belgium
    Court of Cassation, 22, 41, 50-52, 123-125
    development of legal Dutch, 49-52
    development of legal German, 15, 52-53
    language rights, 49, 52
    national languages, 49
    official languages, 49, 52
    plurilingual Constitution, 50, 52, 148
    response to co-drafting, 50, 272
    territorial principle, 49, 52
    Van Dievoet Committee, 50
Bilingual legal drafting, *see also* Co-drafting, 108-110
    is co-drafting translation? 105-108
    new methods of, 87, 99-102
    use of new methods, 102, 182, 272

Canada and Quebec
    bilegal (common law and civil law), 41-43, 69
    bilingual cross-construction, 75-76
    bilingual drafting methods, 101-103
    bilingualism, 42-44, 81
    Canadian National Program, 249, 260, 268, 269, 274
    Commissioner of Official Languages, 45-46, 97
    equal language rights, 41-45, 80
    experiment in co-drafting, 181-194, 272-273
    federal legislation, 69, 78, 128, 181-194
        distinctive style of French text, 182-191, 193-194
        drafting style and rules of interpretation, 192-194
        limits of stylistic diversity, 192-193
    history of legal translation, 41-48
    interpretation of bilingual legislation, 69, 75-79, 94
    legislative process, 56
    jurilinguist, 2, 100, 114
    mixed legal system in Quebec, 42
    plurilingualism in the courts, 80-85
    postgraduate program in legal translation, 115
    production of bilingual legislation, 94, 100-101
    section 8(2) Official Languages Act, 76-78, 247-248, 274